THE CONSTRUCTION LAW LIBRARY FROM WILEY LAW PUBLICATIONS

CONSTRUCTION
FAILURES

CONSTRUCTION FAILURES

ROBERT F. CUSHMAN, Esquire
IRVIN E. RICHTER
LESTER E. RIVELIS, Esquire
Editors

WILEY

Wiley Law Publications
JOHN WILEY & SONS
New York • Chichester • Brisbane • Toronto • Singapore

Library of Congress Cataloging in Publication Data

Construction failures.
    (Construction law library)
    Bibliography: p.
    Includes index.
    1. Liability for building accidents—United States.
I. Cushman, Robert Frank, 1931–   . II. Richter, Irvin E.
III. Rivelis, Lester E. IV. Series.
KF1287.5.B8C655 1989   343.73′07869   89-5767
ISBN 0-471-61506-4   347.3037869

Printed in the United States of America

10 9 8 7 6 5 4 3 2 1

PREFACE

The recent disastrous collapses in Connecticut, one of the L'Ambiance Plaza building in Bridgeport and one of the roof at the Hartford stadium, the MGM hotel fire in Las Vegas, and the failure of the interior walkways at the Kansas City Hyatt Regency Hotel were not acts of God.

The structural engineer for the L'Ambiance Plaza in Bridgeport claims that it had no formal role as inspector written into its contract, that the structural plans called for temporary lateral bracing, and that no lateral bracing was used.

The failure of the Hyatt walkways, which tragically killed 111 persons and caused serious injury to hundreds more, was due to a design that was defective at the outset and was rendered even more defective by design changes during construction. Nearly 120 lawsuits seeking more than $2 billion in damages were filed in the Missouri courts on the design professional and many others.

Construction failures (the pervasive functional failure, the leaking roof, the HVAC system not delivering, the wastewater treatment plant not performing as designed) and construction disasters (the sudden and dramatic collapse) are increasing at an alarming rate. Whether failure or disaster, the basic legal and engineering issues are the same. The complexity of today's sophisticated construction projects in itself leads to poor coordination between designers and contractors. Add to this the pressure of today's economy to get the most bang for the least bucks, and the reasons for these failures become apparent.

Negligence actions involving architects, engineers, construction managers, contractors, and suppliers are also increasing at an alarming rate. Claims in astronomical figures for lost profits, loss of use, delays, disruption, and loss of productivity are now everyday occurrences. Cross-complaints for comparative indemnity abound. In some cases, design professionals are added as defendants to lawsuits without significant merit to warrant such involvement. In other cases, serious design deficiencies may come to light during the construction phase of a project, resulting in the filing of litigation or arbitration against the design professional. The simple fact is that most design professionals and contractors will find themselves involved in a claim based upon allegations of negligence at one time or another.

The double-digit inflation of the 1970s caused owners to examine the methods by which buildings had been designed and constructed. Delivery systems such as fast-track, phased construction, value engineering, and construction management became the vogue. These new concepts created new legal relationships and, as would be expected, new legal problems.

The recession of the 1980s created its own set of problems. Cutbacks in public and private works have caused contractors to go out of business, and, when work is available, the bidder lists are long and the competition is fierce. Because each party in the construction process is on a tight budget, there is a profound unwillingness to voluntarily contribute to the solution of site problems. The trend toward more and more litigation of construction disputes is exacerbated by the present economic climate.

Although physical damage can be repaired and monetary compensation given, lives cannot be brought back, reputations can seldom be entirely restored, permanent disabilities cannot be reversed, and pain and suffering cannot be erased. We must learn from studying construction failures how they can be avoided in the future and how liabilities can be reduced. This is the higher goal for both engineers and lawyers.

This book is the most complete publication yet developed to focus on the liability of architects, engineers, construction managers, contractors and suppliers of construction material, developers, and other claimants for functional failure and tragic collapse. It is not a nuts-and-bolts book. It is a guide to the tough problems pertaining to construction failure and disaster, and to a subsequent understanding and solution to these problems.

May, 1989   ROBERT F. CUSHMAN
                                                     Philadelphia, Pennsylvania

                                                     IRVIN E. RICHTER
                                                     Willingboro, New Jersey

                                                     LESTER E. RIVELIS
                                                     New York, New York

ABOUT THE EDITORS

Robert F. Cushman is a partner in the national law firm of Pepper, Hamilton & Scheetz and a recognized specialist and lecturer on all phases of construction and real estate law. He serves as legal counsel to numerous trade associations and construction, development, and bonding companies. Mr. Cushman is editor and coauthor of *The McGraw-Hill Construction Business Handbook, Construction Litigation: Representing the Owner, Construction Litigation: Representing the Contractor, Architect and Engineer Liability: Claims Against Design Professionals,* and numerous other books in the construction field. A member of the Pennsylvania bar and admitted to practice before the Supreme Court of the United States and the United States Claims Court, he has served as Executive Vice President and General Counsel to the Construction Industry Foundation and the American Construction Owners Association, as well as Regional Chairman of the Public Contract Law Section of the American Bar Association. He is a member of the International Association of Insurance Counsel.

Irvin E. Richter is chairman and chief executive officer of HILL Group, Inc., a 2,300-person engineering, consulting, and environmental science firm headquartered in Willingboro, New Jersey, with 26 offices worldwide.

A graduate of Rutgers University Law School and Wesleyan University, Mr. Richter is a noted construction claims expert, arbitrator, and author. He has written *International Construction Claims: Avoiding and Resolving Disputes,* coauthored the *Handbook of Construction Law and Claims,* and contributed chapters to a number of other works and numerous articles in his field.

Mr. Richter is a member of the New Jersey and Pennsylvania Bars, the Philadelphia Chapter of the Young President's Organization, and the Construction Industry Presidents Forum.

Lester E. Rivelis is a partner in the New York City law firm of LePatner, Gainen & Block. Throughout his professional career he has specialized in all phases of building design and construction; representing architects, engineers, construction managers, sureties and lenders in contract negotiations, litigation, and arbitration. He is often retained to provide business advisory services to meet the specialized needs of the design, construction, and real estate industries on matters such as insurance, cost reporting, project management, contract and claims administration, and scheduling issues.

For five years, he was senior vice president and general counsel of Lehrer McGovern Bovis, a leading construction management/consulting firm. While at Lehrer McGovern Bovis, he was involved with some of the most prestigious and challenging construction projects in the world, such as the restoration of the Statue of Liberty and Ellis Island, EuroDisneyland in Paris, France, Canary Wharf in London, England, and many more.

Because of his significant construction industry experience, he has lectured widely before the ABA Litigation Section Construction Forum Committee, Pratt University, New Jersey Institute of Technology, Construction Litigation Superconferences, and the New York State Bar Association.

SUMMARY CONTENTS

DETAILED CONTENTS

PART I

PREFAILURE CONSIDERATIONS

CHAPTER 1

DRAFTING A CONSTRUCTION CONTRACT

Jerome Reiss, Esquire

Jerome Reiss has been involved since 1954 in the practice of the law devoted to construction, real estate, and supply contract matters representing government, private owners, developers, contractors, sureties, architects, engineers, subcontractors, and suppliers. Mr. Reiss received his Juris Doctor from Harvard University in 1951. He represents the Lefrak Organization, Donald Trump, New York Convention Center Development Corporation, Statue of Liberty/Ellis Island Foundation, The Metropolitan Museum of Art, Madison Equities, Starrett Bros., Cohen Bros., Rose Associates, and many other well-known institutions and companies. Mr. Reiss has had extensive trial experience in many state courts, in various federal courts throughout the country, and before many federal agencies. He has also had extensive experience trying construction arbitration cases involving claims for millions of dollars. He has written numerous articles and has lectured extensively. He is listed in *Who's Who in American Law* and *Who's Who In The World.*

§ 1.1 General Considerations

Drafting a formal legal document requires special knowledge and skills. Because of the number of parties involved, their interrelationships, the unique requirements of each construction project, and the extreme financial exposure of all concerned, construction contracts require the use of a draftsperson who fully understands construction law as well as the fears and needs of the contracting parties.

Construction contracts are not documents that should be used over and over again like a store-bought lease or will. Each construction project has its own particular needs because of the different parties' requirements or the project's complexity, location, magnitude, or even its degree of prestige. Few projects are alike. Differences may be slight, but they are still present and require a contract change, even though it may only be a single provision, sentence, or word. It is rare indeed that no changes would be needed for different projects.

Before drafting an agreement, an attorney should know the background of the contracting parties, the type of construction involved, the specific location, weather conditions in the area, applicable construction law for the project, what the client wants and needs, and the duties and obligations reasonably expected of the contracting parties. Clearly, a project to be constructed in the southwestern part of the United States involves different considerations than one in the northeast, if only because of weather and soil conditions. Similarly, a contract between private parties is quite different from a contract between a public agency and a private party.

Heavy construction and building construction are not the same. Heavy construction may involve a road, tunnel, dam, or bridge and carries legal and factual considerations that differ from building construction, which may involve a school, hospital, high-rise residence, office building, hotel, shopping center, or an industrial or manufacturing plant.

Even the decade in which a project is to be constructed may merit special considerations. Different times have different problems. For example, during the 1960s inflation was a major concern in estimating future costs; in the 1970s the cost and use of energy were important considerations. Today, the cost of insurance and its availability have become a major problems.

The parties to a construction contract have changed over the years. In the early days, the contractor and the architect were one and the same. Whoever built was also the one who designed. Today, that is infrequently the case. Moreover, a new service provider has emerged in the form of a construction manager, whose relationship to the owner is substantially different from that of a general contractor.

The use of the computer has emerged in the construction field, as well as in so many other fields, as an important tool. Most construction progress schedules used to be in the form of a Gant or Bar Chart. Today, the Critical Path Method (CPM) is being used increasingly to schedule construction work, and the computer printout is an integral, important tool to show the early and late start and finishing dates for the hundreds, if not thousands, of separate construction activities.

Systems, equipment, and materials have changed over the years. Designers and owners alike take into account the feasibility and desirability of new systems and materials to use in a project. Contractors must know about the costs of and benefits to be derived from modern pieces of equipment as well as how best to use them.

All of these considerations and more must go into the drafting of a construction contract. Moreover, the attorney should understand that each contract must concern itself with:

1. Concept
2. Form
3. Language.

The most popular construction contracts are printed forms of the American Institute of Architects (AIA). The language in those contracts is generally superb and the form may be acceptable; however, the concept is frequently poor. No preprinted form is geared to cover adequately the particular needs of a project and the parties. Indeed, the cost of drafting a contract is one of the least expensive items in a project, but a poorly drafted contract can result in one of the largest costs of the project.

OWNER/CONTRACTOR CONTRACTS

§ 1.2   Lump Sum Contract

The lump sum contract is the traditional and most common type of contract used in both public and private projects. In a Lump Sum Contract the owner warrants the completeness of the plans and specifications, so that if a contractor follows them the results sought will be achieved.[1] A contractor bids a single lump sum or contract price to do the project. This is normally done after reviewing the plans and specifications and doing what is known as dimensional "take-offs." The contractor also analyzes the General Conditions and other contract documents to determine his own obligations and discern the owner's efforts to exculpate himself against liability for different situations. Other considerations that determine the contractor's ultimate price are the time of performance, the local and general area in which the project is to be constructed, who the owner is, and the owner's ability to pay. After weighing each of these considerations, the contractor may decide not to submit a price proposal.

The contract documents are usually made up of the following:

Information for Bidders (IFB).   This document is provided to bidders and generally contains preliminary information indicating what the owner expects them to do: where to get the bid or contract documents, when and where the bid or price is to be submitted, whether a bid bond will be required, and a warning that the bidder has an obligation to visit the site to become familiar with visual site conditions.

The Proposal.   It is basic law that a contract requires an offer and an acceptance. Although it may be drawn by the owner, the proposal is submitted by the contractor and is deemed to be his offer. Public entities usually permit no variation from the terms of the proposal that they have drafted; however, private parties may permit the proposal to be varied by the contractor without disqualifying the bid. The owner is then left with the option of accepting or rejecting the bid as modified, or engaging in negotiations with the bidder.

General Conditions.   This is considered by many to be the most important contract document. It contains the basic rights and obligations of the parties.

Special Conditions.   From time to time, particularly in connection with work that must be performed by a specialty contractor or that involves a special type of work, special conditions may be drafted. The Special Conditions document would be in addition to the General Conditions document.

Plans or Drawings.   These documents graphically show the work to be done and its general location. Specific locations and details of equipment installation are contained in shop drawings that are submitted during the construction phase by the contractor.

---

[1] J.D. Hedin Constr. Co. v. United States, 347 F.2d 235 (Ct. Cl. 1965); United States v. Spearin, 51 Ct. Cl. 155 (1918).

Specifications.   These describe the nature of the work, the systems to be used, and the class of material required. Together with the drawings they indicate the scope of the work of the project.

Addenda.   If any work or requirement is added, deducted, or modified after the plans and specifications are drawn but before a price is submitted, the owner issues an Addendum or Addenda to show the change in the scope of the work.

Payment and Performance Bonds.   If required by the owner, these bonds become part of the contract documents. A surety then becomes a third party to the contract as a guarantor of the contractor's paying his bills and performing the work as required.

§ 1.3   Guaranteed Maximum Price Contract

A guaranteed maximum price contract is used when an owner wants assurances that the cost of construction will not exceed an agreed-upon amount. An attorney must be sure to spell out what constitutes "costs" in this agreement. To be certain that he will not be forced to absorb any costs above the guaranteed amount, the contractor usually does two things. First, he adds a "cushion" to cover any possible unforeseen contingencies. Second, he explicitly defines "costs" to include many administrative activities for the contract. This form of agreement is frequently used with a Cost Plus Fixed Fee Contract, which usually contains a special incentive provision for the sharing of any savings between the owner and the contractor if the ultimate costs fall below the guaranteed maximum amount.

§ 1.4   Cost Plus Fixed Fee Contract

A cost plus fixed fee contract is generally used in private work, particularly if the project is an unusual one. Here again what constitutes the "cost of the work" needs to be clearly defined. It is also important to determine how the fee is to be paid—that is, whether it should be paid monthly based upon the percentage of the project that has been completed, or whether an equal amount should be paid each month. The latter method of payment, however, is more likely to give rise to a claim for an additional fee if the project's completion is delayed.

§ 1.5   Unit Price Contract

In a unit price contract each work item is defined and a price is separately expressed for each: for example, "common excavation $_____ per cubic yard." A lump sum price contract may also contain unit prices to represent agreed-upon set prices for certain extra or deleted work items.

§ 1.6 Fast Track Contract

The fast track contract is used when the owner wants the work to proceed before the design is complete. Its purpose is to save time and thereby save time-related financial and construction costs. The contractor is aware that the design is incomplete and submits a price based on his understanding of what costs should be for that type of construction. For example, his experience may have shown that normal costs of an office building without tenant work should be $100 per square foot, and the price he submits would be based upon the total square footage of the building. The uncertainty, however, can be in the scope or nature of the work—that is, whether the drawings and specifications, when completed, reflect what both parties agree is normal construction for that type of building, or whether the systems or material called for are what the contractor had expected.

§ 1.7 Design/Build Contract

The design/build contract is one in which the contractor agrees to design and construct the proposed project and turn it over to the owner complete. This is normally called a *turnkey* job. It is usual to combine a cost plus fixed fee contract or guaranteed maximum price contract with this type of contract.

CONTRACTS BETWEEN OTHERS

§ 1.8 Owner/Design Professional Contract

The architect and engineer, each of whom is considered a design professional, are normally deemed agents of the owner. They have no contractual privity with the contractor. The owner is considered to be a disclosed principal and, therefore, is liable to the contractor for breach of contract resulting from the errors and omissions of the design professional.[2] Similarly, the owner is liable to the contractor if the design professional fails to

---

[2] Laburnum Constr. Corp. v. United States, 163 Ct. Cl. 339 (1969); *see also* Joseph F. Egan v. City, 17 N.Y.2d 90, 215 N.E.2d 490, 268 N.Y.S.2d 301 (1966).

process shop drawings within a reasonable time, thereby affecting the time of completion and the cost of the work.[3]

The design professional, however, is neither a guarantor,[4] a warrantor,[5] nor an insurer[6] of the design. Consequently, the provisions in an owner/design professional contract should include, when possible, an indemnification provision, particularly because the design professional usually is unable to obtain adequate insurance coverage.

Years ago it was rare for an owner to sue a design professional. Although there remains some semblance of that reluctance in some owners today, the average owner will seek recourse if he believes he has been injured. Design professionals are acutely aware of that fact; therefore, it has become more difficult to negotiate contracts with them. Architects invariably prefer the AIA form contract with minor modifications. Owners, whose risks have increased substantially, however, should insist on their own version of the contract because they are paying the bills.

There are certain obligations imposed by law upon design professionals. They are usually licensed and regulated by statute.[7] When the design professional enters into a contract, he impliedly represents that he is skilled and capable of providing good design services. He is held to the reasonable skill and knowledge usually exercised by others in his profession. The law does not require him to be perfect.[8] On the other hand, the failure to meet the standard of care of his profession does subject him to liability to the owner.[9] Nevertheless, the wise owner will not rely on tortious conduct to sustain his rights. He should negotiate a contract that reasonably protects those rights, taking into account any special needs of his project.

§ 1.9   Owner/Construction Manager Contract

The retention of a construction manager by an owner is relatively new in the construction industry. It has been said to have arisen as a result of general contractors seeking to avoid the inherent risks in undertaking a lump sum fixed price contract, and of owners seeking the performance of certain administrative functions and design suggestions from a general

---

[3] Public Constructors, Inc. v. State of New York, 55 A.D.2d 368, 390 N.Y.S.2d 481 (1977).

[4] American Sur. Co. v. San Antonio Loan & Trust Co., 98 S.W. 387 (Tex. Civ. App. 1966), *modified,* 104 S.W. 1061 (Tex. 1967).

[5] Chapel v. Clark, 76 N.Y. 62, ___ N.E. ___ (1898).

[6] Gagne v. Bertran, 43 Cal. 2d 48, 275 P.2d 15 (1954).

[7] *See* N.Y. Educ. Law §§ 7200 & 7300.

[8] *See* Major v. Leary, 268 N.Y. 413, 241 A.D. 606 (1934).

[9] 530 E. 89 Corp. v. Unger, 43 N.Y.2d 776, 373 N.E.2d 276, 402 N.Y.S.2d 382 (1977).

contractor. Normally, the duties of a construction manager commence during the design rather than the construction stage. At the design stage, the construction manager may make suggestions relating to the use of systems, materials, and other design considerations that could save the owner millions of dollars and still achieve the purpose of the project.

In return for providing such services, the construction manager acts as the owner's agent even though he contracts directly with the various trades. These trade contracts are frequently incorrectly called subcontracts, but they are actually prime contracts and should be designated as *trade contracts* to avoid confusion. The trade contracts may be between the tradesman and the owner or between the tradesman and the construction manager as agent of the owner.

The construction manager, like the architect, seeks a fee and reimbursement for his costs and expenses. At times, he functions in two capacities. He acts as a trade contractor when he is performing certain construction services such as cleaning, and as a construction manager when he is administering the project. The construction manager also provides and recommends the use of various trade contractors. As an administrator, he presides at job meetings and keeps the minutes, keeps various daily and other job records for the owner, reviews and processes shop drawings and payment requisitions, inspects or monitors the work of the tradesmen, recommends the issuance of Change Orders and the amounts which should be paid, participates in reviewing and making punch lists with which each trade contractor is required to comply, and attempts to coordinate the work of the tradesmen and make them perform in accordance with the plans and specifications of the project within the time prescribed by their contracts.

Construction managers generally submit their own form contracts to the owner. These contracts are, as should be expected, slanted to benefit themselves. A common dispute between the owner and the construction manager is the inclusion of an indemnification provision to cover damages arising out of the construction manager's negligence or breach of the contract. It would seem evident that, notwithstanding the agency relationship with the owner, the construction manager should be liable for any additional costs the owner incurs due to the construction manager's negligence or breach of contract. Nevertheless, construction managers are loath to accept any such responsibility and, when pressed, will seek strenuously to limit their liability arising from their own errors, omissions, or misconduct. The owner, however, is the person who must pay; therefore, the contract should be drafted by the owner, who should insist upon being indemnified if additional costs are the fault of the construction manager. The field is competitive, and there are enough good construction managers available to enable an owner to pick and choose the fair contract provisions he wants.

§ 1.10 General Contractor/Subcontractor Contract

Our system of construction is one of specialties. The plumbing, electrical, mechanical, masonry, carpentry, concrete, and other work are all done by specialty tradesmen who subcontract with the general contractor.

The general contractor stands between the owner and the subcontractors. There is no privity of contract between a subcontractor and an owner. Consequently, the subcontractor cannot sue the owner for breach of contract and must look to the general contractor for his recourse. Thus, the general contractor is responsible to the subcontractors not only for his own acts but also for the improper acts of the owner. Likewise, the general contractor is responsible to the owner for the improper acts of his subcontractors.

The general contractor should be protected in his contracts against any breach or wrongdoing by the subcontractor or the owner. It is more difficult to achieve this goal in the contract with the owner because the general contractor is usually more anxious to enter into the contract, and the owner is not likely to be willing to look to a subcontractor for his recourse because subcontractors are rarely as economically sound as general contractors.

The general contractor, however, can insist on an indemnification provision from his subcontractor for any liability he has to the owner when a problem is caused by the sub-contractors. The problem, of course, is the economic ability of the subcontractor to pay for his mistakes.

DRAFTING THE CONTRACT

§ 1.11 Concept of the Contract

Each party to a construction contract seeks maximum protection, minimum exposure to liability, and maximum economic benefits. Because inherent conflicts exist between the parties, the contracts must be based upon reasonable compromises and concepts. When, how, and under what circumstances a party should reduce his demands or requirements depend upon such considerations as (1) the "responsibility" of the parties, (2) the prestigious nature of the project, and (3) how badly one wants the contract, or the other party, for this project.

The owner must first decide whether he wants to retain a single architect or engineer who will hire the others necessary to design the project or whether he wants to engage each of the design professionals separately. The architect wants to control the design, but he does not want to be responsible for the services performed in the design process by others, such as the structural or soils engineer. The owner, however, is better served by having a single contract with one party who is responsible for the design, rather than contracts with multiple designers. On the other hand, increased insurance coverage may be more easily available with several designers.

The owner must then decide whether he wants a construction manager or general contractor. If the owner is a private developer or institution with little or no construction staff, he is more likely to use a construction manager who can perform the necessary administrative functions during the construction of the project. Construction managers will attempt to use their own contract form. The owner should reject that attempt and contract directly with the tradesmen, particularly because the owner is directly responsible to the tradesmen even when they contract with the construction manager. In this way, the owner is more likely to achieve maximum protection. On the other hand, a trade contractor frequently will accept from a construction manager exculpatory and protective terms that might otherwise be rejected from an owner because of the tradesman's wish to retain a business relationship with the construction manager from whom he expects to obtain repeat business.

§ 1.12   Form of the Contract with Sample Provision Headings

Drafting a contract is an art. This is especially true in a construction contract because of the interrelationships of the parties. It requires a combination of theoretical and practical considerations, delicately balanced and in a different form for different projects.

In owner/architect or owner/construction manager contracts, there is a similarity of form because the services fall into three basic periods: the design period, the bid or preconstruction period, and the construction period. Each phase covers different services that must be defined. Payments may be made differently for each phase. Insurance, termination, and certain miscellaneous considerations must be made part of the agreement to cover all three phases. For example, the following provision headings should be found in an owner/construction manager contract after the preliminary provision which sets forth the date, the identification of the parties, and the appropriate "Whereas" clauses.

Article 1   Plans and Specifications
Article 2   Scope of Work
Article 3   Construction Manager's Status and Duties
Article 4   Owner's Responsibilities
Article 5   Schedule of the Work

Article 6   Cost of the Work
Article 7   Costs Not to Be Reimbursed
Article 8   Construction Manager's Fees
Article 9   Changes in the Work and Custom Tenant Work
Article 10 Payments
Article 11 Insurance
Article 12 Liens and Other Encumbrances
Article 13 Termination
Article 14 Equal Employment Opportunity
Article 15 Assignments
Article 16 Entire Agreement
Article 17 Books and Records
Article 18 Indemnification
Article 19 Additional Provisions.

In a contract between an owner and a general contractor, or a contract between a construction manager acting as the owner's agent and a trade contractor, the following should generally be found after the date of the agreement, the identification of the parties, and the "Whereas" clauses:

Article 1   Contract Documents
            1.1   Definitions
Article 2   Scope of Work, Materials, and Labor
            2.1   Scope of Work
            2.2   Contract Documents
            2.3   Intent of Contract Documents
            2.4   Site Investigation and Completeness of Drawings
            2.5   Title to Materials
            2.6   Contractor's Obligations
            2.7   "Or Equal"/Substitution Clause
            2.8   Quality and Labelling
Article 3   Time of Performance, Progress Schedule, Coordination, Time Extension
            3.1   Contract Time
            3.2   Progress Schedule
            3.3   Coordination with Other Contractors
            3.4   Notice of Delay or Disruption
            3.5   Extension of Time
            3.6   Damages

§ 1.13   Language of the Contract with Primary Rules of Interpretation

Once the concepts of a contract have been determined and the form understood, there remains only the appropriate language to reflect the intention of the parties. History has proven that communication has been a problem throughout our civilization. Consequently, it has been necessary to resort to "rules of interpretation" to determine what is meant by written words. Volumes have been written about the meanings of the writings of William Shakespeare. The same may be said about interpreting the Constitution of the United States. Indeed, even the Bible contains "rules of interpretation," and their similarity to present-day rules in our jurisprudence is amazing.

When writing contracts today, we use the following primary rules of interpretation:

1. Reasonable, Logical Interpretation.

2. Manifest Intent of the Drafter.   One of the important interpretation aids to be considered is the intention of the drafter of the contract as manifested by the words, phrases, symbols, or legends he elects to use.

3. Look to the Whole Agreement of the Contract.   Of all the aids to a reasonable interpretation, none is used more frequently by the courts, including federal administrative appeals boards, than the whole agreement rule.

4. Normal Meaning of Words.   Words, symbols, and marks will be given their common and normal meaning unless it is clearly shown that such words, symbols, or marks (1) have a technical meaning and were used in the contract in their technical sense or (2) have some other special meaning accorded to them by the parties.

5. The Principal and Apparent Purpose of the Contract.   One of the maxims of interpretation to be given great weight in ascertaining a contract's reasonable meaning is the principal apparent purpose of the contract.

6. Custom and Usage.   Custom and usage of the trade is commonly used as an aid to interpretation in two situations: (1) when it is necessary to add a term to the contract without which the obligations of one or both of the parties would be unclear and (2) when a custom and usage is needed to clarify an otherwise ambiguous provision.

7. Knowledge of the Other Party's Interpretation.   This rule—that a contracting party is bound by his knowledge of the other party's interpretation unless he indicates disagreement therewith—is steeped in ethics as well as in law. It is based on the principle that an interpretation is unreasonable if it permits one contracting party to take advantage of another.

8. Concurrent Interpretation.   When there is evidence of a concurrent interpretation (1) by other bidders prior to entering into the contract, (2) by the parties or their representatives during performance and before a controversy arises, or (3) by the contractor's subcontractors before a controversy arises, such an interpretation (unless clearly erroneous) is to be given great, if not controlling, weight.

9. Order of Precedence.   Contracts frequently set forth the precedence to be accorded to words, terms, and drawings should it develop that

conflicts exist between them. For example, contracts often provide and the law prescribes that when there is a conflict in language, (1) the contract prevails over the specifications,[10] (2) the specifications prevail over the drawings,[11] and (3) specific requirements prevail over general requirements.

10. Construction against Drafter.   If the words are ambiguous, the provision will be construed against the party who drafted it. This rule is known as the doctrine of contra proferentem. Ambiguities, which form the basis of many claims, are generally construed against the owner. The following explains the law clearly:

> When the government draws specifications which are fairly susceptible of a certain construction and the contractor actually and reasonably so construes them, justice and equity require that construction be adopted. Where one of the parties to a contract draws the document and uses therein language which is susceptible of more than one meaning, and the intention of the parties does not otherwise appear, that meaning will be given the document which is more favorable to the party who did not draw it. This rule is specifically applicable to Government contracts where the Contractor has nothing to say as to its provisions.[12]

11. Parol Evidence.   The parol evidence rule provides that, when two parties have reduced their agreement to a written contract, all prior negotiations and understandings (whether written or oral) are merged into the contract and thus cannot be considered in interpreting the contract.

12. Duty to Seek Clarification.   When an ambiguity is obvious or patent, a party has an obligation to ask.

13. Changes from the Print.   Typewritten words prevail over inconsistent printed words[13] and handwritten words prevail over inconsistent typewritten or printed words.[14]

The ability to express clearly what the parties intend is of paramount importance. Unfortunately, too many drafters of construction contracts use "scissor provisions" because they do not adequately understand what is needed and, therefore, they do not clearly express what the parties truly intend. The end result is to increase, rather than reduce, the likelihood of disputes.

---

[10] Annotation, *Building Contracts—Alterations and Extras,* 66 A.L.R. 658–59.

[11] Early v. O'Brien, 51 A.D. 569, 64 N.Y.S. 848 (1900).

[12] Peter Kiewit & Sons' Co. v. United States, 109 Ct. Cl. 390 (1947).

[13] Telefson v. Green Bay Packers, 256 Wis. 318, 41 N.W. 201 (1950).

[14] Johnson v. Green Bay Packers, 272 Wis. 149, 74 N.W.2d 784 (1956).

§ 1.14   Whether to Include Specific Provisions

There are certain contract provisions which inevitably form the basis for disputes when negotiating a contract because they may deeply impact the parties. Their ultimate inclusion or exclusion depends upon the circumstances surrounding the contract: for example, the magnitude of the project, the type of owner and his perceived ability to pay, how prestigious the project is, and how badly a party wants the job or, conversely, how difficult it is to obtain someone to do the job.

Following are the provisions which are most likely to be hotly contested in various contracts:

1. Owner/Architect Contract
   a. Warranty of fitness for use of the systems and equipment prescribed
   b. The extent or the requirement of inspection services
   c. Approval or rejection of shop drawings
   d. Payment: how and when made
   e. Reimbursable items: what to include
   f. The amount of insurance required.
2. Owner/Construction Manager
   a. Fee: whether the amount paid monthly should be based upon a percentage of completion or a specific proportional amount of the total fee divided by the anticipated number of months required for completion of the project
   b. The extent or the requirement of inspection services
   c. Reimbursable items: what to include
   d. Distinguishing duties of the construction manager from those of the architect.
3. Owner/Contractor
   a. Differing Site Condition provision
   b. No Damages For Delay provision; the type of progress schedule to use
   c. Termination for convenience and default (obtain approval of union)
   d. Obligation to continue to work despite dispute.
4. Contractor/Subcontractor
   a. No Damages For Delay provision
   b. Termination for convenience and default (obtain approval of union)
   c. Payment only after general contractor receives payment from owner.

CHAPTER 2

INSURING AGAINST THE CONSTRUCTION FAILURE AT A TIME WHEN INSURANCE IS UNAFFORDABLE

Manny D. Buzzell
David A. Verona, Esquire

Manny D. Buzzell has more than 30 years of experience in the insurance industry as an underwriter and broker specializing in problem solving for major clients for Corroon & Black, where he is vice chairman of Advanced Risk Management Services, a national resource to all Corroon & Black offices. Mr. Buzzell is on the faculty of the Risk and Insurance Management Society and teaches techniques of risk financing. An underwriting member of Lloyds of London, Mr. Buzzell received a B.S. in business administration from Jamestown College in North Dakota.

David A. Verona is an assistant vice president in the Advanced Risk Management Services Division of Corroon & Black. Mr. Verona is an attorney admitted to practice in Illinois where he practiced law and served in an in-house counsel capacity in Chicago. He maintains memberships in both the American Bar and Illinois State Bar Associations. Mr. Verona received a B.S. in economics from Ball State University in 1976, a Master of Business Administration from George Washington University in 1980, and a Juris Doctor from IIT/Chicago-Kent College of Law in 1985.

21

§ 2.1   Introduction

Numerous insurance alternatives are available to construction contractors seeking coverage for construction failures. Although certain principles may apply across the board, application of these principles must be considered in light of specific internal and external factors affecting the contractor. This chapter will define construction failure from the contractor's perspective and then examine insurance coverage.

The specific types of failure the contractor may encounter vary with the source of the loss. Although no insurance alternative can indemnify the contractor whose company experiences financial insolvency for whatever reason, insurance alternatives exist for the financial failure of the project or of the parties involved, such as the property owner, the financial institution obligated to pay losses pursuant to a letter of credit relationship between it and the insurer, surety, or in some situations the contractor, a major supplier of material or equipment, a vendor, or even an insurer. All of these possible failures must be evaluated in a liability context so that proper types and amounts of coverage can be secured.

ANALYZING PROJECT-RELATED
FINANCIAL FAILURES

§ 2.2   Failure of Project

A financial failure of the project will probably not affect the liability of the contractor, because typically the owner secures coverage for the project and the contractor secures its own coverage, which is limited to only contractual protection for the project. Furthermore, the owner's insurer may also waive subrogation rights against the contractor or subcontractor for alleged negligent acts or omissions of their respective employees or agents.

One major exception involves an Owner Controlled Insurance Program (OCIP). Under an OCIP, sometimes referred to as a "Wrap-Up," the owner typically procures all coverages protecting both the owner and various contractors involved with the construction project. The most serious risk a contractor being protected under an OCIP experiences is the catastrophic loss that may exhaust the aggregate limits of an OCIP. Owners not uncommonly underestimate these potential losses, and contractors should negotiate the cost of placing more coverage if the OCIP limits are inadequate. Beyond coverage concerns, an OCIP may disrupt a contractor's usual relationships with both insurers and brokers and may cause additional administrative burdens, particularly in the areas of coverage and claims administration coordination.

§ 2.3   Failure of Owner

The financial failure of an owner generally does not affect a contractor unless the contractor has held the owner harmless from ensuing liability. Such a contractor may be exposed for an amount equal to the owner's self-insurance initial layer contribution.

§ 2.4   Failure of Financial Institution

The failure of a financial institution that has issued a letter of credit permitting a contractor to avoid securing a performance bond may possibly affect contractor liability in two ways. Under such a letter of credit, the owner would be the beneficiary (the party that could draw against the letter of credit), and the contractor would contractually be obligated to reimburse the financial institution for all monies the institution paid the owner pursuant to such draws. The contractor in this situation is known usually as the customer or account party.

First, assuming that such a letter of credit arrangement would require the owner to submit documents (such as an architect's certificate specifying default) in order to be paid by the issuing bank, any collateral previously tendered or monies paid to the issuing bank by the contractor would take priority over the depositors and creditors of the insolvent bank under §§ 5-102 and 5-117 of the Uniform Commercial Code (U.C.C.).[1] However, no such priorities between a letter of credit customer's collateral and the creditors and depositors of the insolvent issuing bank exist under the U.C.C. for letters of credit that do not require the beneficiary to tender documents for payment. Thus, if a beneficiary is not required to submit documents to collect under the letter of credit, the contractor who has arranged a letter of credit with a later insolvent bank could forfeit portions of the collateral previously pledged the bank, the amount of such forfeiture being dependent upon the bankruptcy distribution plan ultimately adjudicated in bankruptcy court. The contractor would then also remain fully liable for all monies owed the owner as the beneficiary of the letter of credit.

The second manner by which a contractor could be affected by an insolvent bank that issued a letter of credit on its behalf is if the letter of credit issued by the bank is a negotiation credit rather than a straight credit. Unlike straight letters of credit, negotiation credits can be freely sold in the commercial market just as notes and checking account drafts are sold when a party receives payment and then endorses the backside of the note or check. Should a negotiation credit draft be sold to another institution before it is presented back to the issuing, now bankrupt, financial institution for payment or acceptance, the contractor may then be obligated to also pay such parties who may be holders in due course of the draft.

Under the U.C.C., a party purchasing an instrument such as a letter of credit draft becomes a holder in due course if that party pays value for the draft and has no notice of any defenses the customer may have against the beneficiary.[2] A common situation involves the party drawing against the letter of credit, in this case an owner, who sells its draft at a

---

[1] The U.C.C. governs a variety of commercial transactions including but not limited to sales of goods valued at $500 or more, commercial banking practices, commercial paper such as promissory notes and checking account drafts, letters of credit arrangements, warehousing transactions and related matters such as transporting and shipping of goods, and secured transactions in which a lender obtains certain legal interests in items a borrower pledges the lender as collateral for the loan. The U.C.C. has been adopted in all 50 states although there are some variations across states regarding specific provisions of the Code.

[2] *See* §§ 3-301 through 3-304 of the U.C.C.

discount to a buyer who gives value expecting to then recover the full value of the draft when the buyer presents the draft to the issuing bank at maturity. The purchasing party in this situation has the very favorable status of a holder in due course of a negotiated draft, and that holder may be able to force the contractor to honor the draft, even though the contractor may have paid the owner after being notified of the bank's insolvency. A contractor may therefore avoid the harshness of the due course rule by restricting the negotiability of any drafts drawn against its issuing bank's letter of credit.

The same principles could likewise apply if a contractor makes use of a letter of credit to finance its own levels of insurance retention with a fronting insurance company as the party who would be authorized to draw against the letter of credit. Here, also, a contractor should ensure that the fronting company is restricted from negotiating the drafts to third parties who could become holders in due course.

§ 2.5   Failure of Major Material or Equipment Vendor

The failure of a project vendor will not affect any property coverages on a project, but there could be resulting liability exposure for the contractor under construction contracts in which time is commonly of the essence. Beyond these contract-related exposures, the contractor could also be at risk of business interruption liability should commercial tenants be deprived of their timely use of the premises. However, material changes by the owner to either equipment or materials or their specifications in the construction contract, which in turn delays project completion, are not likely to result in contractor liability. Should such a claim be asserted against the contractor, the contractor would likely avoid liability by impleading the owner, who may actually have been responsible for the resulting delays.

§ 2.6   Failure of Insurer

Insurer failure has become an increasing concern to contractors since the 1970s. The consequences of an insurer failure may include an inability to pay incurred claims and a forfeiture of monies the contractor-insured may have paid pursuant to a retrospective, loss sensitive premium program. Placing coverage with an insurer that may subsequently face liquidation proceedings can best be avoided by choosing only insurers admitted to write coverage in the state in which the project is located and favorably rated by professional insurance societies.

OBTAINING ALTERNATIVE COVERAGE

§ 2.7   A Contractor's Loss of Coverage

Essential to analyzing a contractor that has had its coverage cancelled is determining the cause of the cancellation. The cancellation may have resulted from an excessive number of claims being filed (frequency) or because of a single-shock loss (severity) problem.

A contractor that has lost its coverage or been threatened with a cancellation of coverage should immediately assess the feasibility of either implementing a risk management program or strengthening an existing one. Should such an effort not be likely to abate either claims frequency or severity, the contractor may need to consider implementing a deductible large enough (from an insurer's standpoint) to reduce claims frequency.

Severe losses involving multiple deaths or serious injuries, such as a walkway collapse in a commercial building crowded with people, may cause extraordinary insurer scrutiny because of the high visibility such a loss is likely to generate. A loss sufficiently catastrophic to exhaust a contractor's aggregate coverage may in effect bring that contractor's operations to a standstill. Other owners for whom the contractor is rendering services pursuant to construction contracts may demand assurances of insurance coverage availability. A contractor facing a claim likely to exhaust aggregate limits may not be able to satisfactorily respond to such coverage assurances, causing that contractor to be in potential breach of contract.

§ 2.8   Coverage Options Available to the Contractor

Insurance industry options that will either resolve lack of coverage availability or reduce the coverage to a level of affordability include:

1. Self-Insurance
2. Increased Retention/Deductibles
3. Loss Sensitive Program
4. Captives
5. Risk Retention/Purchasing Groups.

The same criteria must be applied in evaluating all of these options. These criteria include projecting a contractor's projected losses based on previous claims experience, estimating settlement/payment patterns, and determining a contractor's use of monies set aside to pay expected claims. The manner in which such monies are used is dependent upon the duration of expected claims—that is, does the contractor expect claims to average one year, four years, or seven years, or some combination? The expected claims duration likely affects both the type of investments the contractor makes and the economic returns on those investments. Federal tax issues involving insurance premium deductibility from taxable income are also involved, particularly so for a contractor that may choose the fourth option to self-insure by forming a captive insurance company.

The five options referenced above are used to select the optimal risk funding method, and none of them addresses the possibility of eliminating or transferring losses.

The risk management oversight function will become, if it has not already done so, the overriding concern on construction sites. Mitigating losses through loss prevention activities, or by transferring those losses to others by subcontracting, is critically important. Although the best risk management program may be impossible to quantify, avoiding money damages losses and intangible losses (such as negative public relations) can nevertheless be accomplished by effective risk management programs.

The numerous factors involved in the computations of expected losses and loss adjustment expense must be expertly calculated and analyzed to determine the most effective insurance program for any given contractor. It is absolutely essential that the appropriate personnel of any contractor fully understand the insurance program chosen, particularly if the plan is a loss sensitive program where actual premiums may be adjusted for up to several years subsequent to the policy period.

§ 2.9   —Self-Insurance

Self-insuring losses differ from a contractor's decision to "non-insure" and pay losses from retained earnings. **Table 2–1** compares the two options. Although self-insurance may sometimes appear to be the be-all and end-all in managing insurance costs, it may not be the best alternative for every coverage requirement. Each coverage requirement should be assessed individually, based on the strengths and weaknesses of a self-insurance program as listed in **Table 2–2**. Determining whether self-insurance may be the best insurance option can be made only after a feasibility study that addresses these issues has been performed.

Table 2-1

A COMPARISON OF SELF-INSURANCE AND
NON-INSURANCE PROGRAMS

Insurance Element	Self-Insurance	Non-Insurance
Loss probability	Actuarially determined	"Ball park" estimate
Funding	Contributions to separate account based on net present value of expected future losses	From cash flow
Claims administration	Contractually performed by third-party administrator	Performed by company's office manager
Loss prevention	Formal program directed or assisted by professionals	Nonexistent or haphazardly performed
Excess insurance	Placed above actuarially determined retention	Based only on what is available

Table 2-2

SELF-INSURANCE PROGRAMS

Strengths	Weaknesses
Cost directly related to loss experience	May need to qualify program in several states
Excellent cash flow	Administrative responsibilities in claims handling and loss prevention
Control over loss control and claims handling	Excess coverage will still need to be placed
May avoid state taxes and assessments	No appropriate stop-loss in certain states
	May encounter difficulty in securing certificates of insurance
	Financial statements may need to be qualified
	Liquidating fund may be difficult

§ 2.10   —Increased Retention/Deductible

Another method to increase insurance cost control is to increase the internal deductible rather than being covered on a "first dollar" basis. Cash flow may be enhanced to the extent that the insurer actually pays claims within the deductible and then bills the insured-contractor on a quarterly or, better yet, annual basis. The strengths and weaknesses of this arrangement are listed in **Table 2–3**.

All the factors in **Table 2–3** need to be analyzed before choosing to increase the deductible or retention level. One of the tests available under this alternative is the "least cost analysis,"[3] which involves computing various costs at multiple simulations to determine which set will result in the least costly program.

§ 2.11   —Loss Sensitive Premium Rating Plans

There are several kinds of insurance plans in which the premium paid by the insured is loss sensitive—that is, the actual premium paid varies

Table 2–3

INCREASED INTERNAL DEDUCTIBLES

Strengths	Weaknesses
Ease of implementation	Increased volatility of expense
Transfer of risk of losses above the deductible	Premium reduction may not properly correlate to risk assumed
Reduced premium payments	Potential cost of retained losses is unlimited
Loss control incentive	Obtaining excess insurance may be difficult
Friction costs avoided	Large deductibles may require a pledge such as a letter of credit or other collateral
Improved cash flow	Financial statements may need to be qualified
	Loss of some federal income tax deductions

---

[3] Performing a least cost analysis involves simulating coverage cost options after loading differing (1) assumptions for expected losses, (2) time spans for when claims are opened until resolution, and (3) insurance program-related fees and administrative expenses.

with the insured's loss experience and the insured's size of premium. All of these plans are retrospective in nature: the insured's actual premium is calculated after the applicable policy term has expired and is based on actual loss experience. Prospective rating plans calculate the insured's premium at the inception of the policy, resulting in premium determinations based on estimated projections rather than on actual loss experience.

Numerous retrospective plans currently exist, and their continued proliferation appears to be bounded only by the creative ideas of insurance professionals. The underlying computation of a retrospective premium involves a basic premium, an adjustment of incurred losses by a loss conversion factor, an excess loss premium that is usually separately incorporated to mitigate the effect that a multiple-line shock loss may otherwise have on the retrospective basic premium computation, and a tax multiplier that varies by line of insurance coverage and by state. The formula is illustrated in **Figure 2–1**. The computed premium is added to the excess premium that is paid to cover severe shock liability losses. The excess premium is not subject to retrospective adjustment but is exposure-related.

A brief description of some of the more prevalent types of loss sensitive premium plans is shown in **Figure 2–1**.

Divided Plans.   These plans provide for a potential return of the premium to the insured after policy expiration. The dividend may be determined as a flat percentage of the premium, as a percentage of the premium that varies with premium size, or as a return of an unused premium. Flat divided plans are not affected by loss experience occurring within the policy year; sliding scale dividends are loss sensitive in that dividend percentages paid to the insured will be related proportionally to that insured's loss experience. Dividends can never legally be guaranteed by an insurer because of statutory restrictions found universally throughout the states that restrict dividends to be paid only from profits of an insurance company.[4]

$$
\begin{array}{l}
\text{Indicated} \\
\text{Retro} \\
\text{Premium}
\end{array}
=
\left\{
\begin{array}{l}
\text{Basic} \\
\text{Premium}
\end{array}
+
\begin{array}{l}
\text{Converted} \\
\text{Losses}
\end{array}
+
\begin{array}{l}
\text{Excess} \\
\text{Loss} \\
\text{Premium}
\end{array}
\right\}
\times
\begin{array}{l}
\text{Tax} \\
\text{Multiplier}
\end{array}
$$

Figure 2-1. Retrospective premium computation formula.

---

[4] *See, e.g.,* 4050 of the Cal. Ins. Code § 4050 (1963) (dividends payable by domestic mutual insurers limited to net realized savings, net realized earnings, or net capital gains); § 54 of the Illinois Insurance Code, Ill. Rev. Stat. ch. 73, Para. 666 (1959) (dividends payable by domestic mutual insurers limited to earned as opposed to contributed surplus); § 4105 of the N.Y. Ins. Law § 4105 (1939) (dividends of domestic stock insurers payable only from earned surplus); Tenn. ins. code, Tenn. Code Ann. § 56-3-108, 109 (1932) (dividends of insurers payable only from surplus profits and never from unearned surplus).

Tabular Plans. The National Council on Compensation Insurance (NCCI) has developed tables of predetermined retrospective rating plan values. These preset tables comprise four different plans, each with its own retro factors based on the levels of standard premium. These plans apply only to workers' compensation. There are some unique plans in certain states, but the majority of the states utilize the same four programs.[5]

Retrospective Rating Plan D. The NCCI Plan D is similar to the described tabular plans but differs from them in two important aspects. First, a Plan D offers a wider range of available minimums and maximums with respect to standard premiums. Secondly, a Plan D can be used for other lines of coverage beyond workers' compensation, including long-term construction project retrospective plans.

For a long-term construction project to be considered eligible for a retrospective rating Plan D, the estimated standard premium should be at least $250,000 or more per year. These plans may be applied to either long-term construction projects or, in some states,[6] a wrap-up project. Long-term projects are those which are expected to take at least one year to complete. Wrap-up programs are those involving a single coverage policy for multiple parties involved in the project. The parties' exposures under the wrap-up project are excluded from their respective individual insurance programs. Workers' compensation and general liability coverages are typically included in the wrap-up, while automobile coverages are typically not, owing to the inherent likelihood that covered vehicles will be used interchangeably for other projects outside the wrap-up program.

Loss Divisor/Loss Multiplier Plans. These are variations of a retrospective program that produce final retrospective premiums based on incurred losses either divided by a divisor or multiplied by a multiplier. Typically, loss divisors range from .70 to .85 and loss multipliers from 1.20 to 1.40.

---

[5] These four different plans for workers' compensation establish differing retrospective factors based on the respective standard premiums. For retrospective plans involving liability other than workers' compensation insurance, states may require a threshold premium before a retrospective plan can be written. New York, for example, requires any retrospectively rated plan for liability insurance to generate not less than $5,000 in an annual premium. Furthermore, any such plan in New York must contain reasonable factors that give appropriate recognition to the distinct exposures involved in such coverages. *See* N.Y. Comp. Codes R & Regs. tit. 11, subchapter D §§ 161.5 through 161.9 (1987).

[6] South Carolina, for example, has approved a retrospective rating plan D for general liability involving a wrap-up insurance program for large construction projects. Both general and automobile liability can be included if a wrap-up program for workers' compensation involving not less than $500,000 in a standard premium is written by one insurer. *See* S.C. Dep't of Ins. Bulletin No. 74-19 (July 18, 1974).

These programs are generally not used because sophisticated insurance buyers are aware of the inconsistencies of the program.

These various loss sensitive plans are designed to provide an insured-contractor with a mechanism to tie coverage costs as closely as possible to actual loss experience. As suggested earlier, successful risk management and loss prevention programs are critically important for a contractor to reduce insurance costs by means of a retrospectively rated, loss sensitive program.

Unfortunately, a contractor may be very hesitant to seriously consider using these types of insurance programs due to previous adverse outcomes, which may have occurred because the contractor was not fully and properly informed of the mechanics of the program. Inadequate or misinforming explanations have resulted in contractors and, for that matter, every other classification of insureds not realizing that their actual premium for a given policy period may not be determined until five to 10 years after the policy's expiration. The classic case involves an insured's principals who, owing to misinformation, believe that the insured's premiums have been completely paid when in fact a retrospective program may have been written and such premium amount may not be fully determined for as many as two, three, five, or even 10 years beyond the policy's expiration date. Determining a retrospective premium may require considerable time because of the difficulties associated with claims spanning several years from the date of opening to the date of ultimate resolution. The resulting premium adjustment may be quite costly, to the point of threatening the contractor's ability to pay the retrospective premium while continuing to meet expenses on a competitively bid subsequent construction project. Such potential consequences of a loss sensitive program cannot therefore be overemphasized to a contractor.

§ 2.12   —Elements of Loss Sensitive Plans

The key elements of a loss sensitive program are the standard premium, the basic premium factor, the maximum premium percentage (the increase that can be made retrospectively based on loss experience), the loss conversion factor, the per claim loss limit (other than the limit that may be established involving a separate, excess premium to anticipate shock loss), the applicable boards and bureaus percentages, and tax, license, and fee percentages payable for coverage in the state where the construction will take place.

Standard Premium.   The standard premium is based on an estimated exposure base as applied to rates developed by the insurance industry and adjusted with an experience modifier, if applicable. The standard premium is computed prior to the retrospective adjustment which is based on actual claims experience after the policy period as previously explained. Standard premium "rates" quoted should be applied to a contractor's "full expected" exposures.

Basic Premium Factor.   This is an adjustment made for fixed costs that is imposed to the standard premium. It should be an amount at least six percent but not in excess of 12 percent of the standard premium.

Loss Conversion Factor.   The loss conversion factor is applied to the insured's limited losses, which are the actual losses paid and those for which reserves have been set. In addition, limited losses sometimes include losses from occurrences which have happened but for which a claim file has not yet been opened (Incurred But Not Reported, or IBNR). Applying the loss conversion factor to the limited losses enables the insurance company to recapture its loss adjustment expenses (claims adjusters' expenses). The insurance company determines the appropriate charge by an assessment of the exposures involved with the construction project site, the frequency of expected losses, the types of losses, and the magnitude of losses. A loss conversion factor range for common construction projects should normally be between 1.075 and 1.125.

Although increasing the loss conversion factor may result in lowered insurance costs if losses are actually low due to the mathematical formula which provides that increasing the loss conversion factor actually reduces the basic premium factor (thus a one point increase in the former reduces the latter by approximately .7), significantly decreasing the loss conversion factor in anticipation of greater limited losses may result in an unacceptably higher basic premium factor. States' boards and bureaus percentages[7] and percentages for taxes, licenses, and fees vary widely. These percentages can be as low as 3.4 percent (in North

---

[7] Boards and bureaus are organizations that compute assessment percentages across lines of insurance that each insurer within that line must pay the state's insurance commissioner based on its computed percentage of coverage written. Such assessments are then contributed to residual insurance markets or assigned risk pools for high risk insureds who may otherwise be unable to obtain insurance coverage. *Boards* refers to rating boards of states that are usually agencies within the state's insurance department (*see, e.g.,* Oklahoma State Board for Property and Casualty Rates, Rule 18). *Bureaus* are private insurance rating organizations such as the National Council on Compensation Insurance, which computes previously described assessments on behalf of a state insurance commissioner. Such organizations are often called rating organizations. Oklahoma is not unlike several states in that it has its rating board but it also permits insurers to use private rating bureaus which then file rating assessments with the insurance commissioner. *See* Oklahoma Insurance Code, 36 Okla. Stat. Ann. § 332 (1957).

Carolina in 1987) and as high as 8.7 percent (in Montana in 1987).[8] Furthermore, these percentages may vary for insurance companies within the same state based on whether the company is a domestic or foreign (that is, out-of-state) insurer admitted to write coverage in the applicable state.

Maximum Premium Percentage. This is the most an insured will be obligated to pay, and is set as a percentage of the standard premium. There is no set ceiling, but generally previous experience determines a maximum premium percentage. If set too high, it will cause the insured to lose its income tax deduction of the standard premium. Under § 162 of the U.S. Internal Revenue Code[9] the premium may be excessive of the "ordinary and necessary" expenses entitled to income deductions from taxation; furthermore, an excessively high premium may run afoul of the risk shifting and risk distribution doctrine.[10] Maximum premium percentages of 110, 125, and 140 would generally be within the reasonable range, but percentages beyond 140 indicate a concerned underwriter. These maximum premium percentages and related risks are illustrated in **Figure 2–2.**

Loss Limit. Under a loss sensitive program this is the preestablished maximum above which any claim amount cannot affect the insured's cost. If, for example, the limit is $100,000, then all claims up to $100,000 will be computed as limited losses, but single claims in excess of $100,000 will be included only up to the first $100,000 in the computations. Shock loss

[8] *See* Montana Retrospective Rating Plan Manual, State Special Rating Values and North Carolina State Special Rating Values, Retro Rating Plan Manual, prepared by the National Council on Compensation Insurance as a duly licensed advisory organization pursuant to Mont. Code Ann. § 33-16-1001 (1947) and N.C. Gen. Stat. § 58-131.41 (1977), respectively.

[9] 26 U.S.C. § 162 (1954).

[10] The risk transfer doctrine emanated from the U.S. Supreme Court decision of *Helvering v. LeGierse,* 312 U.S. 531 (1941), where it was ruled that, for federal income tax purposes, insurance must involve both risk shifting and risk distribution. Risk shifting involves the transfer of risk to a third party. If the insured under a retrospectively rated plan pays excessive additional premiums beyond the standard premium, the U.S. Internal Revenue Service may deny deductibility because the IRS may then view such a transaction as not satisfying the risk transfer requirement. (*See, e.g., Steere Tank Lines, Inc. v. United States,* 577 F.2d 279 (5th Cir. 1978), *cert. denied,* 440 U.S. 946 (1979) in which it was held that an additional premium, beyond the basic premium, that the insured paid the insurer for purposes of paying claims with excess monies being refunded to the insured, did not constitute a transfer of risk.) As for the risk distribution requirement, the monies paid must be distributed or pooled by the insurer so that adequate funds are available to pay individual insured's losses based on actuarially determined estimated payouts.

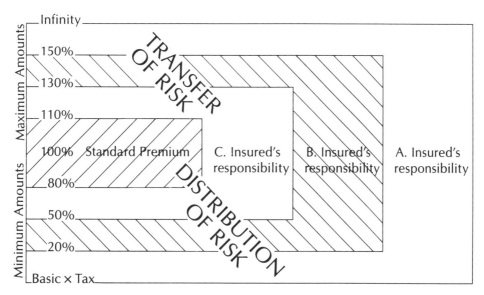

Figure 2–2. Insurance test of transfer and distribution. Every insurance program must meet this IRS test. If (1) the maximum is above 150 percent and the minimum below 20 percent, then the elements are all within the insured's responsibility and thus do not meet the test; (2) the maximum is above 130 percent and the minimum is below 50 percent, then some elements are present—are there enough?, and (3) the maximum is above 110 percent and the minimum is below 80%, there is every reason to believe the test will be met. However, each case is evaluated on its merits and to date the IRS has not specified minimums or maximums.

coverage for claims in excess of the loss limit is covered under excess coverage, which typically involves a separately established premium, as previously discussed. The primary benefit of a loss sensitive program is that premiums are determined and paid based on actual losses. Loss prevention thus translates into reduced insurance costs.

§ 2.13   —Considerations for Choosing Loss Sensitive Plans

The strengths and weaknesses of a retrospective based loss sensitive program are listed in **Table 2–4**. Again, the use of retrospective loss sensitive plans must be clearly understood by a contractor-insured before such an insurance program is established. Adjusting the actual premium long after the policy period has expired may potentially cause serious harm to a contractor that has not anticipated this premium liability.

Table 2–4

RETROSPECTIVE LOSS SENSITIVE PROGRAM

Strengths	Weaknesses
Premium based on actual experience	Premium not determinable for potentially long period of time
Total cost in primary layer is capped	May require security in form of letter of credit or other collateral
Possible favorable payment terms	Deductibility of premium may receive greater IRS scrutiny
Fully insured status advantageous in placing excess coverage	Cancellation may be onerous
	Disputes over reserving may be more likely

§ 2.14   —Captive Insurance Companies

A captive insurance company is formed by a company or group of companies to provide various types of insurance related to their operations. The captive's most common form is as a reinsurance company.

Before any individual company or group of companies ventures into the insurance business, there should be a feasibility study done to assess a captive's advantages and disadvantages, shown in **Table 2–5.**

A group-owned captive typically is operated as a reinsurance company that in turn uses a "fronting company." The fronting company is an insurer admitted in the state where the coverage is needed and it writes the coverage on its "paper." These relationships and the flow of operation are described in **Figure 2–3.**

§ 2.15   —Risk Retention/Purchase Groups

These groups are very similar to group captives, except they are formed and regulated under federal legislation. Under the Product Liability Risk Retention Act of 1981,[11] companies engaged in businesses or activities with similar liability exposures are permitted to join together for purposes of obtaining insurance coverages. These groups can then operate in all states after receiving a charter as a risk retention group in one state, so long as they submit to any state other than their charter state a business

---

[11] *See* U.S. Pub. L. No. 97-45 effective September 25, 1981. The law was amended in 1986 by the Risk Retention Amendments of 1986, Pub. L. No. 99-563. These laws are codified at 15 U.S.C. § 3901 (1981).

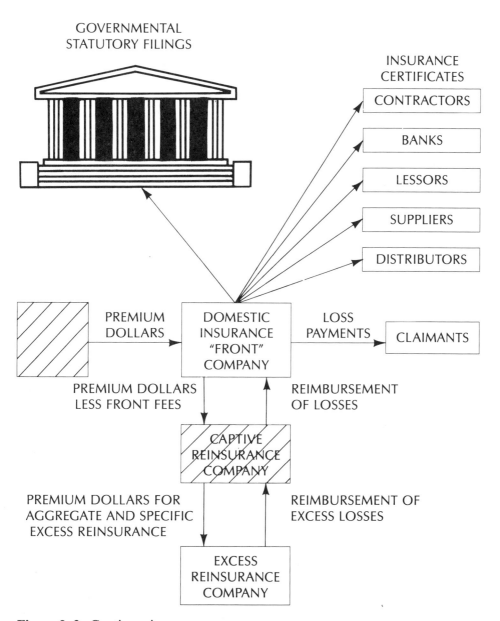

Figure 2–3. Captive reinsurance company.

Table 2–5

CAPTIVE INSURANCE COMPANIES

Advantages	Disadvantages
Premium affordability	Risk sharing and pooling may strain thinly capitalized company
Cash flow	
Coverage availability	Significant managerial commitment required of companies forming captive
Control of administrative expense	
Control of claims	Initial capital contribution significant –minimum capitalization requirement of local law must be established
Operational flexibility	–maximum premium-to-surplus ratio of local law must be met
Limited liability	–maximum retention-to-surplus ratio of local law must be met
Deductibility of premiums if at least 50 percent of coverage written by captive is on unrelated concerns	–sufficient capital may need to be pledged to secure fronting company, if any
	Start-up expenses
	Additional capital contributions owing to potential assessments, if any
	Shareholder dividends typically delayed

Table 2–6

RISK RETENTION GROUP

Advantages	Disadvantages
No fronting company needed	Not available for workers' compensation coverage
Can conduct business in all states	Statutorily mandated guaranty funds[12] inapplicable
	Excess insurance may be difficult to obtain
	State insurance commissioners may generally be unfavorable

---

[12] Guaranty funds are required by some states to provide additional policyholder security in the event an admitted insurer is forced into liquidation proceedings. Each company is assessed and the monies are accordingly paid into the guaranty fund for potential distribution to policyholders of a liquidated insurer.

operating plan (a feasibility study), audited financial statements, and an actuarial report. Any such group must also agree to be subject to each state's premium taxes and possibly to assigned risk pool and joint underwriting assessment funds that may be required by some states. This federal legislation was designed to increase insurance availability in some markets where coverage was either unobtainable or obtainable only by paying exorbitantly priced premiums.

The advantages and disadvantages of a risk retention group are listed in **Table 2–6**.

The risk purchasing group section of the federal risk retention law[13] goes further than permitting similarly situated companies with similar hazards to pool their liabilities and purchase insurance policies. It permits "unrelated" risks to join together to achieve "economies of scale" by collective bargaining. This provision essentially sets aside commonly adopted state insurance regulations addressing the "fictitious groups" of insureds. Before risk purchasing group programs existed, persons in need of similar insurance coverages would seek to become qualified to issue insurance policies by submitting applications indicating fraudulently the validity of their group formation. Since the passage of the Risk Retention Act, after joining together to strengthen their negotiating posture, any group may approach a licensed, admitted insurer who may be capable of combining these assorted exposures under one program that would operate in multiple states. For this scenario to be successful, there must be a motivated member of the group or a sponsor who will commit the necessary time to ensure the program is properly in place, the group must remain cohesive, and the premium charged the group must be at least somewhat profitable for the insurer. These programs can generally withstand a claims severity potential but usually cannot sustain losses owing to claims frequency. **Table 2–7** lists the advantages and disadvantages of a risk purchase group program.

Table 2–7

RISK PURCHASE GROUP

Advantages	Disadvantages
Exempt from state laws prohibiting group insurance purchasing	Completely market dependent
	Little if any control
Low capitalization	
Ease of administration	
Financial security may be desirable	

---

[13] *See* Risk Retention Amendments of 1986, Pub. L. No. 99-563 (15 U.S.C. § 3903) (1986).

Any contractor contemplating any type of coverage through either a risk retention or risk purchase group should consider carefully several matters pertaining to both finance and insurance. First, the potential participant should evaluate the risk involved with the group and compare that risk to the potential return the program may provide. That evaluation must include carefully studying the prospectus, bylaws, and other related documents of the group. Any potential participants should also plan to meet with the group's personnel and become familiar with the persons handling unearned premium and reserves investments. The financial analysis should not emphasize expected return on investment as much as compare the net present value cost of the plan with the costs of alternative insurance programs. A sensitivity analysis should also be performed using various assumptions as to expected losses, discount rates, and payout schedules. Before committing to join the group, the implications of withdrawing from the program and assessment aspects of the program should also be determined.

§ 2.16   Completed Operation Failure

One failure that has not previously been addressed is a completed operation failure that produces a major or catastrophic loss exceeding policy limits.

The failure of a highly valued commercial project could exhaust the policy limits of all parties including the contractor, the owner, and the property manager. An example might be the collapse of a shopping mall walkway during a peak shopping period. Beyond the claims for bodily injury and potentially wrongful death, commercial tenants could sustain tremendous business interruption losses.

To illustrate such a situation, assume that an owner, property manager, and general contractor have current policy limits in the amount of $100 million. Under a worst-case scenario involving the collapse at the shopping mall, the resulting losses could be in the area of $500 million. The insureds will thus need to secure retroactive excess limits in the amount of $400 million. The resulting coverage scenario and affect on the insureds' financial statements might be as depicted in **Table 2–8**. This scenario assumes longer payout periods as the amount of excess claims continues to increase toward the retroactive excess $400 million policy limit. This longer tail period is financially advantageous to the insured because it reduces the amount of monies that need to be set aside to satisfy demands at a later date.

However, should any such tail period be actually shorter than the period forecasted, an insurer may be unable to satisfy claims payment demands because of excessive present value discounting. For example, the excess

Table 2–8

RETROACTIVE COVERAGE THEORY SCENARIO

Loss: $500,000,000
Coverage: $100,000,000

Layer (000)	Probability Penetration	Limit (000)	Probable Payout	Premium (000)	Net Present Value*
$100,000 xs $100,000	100%	$100,000	2–4 years	$83,100	83.1%
$100,000 xs $200,000	80%	$ 80,000	3–5 years	$62,480	78.1%
$200,000 xs $200,000	50%	$100,000	4–6 years	$73,400	73.4%

Maximum Coverage	Possible Payout	Anticipated Premium
$400,000,000	$280,000,000	$218,980,000

*Assumes 6% discount rate.

insurers that wrote the retroactive excess coverage after the MGM Grand Hotel fire in 1980 that killed a number of people experienced this payment capability problem because many large claims were settled far sooner than had been anticipated. The present value discount computation had thus been overstated, causing the interest income earned on the discounted reserves to inadequately accrue. The matter was resolved after MGM sued its excess insurers, which ultimately paid all or some of the claims.

§ 2.17   Informational Sources for Choosing the Best Insurance Program Alternative

A contractor must gather a variety of information to analyze which of the foregoing insurance programs is best suited for its particular exposures.

Any insurer or risk retention/purchase group will require a fully completed insurance application. Such applications typically contain sections on applicant information, general liability, and an umbrella section. It is critically important for a contractor to accurately represent the information contained in the application, because it is this information that receives utmost scrutiny by a court of law that either or both of the parties may call upon to settle coverage-related disputes. Insurers oftentimes prevail in their denial of coverage by successfully demonstrating that an insured materially misrepresented information sought in the application.

The contractor should also compile a brief but complete description of its operations, including operational information about its affiliated or subsidiary entities and joint venture partners. Insurers may also want ownership-related information about such entities and access to related incorporating and governing documents. Many underwriters are also requesting financial information and may therefore want access to certified financial statements, annual reports, and various reports that publicly-owned companies may be required to file with the U.S. Securities and Exchange Commission, such as "10-K" statements.

Loss histories with detailed loss information typically in excess of $50,000 (although some underwriters may want detailed information on losses exceeding $10,000) must also be compiled. Most underwriters prefer loss histories back five years but some are requesting information as far back as 15 years. London underwriters require claims made-equivalent loss data. Exposure history and projections will also be required.

A contractor needs to prepare a list of prior carriers and the premiums paid them. All underlying policy limits and coverages also need to be compiled in addition to copies of current policies and endorsements.

Some underwriters are requiring access to loss control surveys prior to offering terms. Product brochures may also be requested so that statements made therein can be examined lest an injured party subsequently allege that such statements constituted binding contractual terms.

CHAPTER 3

RESPONSIBILITY FOR IDENTIFYING AND REMEDYING DESIGN DEFECTS DURING CONSTRUCTION

John B. Tieder, Jr., Esquire

Julian F. Hoffar, Esquire

William J. Ferguson, Jr., Esquire

John B. Tieder, Jr., is a senior partner in the Vienna, Virginia law firm of Watt, Tieder, Killian & Hoffar, where he specializes in private and public construction contract litigation. He is a visiting lecturer on government contract law at the William & Mary School of Law and a speaker for various associations, including the Construction Specifications Institute and the American Institute of Architects. He has authored various articles on construction contract problems. He is a member of the Federal and American Bar Associations and a participant in the ABA's Section of Public Contract Law and Section of Litigation.

Julian F. Hoffar is a senior partner in the law firm of Watt, Tieder, Killian & Hoffar, with offices located in Washington, D.C. and Vienna, Virginia. For the past 16 years Mr. Hoffar has specialized in the representation of owner-developers, contractors, subcontractors, engineers, and sureties involved in construction disputes in the United States, South America, Mexico, Canada, and the Middle East. His practice primarily involves the evaluation, preparation, negotiation, and litigation of construction contract claims. Mr. Hoffar has developed, presented, negotiated, and litigated numerous construction claims in both the public and private sectors of the construction industry.

William J. Ferguson, Jr., is a partner in the Vienna, Virginia law firm of Watt, Tieder, Killian & Hoffar. He is author of the monthly column in *Electrical Contractor Magazine* entitled "Contractors & The Law." He has also authored and co-authored a number of articles dealing with construction law. Mr. Ferguson has lectured before several industry groups and trade organizations on the subject of construction claims and construction litigation. He is a graduate electrical engineer, a former construction contractor, and a licensed master electrician in four states.

§ 3.1   General Responsibilities

Each construction project is unique in the sense that a diverse team of professionals is assembled to respond to the specific needs of a construction client. Common to most construction projects, however, are the practical concerns of time and money. Few, if any, construction clients can devote unlimited funds to a construction project. Because each project is a financial investment, time is also an important factor in determining whether the financial investment will be successful. It follows that virtually all construction projects are conceived and built by a team of professionals who have made various binding commitments to deliver a quality product at a fair price and within a reasonable period of time.

This chapter focuses on the common concern of those involved with a construction project to see that the project is constructed properly. In a perfect world, safety and functional accuracy should be of primary concern to every construction professional. However, practical considerations of time and money naturally limit each professional's ability to scrutinize his own work product or the work product of others. It is incumbent upon all construction professionals to make certain that a construction project is free of design defects and inherent faults that could result in construction failure. Accordingly, all members of the construction team—including owners, architects, engineers, construction managers, and contractors—must be aware of their responsibilities for identifying and remedying design defects during construction.

Virtually everyone involved with a construction project has a responsibility to look for, identify, and remedy potential causes of construction failure. Often these responsibilities are clearly defined by contract. However, even in the absence of express language in a contract, the law imposes certain responsibilities relating to design defects upon all those who participate in a construction project, whether or not they were directly involved in the preparation of the design documents.

Construction professionals, as well as owners, can be held liable for damages incurred as a result of a design defect or other form of construction failure. A party may recover damages under a number of legal theories, including breach of contract, negligence, breach of implied warranty, intentional misrepresentation, and fraud. Whether one or more of these theories of recovery is applicable in a given instance turns on the legal relationships between the parties, the facts of the particular case, and the legal precedents of the particular jurisdiction.

ROLE OF THE
CONSTRUCTION CONTRACTOR

§ 3.2   Contractor's Responsibility at Bidding Stage

Construction contractors are often in the best position to identify design defects and other potential causes of construction failure. Although owners, architects, engineers, and construction managers have the opportunity to review contract documents before they are released for bid, it is the construction contractor who will inspect the project site and assemble a team of specialty contractors to begin the actual work.

The bidding process is the first opportunity for a construction contractor to scrutinize in detail the various components of the construction work. The bidding process requires the contractor to view the project in its entirety and to determine how the project design, as conceived by a team of architects and engineers, will eventually be implemented, primarily from a perspective of time and cost of performance. The bidding process can serve as an initial "litmus test" to determine whether the design of the project is practical and can be constructed as set forth in the contract documents. Thus, it is incumbent upon the construction contractor to bring readily apparent design defects and other potential causes of construction failure to the attention of the owner and/or the owner's representatives as soon as they are discovered.

It is well established law that the owner impliedly warrants the accuracy and suitability of its plans and specifications for use in performance of the construction work.[1] If the specifications contain errors, omissions, ambiguities, or misdescriptions which significantly delay or hinder

---

[1] See United States v. Spearin, 248 U.S. 132, 39 S. Ct. 59, 63 L. Ed. 166 (1918); M.L. Shalloo, Inc. v. Riccardi & Sons Constr., Inc., 348 Mass. 682, 686–88, 205 N.E.2d 239 (1965).

performance, the contractor may recover his increased performance costs resulting therefrom.[2]

Even though the owner impliedly warrants the adequacy of its plans and specifications, a contractor cannot ignore with impunity defects or deficiencies in the contract documents that are obvious to him. As one court stated:

> If a contractor or a subcontractor is presented with an obvious omission, inconsistency, or discrepancy, he should take steps, by way of his own investigation, or by putting questions to the owner (or owner's representatives), to bridge gaps in the documents. *John F. Miller Co. v. George Fichera Constr. Corp., 7 Mass. App. 494, 499, 388 N.E.2d 1201 (1979).* If, as here, "a person furnishing labor and materials, who examines the specifications reasonably conscientiously, might miss a requirement which is out of sequence or ineptly expressed, the burden of the error falls on the issuer of the specifications. . . ." *Id.* at 498, 388 N.E.2d 1201.[3]

Conversely, if the discrepancy is a subtle one, so that a bidder who examines the specifications conscientiously might miss the error or defect, then the burden of the error falls on the issuer of the specifications, who is normally the owner.[4] Thus, when a bidder recognizes an omission, inconsistency, or discrepancy, he should at least ask the owner for guidance or clarification if he intends "to bridge the crevice in his own favor."[5]

The law requires a contractor to examine the plans and specifications prior to bid with "reasonable diligence" for the purpose of computing his bid.[6] It follows that a contractor who fails to undertake a review of the plans and specifications with reasonable diligence may be held responsible, in whole or in part, for the consequences if an obvious defect in the contract documents later results in a construction failure.

The rule with respect to design defects is similar to the rule regarding patent ambiguities in contract documents prepared by the government. As was stated in *Beacon Construction,*

---

[2] *See, e.g.,* Alpert v. Commonwealth, 357 Mass. 306, 321, 258 N.E.2d 755 (1970); Warner Constr. Corp. v. City of Los Angeles, 2 Cal. 3d 285, 466 P.2d 996, 85 Cal. Rptr. 444 (1970); Souza & McCue Constr. Co. v. Superior Court of San Benito County, 57 Cal. 2d 508, 370 P.2d 338, 20 Cal. Rptr. 634 (1962).

[3] Richardson Elec. Co. v. Peter Francese & Son, 21 Mass. App. 47, 484 N.E.2d 108, 111 (Mass. App. 1985).

[4] *See, e.g.,* Mountain Home Contractors v. United States, 425 F.2d 1260, 1264, 192 Ct. Cl. 16 (1970).

[5] Beacon Constr. Co. v. United States, 314 F.2d 501, 504, 161 Ct. Cl. 1 (1963); *see also* John F. Miller Co. v. George Fichera Constr., 7 Mass. App. 494, 388 N.E.2d 1201 (1979).

[6] *See, e.g.,* State Highway Dep't v. Hewitt Contracting Co., 113 Ga. App. 685, 149 S.E.2d 499 (1966).

The bidder who is on notice of an incipient problem, but neglects to solve it as he is directed to by this form of contractual preventive-hygiene, cannot rely on the principal that ambiguities in contracts written by the Government are held against the drafter. . . . Even more, the bidder in such a case is under an affirmative obligation. He "should call attention to an obvious omission in a specification, and make certain that the omission was deliberate, if he intends to take advantage of it."[7]

§ 3.3 —Site Investigations of Field Conditions

Most construction contracts require a contractor to notify an owner of defects in the contract plans and specifications as soon as the defect is discovered. It is not uncommon for construction contracts to contain a "site investigation" clause that requires prospective contractors to visit the project site prior to making a bid to ascertain the conditions under which the work will be performed.[8] In spite of such contract language, contractors often fail to investigate the site and accept as accurate the owner's representations in the contract documents regarding the site conditions. Courts have upheld owners' defenses that clauses of this nature protect the owner from liability due to inaccuracies in the specifications as to site conditions.[9] Nevertheless, such clauses are not enforced without exception. For example, in *Hollerbach v. United States,*[10] a contractor had entered into a contract with the government to repair a dam. In addition to a requirement that bidders investigate the work site, the contract included the following clause:

> The dam is now backed for about 50 feet with broken stone, sawdust and sediment to a height of within two or three feet of the crest, and it is expected that a coffer dam can be constructed with this stone, after which it can be backed with sawdust or other material.[11]

Once work had begun, the contractor discovered that the material was not of the character that had been represented in the contract documents.

The court concluded that the contractor was justified in relying upon the positive representations in the specifications. The court noted that, if the government had wished to place upon the contractor the burden of

---

[7] Beacon Constr. Co. of Mass. v. United States, 314 F.2d at 504 (citations omitted).

[8] *See, e.g.,* AIA Document A201-1987, art. 1, ¶ 1.2.2.

[9] *See, e.g.,* Zinger Constr. Co., ASBCA No. 26331, 82-2 B.C.A. (CCH) ¶ 15,988 (1982); Stock & Grove, Inc. v. United States, 204 Ct. Cl. 103, 493 F.2d 629 (1974).

[10] 233 U.S. 165, 34 S. Ct. 553 (Ct. Cl. 1914).

[11] *Id.* at 168.

discovering the actual conditions, it should have omitted the unequivocal representation of the character of the filling material.[12]

The construction contractor has a continuing duty to police his work and to inspect installations to make certain that errors, inconsistencies, or omissions are discovered in a timely manner. Most private contracts, as well as federal government contracts, have standard clauses that impose a duty upon the contractor to scrutinize the contract documents and to inspect the work as it is installed. AIA Document A201, for example, contains several provisions that delineate the contractor's responsibilities in this area, including a paragraph entitled "Review of Contract Documents and Field Conditions by Contractor." It reads in pertinent part:

3.2.1 The Contractor shall carefully study and compare the Contract Documents with each other and with information furnished by the Owner pursuant to Subparagraph 2.2.2 and shall at once report to the Architect errors, inconsistencies or omissions discovered. The Contractor shall not be liable to the Owner or Architect for damage resulting from errors, inconsistencies or omissions in the Contract Documents unless the Contractor recognized such error, inconsistency or omission and knowingly failed to report it to the Architect. If the Contractor performs any construction activity knowing it involves a recognized error, inconsistency or omission in the Contract Documents without such notice to the Architect, the Contractor shall assume appropriate responsibility for such performance and shall bear an appropriate amount of the attributable costs for correction.

This contract language places an affirmative duty upon the contractor to carefully study and compare the contract documents and discover errors, inconsistencies, or omissions therein. If the contractor knowingly fails to report such defects to the architect, the contractor may be held partially responsible for the results of such defects.

The requirement set forth in AIA Document A201 that the contractor report to the architect errors, inconsistencies, or omissions discovered in the contract documents, is consistent with the legal standards that have evolved in most jurisdictions regarding a contractor's duty to report known defects in design.[13]

A contractor's knowledge of a defect in the plans or specifications before being awarded the contract will prevent the contractor from recovering any of his increased costs allegedly resulting from the defect. As the Armed Services Board of Contract Appeals has stated, "Defects in specifications

[12] *Id.*

[13] *See, e.g.,* Bethesda Lutheran Church v. Twin City Constr., 356 N.W.2d 344, 349 (Minn. App. 1984) (contractor has a duty to alert the architect to potential defects in the specifications, and his failure to alert the architect would constitute a breach of contract and, possibly, negligence); *see also* Commonwealth of Pa. Dep't of Transp. v. Anjo Constr. Co., 87 Pa. Commw. 310, 487 A.2d 455 (1985).

of which a contractor has actual knowledge prior to bidding must be brought to the Contracting Officer's attention before the opening of bids, or the contractor will be deemed to have assumed the risk."[14]

The contractor's duty to identify design defects prior to bid is limited to obvious errors because the contractor is not normally under a duty to conduct an independent investigation of the contract documents to determine if they are adequate.[15] Accordingly, even if a design defect could have been discovered prior to bid, it will not prevent a contractor from recovering additional costs if it is found that the contractor acted reasonably under the circumstances.[16] However, if a contractor decides to perform work with knowledge of specification defects, he may be precluded from recovering the additional costs involved.[17]

§ 3.4   Shop Drawing Review

The shop drawing submittal process is another area in which a contractor assumes some responsibility for identifying design defects. Indeed, there is a trend towards placing increased responsibility on the contractor for shop drawing compliance with the contract documents even after the architect has approved the shop drawings during the review process. AIA Document A201 characterizes the contractor's responsibilities in this area as follows:

> 3.12.7   By approving and submitting Shop Drawings, Product Data, Samples and similar submittals, the Contractor represents that the Contractor has determined and verified materials, field measurements and field construction criteria related thereto, or will do so, and has checked and coordinated the information contained within such submittals with the requirements of the Work and the Contract Documents.
>
> 3.12.8   The Contractor shall not be relieved of responsibility for deviations from requirements of the Contract Documents by the Architect's approval of Shop Drawings, Product Data, Samples or similar submittals unless the Contractor has specifically informed the Architect in writing of such deviations at the time of submittal and the Architect has given written approval to the specific deviation. The Contractor shall not be relieved of

---

[14] S. Head Painting Contractor, Inc., ASBCA 26249, 82-1 B.C.A. (CCH) ¶ 15,629, *motion for reconsideration denied,* 82-2 B.C.A. (CCH) ¶ 15,886, at 77,204 (1982) (citing Allied Contractors, Inc. v. United States, 180 Ct. Cl. 1057, 1062–64, 381 F.2d 995, 998–1000 (1967)).

[15] *See* John McShain, Inc. v. United States, 188 Ct. Cl. 830, 412 F.2d 1281 (1969).

[16] *See, e.g.,* Johnson Controls, Inc., VACAB 1197, 79-1 B.C.A. (CCH) ¶ 13,763, *rev'd,* 80-1 B.C.A. (CCH) ¶ 14,212 (1979), *aff'd in part, rev'd in part,* 229 Ct. Cl. 445, 671 F.2d 1312, 1313 (1982).

[17] *See* Delphi Indus., Inc., AGBCA 76-160-4, 84-1 B.C.A. (CCH) ¶ 17,053 (1983).

responsibility for errors or omissions in Shop Drawings, Product Data, Samples or similar submittals by the Architect's approval thereof.[18]

The above language imposes a continuing responsibility on the contractor to review the shop drawings, product data, and samples for consistency with the contract documents and to independently approve the materials proposed therein as consistent with the requirements of the work and of the contract documents. However, this contract provision does not relieve the architect of its independent responsibility to review shop drawing submittals for compliance with the contract documents as set forth in the owner-architect agreement.[19]

§ 3.5   Site Inspections

A construction contractor also has responsibility to identify potential causes of construction failure during the inspection phases of the project. Construction contracts often impose a duty upon the contractor to inspect previously performed portions of the work to determine that the work has been properly installed and is ready to receive subsequent work. Many federal construction contracts include a clause entitled "Inspection of Construction." This clause imposes upon the government contractor a quality control requirement:

> (b)   The Contractor shall maintain an adequate inspection system and perform such inspections as will ensure that the work performed under the contract conforms to contract requirements. The Contractor shall maintain complete inspection records and make them available to the Government. All work shall be conducted under the general direction of the Contracting Officer and is subject to Government inspection and test at all places and at all reasonable times before acceptance to ensure strict compliance with the terms of the contract.
>
> (f)   The Contractor shall, without charge, replace or correct work found by the Government not to conform to contract requirements, unless in the public interest the Government consents to accept the work with an appropriate adjustment in contract price.[20]

Thus, it is generally recognized that the contractor has a continuing duty to police the work that he installs to insure that the work complies with the contract documents. If during this process a defect is discovered, then

---

[18] AIA Document A201-1987, art. 3, ¶¶ 3.12.7–3.12.8.

[19] *See, e.g.,* Alabama Soc'y for Crippled Children & Adults, Inc. v. Still Constr. Co., 54 Ala. App. 390, 309 So. 2d 102 (1975).

[20] 48 C.F.R. § 52.246-12 (1987).

the contractor has a duty to alert the owner or the owner's representatives to see that it is corrected.[21]

§ 3.6 Contractor's Responsibility for Correcting Defects—Differing Site Conditions

Once a design defect or construction failure has been identified, an appropriate remedy must be effected. The construction contractor usually plays an important role in seeing this process to a conclusion.

One potential cause of construction failure is a differing site condition. Federal government contracts, as well as AIA Document A201, set forth procedures to be followed when a differing site condition is encountered in the performance of the contract work. A differing site condition is defined in a federal government contract as: "(1) subsurface or latent physical conditions at the site which differ materially from those indicated in this contract, or (2) unknown physical conditions at the site, of an unusual nature, which differ materially from those ordinarily encountered and generally recognized as inhering in work of the character provided for in the contract."[22]

Before a contractor remedies a differing site condition, it is incumbent upon him to give the owner written notice of the condition and to allow the owner an opportunity to investigate the site and determine an appropriate course of action. The owner can then examine and evaluate the conditions encountered, consider changes in design or performance requirements to avoid or minimize the extra cost caused by the differing condition, and oversee the keeping of cost records on the differing conditions.[23]

§ 3.7 —Inspection of Construction Clauses

The method or methods by which a contractor is required to remedy a design defect or potential cause of construction failure is usually set forth in the contract documents. In particular, AIA Document A201 contains several provisions that specifically address the obligations of the contractor to remedy defects and correct faulty work. The document also imposes upon

---

[21] *See, e.g.,* Bethesda Lutheran Church v. Twin City Constr., 356 N.W.2d 344 (Minn. App. 1984); *see also* Delphi Indus., Inc., AGBCA 76-160-4, 84-1 B.C.A. (CCH) ¶ 17,053 (1983).

[22] *See* 48 C.F.R. § 52.236-2 (1987). Chapter 1 of Title 48 of the Code of Federal Regulations is known as the Federal Acquisition Regulations (F.A.R.). The F.A.R. applies to all federal government acquisitions for supplies and services (including construction) as defined in 48 C.F.R. §§ 2.000–2.201 (1987).

[23] *See, e.g.,* Blankenship Constr. Co. v. North Carolina State Highway Comm'n, 28 N.C. App. 593, 222 S.E.2d 452, 460 (1976).

the contractor an obligation to take reasonable precautions for the safety of persons and property and to provide reasonable protection to prevent damage, injury, or loss at the site.[24]

The contractor is generally required to correct potential causes of construction failures when ordered to do so by the owner or the owner's representative. The "Inspection of Construction" clause found in federal government contracts, as well as the "Uncovering and Correction of Work" provision found in Article 12 of AIA Document A201, each contain language that makes it incumbent upon the contractor to correct rejected work. Indeed, in both contracts the owner or the government has the authority to replace or correct the rejected work on its own if the contractor fails to promptly replace or correct the defective or nonconforming work.[25]

§ 3.8   —Contract Warranty Provisions

Most construction contracts contain some form of a warranty provision. The warranty provision obligates the contractor to remedy any defect in equipment, material, or design furnished or workmanship performed by the contractor within the warranty period.[26]

§ 3.9   —Compliance with Shop Drawings

When a construction failure occurs, the question often arises as to who is at fault. For this reason, it is essential that those involved with a construction project keep accurate records to document contract performance.

Shop drawings are one source of information that can be used to determine the cause of a construction failure. If field installations do not coincide with the shop drawings or the contract documents, then a presumption exists that the failure occurred in the implementation of the design and was caused by the contractor or subcontractor performing the work.

Similarly, if the work in the field is consistent with the shop drawings submitted for that portion of the project, but the shop drawings themselves are inconsistent with the actual contract documents, then this may imply that the entity in charge of reviewing the shop drawings for contract compliance did not do its job properly. Under these circumstances, the architect/engineer may be found liable, in whole or in part, for a resulting construction failure.

Finally, if the field installations are consistent with the shop drawing submittals and the original contract documents, a strong implication

---

[24] AIA Document A201-1987, art. 10.

[25] *See generally* 48 C.F.R. § 52.246-12 (1987) and AIA Document A201-1987, arts. 2 & 12.

[26] *See, e.g.,* AIA Document A201-1987, art. 3, ¶ 3.5.1.

exists that the original design itself was defective unless there is evidence of a fault in the materials used or the method of installation.[27]

ROLE OF THE ARCHITECT/ENGINEER

§ 3.10   Architect/Engineer's Responsibility for Design Documents

The responsibility of an architect/engineer to identify potential causes of construction failure must first be viewed in light of his duty to prepare professional quality design documents. As noted in § 3.2, an owner impliedly warrants that its plans and specifications are free from defect and sufficient for the purpose intended.[28] This standard, however, does not apply to an architect/engineer.[29] Thus, unless specifically agreed to in the owner/design professional contract, the architect/engineer does not impliedly warrant that its plans and specifications are free from defect nor does he guarantee that the result of the work will be what the owner intended.

In *Allied Properties v. John A. Blume & Associates, Engineers,*[30] the plaintiff claimed that an engineering firm impliedly warranted that a pier and floats designed by the firm were reasonably suitable for use by small craft. The court held that, because the primary purpose of the transaction was to obtain services, the doctrines of implied warranty and strict liability were not applicable. This is the majority view.

Other states declining to impose an implied warranty of fitness in regard to professional services rendered by architects and engineers include Colorado,[31] Minnesota,[32] Florida,[33] and New York.[34]

---

[27] *See, e.g.,* Alabama Soc'y for Crippled Children & Adults, Inc. v. Still Constr. Co., 54 Ala. App. 390, 309 So. 2d 102 (1975).

[28] *See* United States v. Spearin, 248 U.S. 132, 39 S. Ct. 59, 63 L. Ed. 166 (1918); M.L. Shalloo, Inc. v. Riccardi & Sons Constr., Inc., 348 Mass. 682, 686–88, 205 N.E.2d 239 (1965).

[29] A small minority of jurisdictions applies a stricter standard and holds that the architect/engineer warranted the adequacy of its plans and specifications. *See, e.g.,* Prier v. Refrigeration Eng'g Co., 74 Wash. 2d 25, 442 P.2d 621 (1968); Broyles v. Brown Eng'g Co., 275 Ala. 35, 151 So. 2d 767 (1963).

[30] 25 Cal. App. 3d 848, 102 Cal. Rptr. 259 (Cal. Dist. Ct. App. 1972).

[31] Johnson-Voiland-Archuleta, Inc. v. Roark Assoc., 40 Colo. App. 269, 572 P.2d 1220 (1977).

[32] City of Mounds View v. Walijarvi, 263 N.W.2d 420 (Minn. 1978).

[33] Audlane Lumber & Builders Supply, Inc. v. D.E. Britt Assoc., 168 So. 2d 333 (Fla.), *cert. denied,* 173 So. 2d 146 (Fla. 1965).

[34] Sears, Roebuck & Co. v. Enco Assocs., 43 N.Y.2d 389, 372 N.E.2d 555, 401 N.Y.S.2d 767 (Ct. App. 1977).

As was stated in *City of Mounds View v. Walijarvi,*

> [a]rchitects, doctors, engineers, attorneys, and others deal in somewhat inexact sciences and are continually called upon to exercise their skilled judgment in order to anticipate and provide for random factors which are incapable of precise measurement. The indeterminable nature of these factors makes it impossible for professional service people to gauge them with complete accuracy in every instance. . . . Because of the inescapable possibility of error which inheres in these services, the law has traditionally required, not perfect results, but rather the exercise of that skill in judgment which can be reasonably expected from similarly situated professionals.[35]

Thus, it is well established that an architect/engineer is bound to perform with reasonable care those duties for which he contracts.

§ 3.11 Administration of the Construction Contract

Architects/engineers do not guarantee absolutely perfect plans or specifications, but they do by their contracts imply that they possess requisite skill and ability as professionals and that they will exercise these skills without neglect.[36] It follows that when a design professional obligates himself to inspect the construction work, he exposes himself to liability for breach of contract or for his negligence in failing to detect defects in construction during the inspection process.[37]

In *Kleb v. Wendling,*[38] by oral contract with the owner, the architects undertook to superintend the actual construction of the building. The owner alleged that many defects resulted from the failure of the architects to properly administer the construction work. The appellate court noted that the law in Illinois was well settled with respect to the architect's duties under these circumstances: "It is the architect's duty, when superintending or overseeing the construction of a building, to prevent gross carelessness or imperfect construction. Mere detection of defective workmanship does not relieve him of a duty to prevent it."[39] The appellate court then remanded the case to the trial court to determine what defects, if any, could have been prevented by a vigilant architect.[40]

---

[35] 263 N.W.2d at 424.

[36] *See, e.g.,* Bloomsburg Mills, Inc. v. Sordoni Constr., 401 Pa. 358, 164 A.2d 201 (1960); *see also* Restatement (Second) of Torts § 299 A (1965).

[37] *See, e.g.,* Robert E. Owen & Assocs. v. Gyongyosi, 433 So. 2d 1023 (Fla. Dist. Ct. App. 1983).

[38] 67 Ill. App. 3d 1016, 385 N.E.2d 346 (1978).

[39] 385 N.E.2d at 349 (citing Lothloz v. Fiedler, 59 Ill. App. 379 (1895)).

[40] *Id.*

AIA Document B141

AIA Document B141, "Standard Form of Agreement Between Owner and Architect," requires the architect to provide administration of the contract for construction in several important respects. One duty of the architect is to "determine in general if the Work is being performed in a manner indicating that the Work when completed will be in accordance with the Contract Documents."[41] The architect is also required to "endeavor to guard the Owner against defects and deficiencies in the Work."[42] Thus, when an architect or an engineer assumes an administrative duty relating to a contract for construction, he will be held to the standard of care applicable to his profession and will be subject to an action for breach of contract, or for negligence, if that standard of care is not met.[43]

Under AIA Document B141, by issuing certificates for payment, the architect warrants that the "Work has progressed to the point indicated"[44] and that he believes it to be of appropriate quality. The architect is to review shop drawings and samples to see that they conform with the contract documents, although that review does not relieve the contractor of his contractual responsibility for the systems the contractor designed.[45] The architect has the further authority to reject any nonconforming work.[46]

The document also contains an article entitled "Additional Services." This article allows the owner to contract with the architect for nonbasic services, including the architect's selection of project representatives to assist in carrying out additional on-site responsibilities in order to "provide further protection for the Owner against defects and deficiencies in the Work."[47] Thus, under AIA Document B141, the owner may ask the architect/engineer to assume an expanded role in the administration of the construction contract.

§ 3.12   Shop Drawing Review

As immortalized in the Kansas City Hyatt construction failure, another area of contract administration that architects/engineers are often responsible for is shop drawing review. When an architect/engineer undertakes

---

[41] AIA Document B141-1987, art. 2, ¶ 2.6.5.

[42] *Id.*

[43] *See, e.g.,* Robert E. Owen & Assocs. v. Gyongyosi, 433 So. 2d 1023 (Fla. Dist. Ct. App. 1983); General Trading Corp. v. Burnup & Syms, Inc., 523 F.2d 98 (3d Cir. 1975).

[44] AIA Document B141-1987, art. 2, ¶ 2.6.2.

[45] *Id.,* ¶ 2.6.12.

[46] *Id.,* ¶ 2.6.11.

[47] *Id.,* ¶ 3.2.3.

the obligation to review shop drawing submittals for contract compliance, that obligation necessarily entails a duty to identify nonconforming items which may result in construction failure. For example, in *Jaeger v. Henningson, Durham & Richardson, Inc.,*[48] an architect was required to review shop drawing submittals relating to steel landing pans. The contract documents required all landing pans to be fabricated from 10-gauge steel with angle stiffeners. However, the architect erroneously approved a shop drawing calling for 14-gauge steel for a particular landing pan. The plaintiffs sued for injuries received as a result of a construction site accident proximately caused by the lack of 10-gauge steel and angle stiffeners. A judgment was entered on a jury verdict in favor of the plaintiffs based upon the architect's negligence, and the verdict was affirmed on appeal.

The architect/engineer's obligation to perform with reasonable care the duties for which he contracts should be distinguished from the obligation to supervise the job and employ all reasonable safety precautions, duties which are generally delegated to the contractor. Thus, when injury results due to the construction means, methods, or techniques chosen to perform the work, the contractor and not the architect will usually be responsible.[49]

§ 3.13   Job-Site Supervision

Normally an architect/engineer is not responsible for supervising the construction work unless he has agreed by contract to do so. However, when he does on his own initiative undertake certain activities that constitute supervision of the construction work, a duty to supervise the work may be imputed by law.[50] When he undertakes a duty to supervise the work, that duty may be deemed to include a duty to exercise reasonable care to avoid construction failures that threaten the safety of persons at the job-site.[51]

§ 3.14   Federal Government Contracts

The federal government often seeks indemnification from architects/engineers for design defects that result in additional construction costs.

---

[48] 714 F.2d 773 (8th Cir. 1983).

[49] *See, e.g.,* Waggoner v. W&W Steel Co., 657 P.2d 147 (Okla. 1982).

[50] *See, e.g.,* Hanna v. Huer, Johns, Neel, Rivers & Webb, 233 Kan. 206, 662 P.2d 243 (1983).

[51] *See generally* Annotation, *Liability to One Injured in Course of Construction Based Upon Architect's Alleged Failure to Carry Out Supervisory Responsibilities,* 59 A.L.R.3d 869 (1974).

The Federal Acquisition Regulations prescribe the policies and procedures to be followed by the government when contracting for architect/
engineer services. An architect/engineer's liability to the government
for design errors or deficiencies is described in the following regulatory
provision:

> Architect-engineer contractors shall be responsible for the professional qual-
> ity, technical accuracy, and coordination of all services required under their
> contracts. A firm may be liable for Government costs resulting from errors
> or deficiencies in designs furnished under its contract. Therefore, when a
> modification to a construction contract is required because of an error or
> deficiency in the services provided under an architect-engineer contract, the
> contracting officer (with the advice of technical personnel and legal counsel)
> shall consider the extent to which the architect-engineer contractor may
> be reasonably liable. The contracting officer shall enforce the liability and
> collect the amount due, if the recoverable cost will exceed the administrative
> cost involved or is otherwise in the Government's interest. The contracting
> officer shall include in the contract file a written statement of the reasons for
> the decision to recover or not to recover the costs from the firm.[52]

Not only is a government architect/engineer liable for government costs
resulting from design errors or deficiencies, but other regulations require
him to "make necessary corrections at no cost to the Government when
the designs, drawings, specifications, or other items or services furnished
contain any errors, deficiencies or inadequacies."[53]

The Federal Acquisition Regulations (FAR) require the contracting officer to insert a clause entitled "Responsibility of the Architect-Engineer
Contractor" in all fixed-priced architect-engineer contracts:

> (a)   The Contractor shall be responsible for the professional quality, techni-
> cal accuracy, and the coordination of all designs, drawings, specifications
> and other services furnished by the Contractor under this contract. The Con-
> tractor shall without additional compensation correct or revise any errors or
> deficiencies in its designs, drawings, specifications, and other services.
>
> (b)   Neither the Government's review, approval or acceptance of, nor pay-
> ment for, the services required under this contract shall be construed to
> operate as a waiver of any rights under this contract or of any cause of ac-
> tion arising out of the performance of this contract, and the contractor
> shall be and remain liable to the Government in accordance with the appli-
> cable law for all damages to the Government caused by the Contractor's
> negligent performance of any of the services furnished under this contract.
>
> (c)   The rights and remedies of the Government provided for under this
> contract are in addition to any other rights and remedies provided by law.

---

[52] 48 C.F.R. § 36.608 (1987).
[53] *See* 48 C.F.R. § 36.609-2 (1987).

(d)   If the Contractor is comprised of more than one legal entity, each such entity shall be jointly and severally liable hereunder.[54]

The FAR clearly articulate the duties and responsibilities assumed by architects/engineers on federal government projects. An architect/engineer will be held to a common-law standard of care with respect to these duties and obligations. The standard test has been described as follows:

> At common law, an architect was required to exercise that degree of ordinary and reasonable care, skill, and diligence as would be expected of an average member of the profession. . . . The common law standard was incorporated into the contract by clause 2(b) of the General Provisions [FAR 52.236-23].[55]

Thus, an architect/engineer can avoid liability to the government by exercising that degree of ordinary and reasonable care, skill, and diligence that would be expected of an average member of his profession.

In one interesting case, the government attempted to hold an architect/engineer liable for a defective design relating to a ventilation and incineration system.[56] However, the government did not allow the architect/engineer total discretion in designing the system: he was required to design the system in accordance with a Project Development Booklet prepared by the government. The booklet did not contemplate a system for treating dangerous toluene fumes that were present at the job-site. Rather, the booklet called for a simple ventilation system to exhaust the fumes into the atmosphere.

At the architect/engineer's suggestion, the government added a toluene abatement system to prevent air pollution. The architect/engineer informed the government, in writing, that the toluene abatement system could not prevent an explosive condition after the spraying of toluene. He suggested that the government include an inert gas generator system to eliminate the potential for an explosive condition, and even offered to submit a proposal for the additional engineering services associated with such a system. However, the government declined to discuss his proposal and did not reply to the letter.

Later, an explosion occurred at or near the incinerator during preliminary testing of the equipment and operational procedures. Secondary explosions followed, causing injuries to six persons and extensive property damage to the government facility. The government withheld substantial fees from the architect/engineer based on alleged deficiencies in the

---

[54] 48 C.F.R. § 52.236-23 (1987).

[55] The Eggers Partnership, IBCA No. 1299-8-79, 82-1, B.C.A. (CCH) ¶ 15,630, at 77,207 (1982).

[56] *See* Lockwood, Andrews & Newman, Inc., ASBCA No. 22956, 80-1 B.C.A. (CCH) ¶ 14,311 (1980).

design of the ventilation and incineration system. Nevertheless, the Armed Services Board of Contract Appeals determined that the architect/engineer was entitled to payment. It stated:

> We find that [the architect/engineer] satisfied its contractual obligation by designing a toluene abatement system within guidelines and limitations imposed by the Government and that the Government, when properly alerted by [the architect/engineer] to a potential weakness in the system and to a method for overcoming the weakness, (which method was subsequently commended by [the government's consultants]), accepted the design without improvement as adequately complying with the contract.[57]

It follows that an architect/engineer can avoid liability for a design deficiency provided he satisfies his contractual obligations and exercises the degree of ordinary and reasonable care, skill, and diligence that is expected of an average member of his profession.

Two rules of damage apply in the area of defective design. Normally, the measure of damages is the cost of correcting the defect. However, when the cost of correcting the defect would be unreasonable or disproportionate to the value of the structure, then the proper measure of damages is the difference between the value of the structure, with the defect, and the value that it would have had if it had been properly designed.[58]

§ 3.15   Contractor Actions against the Architect/Engineer

A relatively recent development in construction contract litigation has been contractor actions directly against project architects and engineers. These actions are allowable regardless of the existence of a contractual relationship between the contractor and the architect/engineer:

> The law imposes upon every person who enters upon an active course of conduct the positive duty to exercise ordinary care to prevent others from harm and calls a violation of that duty negligence. The duty to protect others from harm arises whenever one person is, by circumstances, placed in such a position towards another that anyone of ordinary sense who thinks would at once recognize that if he does not use ordinary care and skill in his own conduct with regard to those circumstances he will cause danger of injury to the person or property of the other. The duty to exercise due care may arise out of contractual relations. However, a complete binding contract between the parties is not a prerequisite to suit by a contractor against an architect. . . .

---

[57] Lockwood, Andrews & Newman, Inc., 80-1 B.C.A. (CCH) at 70,530.

[58] *See generally* Leo A. Daly Co., ENG B.C.A. (CCH) No. 4463, 85-1 B.C.A. (CCH) ¶ 17,740 (1984).

Accordingly, we hold that an architect in the absence of privity of contract may be sued by a general contractor or the subcontractors working on a construction project for economic loss foreseeably resulting from breach of an architect's common law duty of due care in the performance of his contract with the owner.[59]

Although most states now recognize that privity of contract is not a prerequisite to a negligence action, some state legislatures have clarified the issue by statute.[60]

When there is an enforceable contract between the parties, it may be possible to sue on both breach of contract and tort theories. Although the distinction between the two claims is not always clear, the court will examine the basis of the claim.

[W]hen the promisee's injury consists merely of a loss of his bargain, no tort claim arises because of the duty of the promisor to fulfill the term of the bargain arises only from the contract. The tort liability of parties to a contract arises from the breach of some positive legal duty imposed by law because of the relationship of the parties, rather than from a mere omission to perform a contractual obligation.[61]

Should a claim meet this description, a contractor may be able to recover in tort despite contract terms—such as allocation of risk clauses—limiting recovery.

The most common negligence claim against architects/engineers involves inadequate or misleading plans and specifications. In a North Carolina case, a general contractor's suit was allowed to proceed against an architectural firm for failing to provide adequate information concerning soil conditions which led to damage to an adjacent property.[62] In that case, an action for negligent misrepresentation was also allowed against the engineers who had performed the initial investigation of the soil conditions. A clause requiring that the contractors conduct a site inspection to gain complete understanding of the conditions did not shield the engineering firm.[63] Similarly, a suit against an architect for negligent and

---

[59] Davidson & Jones, Inc. v. County of Hanover, 41 N.C. App. 661, 255 S.E.2d 580, 584 (N.C. Ct. App. 1979), *cert. denied,* 298 N.C. 293, 259 S.E.2d 911 (1979) (citations omitted).

[60] *See, e.g.,* Miss. Code Ann. § 11-7-20 (1981).

[61] Battista v. Lebanon Trotting Ass'n, 538 F.2d 111, 117 (6th Cir. 1976) (citing Bowman v. Goldsmith Bros., 63 Ohio Law Abst. 428, 109 N.E.2d 556 (Ct. App. 1953)).

[62] Davidson & Jones, Inc. v. County of Hanover, 255 S.E.2d 580 (N.C. App. 1979), *cert. denied,* 259 S.E.2d 911 (N.C. 1979).

[63] *Id.; but see* Savin Bros. v. State, 62 App. Div. 511, 405 N.Y.S.2d 516, 520 (1978), *aff'd,* 419 N.Y.S.2d 969 (1979) (absent a showing of fraud, clause limiting liability concerning soil conditions bars recovery).

improper preparation of a drainage plan for a construction site was allowed to go to trial.[64]

Architects/engineers can also be held liable to contractors for their failure to properly supervise the construction work. In *Normoyle-Berg & Associates v. Village of Deer Creek,*[65] for example, the court held:

> A supervising engineer must be held to know that a general contractor will be involved in a project and will be directly affected by the conduct of the engineer. This relationship of supervising engineer and general contractor gives rise to a duty of care on the part of each party to the other.[66]

In *Bates & Rogers Construction Corp. v. North Shore Sanitary District,*[67] the Illinois court once again held that a supervisory architectural engineer owed a general contractor a duty to conduct his contractual activities in a non-negligent manner. The court in that case assessed the relationship between the architect, the owner, and the contractor and found that the architect did indeed owe the contractor a legal duty of due care in performing the functions which he had agreed to perform. The court stated:

> We have recently held that an engineer owes a contractor a duty of care in the design and administration of the project. . . . We cannot agree, however, that the pleadings show that the Engineers had no duty to the Contractor as a matter of law. To so conclude would conflict with the Illinois cases as well as a majority of the cases in other jurisdictions which have upheld that a duty runs from the architect or engineer who engages in tortious action which hinders and damages the Contractor.[68]

In either a negligent design or negligent supervision type of action against an architect or engineer, a contractor must prove the standard of ordinary care prevalent in the community and that the engineer's lack of care was the proximate cause of the damages incurred. Thus, a plaintiff bank was successful in its breach of contract theory against an architect but did not offer sufficient evidence to prove its tort claims.[69] The cause of action for negligent supervision and a failure to discover problems was not recognized because the bank did not establish the scope of supervision required by the professional standard.[70] The claim that the architect failed to specify the use of a bond breaker was dismissed because ordinary skill

---

[64] Owen v. Dodd, 431 F. Supp. 1239 (N.D. Miss. 1977).

[65] 39 Ill. App. 3d 744, 350 N.E.2d 559 (1976).

[66] *Id.; see also* W.H. Lyman Constr. Co. v. Village of Gurnee, 84 Ill. App. 3d 28, 403 N.E.2d 1325, 1333–34, 38 Ill. Dec. 721 (1980).

[67] 92 Ill. App. 3d 90, 414 N.E.2d 1274 (1980).

[68] Bates & Rogers Constr. Corp. v. North Shore Sanitary Dist., 414 N.E.2d at 1280 (citations omitted).

[69] First Nat'l Bank of Akron v. Cann, 503 F. Supp. 419 (N.D. Ohio 1980).

[70] *Id.* at 439.

did not require such a specification, and proximate cause was not proved because the disbonded caulking was only one of a number of sources from which moisture entered the wall.[71]

It should also be noted that subcontractors on a project can bring a negligence action directly against the architect/engineer. As is the case with general contractors, this action can be for inadequate plans and specifications[72] and improper supervision.[73]

An architect/engineer will not be held liable for a failure to perform duties that he is not required to perform. In one recent case, a Minnesota court ruled that an architect was not hired to inspect construction work in progress and that the architect was not responsible for the collapse of a parapet caused by contractor-initiated deviations from the plans and specifications.[74] The architectural firm had proposed to the owner that it provide detailed construction drawings and construction observation services for a fixed fee. However, the owner elected only to hire the firm to prepare conceptual drawings for the project. After construction began, the owner agreed with the construction contractor's recommendation to make changes to a portion of the architect's design. A construction failure later occurred, resulting in personal injury and extensive property damage.

The court of appeals of Minnesota agreed to dismiss the architect from the lawsuit on a motion for summary judgment. The court noted that the scope of the design professional's responsibilities is determined by his agreement with the project owner. It held that the contractor clearly deviated from the architect's drawings so that the architect could not be held responsible for the resulting damage:

> The Press Bar chose to contract for conceptual plans, for less money, rather than the more expensive arrangement which would have provided supervision. The conceptual plans produced by [the architect] did not include the duty to inspect or supervise. . . . The plans and design of a professional are not the proximate cause of an injury if the work was not constructed or performed according to the plans.[75]

§ 3.16   The Economic Loss Doctrine

The extent of the design professional's liability in the absence of privity of contract remains an unsettled area of the law. In particular, architects/

---

[71] *Id.; see generally* Barton, *Architect/Engineer Liability to Third Parties,* Construction Briefings 80-3 (May 1980).

[72] Gurtler, Herbert & Co. v. Weyland Machine Shop, Inc., 405 So. 2d 660 (La. Ct. App. 1981), *writ denied,* 410 So. 2d 1130 (1982).

[73] Detwelier Bros. v. John Graham & Co., 412 F. Supp. 416, 421 (E.D. Wash. 1976).

[74] *See* Goette v. Press Bar & Cafe, Inc., 413 N.W.2d 854 (Minn. Ct. App. 1987).

[75] *Id.*

engineers have been raising the defense of lack of privity of contract to prevent third-party actions for damages based on architect/engineer negligence when the damages sought are for purely economic losses. *Economic loss* has been defined as "damages for inadequate value, costs of repair and replacement of the defective product, or consequent loss of profits—without any claim of personal injury or damage to other property."[76]

Thus, when an architect/engineer is sued in negligence for a construction failure, a threshold legal issue is whether the law of the jurisdiction permits a party to be sued in tort for purely economic losses. One court has characterized the issue as being whether a third party who may be foreseeably injured by the negligent performance of an architect/engineer has a cause of action in negligence against the architect/engineer despite a lack of privity of contract.[77] In most states, third parties may sue an architect/engineer for the foreseeable economic harm caused by his negligence without the need to show personal injury or property damage. States that have allowed such actions include Arizona, California, Florida, Louisiana, Michigan, Missouri, New Jersey, North Carolina, Rhode Island, Washington, and Wisconsin. However, other states have applied the economic loss doctrine to bar third-party tort claims. These states include Alabama, Alaska, Georgia, Illinois, New York, Pennsylvania, Texas, and Virginia.

Some states have had difficulty applying the economic loss doctrine in a consistent manner. For example, Illinois courts generally have recognized that an architect/engineer owes a contractor a duty of care in the design and administration of a project.[78] However, in 1982 the Supreme Court of Illinois reviewed the background and history of the economic loss doctrine and held that a plaintiff cannot recover for purely economic losses under the tort theories of strict liability, negligence, and innocent misrepresentation.[79]

That leading Illinois case involved a products liability action brought by Moorman Manufacturing Company (Moorman) against the manufacturer of a grain storage tank, National Tank Company (National), and its parent company. Moorman sought to recover for economic losses caused by a crack that developed in one of the steel plates on the second ring of a grain storage tank it purchased from National. Moorman sued National under

---

[76] Note, *Economic Loss and Products Liability Juris Prudence,* 66 Colum. L. Rev. 917, 918 (1966).

[77] Forte Bros. v. National Amusements, Inc., 525 A.2d 1301 (R.I. 1987).

[78] *See* Normoyle-Berg & Assocs. v. Village of Deer Creek, 39 Ill. App. 3d 744, 350 N.E.2d 559; W.H. Lyman Constr. Co. v. Village of Gurnee, 84 Ill. App. 3d 28, 403 N.E.2d 1325, 38 Ill. Dec. 721; Bates & Rogers Constr. Corp. v. North Shore Sanitary Dist., 414 N.E.2d 1274 (Ill. App. 1980).

[79] *See* Moorman Mfg. Co. v. National Tank Co., 91 Ill. 2d 69, 61, 435 N.E.2d 443, Ill. Dec. 746 (1982).

several legal theories, including strict liability in tort, misrepresentation, and negligence. The court held that the plaintiff's remedy for economic loss lay in the area of contract law and that the tort theories of strict liability, negligence, and misrepresentation were more appropriately suited for claims involving personal injury or property damage.[80] Significantly, the *Moorman* court identified two exceptions to this general rule: (1) when a tortfeasor intentionally makes false representations and (2) when one who is in the business of supplying information for the guidance of others in their business transactions makes negligent representations.[81]

Since the *Moorman* decision, several Illinois cases have dealt with a third party's right to sue an architect/engineer for economic losses resulting from the architect/engineer's negligence. These cases have focused on the second exception to the general rule established in *Moorman,* that economic losses may be recovered in tort when the tortfeasor is in the business of supplying information for the guidance of others in their business transactions. The Appellate Court of Illinois for the Second District issued four decisions holding that a party not in privity of contract with an architect/engineer is precluded from suing him for economic losses resulting from the architect/engineer's negligence.[82]

In contrast to the above, the First and Third Districts of the Appellate Court of Illinois have issued decisions allowing a party to sue an architect/engineer for economic losses resulting from the architect/engineer's negligence when (1) the party was not in privity of contract with the architect/engineer,[83] and (2) the party was in privity of contract with him.[84]

The most recent decision in Illinois regarding the economic loss doctrine is *Oldenburg v. Hagemann.*[85] The *Oldenburg* court attempted to reconcile the other appellate decisions addressing this doctrine by focusing on the contract remedies that were available to the plaintiffs at the time their actions were instituted. The court concluded that a third party may not recover against an architect/engineer for economic losses caused by the architect/engineer's negligence if there is an adequate contractual remedy

---

[80] 91 Ill. 2d at 86.

[81] 91 Ill. 2d at 88–89.

[82] *See* Palatine Nat'l Bank v. Charles W. Greengard Assocs., 119 Ill. App. 3d 376, 456 N.E.2d 635 (1983); Bates & Rogers Constr. Corp. v. North Shore Sanitary Dist., 128 Ill. App. 3d 962, 471 N.E.2d 915 (1984), *aff'd on other grounds,* 109 Ill. 2d 225, 486 N.E.2d 902 (1985); Santucci Constr. Co. v. Baxter & Woodman, Inc., 151 Ill. App. 3d 547, 502 N.E.2d 1134, 104 Ill. Dec. 474 (1986); Oldenburg v. Hagemann, 159 Ill. App. 3d 631, 512 N.E.2d 718, 111 Ill. Dec. 329 (1987).

[83] *See* Ferentchak v. Village of Frankfort, 121 Ill. App. 3d 599, 459 N.E.2d 1085 (1984), *rev'd on other grounds,* 105 Ill. 2d 474, 475 N.E.2d 822 (1985).

[84] *See* Rosos Litho Supply Corp. v. Hansen, 123 Ill. App. 3d 290, 462 N.E.2d 566 (1984).

[85] Oldenburg v. Hagemann, 159 Ill. App. 3d 631, 512 N.E.2d 718, 111 Ill. Dec. 329.

available to the third party.[86] The *Oldenburg* court failed to mention, however, a prior decision by the Illinois Supreme Court holding that a plaintiff seeking to recover for purely economic losses associated with a commercial bargain cannot recover in tort regardless of the plaintiff's inability to recover under an action in contract.[87] This apparent inconsistency in Illinois case law will have to be resolved in future decisions addressing the economic loss doctrine.

Other jurisdictions have also found it difficult to apply the economic loss doctrine in a consistent manner. For example, recent federal opinions in New York have disallowed suits against an architect/engineer for economic loss because of a lack of privity of contract.[88]

In one case, the appellate division of the Supreme Court of New York held that, without privity of contract, a contractor may not maintain an action based on professional negligence against an engineer who was under contract with a county.[89] However, there are conflicting decisions at the state court level regarding a contractor's right to sue an architect/engineer in negligence for economic loss.[90] Thus, although the clear trend in New York is to recognize the validity of the economic loss defense, there still is conflicting precedent at the state court level.

Finally, at this writing, there is a split of authority in Minnesota regarding the validity of the economic loss defense. In particular, one Minnesota appellate court has held that a contractor could not bring a tort claim against an architect because the architect's project duties were defined by his contract with the owner.[91] The court noted that when "the parties duties and remedies are imposed by contract," a cause of action between them is barred as a matter of law.[92] In contrast, another Minnesota appellate court has held that a supplier can sue an engineer for a negligent interpretation of the contract documents.[93] Accordingly, it remains for the

---

[86] 512 N.E.2d at 727.

[87] Anderson Elec., Inc. v. Ledbetter Erection Corp., 115 Ill. 2d 146, 149–50, 503 N.E.2d 246, 104 Ill. Dec. 689 (1986).

[88] *See* Widett v. The United States Fidelity & Guar. Co., 815 F.2d 885 (2d Cir. 1987); Morse/Diesel Co. v. Trinity Indus., Inc., 664 F. Supp. 91 (S.D.N.Y. 1987).

[89] *See* Edward B. Fitzpatrick Jr. Constr. Corp. v. Suffolk County, 138 A.D.2d 446, 525 N.Y.S.2d 863 (1988).

[90] *See* Northrup Contracting, Inc. v. Village of Bergen, 129 A.D.2d 1002, 514 N.Y.S.2d 306 (1987) (affirming a contractor's right to sue an architect/engineer for economic loss even without privity of contract); Ossining Union Free School Dist. v. Anderson, 135 A.D.2d 518, 521 N.Y.S.2d 747 (1987) (a contractor cannot sue an architect/engineer for economic loss resulting from professional negligence absent privity of contract).

[91] *See* Prichard Bros. v. Grady Co., 407 N.W.2d 423 (Minn. Ct. App. 1987).

[92] *Id.*

[93] Waldor Pump & Equip. Co. v. Orr-Schelen-Mayeron & Assocs., 386 N.W.2d 375 (Minn. Ct. App. 1986).

Minnesota Supreme Court to determine the scope and validity of the economic loss doctrine in that jurisdiction.

§ 3.17   Architect/Engineer's Contractual Responsibility for Correcting Defects

Most architect/engineer contracts contain provisions that describe the methods and procedures to be followed by the architect/engineer when remedying design defects and other causes of construction failure. According to AIA Document B141 entitled "Standard Form of Agreement Between Owner and Architect," "[t]he Architect shall provide administration of the Contract for Construction as set forth . . . in the General Conditions of the Contract."[94] In AIA Document A201 the authority an architect has to administer the contract work and to remedy defects and deficiencies during construction is delineated.

The General Conditions to AIA Document A201 impose the following responsibilities upon the Architect:

1. The architect will be the owner's representative during construction.[95]

2. "[T]he Architect will keep the Owner informed of progress of the Work and will endeavor to guard the Owner against defects and deficiencies in the Work."[96]

3. The architect can reject nonconforming work.[97]

4. "The Architect will review and approve or take other appropriate action upon the Contractor's submittals such as Shop Drawings, Product Data and Samples, but only for the limited purpose of checking for conformance with information given and the design concept expressed in the Contract Documents."[98]

5. "The Architect's review shall not constitute approval of safety precautions or, unless otherwise specifically stated by the Architect, of any construction means, methods, techniques, sequences or procedures. The Architect's approval of a specific item shall not indicate approval of an assembly of which the item is a component."[99]

6. The architect may prepare a written "Construction Change Directive" to be signed by the owner and the architect "directing a change

---

[94] AIA Document B141-1987, art. 2, ¶ 2.6.2.

[95] AIA Document A201-1987, art. 4, ¶ 4.2.1.

[96] *Id.,* ¶ 4.2.2.

[97] *Id.,* ¶ 4.2.6.

[98] *Id.,* ¶ 4.2.7.

[99] *Id.*

in the Work and stating a proposed basis for adjustment, if any, in the Contract Sum or Contract Time or both."[100]

7. The architect may issue a Certificate of Payment by which he represents "that the Work has progressed to the point indicated" and that "the quality of the Work is in accordance with the Contract Documents."[101]

8. The architect may issue a final Certificate of Payment when he believes the work has been appropriately completed.[102]

The General Conditions to AIA Document A201 also provide that "[t]he Architect may . . . decide not to certify payment, or, because of subsequently discovered evidence or subsequent observations, may nullify the whole or a part of a Certificate for Payment previously issued, to such extent as may be necessary in the Architect's opinion to protect the Owner from loss because of . . . defective work not remedied."[103] Thus, the AIA contract documents impose significant responsibilities upon the architect to identify and remedy design defects during construction. They also allow the architect broad discretion in determining when the work is acceptable under the contract documents and when payments should be issued to the contractor.

§ 3.18 —Indemnification Clauses

Architects/engineers should be aware of the special limitations contained in the indemnification clause that is found in AIA Document A201. In particular, paragraph 3.18 provides, among other things, that the contractor shall indemnify and hold harmless the owner and architect from claims, damages, losses, and expenses arising out of or resulting from the performance of the work. Nevertheless, this obligation of the contractor is expressly limited:

> The obligations of the contractor . . . shall not extend to the liability of the Architect, the Architect's consultants, and agents and employees of any of them arising out of (1) the preparation or approval of maps, drawings, opinions, reports, surveys, Change Orders, designs or specifications, or (2) the giving of or failure to give directions or instructions by the Architect, the Architect's consultants, and agents and employees of any of them provided such giving or failure to give is the primary cause of the injury or damage.[104]

---

[100] Id., art. 7, ¶ 7.3.1.

[101] Id., art. 9, ¶ 9.4.2.

[102] Id., ¶ 9.10.1.

[103] Id., ¶ 9.5.1.

[104] Id., art. 3, ¶ 3.18.3.

Thus, the broad form indemnification provision contained in AIA Document A201 does not extend to those duties and responsibilities that are normally assumed by the architect.

ROLE OF THE CONSTRUCTION MANAGER

§ 3.19   Duty Owed by the Construction Manager

The term *construction management* refers to a system in which each of the construction trades on a particular project has a direct contract with the owner, and the work is administratively controlled by a separate entity that performs little or no direct construction work: the construction manager.[105] The role of the construction manager is fairly clear: he administers the construction for the owner; however, the status of the construction manager is a subject of considerable controversy. Is he a professional and thus susceptible to the same liabilities as, for example, architects and engineers, or is he a general contractor? On most projects, he enters into a contract with the owner for administration of all or some portion of the overall construction project. Thus, the standard of care owed by the construction manager to third parties on a project will be discussed in light of this typical form of owner/construction manager agreement.

Unlike the traditional positions of design architect or supervisory engineer, the status of the construction manager has not yet been clearly defined by statute, case law, or industry practice. In order to identify the standard of care he owes to third parties on a project, it must first be determined if he is functioning as a design professional or as a general contractor. This distinction is important because it establishes the basic standard of care to which he will be held.

As stated in §§ 3.10 through 3.14, an architect/engineer or other design professional owes the duty of ordinary skill and competence of members of that profession.[106] This standard applies to both the design and administration of the project. If that duty is not met, the design professional will be subject to liability for negligence. In the absence of a specific contractual agreement to the contrary, a design professional is not required to provide a perfect design or to perform other engineering services to perfection but is only liable for a failure to exercise reasonable care and skill in the design or supervision of the work.[107] Moreover, the standard by

---

[105] Conners, *Contracting for Construction Management Services,* 46 Law & Contemp. Probs. 5 (Winter 1983).

[106] *See, e.g.,* Gravely v. Providence Partners, 549 F.2d 958 (4th Cir. 1977).

[107] See §§ 3.10–3.14.

which the professional will be judged is variable, depending upon the nature and location of the work.[108]

The standard of care owed by a design professional must be contrasted with the standard of care owed by a general contractor. A general contractor's duty to third parties is one of ordinary and reasonable care.[109] It should be noted, however, that some jurisdictions hold that the duty of care owed by a contractor, or any other party possessing special knowledge or skill, is commensurate with the circumstances.[110] In these jurisdictions, even if the construction manager were regarded as a general contractor, he would be held to a greater standard than ordinary care. The standard of care will depend upon such matters as the complexity of the project, the skill and expertise needed to effect the work, and similar surrounding circumstances. Thus, the determination of whether a construction manager is acting as a design professional or a general contractor establishes the standard of care he owes to third parties.

§ 3.20 Determining the Standard of Care
Owed by the Construction Manager

The question of whether a construction manager is performing as a design professional or as a contractor can be resolved, in part, by the method under which his services are procured. On public contracts, the issue of his classification and the resultant standard of care can at least be narrowed, if not resolved, by reference to the procurement codes and building requirements of the particular public body soliciting the contract. These codes frequently limit the types of services for which a public body can contract or, at least, categorize the construction manager as either a design professional or a contractor.

Some states have specific statutes providing for the procurement of construction management services and define the procedure by which the services must be procured.[111] In most states, however, the method of procurement of construction management services is not specifically set forth. The courts have, therefore, taken a pragmatic view in determining

---

[108] Mounds View v. Walijarvi, 263 N.W.2d 420, 424 (Minn. 1978).

[109] Green Constr. Co. v. William Form Eng'g Corp., 506 F. Supp. 173, 177 (W.D. Mich. 1980); Hawthorne v. Kober Constr. Co., 196 Mont. 519, ___ Mont. ___, 640 P.2d 467, 470 (1982); Harris v. Chisamore, 5 Cal. App. 3d 496, 85 Cal. Rptr. 223 (1970).

[110] See, e.g., La Vine v. Clear Creek Skiing Corp., 557 F.2d 730 (10th Cir. 1977); Redgrave v. Boston Symphony Orchestra, Inc., 557 F. Supp. 230 (D. Mass. 1983); see generally Prosser, Law of Torts § 34 (4th ed. 1971).

[111] See, e.g., S.C. Code Ann. § 11-35-3220 (1982); see generally L.D. Philips, The Legal Status of the Construction Management Project Delivery System in the United States (unpublished paper, Mich. Technological Univ., May 1984).

whether a contract should be competitively bid as a construction contract or negotiated as a design professional contract. In California, for example, the supreme court held that a construction management contract guaranteeing the maximum contract price was "too closely akin to traditional lump sum general construction contracting to be held exempt from the statutory competitive bidding requirements."[112] The Indiana court of appeals reached a different conclusion in the case of an agency construction management contract, holding that the contract at issue was for a professional service.[113]

§ 3.21   Construction Manager's Contract with the Owner

Although the standard of care owed by the construction manager is determined first by his classification as a design professional or a general contractor and then by the degree of care owed based upon the nature and locale of the project, the duty he owes depends primarily upon his specific undertaking on a project.[114] Thus, for the most part, his obligations are set forth in his contract with the owner.[115] The construction manager's contract and the applicable statutes, regulations, and standards define the scope of the construction manager's duties. As noted in § 3.13, a party may also be held liable for negligently performing duties that he voluntarily or gratuitously assumes.[116] It is important to note that the majority of the cases dealing with the construction manager's liability for such de facto duties are in the area of safety at the worksite.[117]

The construction manager is not generally responsible for the overall design of a construction project. He may, however, participate in design reviews and make recommendations to the owner for changes or improvements. Although there have been no cases to date in which a contractor has sued a construction manager for design defects, it is clear that such a cause of action could be allowed. This conclusion is based on two lines of cases which have already fully developed: (1) contractor claims

---

[112] City of Inglewood-Los Angeles Co. Civic Center Auth. v. Superior Court, 7 Cal. 3d 861, 500 P.2d 601, 604, 103 Cal. Rptr. 689 (1972).

[113] Attlin Constr., Inc. v. Muncie Community Schools, 413 N.E.2d 281 (Ind. Ct. App. 1980).

[114] See, e.g., Plan-Tec v. Wiggins, 443 N.E.2d 1212 (Ind. 1983).

[115] Krieger v. J.E. Griner Co., 282 Md. 50, 382 A.2d 1069 (1977).

[116] See, e.g., Plan-Tec v. Wiggins, 443 N.E.2d at 1219.

[117] See, e.g., Caldwell v. Bechtel, 631 F.2d 989 (D.C. Cir. 1980); Hammond v. Bechtel, Inc., 606 P.2d 1269 (Ala. 1980); Plan-Tec, Inc. v. Wiggins, 443 N.E.2d 1212 (Ind. Ct. App. 1983).

against design architects/engineers[118] and (2) owner claims against construction managers for their participation in the design process.[119] Thus, it seems clear that the construction manager can be liable for a defective design.

§ 3.22   Construction Manager's Duty to Review Shop Drawings

One of the construction manager's duties can be to review and approve the shop drawings submitted by the contractor. This activity can result in the construction manager's liability in three situations: (1) when he rejects drawings that should have been approved, (2) when he approves drawings that should have been rejected, and (3) when he delays the approval of drawings. Just as in the case of an architect/engineer, when a construction manager undertakes an obligation to review shop drawing submittals for contract compliance, that obligation necessarily entails a duty to identify nonconforming items that could result in construction failure.[120] A breach of this duty may subject the construction manager to a cause of action in contract or negligence for any resulting construction failure.

§ 3.23   Construction Manager as Agent of the Owner

It may be possible for a construction manager to argue that because he is performing as an agent of an owner, he is not independently liable for his negligence. The general test for the existence of an agency relationship is whether the owner has the right to control and direct the work, not only as to the final result but also as to the manner and means by which that result is accomplished.[121] To date, there have been no cases in which a construction manager avoided liability to a contractor or other party because he asserted that he was acting as an agent of the owner. If he is functioning

[118] *See, e.g.,* Conforti & Eisele, Inc. v. John C. Morris Assocs., 175 N.J. Super. 341, 418 A.2d 1290 (1981), *aff'd,* 199 N.J. Super. 498, 489 A.2d 1233 (1985); James McKinney & Son, Inc. v. Lake Placid 1980 Olympic Games, 61 N.Y.2d 836, 462 N.E.2d 137, 473 N.Y.S.2d 960 (1984).

[119] *See, e.g.,* American Employers Ins. Co. v. Maryland Casualty Co., 509 F.2d 128 (1st Cir. 1975); *see generally* R. Cushman, Construction Litigation: Representing the Owner 105 (John Wiley & Sons, 1984).

[120] *See generally* Jaeger v. Henningson, Durham & Richardson, Inc., 714 F.2d 773 (8th Cir. 1983).

[121] S. Williston, A Treatise on the Law of Contracts § 1012A (3d ed. 1967).

as the owner's agent, however, he may be able to obtain indemnification from the owner for any damages sought by a contractor.[122] Likewise, he may be able to avail himself of all defenses available to the owner.[123]

§ 3.24   The AIA Standard Form Agreement

"Standard Form of Agreement Between Owner and Construction Manager" (AIA Document B801) is intended to be used in conjunction with several other AIA documents, including Document A201/CM, the General Conditions of a construction contract on projects involving a construction manager. The document allocates certain duties and responsibilities to the construction manager, including the obligations to:

1. Review designs during their development[124]
2. Administer the contract[125]
3. Recommend changes to the owner or architect[126]
4. Determine whether a contractor's work complies with the contract in order to safeguard against defects[127]
5. Reject nonconforming work, subject to the architect's review[128]
6. "Receive from the Contractors and review all Shop Drawings, Product Data, Samples and other submittals. Coordinate them with information contained in related documents and transmit to the Architect those recommended for approval. In collaboration with the Architect, establish and implement procedures for expediting the processing and approval of Shop Drawings, Product Data, Samples, and other submittals."[129]
7. Maintain site records[130]
8. Assist the architect in conducting inspections[131]
9. Coordinate any necessary corrections.[132]

---

[122] Restatement (Second) of the Law of Agency § 439 (1958).

[123] *Id.* § 334.

[124] AIA Document B801-1980, art. 1, ¶ 1.1.2.

[125] *Id.,* ¶ 1.2.1.

[126] *Id.,* ¶ 1.2.3.3.

[127] *Id.,* ¶ 1.2.7.

[128] *Id.*

[129] *Id.,* ¶ 1.2.10.

[130] *Id.,* ¶ 1.2.11.1.

[131] *Id.,* ¶ 1.2.14.

[132] *Id.*

The provisions of AIA Document B801 also obligate the construction manager to establish and implement procedures for remedying design defects and other causes of construction failure in conjunction with the architect. It follows that he can be sued for breach of contract, and/or in negligence, for a failure to perform the duties set forth in his contract with the owner. The standard of care applicable to the construction manager in a particular case will be determined by the nature and location of the work and whether he is deemed to be a design professional or general contractor.

§ 3.25   The Economic Loss Doctrine

Although there is little doubt that a construction manager can be sued for negligence, there is considerable controversy over whether he can be liable for economic loss. As discussed in § **3.16**, some jurisdictions hold that a design professional is liable for economic loss only to his client—that is, the owner or the other party with whom he has a contract.[133] Other jurisdictions, however, have held that design professionals are liable for economic loss.[134]

ROLE OF THE OWNER

§ 3.26   Owner's Implied Warranty

An owner impliedly warrants the adequacy of his plans and specifications for use in performing construction work.[135] The owner's implied warranty consists of both a warranty of accuracy and a warranty of suitability.[136]

An owner is generally liable for the additional costs incurred by a contractor in attempting to comply with defective contract documents.[137] In

---

[133] *See, e.g.,* Local Joint Executive Bd. of Las Vegas v. Stern, 98 Nev. 409, 651 P.2d 637 (1982); Blake Constr. Co. v. Alley, 233 Va. 31, 353 S.E.2d 724 (1987); Aikins v. Baltimore & Ohio R.R., 348 Pa. Super. 17, 501 A.2d 277, 279 (1985); Bernard Johnson v. Continental Constructors, 630 S.W.2d 365 (Tex. Civ. App. 1982).

[134] See § **3.16**.

[135] United States v. Spearin, 248 U.S. 132, 136 (1918); Bates & Rogers Constr. Corp. v. North Shore Sanitary Dist., 92 Ill. App. 3d 90, 414 N.E.2d 1274, 1278 (1981); M.L. Shalloo, Inc. v. Riccardi & Sons Constr., Inc., 348 Mass. 682, 686–88, 205 N.E.2d 239 (1965).

[136] United States v. Spearin, 248 U.S. 132, 136 (1918); *see generally* Patten, *The Implied Warranty That Attaches to Government Furnished Specifications,* 31 Fed. B.J. 291 (1972).

[137] *See, e.g.,* Consolidated Diesel Elec. Corp., ASBCA 10486, 67-2 B.C.A. (CCH) ¶ 6669 (1967).

the case of the government as owner, the law in this area has been described as follows:

> It is well settled that where the government orders a structure to be built, and in so doing prepares the project's specifications prescribing the character, dimension, and location of the construction work, the government implicitly warrants, nothing else appearing, that if the specifications are complied with, satisfactory performance will result. This rule rests on the presumed expertise of the government where it sees fit to prescribe detailed specifications. "This implied warranty is not overcome by the general clauses requiring the contractor[,] to examine the site, to check up the plans, and to assume responsibility for the work until completion and acceptance." *United States v. Spearin* [248 U.S. 132, 137 (1918)]. Moreover, this implied warranty is not defeated by a contract clause permitting the prospective bidders to conduct independent subsurface investigations, if such explorations could not reasonably be completed before the bids were to be submitted. However, an experienced contractor cannot rely on government-prepared specifications where, on the basis of the government furnished data, he knows or should have known that the prepared specifications could not produce the desired result for ". . . he has no right to make a useless thing and charge the customer for it." *R. M. Hollingshead Corp. v. United States* [124 Ct. Cl. 681, 683, 111 F. Supp. 285, 286 (1935)]. If faulty specifications prevent or delay completion of the contract, the contractor is entitled to recover delay damages for defendants breach of its implied warranty, and this breach cannot be cured by the simple expedient of extending the time of performance.[138]

This rule was recently affirmed in *Department of Natural Resources of Montana v. United States,*[139] in which the contractor was allowed to recover an equitable adjustment for defective plans and specifications furnished by the government. The court found that in the absence of clear, express, and direct language to the contrary, the government warranted and the state was entitled to assume that the plans which the government furnished were free from defect.

Generally, a contractor is entitled to an equitable adjustment for the increased costs he incurs in attempting to comply with defective plans or specifications. However, if the contract provides that details are left for the contractor's resolution and the contractor has been warned to investigate conditions affecting the work, the owner's implied warranty of design adequacy and sufficiency does not apply and the contractor will be barred from recovery.[140]

The scope of the owner's implied warranty in the contract documents often depends on the type of specifications involved. Design specifications

---

[138] J.D. Hedin Co. v. United States, 347 F.2d 235, 241 (Ct. Cl. 1965) (citations to nonquoted material omitted).

[139] 1 Ct. Cl. 727 (1983).

[140] Algernon Blair, ASBCA No. 26761, 82-2 B.C.A. (CCH) ¶ 16,029 (1982).

detail the manner or method of the contractor's performance. They must be contrasted with performance specifications, which leave to the contractor's discretion the details of the work. One court has recognized this distinction in the following manner:

> The specifications, which were prepared by the [government], are a classic example of 'design' specifications and not 'performance' specifications. In other words, in these specifications, the [government] set forth in precise detail the materials to be employed and the manner in which the work was to be performed, and [contractor] was not privileged to deviate therefrom, but was required to follow them as one would a road map. In contrast, typical 'performance' type specifications set forth an objective or standard to be achieved, and the successful bidder is expected to exercise his ingenuity in achieving that objective or standard of performance, selecting the means and assuming a corresponding responsibility for that selection.[141]

An owner is generally not liable for a contractor's increased costs in attempting to satisfy the performance requirements set forth in a performance specification unless the specifications contain requirements that are objectively impossible or commercially impracticable to achieve.[142] With respect to performance specifications, the court in *Intercontinental Manufacturing Co. v. United States* stated:

> [A] case for defective specifications could exist only if performance had proven impossible, either actually or from a standpoint of commercial impracticability (i.e. commercial senselessness). Short of these extremes, however, the risks of unanticipated performance costs remain upon the contractor's shoulders alone.[143]

Thus, an owner more often is held responsible for a contractor's increased costs in attempting to comply with a defective design specification as opposed to a performance specification.

§ 3.27 Contractual Obligations of the Owner

In the context of a federal government contract, the changes clause found in fixed-price construction contracts makes it abundantly clear that the government is responsible for all increased costs relating to a defective specification. The clause states in pertinent part:

---

[141] J.L. Simmons Co. v. United States, 188 Ct. Cl. 684, 689, 412 F.2d 1360 (1969) (footnote omitted).

[142] Intercontinental Mfg. Co. v. United States, 4 Ct. Cl. 591, 592 (1984).

[143] *Id.; see also* Rolin v. United States, 142 Ct. Cl. 73, 82–83, 160 F. Supp. 264 (1958).

(d)   If any change under this clause causes an increase or decrease in the Contractor's cost of, or time required for, the performance of any part of the work under this contract, whether or not changed by any such order, the Contracting Officer shall make an equitable adjustment and modify the contract in writing. However, except for an adjustment based on defective specifications, no adjustment for any change under paragraph (b) of this clause shall be made for any costs incurred more than 20 days before the Contractor gives written notice as required. In the case of defective specifications for which the Government is responsible, the equitable adjustment shall include any increased cost reasonably incurred by the Contractor in attempting to comply with the defective specifications.[144]

The standard contract forms produced by the American Institute of Architects also require the owner to identify potential causes of construction failure at the earliest possible moment. In particular, AIA Document B141 provides that the owner shall promptly notify the architect in writing of any defect of which it becomes aware.[145] Similarly, AIA Document B801 states that the owner has the same obligation to give prompt written notice to the architect and construction manager of design defects and other potential causes of construction failure known to the owner.[146]

§ 3.28   Owner's Right to Demand Strict Compliance with the Contract Documents

The owner is generally entitled to require that the contract documents be strictly complied with. The standard inspection clauses in most construction contracts contain broad statements that permit the owner to reject nonconforming work and to order the contractor to correct any defects found during the inspection process. Occasionally, acceptance of the defective work with an equitable reduction in the contract price will be a more sensible remedy for the owner. As stated in AIA Document A201,

[i]f the Owner prefers to accept Work which is not in accordance with the requirements of the Contract Documents, the Owner may do so instead of requiring its removal and correction, in which case the Contract Sum will be reduced as appropriate and equitable. Such adjustments shall be effected whether or not final payment has been made.[147]

When the defect or potential construction failure is discovered before the work is performed, the owner and its representatives have broad latitude

---

[144] 48 C.F.R. § 52.243-4 (1987) (emphasis added).

[145] AIA Document B141-1987, art. 4, ¶ 4.10.

[146] AIA Document B801-1980, art. 2, ¶ 2.9.

[147] AIA Document A201-1987, ¶ 12.3.1.

in fashioning a remedy. For example, the federal government as owner may reject shop drawings proposing work that is not in strict conformance with the contract documents.[148] However, after the work has been installed, the strict compliance rule must be considered in light of the common law doctrines of substantial performance and economic waste. Thus, if the repair or replacement is economically wasteful and the owner receives work that substantially complies with the contract, the owner's remedy should be limited to damages based upon the loss of value in the installation or the savings to the contractor.[149]

§ 3.29 Standard Inspection Clauses

The federal government inspection clause for a fixed-price construction contract requires the contractor to "without charge, replace or correct work found by the Government not to conform to contract requirements, unless in the public interest the Government consents to accept the work with an appropriate adjustment in contract price."[150] Similar language is also found in paragraphs 3.5.1, 4.2.6, and 12.2 of AIA Document A201. Thus, prior to acceptance of the work the owner will generally be able to require the contractor to replace, repair, or remedy defects in construction. The standard inspection clauses also provide that if the contractor fails to promptly replace or correct rejected work then the owner may, after proper notice, effect the repairs itself.[151]

§ 3.30 Acceptance by the Owner

Acceptance plays a crucial role in construction contract administration. Under AIA Document A201, the issuance of a final certificate for payment by the architect constitutes a representation that "the Work has been completed in accordance with the terms and conditions of the Contract Documents and that the entire balance found to be due the Contractor and noted in said final Certificate is due and payable."[152] A similar provision

---

[148] See Robert McMullan & Son, Inc., ASBCA 21159, 77-1 B.C.A. (CCH) ¶ 12,453 (1977).

[149] See, e.g., Valley Asphalt Corp., ASBCA 17595, 74-2 B.C.A. (CCH) ¶ 10,680 (1974); see also East Lake Constr. Co. v. Hess, 102 Wash. 2d 30, 686 P.2d 465 (1984); see generally Annotation, Modern Status of Rule as to Whether Cost of Correction or Difference in Value of Structures is Proper Measure of Damages for Breach of Construction Contract, 41 A.L.R.4th 131 (1985).

[150] 48 C.F.R. § 52.246-12(f) (1987).

[151] See AIA Document A201-1987, art. 2, ¶¶ 2.3.1, 2.4.1; 48 C.F.R. § 52.246-12(g) (1987).

[152] AIA Document A201-1987, art. 9, ¶ 9.10.1.

is found in the FAR governing fixed-price construction contracts: "Acceptance shall be final and conclusive except for latent defects, fraud, or gross mistakes amounting to fraud or the Government's rights under any warranty or guarantee."[153] Thus, acceptance is an important legal event on a construction project. In fact, once the federal government issues final acceptance, it has no rights against the contractor for patent defects except under a warranty provision.[154] This is true whether the government accepted the work with knowledge of a patent defect or whether it lacked knowledge of the defect.[155]

§ 3.31 Warranty Provisions

The use of warranty clauses in government contracts is optional. The standard warranty of construction clause in fixed-price construction contracts is found in the FAR,[156] which provide for a warranty period of one year from the date of final acceptance of the work. In addition, AIA Document A201 provides for a one-year warranty period.[157]

The scope of the warranty depends upon the language used in the particular contract. Normally, the warranty clause requires the owner to give the contractor notice of the existence of a defect in the work within a specified warranty period. Once it is established that the most likely cause of the defect relates to the contractor's performance, the contractor must establish that he had no responsibility for the defect or that the defect did not exist.[158]

Remedies for breach of warranty are generally more specific than the remedies set forth in the standard inspection clauses. Warranty provisions are also strictly construed in most instances. Therefore, each warranty clause will be enforced according to its own terms. The most commonly used warranty clauses contain language stating that the rights set forth therein are in addition to, and not in limitation of, the rights contained in the inspection clause.[159]

Once final acceptance has been issued by the owner and the warranty provisions have expired, the owner may only retract its acceptance by establishing that a latent defect existed at the time of acceptance or that acceptance was issued by fraud or through gross mistake.

---

[153] 48 C.F.R. § 52.246-12(i) (1987).

[154] *See* C.H. McQuagge v. United States, 197 F. Supp. 460 (W.D. La. 1961).

[155] H.P. Carney, ASBCA 8222, 1964 B.C.A. (CCH) ¶ 4149 (1964).

[156] 48 C.F.R. § 52.246-21 (1987).

[157] *See* AIA Document A201-1987, arts. 3, 9 & 12, ¶¶ 3.5.1, 9.9.1 & 12.2.

[158] *See* George E. Jensen Contractor, Inc., ASBCA 23284, 81-2 B.C.A. (CCH) ¶ 15,207 (1981).

[159] *See, e.g.,* Gresham & Co., ASBCA 13812, 70-1 B.C.A. (CCH) ¶ 8318 (1970), *rev'd on other grounds,* 200 Ct. Cl. 97, 470 F.2d 542 (1972).

CHAPTER 4

PREVENTING CONSTRUCTION FAILURES THROUGH EFFECTIVE RELATIONSHIPS

Richard L. Tomasetti

Richard L. Tomasetti is senior vice president of Thornton-Tomasetti and Lev Zetlin Associates in New York City. A civil and structural engineer, Mr. Tomasetti holds a B.S. degree from Manhattan College, an M.S. degree from New York University, and has completed additional postgraduate studies at the University of Connecticut and Polytechnic Institute of New York. He has authored numerous technical papers, lectured at universities, has been active on industry and professional committees and advisory boards and is co-author of the chapter on shop drawings in the new ASCE Manual, *Quality in the Constructed Project.*

Mr. Tomasetti has twice won the Lincoln Arc Welding Foundation Gold Award, and in 1982 he received the *Engineering-News Record's* annual citation for "Those Who Made Marks" for developing the innovative stressed-skin tube structure for the One Mellon Bank Center in Pittsburgh, Pennsylvania. He has been involved in major investigations such as the New York Thruway Schoharie Bridge Collapse, the L'Ambiance Plaza Collapse in Bridgeport, Connecticut, and the Journal Square suspended ceiling failure in New Jersey.

§ 4.1   Defining Responsibilities of the Parties

"I can't sign the contract," I told a client in a recent negotiation. "It says I must indemnify you if anything goes wrong with the structure. It does not say I must indemnify you for problems due to my errors, omissions, or negligent acts. I'm not an insurance company. I can only indemnify you for my negligence. That's all I have insurance for."

The attorney for the developer with whom I was negotiating our contract for structural engineering services simply stated, "I will modify the indemnity clause so that it holds only for your errors, omissions, or negligent acts." I said to him: "Three years ago in discussions with your firm regarding another project, we agreed to modify the same clause in the exact same way. It seems this clause has been in your standard contracts since then. How can a professional agree to indemnify you unless it's for his negligence? Do any professionals ever sign this contract with this clause?" His response: "All the time."

Construction contracts between owners and design professionals seem to put more emphasis on what a design professional and/or contractor is liable for than on what they are responsible for. Is there a difference? According to Webster's Dictionary, "liable" and "responsible" are synonyms but imply different things. *Liable* implies "a possibility or probability of incurring something because of position, nature or particular situation." *Responsible* implies "holding a formal organizational role, duty or trust." Responsibility relates more to the scope of services.

Considering these implications, it seems that some owners today are more concerned about architects and engineers acting as insurance companies and less concerned about developing the most appropriate relationship among all parties involved in the construction project to assure a minimum chance of failure. For this reason, design professionals must be alert to altering standard contract language to provide that the design professional indemnify the owner only for the designer's errors, omissions, or negligent acts (the only thing for which she is insured). Owners and their attorneys are developing onerous contracts. A more effective relationship with the design professional can be forged by directly developing the scope and responsibility of the design professional's service and its interface with the service of others, rather than by writing contractual clauses to make her liable for as much as possible.

§ 4.2   Coordinating Responsibilities of
Various Parties

Many construction failures have been caused by a lack of proper coordination at the interface between the services of two parties on the construction team. Examples include the interface between the architect's work and the engineer's work when a curtain wall is attached to the structure, or the interface between the fabricator's work and the structural engineer's work concerning the designing and detailing of connections on shop drawings. Clear definitions of each party's scope of work and responsibility are important at an interface to be sure that nothing gets missed. Precise language in specifications can define responsibilities so as to remove any uncertainties regarding whose task it is to perform them. The shop drawing section of our firm's structural steel specifications illustrates this point:

> The shop drawings shall be prepared under the supervision of a professional engineer licensed in the State of the project and shall have the signature and seal of the professional engineer. The shop drawings shall contain all dimensional and geometrical information, grade of steel, shop surface treatments and shop connections. Materials shall not be ordered, fabricated, or delivered to the site before the shop drawings have been reviewed and returned to the Contractor.

> Prior to review of the shop drawings by the Engineer such shop drawings shall have been reviewed and approved by the Contractor. Such approval by the Contractor shall constitute Contractor's representation that the Contractor has verified all quantities, dimensions, specified performance criteria, installation requirements, materials, catalog numbers and similar data with respect thereto and reviewed or coordinated each drawing with other drawings and samples and with the requirements of the Work and the Contract Documents. . . .

> Reviewed Drawings: The review and approval of shop drawings by the Engineer shall be for general conformance with contract documents only and will not in any way relieve the Contractor from (a) responsibility for the adequacy of the design of those connections designed by the Contractor's licensed engineer, (b) all required detailing, (c) responsibility for the proper fitting of construction work in strict conformance with the contract requirements or (d) the necessity of furnishing material and workmanship required by contract drawings and specifications which may not be indicated on the shop drawings.

This clearly states that the fabricators have responsibility for connections they design, the contractors must coordinate the trades, and the engineers are responsible for reviews and approvals. See also § **4.8**.

Equally important is appropriate protection from liability to encourage each party to get involved in another's work. Contracts which overemphasize liability, as opposed to responsibility, do not encourage a teamwork effort and can contribute to an item's getting missed. The more each party reviews the work of others, the better off all parties will be. Mutual review can be encouraged by making it less threatening for a party to get involved in and/or comment on another's work.

Let's look at some examples. A cement ceiling fell down in 1983 in Journal Square in Jersey City, New Jersey, killing two people and injuring many others. The ceiling was hung with wire hangers that were attached to metal tabs protruding from a steel deck topped with concrete above. The failure resulted from overloading the tabs. The contract documents and the fabricator's shop drawings clearly stated the load restrictions on the tabs. The ceiling was installed, with the knowledge of the members of the design team and the construction manager, with a four-foot-by-four-foot grid of hangers. No one felt it was their responsibility to do a simple calculation that would show that the grid would overload the tabs. There also was a definite lack of involvement by many of the parties concerning the interface between the ceiling and the structure. Everyone thought it was another person's responsibility. A contract with clearly delineated responsibilities can prevent such a situation.

Another example is the 1984 Hyatt Regency walkway bridge collapse that killed 114 people. The case revolved around who was responsible for the design of a failed connection, the engineer of record or the fabricator who prepared the shop drawings. This case demonstrated an industrywide problem. For years fabricators had been designing connections and relying on the engineer's review and approval during the shop drawings stage to relieve them of any design responsibility. However, when the engineer of record would review and/or approve the shop drawings, that engineer would clearly state on the shop drawing stamp and/or through the specifications that the review was only for general conformance with the design concept and the information given in the contract documents. Who then had the responsibility for the design of the connections?

Another tragic example was the L'Ambiance Plaza lift slab concrete construction failure in 1987. Numerous concrete slabs, some held temporarily in position, came sliding down their columns, killing 28 people. In this case the contractor had the responsibility for all temporary support of the structure. The engineer of record developed a design for the final configuration of the structure and specified the option of a lift slab method of construction through a performance specification. All methods of performing the construction, including the temporary support for each of the slabs until they were in their final positions and the overall resistance to lateral sway of the building during construction, were performed by the contractor. Typically, the engineer of record does not get involved in that process, nor does the engineer review and/or approve what the contractor is doing. It is not considered the engineer's responsibility. The question is whether it should be. Is there a way to encourage the engineer to be involved without assuming all of the contractor's responsibility or without feeling that the amount of liability that will be added because of this review process cannot be justified?

What each of these failure cases had in common was an interface prob-lem and a lack of involvement of people close to that interface. Owners would be better served if they could get all parties more involved at the interface with the other parties' work. However, the problem is a very old one. It's the Good Samaritan question: If someone goes out of her way to help someone else and then that person gets injured, will the Good Samar-itan be responsible for the injury? Protection for the Good Samaritan en-courages involvement whereas exposure discourages involvement.

§ 4.3 Additional Exposure

Let's look at an example. Many owners feel very comfortable thinking that the engineer of record on their project is overseeing some of the contrac-tor's safety precautions when visiting the project. This is understandable. However, one must face the realities of the situation. For the engineer of record to be involved in any form of the contractor's construction means and methods and safety procedures, her scope of work must keep her in-volved during the design of these procedures and their inspection, and she must have control over such. This is a major undertaking requiring time, effort, and cost.

Some owners are trying to include words in the contract that add expo-sure for the architect and engineer. Typically, architects and engineers have not been responsible for construction means and methods and safety precautions. But recently I have seen contracts stating that "although the architect and engineer are not responsible for such, if they see or are aware of some safety problem they must bring it to the attention of the owner." All this means to the architect and engineer is that they will be kept in more lawsuits: there will always be a question of fact as to whether they were aware of the problem. What does it mean to the owner? The owner is not giving the architect and engineer any more responsibility. There is no additional item of work specifically listed in the scope of services to be performed for the owner's protection and for which the architect and engi-neer would be compensated. But what the owner has done is add more exposure and liability to the architect and engineer. This causes the archi-tect and engineer to be more cautious than ever; they would hesitate to have any involvement at all in the construction means and methods or to suggest any improvements. It motivates them to keep their eyes closed as they walk by any safety procedures.

Ironically, the owner would be better served to indemnify the architect and engineer for claims arising out of construction means and methods—these are not within the design professional's scope of work. Such protec-tion would make the architect and engineer more comfortable to involve themselves in that process, to give suggestions, and to keep their eyes open to everything when walking the site.

It should be noted that courts are realizing now that design professionals cannot be held responsible for items over which they have no control; they are not insurance companies. For example, the Alabama Supreme Court found that an engineering firm was not liable when an employee of a contractor was killed in a trench cave-in while a telephone cable was being laid.[1]

> According to the [Alabama Supreme Court], in order for [the engineering firm] to be held responsible for the actions of [the contractor] in digging the defective trench, it would have to have the control over the manner in which the contractor did its work. The court concluded that [the engineering firm] did not have such control.
>
> Although [the engineer's] agreement with [the owner] required it to make sure that [the contractor] was complying with the terms of its contract, said the court, [the engineering firm] had no right to control the way in which [the contractor] performed any of its work of running the telephone cables. [The contractor's] employees took their directions in the laying of the pipe exclusively from [the contractor], the court noted. Thus [the engineering firm] was not in control, and could not be held liable for [the employee's] death.[2]

This case illustrates that attempts to increase a design professional's exposure, in connection with events not included in the scope of services and over which she has no control, may be self-defeating. Not only do such attempts further the design professional's reluctance to become involved in various aspects of the work, but they also work to the owner's detriment by seeming to provide the owner with contractual protection which may not exist.

§ 4.4   Additional Protection

A new trend is developing in which design professionals are willing to become more involved and take more responsibility as long as there is some degree of protection. For example, in the past many structural engineers would not review the calculations and detail designs of a curtain wall for an architect. Typically these calculations and designs were submitted by a manufacturer and were not submitted under the seal of a professional engineer licensed in the state of the project. Thus, after spending just several hours of review, the structural engineer was the only professional who

---

[1] Pugh v. Butler Tel. Co., 512 So. 2d 1317 (Ala. 1987).

[2] *Id.*

was involved in the process of approving these calculations. The engineer therefore faced tremendous liability. If she is the only professional involved, would anyone ever hold the people who originally prepared the design calculations accountable? That would be analogous to the surgeon's blaming the nurse. The higher form of authority will always get the blame.

Today it is quite common for structural engineers to review the calculations and design work for a curtain wall. Both the structural engineer and the architect insist, and owners are beginning to understand, that, prior to the structural engineer's review of the calculations, they must be submitted under the signature of a professional engineer licensed in the state of the project. Quality must be built in; it cannot be accomplished through a review process. In addition, it should be clear from the specifications that the structural engineer's review does not relieve the manufacturer and/or her professional engineer of responsibility. This type of arrangement encourages a "get involved" attitude because it has the appropriately stated responsibilities and liabilities.

An example of the types of provisions that involve the design professional in expanded duties but offer greater protection can be found in an architect's specifications to a curtain wall manufacturer:

The detail design drawings shall include proposed typical framing members, glass and other components, together with two copies of structural calculations, including calculations for glass, prepared by a professional engineer licensed in the state of the project. Structural calculations shall be referenced to the Shop Drawings. Engineer shall certify both structural calculations and Shop Drawings.

The Architect's review shall be for the purpose of determining conformance to the design concept and for general arrangement, only, and such review shall not relieve the Contractor of any of the responsibilities as stated herein or any other applicable items herein specified.

§ 4.5   Owner's Contingency Fund

Many owners have the attitude that, if something goes wrong, it cannot be their fault, it must be somebody else's. The owner has a fundamental obligation to set up appropriate relationships among all the parties. A project's atmosphere should encourage the architect, engineer, and contractor to work together to resolve problems for the owner's benefit, not to sit back and constantly point a finger at each other every time some minor item goes wrong.

Many owners expect the architect, engineer, and contractor to be perfect. There is no such thing as a perfect set of drawings, however. There is also no such thing as a perfect location of piles. Construction projects will always need constant coordination among all the members of the design team and the contractors throughout the entire project, right to the very end.

By its very nature, the construction process is problematic. But every time something goes wrong, it doesn't have to be somebody's fault. What is really needed is a contingency fund, established by the owner, recognizing that construction is an imperfect process. The fund would apply irrespective of the fault of any party on the project. The owner should establish this contingency fund and agree not to look for any other forms of funding to resolve minor problems until the fund has been exhausted. This would encourage a much more cooperative atmosphere between the design team and the contractor and provide a cohesively managed project. The owner has everything to gain and nothing to lose.

In the Design Professionals Insurance Companies' *Guide to Better Contracts,*[3] it is suggested that the design professional must educate the owner "on the possibility of errors and omissions in the plans and specifications which may lead to unanticipated costs" and urge the owner to establish the contingency fund to cover such emergencies. The *Guide* offers a possible clause that could be negotiated, based on a "percentage of the construction budget that would be an appropriate contingency amount":[4]

CONTINGENCY FUND

If, as a result of any errors, omissions or negligent acts, for any of which the DESIGN PROFESSIONAL has legal responsibility, the OWNER incurs an accumulation of excess costs over two percent (2%) of the actual project construction cost, the DESIGN PROFESSIONAL shall bear the burden of such accumulation of excess costs over the 2%; provided said accumulation of excess costs shall not include any improvement costs or betterment costs and shall not exceed the difference between (1) the actual construction costs resulting from such errors, omissions, and negligent acts of the DESIGN PROFESSIONAL and (2) an estimate of what such costs would have been at the time of the signing of the construction contract. The DESIGN PROFESSIONAL shall have no liability for any such excess costs which are less than two percent (2%) of the actual project construction costs.[5]

The *Guide* points out that the design professional would be liable for any costs above the amount in the fund, so it instructs the design professional that it is

---

[3] Design Professional Insurance Companies, Guide to Better Contracts 23–24 (1987). These clauses are not intended as legal advice. If legal advice or other expert assistance is required, the services of a competent professional person should be obtained.

Copyright © 1987 by Design Professionals Insurance Company. Reprinted from DPIC Companies' Guide to Better Contracts. All rights reserved.

[4] *Id.*

[5] *Id.*

imperative for your safety that the percentage figure be realistic. If the client refuses to agree to the figure you feel is appropriate you may want to revise the clause to just provide for the contingency fund without stating your liability for costs in excess of the agreed upon percentage.[6]

§ 4.6   Suggested Designations of Responsibility

On a building project, some of the areas that most typically cause problems are:

1. The structural integrity of the facade system and its interface with the structural system of the building
2. The interface between a fabricator's design and detailing of steel connections on shop drawings and the engineer's review and approval of them
3. The definition of the contractors', architects', and engineers' responsibilities during the construction and inspection stages of a project.

Sections 4.7 through **4.9** discuss the roles and responsibilities of the appropriate parties for these areas and include some suggestions to clearly define responsibilities and encourage involvement by all parties to assist the owner in minimizing problems.

§ 4.7   —Wall Structure Interface

Traditionally, the architect designs and/or specifies facade systems of a building. If it is brick or other forms of masonry or stone, the architect typically designs it in detail on the drawings. For a curtain wall, she would sketch the overall requirements on the drawings but basically provide a performance specification that the curtain wall supplier must follow. The curtain wall supplier then does the detail design and analysis of the wall system for both its weather integrity and structural integrity. The structural engineer's prime responsibility is to be sure that any loads imposed upon the structure due to these wall systems can be accommodated by the structure.
   The approach that works the best for a curtain wall is this:

1. The architect prepares her drawings and her specifications, stating all performance requirements for the wall system
2. The engineer assists the architect in determining loading requirements for the wall system. In addition, the engineer should define all

---

[6] *Id.*

floor-to-floor differential movements of the structure that the wall system will have to accommodate

3. For a curtain wall, the architect's specifications should make it clear that the manufacturer must have the curtain wall designed by a professional engineer licensed in the state of the project

4. The curtain wall engineer should certify to the integrity of the wall system, and the architect and the structural engineer should review the curtain wall system.

This system works because there is a specific scope of work that is clearly defined. Each party on the design team knows that she is involved in the elements of the interface as well as the interface itself. Although the engineer of record may have additional exposure by reason of the review of the curtain wall, it is an appropriate amount—she is not picking up all of the responsibility, because the curtain wall was originally designed by another engineer. This combination of responsibility provides the owner maximum protection by encouraging maximum involvement of the design team members.

§ 4.8 —Connection Design in Steel Buildings

The problem here has typically been a lack of clear definition of responsibilities during the connection design. The more effective procedure that is becoming popular now is:

1. The engineer of record takes responsibility for the overall structural design of the project, including connections. This engineer defines the loads for the connections and is responsible for the review and approval of the fabricator's work on such designs and detailing.

2. The engineer may, however, specify, as is common on the east coast, that the fabricator perform the design work for the connections based on the loads given and that the fabricator take responsibility for the design work. If the fabricator is doing such design work, it should be done under the supervision of a licensed professional engineer in the state of the project. This engineer should certify in writing that the connection designs on the shop drawings were done under her supervision.

3. The engineer of record should still review and approve the shop drawings to be sure that they meet the overall requirements of the contract documents and can support the loads which she has specified. Her review and approval is a serious one and she must take responsibility for it. It is not a general overview. However, this review

and approval should not relieve the fabricator and her professional engineer of their design responsibility. Each takes responsibility for her own work.

4.   The difference between designing and detailing must be recognized. If the engineer of record does all of the design of the connections on her drawings (such as showing the spacing of the bolts, the number of bolts, and the pattern and sizes of welds), then she requires only detailing from the fabricator. In this case, the fabricator does not have to have an engineer involved in the design of the connections and the fabricator should thus have no responsibility for the connection design. She is still responsible for her detailing work. This procedure is common on the west coast.

This procedure makes sense because each person recognizes clearly her responsibility at the work interface.

§ 4.9   —Construction and Inspection

During construction it must be very clear that the party who has control must have responsibility.

1.   The contractor has control over how she does this work. No one else can tell her what the construction means and methods are. No one tells the contractor the size or number of her shores or controls the detail design of her shoring system. It is traditionally the contractor's work. She therefore has all the responsibility for construction means and methods.

2.   The engineer of record has no control over construction means and methods and safety precautions and therefore should be relieved of any related liability. She cannot simply walk through the site and start noticing what is safe and what is not safe; she has not been involved in the contractor's methodology or in determining the sizes and configurations of shoring systems.

3.   The other item that should be clear is that it is the contractor's responsibility to do the work in accordance with the contract documents. The engineer's review and/or inspection of that work does not relieve the contractor of the duty of doing it properly. The engineer is not responsible for the contractor properly conducting her work. The contractor must realize that inspection is for the owner's benefit, and she cannot rely on the inspection as an excuse for any improperly performed work. The owner could choose, for example, not to have an inspection. This would not relieve the contractor of her responsibility.

On the other hand, the engineer of record must take responsibility for her review of the work relative to it meeting the design requirements. If she is on site and she sees something wrong, it is her responsibility to call it to the attention of the owner. If the contractor does make a mistake and the engineer does not spot it when she is reviewing the work, then both have a responsibility.

Again, the concept is that each party takes responsibility for her own work.

PART II

WHEN FAILURE OCCURS

CHAPTER 5

WHAT TO DO WHEN THE PHONE RINGS: HOW TO SURVIVE THE CONSTRUCTION FAILURE*

Frank A. Shepherd, Esquire
Stuart J. McGregor, Esquire

Frank A. Shepherd is the executive vice president of Kimbrell & Hamann, P.A., a firm of 50 lawyers and one of the oldest in Miami, Florida. Mr. Shepherd heads a section of litigation practitioners who specialize in general commercial litigation with a heavy emphasis on construction and real estate disputes. Throughout his career, Mr. Shepherd has represented owners/developers, design professionals, contractors, and subcontractors in the preparation and trial of commercial construction disputes. Mr. Shepherd has lectured in his field both in Florida and nationally.

Mr. Shepherd is a member of the Florida Bar, the District of Columbia Bar, the United States District Court of the Southern, Middle, and Northern Districts of Florida, and the United States Courts of Appeal for both the Fifth and Eleventh Circuits. His civic and bar activities include the Greater Miami Chamber of Commerce (Chairman, Legislative Liaison Meeting Group), the Florida Bar Association, the American Bar Association's Sections on Litigation, Corporations, Banking and Business Law, the Dade County Bar and Defense Bar Associations, and the Dade County Republican Party Executive Committee.

Mr. Shepherd was born in West Palm Beach, Florida, and received his Bachelor of Arts degree from the University of Florida in 1968. He holds a Master of Arts degree from the University of Massachusetts and obtained his Juris Doctor degree from the University of Michigan in 1972.

*The authors would like to acknowledge Jeffrey D. Kottkamp, an associate with Kimbrell & Hamann, P.A., for his assistance in preparing this chapter.

Stuart J. McGregor concentrates his practice in general corporate representation and presently is in charge of the office practice section of Kimbrell & Hamann, P.A. He has also had considerable experience in construction and commercial litigation. He has participated in the litigation of major construction disasters for both plaintiffs and defendants, has authored articles, appeared on media, and spoken at seminars on legally related topics.

Mr. McGregor is a member of the Florida and New York Bars, the United States District Court for the Southern District of Florida, the United States Court of Appeals for the Eleventh Circuit, and the Trial Bar for the Southern District of Florida. His civic and bar activities include being director of the Dade County Defense Bar Association, and membership with the Florida Bar Association and the American Bar Association's Litigation and Corporation, Banking, and Business sections. He has served as editor of the *Florida Real Estate and Construction Law Quarterly* and attended the National Institute of Trial Advocacy. He is the founder and chairman of the board of Biblio Juris, Inc., a New York not-for-profit corporation that provides law books to students at Fordham Law School.

Mr. McGregor received his Bachelor of Science degree from Boston College in 1966. He obtained his Juris Doctor degree from Fordham University in 1976 where he was president of the Student Bar Association.

§ 5.1   Dealing with Disasters

The collapse of Connecticut's Mianus Bridge at 1:05 A.M. on June 28, 1983, was every highway department manager's nightmare. A 100-foot span on one of the Northeast's most heavily traveled highways suddenly gave way, plunging four vehicles into the Mianus River and killing three motorists.

J. William Burns, Commissioner of the Connecticut Department of Transportation (DOT), was awakened at 1:25 A.M. (20 minutes after the accident occurred), and by 4:00 A.M. he and other DOT officials arrived at the accident site (less than three hours after the accident occurred). By the next workday, Burns and his staff had already set up headquarters in a nearby motel, ordered an investigation of the 300 other bridges along the Connecticut turnpike, and hired outside consultants to investigate the failure and begin rebuilding the damaged bridge.[1]

At the same time, Burns had to cope with stunned public officials, reporters, residents, and motorists demanding an explanation of why the bridge collapsed. One of the commissioner's first decisions was to open all bridge records for inspection. In addition to holding scheduled daily and twice-daily press conferences, DOT officials also made themselves accessible for media questions on a 24-hour basis. "The principal factor in being able to handle that crisis was to level with everybody," Burns later said. "[I]t eliminated any suspicion that things weren't as they seemed."[2]

The commissioner also had to cope with nervous DOT staff members, who were worried about possible witch hunts. To calm their fears, he met with all agency bridge inspectors the day after the collapse and continued daily meetings with key staff members. Burns made every effort to assure his staff that no "lynch mob" would come after them.[3]

Dealing with disasters like the Mianus collapse is something with which more construction industry agencies and companies are coming to grips. Major catastrophes such as the L'Ambiance Plaza and Hyatt Regency collapses and the accident at the Three Mile Island Nuclear Station illustrate that the unthinkable can happen. Janine Reid, a crisis management consultant for Fails Management Institute in Denver, has stated that crisis construction is no longer the exception, but is the expected.[4]

San Antonio-based Texstar Construction Corporation is still reeling from the collapse of the L'Ambiance Plaza Apartment Building in Bridgeport, Connecticut, in April of 1987, which killed 28 workers and prompted a $2.5 million government fine against the project's lift-slab subcontractor. The disaster was the worst construction accident in New England history, and an executive vice president of Texstar later stated that Texstar was unprepared for the upheaval caused by the construction failure.[5]

---

[1] Rubin, Campbell & Lawson, *From Collapse to Corruption: Managing Company Crisis,* Eng'g News-Record (Feb. 1988).

[2] *Id.*

[3] *Id.*

[4] *Id.*

[5] *Id.*

In July 1981, two 75-yard-long concrete walkways, suspended from the ceiling by steel cables, collapsed into a lobby where 1500 people were dancing at the Hyatt Regency Hotel in Kansas City, Missouri. One hundred and fourteen people were killed and nearly 200 others were injured. The Hyatt structural engineer, VCE International, Inc., made efforts to blunt the impact of the disaster on its clients and employees but was eventually forced to sell its assets to a Denver-based structural engineer.[6]

In January 1978 the Hartford, Connecticut, Civic Center Coliseum roof collapsed just hours after 5,000 people had occupied the building to watch a college basketball game. A major catastrophe was narrowly avoided. Repair costs of the project topped the $30 million mark.

Indeed, construction failure and disaster occur periodically all around us, although not all accidents are the results of structural failure. There are operational failures caused by the action or inaction of people in positions of responsibility. Examples include the ferry that capsized in Belgium in March of 1987 after trying to leave port with the bow doors open, killing nearly 200 people; the accident at Three Mile Island in 1979; and the catastrophe at Chernobyl in 1986, which caused the deaths of 31 people.

Planning ahead for construction failure and disaster is just another part of the growing complexity and sophistication of the construction business. Today more and more companies are involved in crisis management planning in an effort to minimize the ill effects of construction failure. Even smaller firms are moving in that direction as they become more successful, realizing that as their companies grow so do their risks. Experts now contend that such planning is critical in today's uncertain construction environment. At least one crisis management expert has said that "forward thinking companies that want to be in business tomorrow must spend more time preparing for the inevitability of crisis. Any company that says it's immune to crisis will surely wind up with one."[7]

Thus, the essence of survival when you learn of a construction failure is planning. Planning for the possibility of construction failure and disaster will prepare you for the phone call at 1:05 A.M. with news of disaster. You won't be left dumbfounded and nervously thinking, "What do I do now?" Instead, through planning and preparation you can eliminate much of the chaos and adverse effects of construction failure by attacking the disaster head-on.

---

[6] *Id.*

[7] *Id.*

This chapter discusses the "how to" of crisis management. Although the bulk of the chapter addresses the needs of property owners, it applies equally to contractors, architects, and attorneys.

§ 5.2 Create a Construction Crisis Management Team

Just as J. William Burns, the commissioner of the Connecticut Department of Transportation, arrived at the Mianus Bridge accident site in less than three hours after that tragic event, it is imperative that those involved in a construction failure get to their construction site immediately in the event of failure. The need for immediate action requires that you plan ahead for such a disaster by creating a construction crisis management team.

The construction crisis management team should be a group of individuals, selected prior to the occurrence of any construction failure, who will take charge when a disaster occurs. The crisis management team is the equivalent of the SWAT team that takes over in police matters involving emergency situations. Just as the SWAT team is called in when drastic measures must be taken, so too, the crisis management team must take all necessary steps to guide you through the turmoil caused by construction failure.

Much thought should be put into organizing the team. It should be composed of people who know how to get the job done. More importantly, team members must think and act well under pressure. To be sure, when construction failure and disaster strike, the pressure is on.

Among those chosen for the team should be one insider. This is the person who knows the nuts and bolts of your operation. He should have hands on experience with the failed project. When questions arise regarding specifics, the insider should be able to provide the answers.[8]

Additionally, one team member should have the ability to think beyond the immediately foreseeable. This member assists in preparing for specific instances of crisis before they ever happen. This team member must be able to look into his crystal ball and imagine worst case scenarios. His role is vital in eliminating the element of surprise that accompanies construction failure. Make no mistake about it, the failure itself is all the surprise you will want to deal with.[9]

Your construction crisis management group also needs someone to play devil's advocate. This team member will be the one constantly saying

---

[8] G. Meyers, When It Hits The Fan 223 (1986).

[9] *Id.* at 224.

"What if?" Your devil's advocate will play the vital role of keeping the group on the right track. A construction crisis is no time for your decision-makers to get tunnel vision. When possible, this member should be someone who is unconnected to your company but is familiar with your type of construction business. Someone who has faced similar problems in the past can provide a wealth of knowledge during the management of a construction failure.[10]

Finally, your construction crisis management team must have a chairman—someone to lead. This person must have three vital abilities: (1) to listen well, (2) to be a strong leader of people, and (3) to act effectively under intense pressure. Your committee chairman will be the one who pulls it all together to create an organized, cohesive effort against the chaos.

After getting the proper members on your construction crisis management team, you must train them. Although there are no formal training centers to teach your committee members construction crisis management skills, a local university or consulting firm could assist you. A less expensive approach would be for your committee members to study the facts surrounding previous construction failures. Team members can learn a lot about handling construction crisis simply by talking to those who have already experienced it. In fact, a whole network of information could be developed by those who have suffered through construction failure, to assist those who will someday face the same problems.[11]

Once you have determined the members of your construction crisis management team and have trained them, you must organize a crisis control station. This will be the location where members meet and from where they will run the project. The crisis control station should be secluded enough to close out all interruptions save for those related to the disaster. The station should be well stocked with necessary supplies and equipment: telephones, computer terminals, blackboards, organization charts, building designs, and the like.[12] In addition, you should keep a list of important addresses and phone numbers at the station, as well as preplanned emergency instructions.[13]

In summary, then, one should organize a construction crisis management team now, before construction failure strikes. If disaster does cross your path, you are then ready to go to the site immediately and in a mobilized fashion. When all team members are in position, you will be ready to take the next step in managing a construction failure: implementing your construction crisis management plan.

---

[10] *Id.*

[11] *Id.*

[12] *Id.* at 225.

[13] *Id.* at 226.

§ 5.3   Prepare a Construction Crisis Management Plan

A construction crisis management plan is nothing more than a set of instructions for the construction crisis management team to follow if a construction failure should ever occur. You want to be prepared for the worst. Once a construction failure strikes, you will have little time to think about what actions to take. The key benefit of preplanning for construction disaster is that you can predetermine decisions on the mechanical level of the disaster (those aspects that usually remain the same), which will leave you with more time to manage the heart of the matter.[14]

When developing your plan, keep in mind the question, "What if?" Try to imagine all of the actions that will be required during a construction crisis, and then try to predetermine as many of those actions as possible: for instance, (1) call medical/fire assistance, (2) fence off site, (3) begin cleanup, and so on. The key to a successful plan is that it should be very specific so that the actions become mechanical.

Stephen Fink, president of Lexicon Communications Corporation, a Los Angeles-based public relations and management consultant firm that offers specialized crisis management counseling, discusses the development of crisis management plans in his book *Crisis Management.* Fink points out that a crisis management plan is necessary not only for your company's well-being but also for the well-being of others.[15] Consider the domino effect of a construction crisis in your community. It could affect other companies, your customers, hospitals, schools, and shops. With so much at stake, planning ahead is an absolute necessity.[16]

Creating a construction crisis management plan is not unlike the thought process required for airplane travel. It is not unusual when on an airplane to look for the emergency exit areas and then create a mental image of your escape out that exit in the event of a crisis on the airplane. It is that sort of "what if" thinking that is at the heart of all crisis management planning.

Thus, once a construction crisis management group has been selected, time should be spent forecasting the possible types of crisis with which your company could be faced. The next step is to prepare for those crises before they occur. If and when construction failure occurs, your construction crisis management committee will be prepared for the worst. The ill effects of construction failure can thus be minimized.

---

[14] S. Fink, Crisis Management 55 (1986).

[15] *Id.* at 54.

[16] *Id.*

§ 5.4   Take Charge of the Disaster Site

It is imperative not only that the crisis management chairman mobilize the team and go immediately to the construction site upon notice of a construction failure but also that the site be secured as soon as possible if that is within your control. Make sure those selected for the job are familiar with the area. In most instances this responsibility falls into the hands of the property owner.

The most effective method of securing the site is usually to fence it off and create controlled access points. In this way records can be kept not only of who is on the site, but also how many people are on the site. By controlling access to a construction failure site, much of the apparent chaos caused by many people proceeding in all directions can be avoided.

The team chairman, especially, must bear in mind the needs of fire, rescue, and medical workers. The immediate concern at any construction failure site must be care for the injured and control of the danger. Once these concerns have been addressed, a firm effort to secure the site must be made. Remember that crucial evidence as to the cause of any construction failure can be moved, altered, or even destroyed if adequate measures to secure the site are not made. Even inadvertent destruction of evidence caused by a failure to secure the site could play a crucial role in determining the liability of the parties later when lawsuits ensue.

Although it is crucial to secure the site and to take charge of it, one must at the same time be accessible to those who are directly affected and involved with the failure. Special attention should be devoted to those who have been injured, if any, and their families.

The period immediately following a construction failure is not the appropriate time to make statements to the media; however, it is the time to contact all interested parties including victims and their families. This means notifying employees who will be interested in whether they should report to work, government and community leaders who will be interested in the extent and impact of the construction failure on the area, insurance companies who will want to send out investigators, customers who will be interested to know if the failure will in any way effect their relationship with your company, and investors and bankers.[17]

Keep in mind that the period immediately following a construction disaster is not the appropriate time to speak to the public. You must provide yourself an opportunity to put your construction crisis management plan into action and to control the area first. Only when the situation is being addressed on your terms and you have had an opportunity to conduct a preliminary investigation will you be able to make a meaningful statement to the public.

---

[17] *Id.* at 99.

§ 5.5 Survey the Facts

Upon learning of a construction failure, it is crucial that you secure your own files and materials on the site and elsewhere. Although the importance of this may not be immediately apparent, years later if you happen to be in a trial trying to establish another's liability for the accident, the importance of this step will be clear. Further, it is vital that all information be gathered and secured so that your professionals and crisis management team can make informed decisions.

It is at this stage, too, that you should determine the experts that you will need. Generally, this will include at a minimum your lawyers, a photographer, design professionals, and construction professionals.

Furthermore, steps should be taken to seek documents and materials from others as necessary. Again, the purpose is to create a complete and accurate pool of information which will assist informed decisionmaking and eliminate surprise.

§ 5.6 Investigate and Preserve Evidence

Investigation of a construction failure must begin as soon as possible, and any investigation must be coordinated by your attorneys. Thus, it is imperative that immediately upon learning of construction failure you contact all needed professionals and get them to the site with any needed tools. This is particularly true for property owners, general contractors, and anyone else who might find themselves liable to others as a result of construction failure.

Steps must be taken to lock up, guard, or photograph important items. You must protect yourself from the alteration or destruction of crucial evidence which may play a vital role in the determination of the causes of and liability for the construction failure.

You may also find it helpful to videotape all investigations. This will provide you with a complete and accurate depiction of the evidence and of your investigation procedures. Furthermore, it may help protect you against later claims that you have altered or damaged evidence.

Moreover, you should be prepared to make any and all necessary repairs to the area of the construction site. You may have to take steps to insure the safety of those investigating the site.

Some attention must be given to proceeding with the investigation in a way that is fair to all parties involved. Every attempt should be made to avoid duplicating or creating hardship on any of the parties. Of primary importance during a site investigation is the procurement of samples of failed components and representative materials, which will be later tested. All parties involved will demand an equal opportunity to collect such material for testing purpose, thus all efforts should be made to conduct your investigation in a cooperative spirit.

Finally, keep in mind that attorneys representing the injured and your customers are likely to arrive at the scene nearly as quickly as your own attorneys. This will create problems regarding access to the site and investigation of the evidence.

You may be faced with motions seeking temporary restraining orders. Do not hesitate to use the court processes when disputes arise regarding how the investigation process should be orchestrated.

§ 5.7 Protect and Investigate through the Use of the Attorney-Client Privilege and Work Product Doctrine

Few rules of law are more widely evoked and frequently misused in construction failure litigation than that of Rule 26(b)(1) and (b)(3) of the Federal Rules of Civil Procedure.

The attorney-client privilege, the oldest of the privileges for confidential information, is incorporated in Rule 26(b)(1), which explicitly recognizes that privileged matters are not obtainable: "parties may obtain discovery regarding any matter, not privileged, which is relevant to the subject matter involved in the pending action."

The attorney work product doctrine is designed to promote the adversarial system by protecting attorney-prepared trial materials from discovery. Unlike the attorney-client privilege, which exists to protect the client in his right to confidential advice, the work product doctrine works primarily for the benefit of attorneys in protecting from disclosure their candid assessments in matters involved in litigation. Outside the context of litigation, the doctrine has no application.

§ 5.8 —Attorney-Client Privilege

The attorney-client privilege is considered a critical tool by which the legal profession provides effective service to clients. It is recognized that, if the traditional privilege for attorney-client communications applies to a particular writing that may be found in a lawyer's file, the privilege exempts it from pretrial discovery proceedings.[18]

When a construction failure occurs, there is an immediate investigation by federal and state authorities, corporate agents, corporate counsel, retained outside legal counsel, insurance claims agents, retained experts in various fields, the media, and many others concerned with the discovery

---

[18] Upjohn Co. v. United States, 449 U.S. 383 (1981).

of the cause of the collapse or failure. Protecting the information in your attorney's possession can therefore be vital to your survival.

Addressing the role of the parties with direct responsibility on the failed project, the law with regard to privilege was significantly broadened by the *Upjohn v. U.S.* decision. In *Upjohn,* the Supreme Court was concerned with which "employees" within the corporate structure were considered clients so that their communication with the corporate counsel remained privileged. Prior to the *Upjohn* decision, the courts had developed two tests designed to identify which corporate employees could communicate with the corporate attorney in confidence: the "control group" test and the "subject matter" test.

Under the control group test only communications between the corporate counsel and upper level management personnel capable of effecting decisionmaking were privileged. Those employees within the lower echelons of the corporate structure did not qualify as clients. Thus, their communications with the corporate attorney were not privileged.[19]

Under the subject matter test communications to the corporate attorney were privileged when made by any employee at the direction of his superiors about matters concerning corporate activity.[20]

In the *Upjohn* decision, the Supreme Court attempted to alleviate some of the confusion in the lower courts by clarifying which employees could communicate in confidence with the corporate attorney. In so doing, the Court specifically rejected the control group analysis as being too rigid and difficult to apply. Although the Court declined to establish a specific test, it did make clear that under the appropriate circumstances the privilege was available to all corporate employees. Among the relevant factors considered by the Court were the following:

1. the communications were by a corporate employee to the corporate counsel upon the directions of his superiors
2. the information communicated concerned matters within the employee's corporate duties
3. the employee was aware that the reason for his communication was so that the corporation could obtain legal advice.

With all of these circumstances present, the Court in *Upjohn* felt it was unreasonable to restrict the scope of the privilege to only those employees in the control group. As a result, the Court held privileged all communications between the corporate counsel and any employee of the corporation fulfilling the appropriate criteria. Therefore, protection was increased by the *Upjohn* decision in that once it has been determined that a corporate

---

[19] Philadelphia v. Westinghouse Elec. Corp., 210 F. Supp. 483 (E.D. Pa. 1962).

[20] Harper & Row Publishers, Inc. v. Decker, 423 F.2d 487 (7th Cir. 1970).

counsel is acting in a legal capacity, the scope of his privilege may extend to all corporate employees, not just those employees in upper level management positions. However, an *Upjohn* analysis is not appropriate until it has in fact been determined that the matter sought to be protected concerns legal affairs and is not related to the corporate counsel's managerial corporate responsibilities.

The difficulty in applying these distinctions comes when there exists a report made by a nonattorney employee concerning the results of an investigation of facts pertinent to some matter that later becomes the subject of litigation. The problem frequently arises in connection with the discovery of accident reports prepared by employees, lists of eyewitnesses, signed statements of witnesses attached to such reports, or statements secured separately by employees or investigators employed in the party's claims department. Routine reports of agents made in the regular course of business, before suit is brought or threatened, have been treated as preexisting documents that are not privileged in the client's hands and do not become so when delivered into the possession of his attorney.

Note that the *Upjohn* decision was decided under federal common law. Federal Rule of Evidence 501 dictates that a federal court in a diversity action applies state law to any privilege claim. As a result, *Upjohn* is not binding precedent on state courts.

In order to anticipate and avoid future problems in this area, you should determine how the state law in your jurisdiction will view this attorney-client privilege. Proper procedures for investigations in the event of a future collapse or failure can then be put in place.

§ 5.9 —Work Product Doctrine

The work product doctrine was first clearly articulated by the United States Supreme Court in *Hickman v. Taylor*[21] in which the Court recognized that "it was essential that a lawyer work with a certain degree of privacy, free from unnecessary intrusion by opposing parties and their counsel."

In *Hickman* the Supreme Court refused to allow the plaintiff to obtain copies of statements made by witnesses to an accident in which the plaintiff was injured on the grounds that the plaintiff had failed to show justification or necessity for invading the files and work product of the defendant's attorney. The Court reasoned that if interviews, statements, memoranda, correspondence, briefs, mental impressions, and personal beliefs (the work product of the lawyer) were open to opposing counsel on mere demand, much of what is now put down in writing would

---

[21] 329 U.S. 495, 67 S. Ct. 385 (1947).

remain unwritten. Thus, *Hickman* held that a party is not entitled to discovery of written statements in the files of an attorney for the adverse party and of memoranda made by him in anticipation of litigation without any showing of the necessity for production of such materials or any demonstration that denial of production would cause hardship.

The work product doctrine is now codified in Rule 26(b)(3) of the Federal Rules of Civil Procedure, which provides:

> A party may obtain discovery of documents and tangible things otherwise discoverable . . . and prepared in anticipation of litigation or for trial by or for another party or by or for that other party's representative, including his attorney, counsel, consultant, surety, indemnitory, insurer, or agent only upon a showing that the party seeking discovery has substantial need of the materials in the preparation of his case and that he is unable without undue hardship to obtain the substantial equivalent of the matters by other means. In ordering discovery of such materials when the required showing has been made, the court shall protect against disclosure of the mental impressions, conclusions, opinions, or legal theories of an attorney or other representative of a party concerning the litigation.

Although the attorney-client privilege applies to written and verbal communications, the work product doctrine takes into account only documents and tangible objects. If a document is covered by the attorney-client privilege, there is obviously no need to discuss the work product effect. It is only when an attorney-client privilege or some other evidentiary exclusion is inapplicable that the work product doctrine comes into play. Thus, if you cannot meet the test of attorney-client privilege, the material may still be recognized as work product prepared in anticipation of litigation or for trial.

"In anticipation of litigation" has been construed quite liberally by the courts.[22] Despite this broad construction, distinctions are continually made on the basis of how routine is the preparation of the reports, what mention is made of the possibility of litigation, and so on. Such decisions are made on a case-by-case basis. The suggestions mentioned in § 5.8 to support an attorney-client privilege are applicable to a work product determination as well.

§ 5.10   —Procedures for Protecting Information

Regardless of whether it is a control group test or an *Upjohn* determination for an attorney-client privilege or a work product doctrine issue, certain procedures should be followed to protect the initial investigation information following the construction failure:

---

[22] Upjohn Co. v. United States, 449 U.S. 383 (1981).

1. Use attorneys whenever possible to obtain facts or conduct investigations. If an employee other than an attorney conducts an investigation, all materials should be delivered to counsel. That employee should operate under clear, written instructions from corporate counsel or outside legal counsel.

2. Identify all communications with a stamp indicated "Confidential/ Legal" or some other legend.

3. Maintain a separate, segregated file in a restricted access area. Avoid maintaining duplicate files or copies of correspondence in other areas of the office.

4. Originate the file with documentation indicating that the investigation to be conducted is in anticipation of litigation.

Finally, consideration should be given to the extent to which the attorney-client privilege and work product doctrine are utilized once suit is filed and the discovery process begun. Remember that the failure of a party to allow pretrial discovery of confidential matters it intends to use at trial will preclude introduction of that evidence.[23] Additionally, a party may not insist on the protection of the attorney-client privilege or work product doctrine for damaging communications while disclosing other selected communications because they are self-serving. A client who chooses to disclose secrets falling within the attorney-client privilege waives the privilege and cannot later insist upon his own or his attorney's silence.[24]

The attorney-client privilege and work product doctrine should not be used to preclude full discovery of the facts and circumstances surrounding a construction collapse or failure. They are vehicles for protecting the efforts of a party and its legal counsel who have made a thorough investigation, examination, and determination of the reasons for the collapse or failure. A prompt determination is critical today when the economic stakes of the potential litigation that frequently follow such a collapse or failure can be devastating.

§ 5.11   Cooperate with Enforcing Authorities

In the event of a construction failure, be aware that federal authorities will likely be on the scene very quickly. These authorities may include inspectors for the Occupational Safety and Health Administration (OSHA). You must make every effort to cooperate with OSHA officials and be aware that they have authority not only to inspect an accident scene but also to

---

[23] Fed. R. Civ. P. 37(b)(2)(b).

[24] International Tel. & Tel. Corp. v. United Tel. Co. of Fla., 60 F.R.D. 177 (M.D. Fla. 1973).

impose heavy fines. The $5.11 million in fines levied by OSHA after the L'Ambiance Plaza construction disaster is an example of how harsh OSHA fines can be.

You may also encounter authorities from the Federal Emergency Management Agency (FEMA). The powers of FEMA authorities stretch beyond mere inspection to actual debris removal. However, FEMA will not become active in a construction failure unless a request is made by your state's governor to the President. Such a request must be based upon the governor's finding that the situation is of such severity and magnitude that effective response is beyond the capabilities of state and local governments. Based upon the governor's request, the president must determine whether an emergency exists which warrants federal assistance.[25]

State and local authorities are also very interested and concerned with construction failure. State prosecutors will be on hand to investigate and search for any signs of criminal wrongdoing. Likewise, local building authorities will be on the scene to determine if any applicable building codes have been violated.

When possible, legal counsel should tour the site with federal and state authorities while they conduct their investigations. Try to determine whether you are the target of their investigations. If you are, make it apparent that you will fully cooperate with them.

§ 5.12   Cooperate Cautiously with Others

Although cooperation with federal and state authorities is necessary to reduce the possibility of a fine or even criminal prosecution, a more cautious approach should be used when cooperating with others. Design professionals, general contractors, subcontractors and suppliers, insurers and claim representatives, and investigators sent by others should all receive cordial, yet cautious, cooperation.

In addition, counsel for all of the above should receive cautious cooperation. The period after a construction failure is neither a time to "hide the ball" nor a time to "spill the beans." Make an effort to assist others in the performance of their duties, but bear in mind that the issue of liability for construction failure is ever present.

§ 5.13   Dealing with the Media

During a construction crisis, it is imperative that you maintain a good rapport with the media. Not only will this be important with respect to

---

[25] 42 U.S.C. § 5141.

how your company is perceived by the public *during* the crisis but it will play a vital role *after* the crisis. Your company's future may depend on how well you handle a construction failure. The media can make or break you in that regard.

Your first step in planning for a positive relationship with the media is to select a spokesperson. This should be done at the same time you select your construction crisis management team. You must have one spokesperson so that your company's message is heard from one unified source.[26]

Put some time and thought into whom you select as your spokesperson. Your spokesperson should be the kind of person who gets along with people and can establish a positive relationship with the press. That person needs to sound and look the part. Remember, the public image of your company will be molded by its impression of your spokesperson. As for practical pointers, make sure your spokesperson looks professional. This means no chewing gum or sunglasses, for example.

Once you have selected a spokesperson, you need to decide how, where, and when to meet with the press. You want to call the shots. It may be best to consider regularly scheduled interviews at the construction failure site. This creates the image that you are on hand and concerned about the construction failure. Interviews from remote office sites that tend to create a "business as usual" image should be avoided.

Begin making your case to the public as soon as news of the construction failure surfaces. Make it clear that you have a construction crisis management group organized and at work. Project an image of concern and confidence. Provide the press with information you are 110 percent sure is accurate. Never guess and never give answers based on hypothetical questions. There will be a period of time when you have no answers. That is the time to make it clear that every effort is being made to deal with the crisis.

Even prior to a construction failure, much of what you should discuss with the media can be prepared. One of the most frustrating positions to be in is when the news media ignore all the positive things you do and just report the negative. To counter this possibility, keep safety records on hand. For instance, you may be able to report that "prior to this construction failure our firm had not lost one man-hour of work due to an accident in the last six years." Positive OSHA reports may also help bolster your prior record of safety.[27]

In addition, have at your fingertips the service records on all equipment that may be involved in a construction failure. In this way you can stress that every reasonable effort has been made to use safe equipment that has been regularly serviced.

---

[26] G. Meyers, When It Hits The Fan 55 (1986).

[27] S. Fink, Crisis Management 55 (1986).

Finally, you can bolster your image by reciting the sheer volume of prior business you have had without a construction failure. This type of information can be easily compiled and updated at some regular interval so that in the event of a construction failure it can quickly and accurately be disseminated to the press.

One more practical pointer: keep in mind the needs of the various news media. Television and radio will be interested in 60 to 90 seconds of news, so give them the most important facts in a simplified form. Newspapers, on the other hand, require detail, and you can get into specifics with their reporters. When your spokesperson talks to reporters remind him to get to the point. He should reduce your arguments down to a few sentences, without any legalese supplied by lawyers. Besides increasing your chances of making the news, you also increase your chances of being understood, because there is less for the reporter to paraphrase or ignore.[28]

§ 5.14 Tell the Truth

Whether you find yourself in a one-on-one interview at the site of a construction failure or at a huge press conference downtown, facing friendly or hostile press, honesty is of vital importance.[29]

Being dishonest or less than honest with the media will only escalate your crisis into proportions that will stagger you. It will serve to destroy your present and future credibility with the media. It will undermine your efforts to ameliorate that adversarial relationship often existing between you and the media. In short, trying to be less than honest with the media, especially during a crisis, is suicidal.[30]

As a practical matter, your communications with the media, federal and local authorities, opposing counsel, employees, and others must be truthful. When dealing with the media in particular not only should you tell the truth, you should never say that anything is "off the record," never say anything that you don't want reported, never say "no comment," never be trapped into predicting the future, and, above all, stay away from liability issues.[31]

Bear in mind that, although the truth may hurt, no agony from telling the truth can equal the upheaval caused by coverups and lies.

---

[28] Boles & Heaviside, *When A Reporter Calls*, A.B.A. J. (June 1, 1987).

[29] S. Fink, Crisis Management 112 (1986).

[30] *Id.*

[31] *Id.* at 114.

CHAPTER 6

CONSTRUCTION FAILURES FROM LATENT ENVIRONMENTAL HAZARDS

Peter J. Wallace, Esquire

Alann M. Ramirez, Esquire

Kevin R. Bryson, Esquire

Peter J. Wallace is a senior vice president with Hill International, Inc., a construction consulting firm headquartered in Willingboro, New Jersey.

A graduate of Rutgers Law School and Northeastern University, Mr. Wallace has extensive experience in the preparation, arbitration, and litigation of claims on a wide variety of projects including commercial, industrial power, and public works. Mr. Wallace has also lectured on construction claims and troubled projects.

Mr. Wallace is a member of the New Jersey and Pennsylvania Bar and has been appointed to the Panel of Arbitrators of the American Arbitration Association.

Alann M. Ramirez is a registered professional engineer and attorney. As a managing consultant with Hill International, he has been involved in providing construction claims services for power generation, transportation, and municipal utility clients. His experience includes review and interpretation of design specifications and contract documents, liability analysis, and schedule delay claim analysis. He is a member of the American Society of Mechanical Engineers, American Nuclear Society, American Bar Association, New Jersey State Bar Association, and the Pennsylvania Bar Association.

Kevin R. Bryson is a project director with Hill International, Inc. As a registered professional engineer and a lawyer, he has been involved with the regulatory and engineering aspects of environmental matters throughout his career. Mr. Bryson is a graduate of the University of Lowell and Suffolk University Law School. He is a member of the New Jersey Bar, the Environmental Law Committee of the New Jersey Bar Association, and the American Bar Association.

§ 6.1 Introduction

Construction failures are most commonly associated with design errors and omissions, poor workmanship, defects in manufactured components or equipment, labor problems, or other internal or external conditions that cause a project to fail in a physical or economic sense. These failures can occur on a diversity of projects, such as an office building that experiences a structural failure, a process or manufacturing plant that does not meet its intended performance or output requirements, or a sewage treatment plant that does not meet the effluent standards imposed by its permit. In many of these cases the failure could have been avoided or its impact mitigated by appropriate management and claim avoidance techniques during the design or construction phase.

In contrast, there are few ways to avoid failures caused by the existence of an environmental hazard. If the hazard is discovered prior to purchasing and developing the site, the choice may be very simple: locate the project on a different site. However, if the hazard is discovered after the site has been purchased and site development or construction has begun, the only option is to suspend work at the site and enter a cleanup program before the project can proceed. In many cases this option destroys the economic feasibility of the project, because it may take years to gain approval for and implement the cleanup program and it may cost millions of dollars.

An environmental consultant has estimated that, in one particular state, up to 85 percent of all subsurface construction at or near industrial sites and up to 40 percent of undeveloped residential sites (former farmland) will encounter latent environmental hazards.[1] Another national environmental consultant has estimated that one in three major real estate transactions will involve property with some contamination.[2]

When a construction project is undertaken and latent hazardous substances are found, substantial potential liability exists. An owner can be held strictly liable for all cleanup costs; the architect/engineer may be liable for negligence in not conducting site tests or finding the subsurface environmental hazards; the construction manager who directs construction site operations may be held strictly liable for cleanup costs jointly and severally with the owner; the construction contractor who excavates the site or

---

[1] Aguilar Assocs. & Consultants, Inc., Morganville, N.J.

[2] Warner, *When Real Estate Is a Vast Wasteland,* The Philadelphia Inquirer, Dec. 25, 1988, § L at 1, col. 3 (statements made by George Pilko).

transports material may be held strictly liable for spreading the hazardous substance that was released. These burdens exist in addition to the construction project schedule delay.

Construction projects with latent environmental hazards can create a variety of other problems. Some examples of real and potential problems are:

1. Prior to the construction of a portside redevelopment project outside New York City involving luxury condominiums, a marina, and a shopping mall, the owners were aware of soil and groundwater contamination but underestimated the cleanup effort. The owners could not turn over designated site areas to the contractors as planned, resulting in schedule delays and potential delay claims by the contractors.

2. At a prison expansion project in Michigan, the excavation of the site adjacent to the existing facility uncovered hazardous substances. Work was suspended and preliminary analysis estimated hundreds of thousands of dollars would be spent in the cleanup effort before the project could resume. Prisoners at the nearby existing facility also asserted toxic tort claims. The potential existed for delay claims by the contractors.

3. After an office condominium complex was constructed and units sold, it was discovered that the underlying soil was contaminated with heavy metals and radium. The original owners, the developer, and the general contractor were liable for the cleanup costs of the site where the contaminated soil was transported and for potential toxic tort claims by employees, the present owners, and their employees.

4. A commercial office complex was being erected by a developer at a former farm site. During site excavation, drums of hazardous substances were found, several of which were releasing hazardous substances into the ground. (This same scenario could apply to a building rehabilitation project where asbestos is found.) The developer was liable for the site cleanup costs and for costs incurred by neighbors for cleanup of their properties due to groundwater contamination.

5. A developer bought two lots in a business park. When excavation began, a network of trenches filled with "blue goo" was found. The substances were later determined to be waste oil, cyanide, and other hazardous materials that were illegally buried. The subsequent cleanup cost the developer and a neighboring landowner $1.6 million. The developer attempted to recoup response costs by suing other responsible parties.[3]

---

[3] *Id.* at 1, col. 1.

Given the risks of environmental hazards, before purchasing or developing a property an owner should make the preparation of an environmental impact survey a key element in its evaluation of the economic viability of the project. An owner who ignores these risks may be exposed to liability for a multimillion dollar cleanup effort and numerous personal injury claims.

This chapter will discuss how failures can occur because of latent environmental hazards, the potential liabilities of the project participants, and avoidance measures that can minimize liability and mitigate damages when a failure occurs.

§ 6.2 Required Actions When Hazardous Materials Are Encountered

The term *construction failure,* as used in this chapter, refers to the occurrence of unanticipated events or conditions that effectively destroy the economic or functional use of the project for its intended purpose. Such failures cannot be remedied without a substantial expenditure of capital and time. Construction projects that encounter latent hazardous substances can typically suffer lengthy schedule delays, enormous cost increases, or a project cancellation. In addition, the site owner and others are exposed to potentially enormous unexpected liability.

A decade ago, under the same circumstances, the site owner may not have taken any action when latent hazardous substances were found and may not have even recognized a problem existed. When hazardous substances are found on the jobsite today the owner cannot ignore or quietly dispose of the contamination. Significant civil and criminal penalties apply for noncompliance with environmental regulations.[4]

---

[4] A fine of up to $10,000 and/or one year imprisonment may be imposed for knowingly failing to notify the Environmental Protection Agency (EPA) of a facility that has had hazardous waste releases (42 U.S.C. § 9603(c) (1982)). In addition, the convicted person forfeits any rights on limitations to cleanup liability and the use of any statutory defenses available under 42 U.S.C. § 9607. The sanctions for being convicted of failing to report a "spill," or present release, which a potentially responsible party (PRP) has knowledge of or for reporting false or misleading information can result in a fine of $250,000 for an individual, $500,000 for a corporation, and/or three years' imprisonment for a first conviction and five years for subsequent convictions. Civil penalties may also be imposed in administrative or judicial proceedings when a person violates the spill reporting requirements. The civil penalties can be $25,000 per violation, or per day for each day the violation continues, or $75,000 each day for subsequent violations. Civil penalties are found in 42 U.S.C. § 9609 and criminal penalties are covered in 42 U.S.C. § 9603. 42 U.S.C. § 9607(c)(3) imposes treble charges against persons who fail without sufficient cause to act on an EPA or judicial order under 42 U.S.C. § 9604 or § 9606 (1982).

Today, the federal government has a comprehensive, broad-based program consisting of several legislative enactments that attempt to minimize the danger to the public health and environment and to force liable parties to pay for any required hazardous waste cleanup. The key elements of the federal hazardous waste program are the Resource Conservation and Recovery Act (RCRA)[5] and the Comprehensive Environmental Response, Compensation, and Liability Act (CERCLA).[6]

§ 6.3   Resource Conservation and Recovery Act

The RCRA provides a federal statutory system governing the disposal of solid wastes and hazardous wastes. It created an extensive regulatory program for handling hazardous wastes from "cradle to grave."[7] The Act also regulates the management of disposal, storage, and treatment facilities that have continued to operate after its enactment. It attempts to avoid the creation of new inactive waste sites by controlling activities at existing operating waste sites. As a general rule, with the exception of the imminent hazard provision[8] discussed further in § 6.5, RCRA does not provide for the regulation of hazardous wastes now located at inactive sites, such as construction projects with latent hazards. The Comprehensive Environmental Response, Compensation, and Liability Act covers this gap in RCRA.[9]

In most of the situations discussed in § 6.1, an unsuspecting owner or contractor will undoubtedly be able to successfully show that she is not a contributing party under RCRA. However, there is the strong potential that she may find herself caught in the web of litigation during the early phases of a hazardous waste cleanup situation and may incur substantial expenses to extricate herself from the process. For this reason, any owner and/or contractor doing business today should be aware of this law and its requirements.

---

[5] Resource Conservation and Recovery Act, 42 U.S.C. §§ 6901–6987 (1982) [hereinafter RCRA].

[6] Comprehensive Environmental Response, Compensation And Liability Act, 42 U.S.C. §§ 9601–9657 (as amended by Superfund Amendments and Reauthorization Act of 1986, Pub. L. No. 99-499, 100 Stat. 1613 (1986)) [hereinafter CERCLA].

[7] 1980 U.S. Code Cong. & Admin. News (94 Stat.) 6119, 6120.

[8] Dore, *The Standard of Liability for Hazardous Waste Disposal Activity: Some Quirks of Superfund,* 57 Notre Dame Law. 260, 266 (1981).

[9] United States v. Northeastern Pharmaceutical & Chem. Co., 25 Env't Rep. Cas. (BNA) 1385 (8th Cir. 1986); United States v. Conservation Chem. Co., 20 Env't Rep. Cas. (BNA) 1008 (W.D. Mo. 1985). See § 6.4 for a discussion of CERCLA.

§ 6.4 —Identifying Hazardous Materials

The Resource Conservation and Recovery Act[10] was enacted in 1976 as the primary statute for the regulation of solid and hazardous waste. The Act is a multifaceted approach to solving the problems associated with solid waste disposal in this country. The regulation of hazardous waste was the overriding concern of Congress when enacting RCRA because this legislation was seen as closing the loop of environmental protection.[11] This Act and its amendments were designed to achieve the safest disposal of discarded materials and to regulate the management of hazardous waste from the time it is generated until the time it is finally disposed of properly.

The RCRA hazardous waste program was a major federal undertaking. Under the program, the Environmental Protection Agency (EPA) was required to develop comprehensive regulations to administer the program. However, it was not until after litigation that the EPA promulgated the basic regulations of the hazardous waste program on May 19, 1980.[12]

To meet the requirements of this program, the EPA developed regulations that: identify hazardous waste;[13] establish notification procedures for those persons managing hazardous waste;[14] and establish standards for generators,[15] transporters,[16] and the treatment, storage, and disposal facilities (TSDF)[17] associated with hazardous waste. In addition, regulations were established that require owners and operators of a TSDF to obtain a permit to operate such facilities.[18] A most significant part of the program is the manifest system, which requires tracking of hazardous waste from its inception to its final resting place, the so-called "cradle to grave" requirement of RCRA. The Resource Conservation and Recovery Act also gives

---

[10] Pub. L. No. 94-580 (codified at 42 U.S.C. § 6901 (1976) *as amended by* Quiet Communities Act of 1978, Pub. L. No. 95-609, 92 Stat. 3079); Solid Waste Disposal Act of 1980, Pub. L. No. 96-482, 94 Stat. 2334; Used Oil Recycling Act of 1980, Pub. L. No. 96-463 (codified at 42 U.S.C. § 6901); Comprehensive Environmental Response, Compensation and Liability Act of 1980, Pub. L. No. 96-510 (codified at 42 U.S.C. § 9601); 1984 Hazardous and Solid Waste Amendments, Pub. L. No. 98-616 (Nov. 9, 1984).

[11] H.R. 1491, 94th Cong., 2d Sess. at 3–4 (1976).

[12] State of Illinois v. Castle, 12 Env't Rep. Cas. (BNA) 1597 (1979).

[13] *See generally* 40 C.F.R. § 261 (1986).

[14] 42 U.S.C. § 6930 (1982). 50 Fed. Reg. 614 (1985), as amended by 50 Fed. Reg. 14216 (1985).

[15] *See generally* 40 C.F.R. § 262 (1986).

[16] *See generally id.* at § 263.

[17] *See generally id.* at § 264.

[18] *Id.*

the EPA broad and comprehensive powers to provide for civil and criminal
sanctions for violations of the RCRA hazardous waste programs.

Under RCRA, a hazardous waste must first be shown to be a solid
waste. *Solid waste* is specifically defined in RCRA at § 1004(27)[19] to include not only solids but also gases, liquids, and semisolids. This definition was expanded in regulations developed specifically for Subtitle C.[20]
Additional provisions and regulations developed under the act provide for
exclusions to this definition of solid waste.[21]

Once a material is determined to be a solid waste, it must then be determined if it is a hazardous waste. Using legislatively mandated factors, the
EPA established criteria upon which to determine characteristics of hazardous waste.[22] Based upon these characteristics, lists of hazardous waste
were established. Under these regulations, a waste is hazardous if it exhibits one or more of the following characteristics:

1. Ignitability
2. Corrosivity
3. Reactivity
4. Extraction Procedure (EP) Toxicity (leading test).[23]

In addition to these characteristics, the EPA promulgated regulations
that listed various chemicals and groups of chemicals that they consider
hazardous.[24]

§ 6.5   —Enforcement Provisions

To provide assurances that the regulatory scheme provided for under
RCRA will be carried out, RCRA contains within it statutory provisions
for a strong enforcement scheme. Included are provisions for administrative, civil, and criminal actions, and injunctive relief as appropriate. Actions in these matters may be brought to correct either past or present
violations and may be brought by the administrator or the appropriate
state authority when a state has delegated authority. Penalties for violation
of such activities may reach as high as $25,000 per day per violation. In
addition, RCRA also provides for individual citizens to commence civil

---

[19] 42 U.S.C. § 6914 (1982).

[20] 40 C.F.R. § 261.2 (1986) (all references to C.F.R. are to 1986 unless otherwise indicated).

[21] *Id.* at § 261.4.

[22] 42 U.S.C. § 6931 (1982); 40 C.F.R. § 261.11.

[23] 40 C.F.R. §§ 261.20, 261.21, 261.22, 261.23, 261.24.

[24] *Id.* at §§ 261.30, 261.31, 261.32, 261.33.

suits against any persons, including the United States, if such parties are violating or have violated certain provisions of RCRA or if the appropriate agency is failing to act.[25]

Criminal liability may attach under RCRA to any person who, among other things, "knowingly" transports or causes to have transported a hazardous waste to a facility that does not have a permit or who transports wastes without first having the proper manifest documents or EPA identification number.[26] Criminal liability may also be imposed upon any person who knowingly endangers another by placing another in danger of death or serious bodily injury.[27] An individual convicted of violating this provision faces a fine up to $50,000 per day and/or two years imprisonment, and a fine of up to $250,000 per day and/or up to 15 years in prison for knowing endangerment.[28]

The knowing requirement of these statutes is significant in proving guilt. As the EPA guidance manual on enforcement notes, the agency must carefully consider several specific factors before proceeding with the criminal prosecution. Among them is that the EPA must determine that the violator knowingly or willfully violated the statute. There must be "evidence of intent in the commission of the violative act rather than it merely being the result of accident or mistake."[29]

RCRA further provides "that upon receipt of evidence that the past or present handling, storage, treatment, transportation or disposal of any solid or hazardous waste may present an imminent and substantial endangerment to health or the environment," the EPA administrator may bring a suit in the appropriate district court against any person (including any past or present generator, past or present transporter, or past or present owner or operator of a treatment, storage, or disposal facility) who has contributed or who is contributing to such handling, storage, treatment, transportation, or disposal action for injunctive relief to stop or remedy such activities.[30]

In early cases interpreting this legislation, the courts were unable to reach unanimous agreement regarding the scope and breadth of its application. However, in *United States v. Northeastern Pharmaceutical & Chemical Co.,*[31] the court cited the House report that accompanied the

---

[25] 42 U.S.C. § 6972 (1982).

[26] *Id.* at § 6938.

[27] *Id.*

[28] *Id.*

[29] U.S. EPA, Compliance/Enforcement Guidance Manual 5–11 (Government Inst. Inc., 1984).

[30] 42 U.S.C. § 6973(a) (1982).

[31] 25 Env't Rep. Cas. (BNA) at 1396 n.5 (8th Cir. 1986).

1984 amendments to RCRA as a clarification to existing law and imposed liability that is joint and several and strict to all parties named in the section.

The EPA is required to provide notice to any affected state whenever an agreement between the EPA and a responsible party indicates that there is a covenant not to sue or to forbear from a suit to settle any claim arising under the imminent danger section. In addition, EPA is required to provide a notice and opportunity for public hearing in the site area along with a reasonable opportunity to comment on the proposed settlement prior to its final entry.[32] Upon receipt of information that there is an imminent danger at any given site, the administrator must provide immediate notice to the local government and require that notice of such endangerment be promptly posted at the particular site.[33]

§ 6.6 Comprehensive Environmental Response, Compensation, and Liability Act

The fundamental purpose of the Comprehensive Environmental Response, Compensation, and Liability Act (CERCLA) is to provide for the cleanup of inactive hazardous waste sites by establishing a mechanism to reimburse those who incur cleanup costs.

The Act applies to any person or facility that causes a hazardous substance[34] to be released into the environment.[35] State, local, and federal government agencies are not immune from CERCLA liability.[36] The Act

---

[32] 42 U.S.C. § 6973(a) (1982).

[33] *Id.* at § 6973(c).

[34] 42 U.S.C. § 9601(14) defines hazardous substance as a variety of substances including RCRA hazardous waste and substances listed in the Clean Air Act, Clean Water Act, and Toxic Substances Control Act except natural gas and other exempted petroleum products.

[35] *Environment* is defined in 42 U.S.C. § 9601(8) and includes navigable waters, ocean waters, any other surface water, ground water, drinking water supply, land surface or subsurface strata, or ambient air within the United States.

[36] Many municipalities have been exposed to CERCLA liability for owning, operating, or using a landfill that is found to release hazardous substances. *See* City of Philadelphia v. Stepan Chem. Co., 544 F. Supp. 1135 (E.D. Pa. 1982); City of New York v. Exxon Corp., 633 F. Supp. 609 (S.D.N.Y. 1986); Artesian Water Co. v. Government of New Castle County, 605 F. Supp. 1348 (D. Del. 1985) ("Artesian I") and 659 F. Supp. 1269 (D. Del. 1987) ("Artesian II"); Mayor & Bd. of Alderman of the Town of Boonton v. Drew Chem. Corp., 621 F. Supp. 663 (D.N.J. 1985). Artesian I held that New Castle County's claim of sovereign immunity was invalid under CERCLA and that a private right of action exists for CERCLA cost recovery. Artesian II considered specific damage claims to determine if the damages were necessary costs of response under 42 U.S.C. § 9607.

created a federal cause of action for liability for hazardous substance disposal, providing a uniform standard of care across the nation.[37]

Reimbursement for cleanup costs is to be recovered from the parties who are statutorily liable, regardless of whether they contributed to the original contamination. If these parties are no longer available, a financing mechanism, the Superfund,[38] supplies the funds for the cleanup effort.

§ 6.7   —Liability of the Parties

Section 107(a)[39] of CERCLA provides that the following entities are statutory liable for hazardous substance response costs:

1. An owner or operator of a facility
2. Any person who owned or operated a facility at the time when hazardous substances were disposed
3. Any person who arranged (in any manner) for disposal, treatment, or transportation of hazardous substances whether or not he owned the substances (commonly referred to "Generator" liability)
4. Any person who accepted any hazardous substances for transportation to a disposal or treatment facility from which there is a release or a threatened release (commonly known as "transporter" liability).

These entities are referred to as potentially responsible parties (PRPs) and are held strictly liable for the following:

1. All costs of removal or remedial[40] action by the United States, a state or Indian tribe, not inconsistent with the national contingency plan (NCP—see § 6.14)

---

[37] United States v. Chem-Dyne Corp., 572 F. Supp. 802, 809 (S.D. Ohio 1983).

[38] Superfund, as amended by the Superfund Amendments and Reauthorization Act of 1986 [hereinafter SARA] is an $8.5 billion fund that can be used to finance government response costs, to reimburse parties for response costs incurred, and for other limited uses. Superfund is designed to have the industries that profit from the production of hazardous substances provide the revenues to support cleanup efforts. This is accomplished primarily through taxes imposed on petrochemical production.

[39] 42 U.S.C. § 9607(a) (1982).

[40] 42 U.S.C. § 9601(25) defines *response costs* as costs incurred in carrying out removal or remedial action. *Remedial actions* are those actions with a permanent remedy (42 U.S.C. § 9601(24)). *Removal actions* are those necessary steps taken in the event of a release or threat of release of hazardous substances and can include monitoring, assessing, evaluating the release or threatened release, or cleanup to mitigate damage prior to remedial action (such as removing sealed barrels of waste or erecting protective barriers and signs) (42 U.S.C. § 9601(23)).

2. Any other necessary response costs incurred by any other person consistent with the national contingency plan
3. Damages for injury, destruction, or loss of natural resources[41] including the reasonable costs of assessing the damage
4. The costs of any CERCLA-defined health assessment or health effects study performed.[42]

The statutory limit to this liability is "the total of all costs of response plus $50,000,000 for any damages."[43]

The standard of liability under CERCLA, when it attaches, is strict liability without regard to causation.[44] The courts have also established a rule of applying joint and several liability when appropriate: "Where the conduct of two or more persons liable under § 9607 has combined to violate the statute, and one or more of the defendants seek to limit his liability on the ground that the entire harm is capable of apportionment, the burden of proof as to apportionment is on each defendant."[45]

THE CONSTRUCTION FAILURE

§ 6.8   The Hypothetical Failure Due to Latent Environmental Hazards

A case study has been developed to illustrate the extent of liability under RCRA and CERCLA and how a construction failure can occur when latent environmental hazards are found on the construction site.

---

[41] *Natural resources* are defined in 42 U.S.C. § 9601(16) and include those resources belonging to, managed by, held in trust by, appertaining to, or otherwise controlled by the United States, any State, or local government.

[42] *Id.* at § 9607.

[43] *Id.* at § 9607(c)(1)(D). If (1) the hazardous substance release or threat of release was the "result of willful misconduct or willful negligence within the priority of knowledge" of a person, (2) "the primary cause of the release was a violation (within the privity or knowledge of such person) of applicable safety, construction, or operating regulations," or (3) a person fails or refuses to "provide a reasonable cooperation and assistance requested by a public official in connection with response activities," then the PRP is liable for the full and total costs of response and damages (*id.* at § 9607(c)(2)).

[44] City of Philadelphia v. Stepan Chem. Co., 544 F. Supp. 1135, 1140 n.4 (E.D. Pa. 1982). *See* 42 U.S.C. § 9601(32) (1982), which expressly incorporates the standard of liability under 33 U.S.C. § 1321 (Clean Water Act of 1977).

[45] United States v. Chem-Dyne Corp., 572 F. Supp. 802, 810 (S.D. Ohio 1983).

Case Study

A land developer, Ace Developers, bought 150 acres of farmland (Site A) ten years ago and has decided the time is ripe for development. Ace hired Bear Consultants, an architectural/engineering firm, to prepare the detailed plans and specifications and to assist Ace in managing the project. The General Contracting Corporation (GCC) was the successful bidder as general contractor.

The project includes two commercial office complexes, a strip shopping center, a senior citizens condominium complex, a dedicated space for a town recreational facility, and the roads and utility infrastructure required of a development of this magnitude. The project is scheduled to require 18 months to complete and is to be completed in the following sequence: infrastructure and site preparation to be complete by month four; commercial complex development to be complete by month 14; and finally the senior citizens complex. To date, 40 percent of the commercial and retail space has been leased, to begin in month 14. Three months into the project, while excavating for building foundations, the subsoil was found to be visibly laden with a dark liquid substance. After laboratory tests, the liquid was confirmed to be toxic industrial waste previously deposited on the site by unknown persons. Several truckloads of this soil had been previously transported to another Ace Properties jobsite (Site B) for use as fill dirt. Assume the American Institute of Architects (AIA) General Conditions for the Contract of Construction[46] has been executed between Ace Developers and GCC.

§ 6.9 Liability under RCRA

In view of the discussion in **§ 6.5** regarding penalties for violating RCRA provisions, it is unlikely that any contractor or owner who unwittingly removes or places contaminated material in a site during construction activities would be held liable for the criminal sanctions of RCRA. However, if an owner or contractor discovered that the material was contaminated and concealed that fact from the appropriate authority or caused that material to be removed from the site and transported to an unauthorized facility for disposal, it would undoubtedly face liability.

Whether the owner or contractor would otherwise become subject to RCRA sanctions if it causes hazardous substances to be removed from or brought to the site, or otherwise unwittingly causes an unknown existing site condition to become exacerbated, is an open question. However,

---

[46] AIA Document A201-1987.

given that under certain provisions of RCRA,[47] the standard of liability is strict (that is, without fault) and the scope of coverage of persons who may be liable is expansive, it would be relatively easy to postulate a scenario in which an owner or contractor could become entangled in a hazardous waste litigation situation. Admittedly, either may be able to raise a defense that successfully shows that it does not meet the criteria of "any person who contributed" to the problem or is otherwise not subject to RCRA. However, this defense may not avoid protracted and expensive litigation. This is particularly true in light of the fact that most actions for injunctive relief under the imminent danger provisions of RCRA[48] will be accompanied by a § 106 and other CERCLA orders, thereby further compounding the party's legal situation.

In summary, it would be prudent for a site owner to ascertain whether any hazardous waste conditions exist at a site, and a contractor would be well within her rights to insist that this be accomplished as a condition subsequent to her beginning work. One such approach to performing the site investigation is discussed in § **6.26**.

§ 6.10   Liability under CERCLA: Owner or Operator Liability

In the hypothetical failure situation, Ace Developers is strictly liable under CERCLA because it is the present owner of facilities where the hazardous substance releases occurred (Site A where the hazardous waste was found and Site B where the fill dirt was dumped). An *owner* or *operator* under CERCLA § 101(20)[49] includes a present facility owner, a person who had title or control of activities at the facility before conveyance, or any person who owned or otherwise controlled activities at the facility immediately before conveyance. This definition allows Ace Developers to sue the prior owners for contribution for any hazardous wastes that were deposited on the site prior to Ace's purchase of the property.

Each PRP under CERCLA has the right of contribution against other PRPs.[50] When CERCLA liability is also joint and several, it is recognized that a PRP who accepts responsibility for cleanup should be encouraged to take early action to remedy the release. The right of contribution to recover a portion of the response costs from other PRPs was intended to

---

[47] *Id.* at n.30.

[48] *Id.* at n.29.

[49] 42 U.S.C. § 9601(20) (1982).

[50] *Id.* at § 9613(f). *See also* City of Philadelphia v. Stepan Chem. Co., 544 F. Supp. 1135 (E.D. Pa. 1982); United States v. New Castle County, 642 F. Supp. 1258 (D. Del. 1986).

entice PRPs to perform cleanups on their own initiative knowing the full cost would be shared by the other PRPs.[51]

Ace Developer's entitlement to contribution would depend on whether it could prove that the hazardous wastes were dumped at Site A when the prior owner had title.[52] Because Ace Developers had held the property for speculation for over 10 years, it would be a particularly difficult burden to prove the wastes were present when Ace bought the land and were not deposited during Ace's ownership, for example, by unknown midnight dumpers. If the wastes were dumped during Ace's ownership of the property, Ace would not have a right of contribution from the prior owner.

Because Ace Developers was in control of the facility and actively managing Site A through its agent, Bear Consultants, a separate operator is not available as a PRP. An *operator* includes any person who actively participates in the management of a facility. Even stockholders and company officers of a corporation can be held personally liable as an operator, without piercing the corporate veil, if they participate in the activities and management of the affected facility.[53] If Bear Consultants were construction managers responsible for controlling job site activities including disposal of materials, it could be argued that they would fall into the CERCLA operator category. Generally, operator liability has been used against persons who are engaged in activities such as operating a landfill or waste management and who exercise control over waste disposal.[54]

---

[51] United States v. New Castle County, 642 F. Supp. 1258 (D. Del. 1986).

[52] *See* Cadilac Fairview/Cal., Inc. v. Dow Chem. Co., 14 Envtl. L. Rep. (Envtl. L. Inst.) 2076 (C.D. Cal. 1984).

[53] *See* United States v. Conservation Chem. Co., 619 F. Supp. 162, 186–87 (W.D. Mo. 1985); State of N.Y. v. Shore Realty Corp., 759 F.2d 1032, 1052–53 (2d Cir. 1985). *But see* United States v. Northeastern Pharmaceutical & Chem. Co., 579 F. Supp. 823 (W.D. Mo. 1984), *aff'd in part and rev'd in part,* 810 F.2d 726 (8th Cir. 1986) (Northeastern Pharmaceutical and Chemical Company) (NEPACCO), in which two former officers of a chemical manufacturer were found individually liable as "contributors" under RCRA because of their position in the company. The NEPACCO president was the person in charge of and directly responsible for all of the company's operations, and because of his authority to control hazardous substance approval he was found to be a "contributor." The court rejected the lower court's decision of finding them liable as CERCLA "owner or operators." *See also* United States v. Mirabile, 16 Envtl. L. Rep. (Envtl. L. Inst.) 20992 (E.D. Pa. 1985); United States v. Maryland Bank & Trust Co., 632 F. Supp. 573 (D. Md. 1986). Construction lenders who become involved in the daily operation of construction projects may be liable as CERCLA § 107 "operators." Sureties who take over projects are ripe for CERCLA "owner/operator" liability.

[54] *See* Artesian Water Co. v. Government of New Castle County, 605 F. Supp. 1348 (D. Del. 1985); United States v. Ottati & Goss, Inc., 630 F. Supp. 1361 (D.N.H. 1985). *But see* Edward Hines Lumber Co. v. Vulcan Materials Co., 861 F.2d 155 (7th Cir., Nov. 7, 1988), in which an independent contractor who designed and built a wood treatment facility, and supplied the chemicals, was found not to be an operator.

However, CERCLA liability is broadly construed, and owner and operator liability is essentially absolute. If the facts of the case study were modified to reflect that Bear Consultants acted as the construction manager, Bear Consultants may be a PRP jointly and severally with Ace Developers. Given the original facts, however, with Bear Consultants as Ace's agent, Bear Consultants would not likely be liable as an operator.

§ 6.11   —Generator Liability

Ace Developers would also be liable for the response costs at Site B where contaminated fill dirt was dumped, both as an owner and as a generator because·it arranged for the fill dirt to be taken from one facility to another. If the contaminated fill were purchased by a third party who took the dirt to an undisclosed location, Ace Developers would still be liable as a generator because it arranged for disposal.

Generator liability is not dependent on PRPs knowing that the wastes were hazardous. Generator liability elements are:

1. The generator's hazardous substances were shipped to the facility (generator owned or possessed the substances)
2. The generator's hazardous substances or similar substances are present at the facility
3. A release or threatened release exists at the facility
4. The release or threatened release created response costs.[55]

General liability has been found even when the generator did not know where the wastes were going,[56] and when the generator sold the wastes as a product.[57]

§ 6.12   —Transporter Liability

Under the case study fact pattern, GCC would be strictly liable, jointly and severally with Ace Developers, as a transporter for response costs at Site B where contaminated soil was received. GCC removed the contaminated

---

[55] United States v. South Carolina Recycling & Disposal, Inc., 20 Env't Rep. Cas. (BNA) 1753, 1756 (D.S.C. 1984). *See also* United States v. Ottati & Goss, Inc., 630 F. Supp. 1361, 1401–02 (D.N.H. 1985); United States v. Wade, 577 F. Supp. 1326, 1337 (E.D. Pa. 1983).

[56] United States v. Conservation Chem. Co., 619 F. Supp. 162 (W.D. Mo. 1985).

[57] New York v. General Elec. Co., 592 F. Supp. 291 (N.D.N.Y. 1984).

soil from the active facility (Site A) and transported it to another facility (Site B) where it is likely to be spread over a wide area.

§ 6.13   —Liability to Third Parties

Potentially responsible parties can also be liable under CERCLA § 107(b)[58] to any third person who incurs response costs due to the release. If a neighboring landowner is required to undertake groundwater monitoring costs because of contamination from Site A, Ace Developers would be liable to the neighbor for all response costs undertaken consistent with the national contingency plan.[59]

If the groundwater contamination reached parklands, or other areas that are classified as "natural resources," Ace Developers would be liable to the United States for any damages under CERCLA § 107(a)(4)(c).[60]

THE CLEANUP PROCESS

§ 6.14   Cleanup Action by Federal Agency

Has a construction failure occurred in the hypothetical situation? It has indeed, because the project schedule is likely to be delayed by many months or years and the projected cost has increased significantly to cover unexpected CERCLA response costs. If Ace Developers can absorb the schedule delay and additional costs and still maintain a profitable venture, it would be in its best interest to undertake an active role in the cleanup process in an attempt to minimize the impact.

Once the EPA has been notified of a hazardous substance release at a facility, the National Oil and Hazardous Substances Pollution Contingency Plan (NCP)[61] must determine how to clean up the sites.[62] The NCP

---

[58] 42 U.S.C. § 9607(b) (1982).

[59] *See* Wickland Oil Terminals v. Asarco, Inc., 792 F.2d 887 (9th Cir. 1986); Dedham Water Co. v. Cumberland Farms Dairy, Inc., 805 F.2d 1074 (1st Cir. 1986); NL Indus. v. Kaplan, 792 F.2d 896 (9th Cir. 1986).

[60] 42 U.S.C. § 9607(a)(4)(c) (1982). *See also* Mayor & Bd. of Alderman of the Town of Boonton v. Drew Chem., 621 F. Supp. 663 (D.N.J. 1985) and City of N.Y. v. Exxon Corp., 633 F. Supp. 609 (S.D.N.Y. 1986) for the right of local governments to sue PRPs for natural resource damages.

[61] 40 C.F.R. § 300.

[62] *See also EPA Interim Guidance to Agency Regional Offices Discussing Issues Related to Selecting Superfund Site Remedies,* 17 Env't Rep. 1603 (Jan. 16, 1987).

requires several activities that identify the magnitude of the response action, which translates into the projected construction schedule delay and cost impact.

First, PRPs have an affirmative obligation under CERCLA to notify the National Response Center of the hazardous substance releases. Immediately upon discovery of a *present release,* or spill, CERCLA § 103(a)[63] requires PRPs to notify the National Response Center (telephone number 800-424-8802). Spill reporting requirements do not normally apply to past releases unless the past release results in a present release to the environment. The Act also has a facility[64] notification requirement that applies when past releases of hazardous wastes[65] are found. For facility notification, the EPA must be notified on the EPA form entitled "Notifications of Hazardous Waste Site"[66] in a good faith, timely manner.[67] The NRC will notify the EPA's designated on-scene coordinator to direct response action for the facility.

In general, the EPA has several options on proceeding with cleanups at hazardous waste sites. The EPA can:

1. Perform remedial action at National Priority List sites using Superfund, then sue the PRPs for response costs under CERCLA § 107[68]

2. Issue an administrative order or initiate litigation to compel the PRPs to perform remedial work under CERCLA § 106[69]

3. Seek settlement negotiations with PRPs to get them to perform or pay for any or all of the remedial action.

The NCP requires the EPA's on-scene coordinator to determine if a threat to the public health or welfare or to the environment exists sufficient

---

[63] 42 U.S.C. § 9603(2) (1982).

[64] *Facility,* as defined by 42 U.S.C. § 9601(9), includes any building, structure, installation, equipment, pipe, well, pit, pond, lagoon, impoundment, ditch, landfill, storage container, motor vehicle, rolling stock, aircraft, or any site or area where a hazardous substance was deposited, stored, or disposed of except consumer products in consumer use, and does not include vessels.

[65] "Hazardous wastes" for purpose of facility notification under 42 U.S.C. § 9603(c) only refers to 42 U.S.C. § 6903(5) definition of hazardous waste, not the 42 U.S.C. § 6901(14) definitions of "hazardous substances."

[66] U.S. Government Office of Management & Budget Form No. 20000138.

[67] Facility notification under 42 U.S.C. § 9603(c) for known past releases are required to be filed in a good faith timely manner while release or spill notification under 42 U.S.C. § 9603(c) must be reported immediately. Penalties have been amended for delays of a few hours in reporting under 42 U.S.C. § 9603(c).

[68] *Id.* at § 9607.

[69] *Id.* at § 9606.

to require prompt removal action.[70] If a present threat exists, the EPA will promptly perform a preliminary assessment to identify the source, evaluate the magnitude of the potential threat, and determine if removal action is required.[71] If removal action is required, the EPA will attempt to identify the PRPs and get them to perform the necessary action.[72] However, the EPA is still responsible for taking "any appropriate action to abate, minimize, stabilize, mitigate, or eliminate the release" and will do so when exigent circumstances exist.[73]

§ 6.15   Cleanup Action by Owner

Ace Developers does not need to wait for the EPA to request removal action from the PRPs. Any PRP or any person can provide appropriate response action if the steps taken are consistent with § 300.365 of the NCP. Section 104(a)(1) of CERCLA[74] gives the EPA authority to allow a PRP to undertake remedial action when the EPA determines that:

1. "[S]uch action will be done properly and promptly"
2. The PRP is "qualified" to conduct a remedial investigation and feasibility study (RI/FS)
3. The EPA contracts a "qualified person" to assist the EPA in overseeing and reviewing the conduct of the RI/FS
4. The PRP agrees to reimburse the EPA for the cost of the management oversight.

In our case study, the mechanical removal of the contaminated soil and placing the soil in dumpsters may be appropriate removal action for Site B. Because of the greater extent of contamination at Site A, removal action may be limited to erecting barriers, signs, drainage controls, etc., to prevent any further release.[75] By undertaking prompt response action itself, Ace Developers may limit the spread of contamination by acting quicker than the EPA could respond. In addition, if the EPA provided the appropriate response action, Ace Developers would be responsible for all costs expended by the EPA in accordance with CERCLA § 107.[76] Because Ace

---

[70] 40 C.F.R. § 300.63(d)(1) & (2) (1986).

[71] Id. at § 300.64(a).

[72] Id. at § 300.65(a)(2).

[73] Id. at § 300.65(b)(1).

[74] 42 U.S.C. § 9604(a)(1) (1982).

[75] See 40 C.F.R. § 300.65(c) (1986) for general, appropriate removal actions.

[76] 42 U.S.C. § 9607 (1976).

Developers has a mobilized work force (GCC), the difference in cost between the EPA and Ace Developers performing the work could be substantial.

One significant roadblock that Ace Developers may face in attempting to perform the response action itself is that GCC may refuse to perform such response action. A prudent general contractor would have included contractual provisions such as AIA Document A201 ¶¶ 10.1.1 through 10.1.4 as modified to apply to hazardous substances and wastes as well as asbestos and PCBs. If this were the case, ¶ 10.1.3[77] would allow GCC to refuse to accept a change order[78] or construction change directive.[79]

§ 6.16   Remedial Investigation/Feasibility Study

If the EPA determines that the Ace Properties facility is sufficiently hazardous to warrant remedial action, a lengthy and costly site evaluation must be conducted before any remedial action is performed.[80] If a preliminary assessment has not been previously prepared, it must be done.[81] A site inspection is then conducted to collect data, determine which releases pose threats to the public, and determine if any immediate threat exists.[82] These data are then used in the Hazard Ranking System,[83] which scores sites based on their threat potential. Those sites that achieve a certain score are added to the National Priority List.[84] Only those sites on the List are eligible for using Superfund as a source for cleanup efforts.[85] Including a facility on the National Priority List is not necessary for CERCLA § 107[86] liability to attach, nor is it a prerequisite for a PRP to perform remedial action.

A detailed work plan is prepared to define an approach to study remedies. After approval of the work plan and before any remedial action can be taken by any party, an RI/FS must be undertaken to determine the nature and extent of the threat and evaluate potential remedies.[87] The

---

[77] AIA Document A201-1987 ¶ 10.1.3 states "The Contractor shall not be required pursuant to Article 7 to perform without consent any Work relating to asbestos or polychlorinated biphenyl (PCB)."
[78] Id. at ¶ 7.2.
[79] Id. at ¶ 7.3.
[80] 40 C.F.R. § 300.66 (1986).
[81] Id. at § 300.66(a)(3).
[82] Id. at § 300.66(a)(4).
[83] Id. at § 300.66(b).
[84] Id. at § 300.66(c).
[85] Id. at § 300.66(c)(2).
[86] 42 U.S.C. § 9607 (1982).
[87] 40 C.F.R. § 300.68(d) (1986).

RI/FS examines the type of response actions that may be required, develops several alternatives, and evaluates the alternatives as to cost and effectiveness. The RI/FS is a significant technical effort averaging $800,000.[88]

§ 6.17   Selection of Remedial Actions

The EPA then selects a cost-effective permanent remedy[89] that meets the appropriate cleanup standards.[90] The selected remedy, whether performed by Ace Developers or EPA contractors, must assure that cleanup standards are met and also be cost-effective. The EPA selection is then published in a Record of Decision and a formal public participation process is undertaken. A final Record of Decision will be issued after the public comment period which further defines the basis for the EPA's decision. This will include conceptual cost estimates for the cleanup effort. Detailed plans and specifications are then prepared for selected remedial action. Costs for this can be in the millions of dollars and take a year.[91] When the engineering is complete, construction contracts will be awarded for the remedial action.

Bear in mind that Ace Developers would be liable to the EPA for all costs incurred in preparing the preliminary assessment, RI/FS, Record of Decision, and public communication phases, the detail designs, actual construction, and future operation and maintenance costs.

Ace Developers can potentially reduce the schedule and cost impact by agreeing to undertake remedial action. Ace Developers has to prepare the RI/FS and follow the same process as listed in § 6.16 to comply with the NCP.

By undertaking the remedial action, Ace Developers may be in a stronger position to protect its interests. The administrative record that is developed during the study and decisionmaking process is an important feature in any challenge to EPA decisions and in future litigation. By participating in the development of the administrative record, Ace Developers can better protect its position.

§ 6.18   Negotiating a Settlement

Ace Developers may benefit by choosing to seek a settlement with the EPA and participating in the response action itself. The Superfund Handbook[92] identifies the benefit and disadvantages as:

---

[88] Environmental Law Handbook 111 (9th ed. Gov't Insts., Inc. 1987).

[89] 40 C.F.R. § 300.68(i) (1986).

[90] Standards for "How Clean Is Clean" is covered in 42 U.S.C. § 9621 (1982).

[91] Environment Law Handbook 111 n.78 (9th ed. Gov't Insts., Inc. 1987).

[92] ERT/Sidley & Austin, Superfund Handbook 62–63, (2d ed. Apr. 1987).

Benefits	Disadvantages
Cost savings	Unfair burden
Time savings	Ongoing liability
Control	
Negotiating leverage	
Avoidance of adverse publicity	
Avoidance of toxic tort liability	

If Ace Developers intends to continue project construction after the cleanup has been completed, then the benefits clearly outweigh the disadvantages, because the disadvantages would be present regardless of who cleaned up the site.

The EPA has broad discretionary powers to enter into settlement agreements with PRPs if such agreements are in the public interest.[93] (In any CERCLA enforcement action, if the EPA decides not to seek settlement agreements it must notify the PRPs.) The "public interest" is primarily a function of the technical aspects of remedial action.[94]

The EPA has discretion to provide a covenant not to sue or place a limit on the liability of the PRP as part of the settlement negotiations.[95] The covenant not to sue can be granted if it is in the public interest, it would expedite response actions consistent with the NCP, the response action has been approved by the EPA, and the defendant fully complies with the enforcement consent decree.[96] In order for the covenant not to sue for future liability to be effective, the EPA must certify satisfactory completion of the remedial action.[97] The covenant not to sue is subject to a "reopener" exception that allows the United States an action for releases or threatened releases that resulted from conditions unknown to the EPA when the remedial action was certified as complete.[98]

---

[93] 42 U.S.C. § 9622(a) (1982).

[94] *Id.* at § 9622(f)(4) lists factors the EPA is to consider in determining if it is within the public interest to grant a discretionary covenant not to sue:

1. The effectiveness and reliability of the remedial action, considering the alternatives

2. The nature of the remaining potential risks at the facility

3. The extent the cleanup effort provides a complete remedy

4. The effectiveness of the response action technology

5. Whether Superfund or other sources would be available for additional future remedial action that may be required

6. The extent the PRP participates in the remedial action.

[95] *Id.* at § 9622(f).

[96] *Id.* at § 9622(f)(1).

[97] *Id.* at § 9622(f)(3).

[98] *Id.* at § 9622(f)(6)(A). Remedial action settlement agreements and consent decrees are not acknowledgments of liability and are not admissible, except as otherwise provided for in the Federal Rules of Evidence.

Settlements are an attempt to get the PRPs to participate in the cleanup efforts, thereby reducing the overall effort required by the EPA. The covenant not to sue and liability limitations available in a settlement provide Ace Developers with a means to quantify its potential liability at an earlier stage than waiting for litigation under CERCLA § 107.[99]

§ 6.19   —De Minimis Settlement Provision

One additional avenue that may become available, especially for contractors or architect/engineers who are third-party PRPs, is the new de minimis settlement provision.[100] The EPA is authorized to reach final settlement with a PRP if it is in the public interest when the PRPs response costs are minor, and when either (1) the amount and toxic/hazardous effect of the substances the PRP contributed to the facility is minimal or (2) when the PRP is the owner and did not conduct or permit hazardous waste generation, transportation, storage, treatment, or disposal and did not contribute to the release of the hazardous substances by an act or omission. This provision does not include a subsequent purchaser with actual or constructive knowledge of hazardous substance releases.

The de minimis settlement provision gives the PRP an opportunity to cut its losses if it was a noncontributor or minimal contributor. A PRP who settles with the EPA is not liable for claims for contributions for matters addressed in the settlement.[101] For example, because GCC excavated Site A, was unaware the soil was contaminated, and transported the cut soil to clean areas of Site A and Site B, it would be in GCC's interest to pursue a de minimis settlement with the EPA, because GCC did not cause the initial hazardous substance release but was responsible for transporting the hazardous substances to other areas (thereby causing a release).

§ 6.20   Third-Party Defense to CERCLA Liability

The Comprehensive Environmental Response, Compensation, and Liability Act does provide limited affirmative defenses to response cost liability. The PRP must establish by a preponderance of the evidence that the release or threatened release was caused solely by an act of God, an act of war, a third party, or any combination of these.[102] The third-party defense is met by proving the release was caused solely by an act or omission of a third party other than an employee, agent, or entity whose act or omission

---

[99] *Id.* at § 9607.

[100] *Id.* at § 9622(g)(1).

[101] *Id.* at § 9622(g)(5).

[102] *Id.* at § 9607(b).

occurred in connection to a direct or indirect contractual relationship with the PRP, and that the PRP exercised due care and took precautions against foreseeable acts or omissions by the third party.

The third-party defense can also be asserted by property owners under a certain set of facts known as the "innocent landowner exception." Section 101(35) of CERCLA[103] allows the third-party defense's contractual relationship a liability exception if it can be shown by a preponderance of the evidence that (1) when the landowner obtained title she "did not know and had no reason to know that any hazardous substance which is the subject of the release or threatened release was disposed of on, in, or at the facility," or (2) the landowner is a government entity who acquired the property involuntarily or by eminent domain or condemnation, or (3) the owner acquired the facility by inheritance or bequest.[104] But to take advantage of this exception, the "innocent" purchaser must have undertaken an inquiry into the past owner and its uses of the property prior to the purchase.[105]

Except for residential real estate transfers,[106] this requirement places a significant technical burden on all land transfers. In residential real estate transfers, it is not reasonably foreseeable or expected to find hazardous substance releases. However, in transfers of commercial, industrial, or undeveloped real estate, the new purchasers should undertake investigative measures to determine if the properties are a CERCLA liability. In light of the increase in legal literature and seminars presented in recent years on this topic, it would be difficult for any purchaser of commercial, industrial, or undeveloped real estate to assert the innocent landowner exception if she did not undertake a due diligence investigation, because such investigations may now be considered to be the required "due care" and reasonable "precautions."[107]

AVOIDANCE MEASURES

§ 6.21   Avoidance Measures Generally

Construction failures are usually associated with technical, managerial, or logistical errors or omissions. However, the genesis of a construction failure may be present long before the project has commenced if the site

---

[103] *Id.* at § 9601(35).

[104] *Id.* at § 9607(b)(3).

[105] *Id.* at § 9601(35)(B).

[106] *See generally* S.A. Tasher, Impact of Environmental Law on Real Estate Transactions (Gov't Insts., Inc. 1986).

[107] 42 U.S.C. § 9607(b)(3)(a), (b) (1982).

selected for development contains latent underground hazardous substances. The only effective way to avoid a construction failure due to latent environmental hazards is to properly investigate the site before commencing the project. Once CERCLA or RCRA liability attaches, the owner/developer is exposed to substantial costs and delays and the project has thereby experienced some degree of failure. Even if an owner can meet the CERCLA third-party defense elements discussed in § 6.20, it has only avoided its personal liability for the hazardous substance release and still has a project subject to cleanup delays.

Sections 6.22 through 6.26 discuss avoidance measures that can be utilized by owners and contractors. Owners/developers can minimize their exposure to latent environmental hazards by performing an environmental site investigation prior to purchasing the property, or before agreeing to manage a project for the landowner. Contractors can protect themselves by having appropriate terms in their general agreements with the owner. When response actions are undertaken by contractors, they can seek protection from liability through negotiation with the EPA.

§ 6.22 Contractual Contractor Liability Provisions

The 1987 edition of the AIA Document A201, General Conditions of the Contract for Construction, includes provisions that assist the contractor in avoiding problems as a result of finding latent asbestos and polychlorinated biphenyls (PCBs) on the jobsite. Paragraph 10.1.2 allows the contractor to immediately stop work in areas where she reasonably believes contains asbestos or PCBs if they are not rendered harmless. Paragraph 10.1.3 allows the contractor the option of not accepting a change order[108] or construction change directive[109] to perform work relating to asbestos or PCBs. In paragraph 10.1.4, the owner agrees to indemnify the contractor and architect and their agents and employees from any damages or claims related to performing work in the areas containing harmful PCBs and asbestos if caused by the owner's negligence. These clauses should be expanded to cover hazardous wastes and substances, pollutants, and contaminants as defined in RCRA and CERCLA, and other pertinent environmental laws.

The term "owner negligence" in paragraph 10.1.4 is subject to differing interpretations. However, in light of the recent heightened awareness of the impact of environmental regulations on real estate transactions,[110]

---

[108] See AIA Document A201-1987, ¶ 7.2.

[109] See id. at ¶ 7.3.

[110] Since 1986, numerous continuing education courses and seminars have been presented on the impact of environmental regulations on real estate transactions. The reader can contact the following: Government Institutes, Inc. (301/251-9250), American

a reasonably prudent industrial or commercial real estate developer should undertake an environmental investigation of the property to protect herself and foreseeable third parties like contractors or subsequent purchasers.

In the absence of contract terms expressly providing these rights to stop work and to refuse to perform in affected areas, the contractor would probably be successful in stopping work based on a safety clause similar to paragraph 10.2.1 of AIA Document A201-1987. In such a clause, the contractor is provided the right to "take reasonable precautions for the safety of, and shall provide reasonable protection to prevent damage, injury or loss to . . . employees [and] other property at the site or adjacent thereto."[111] In addition, the contractor must comply with all applicable laws,[112] regulations, and orders of public authorities, and erect or maintain reasonable safeguards for protection.[113] This type of broad safety provision allows the contractor to stop work and take reasonable measures to protect the public.

If the owner directs the contractor to perform removal action, the contractor may be able to successfully assert that such work would be a cardinal change[114] to their agreement and refuse to perform the work on the basis that the change is beyond the scope of the contract as originally contemplated by the parties.[115]

Law Institute-American Bar Association (215/243-1661), and Practising Law Institute (212/765-5700). In addition, numerous articles and books have been written on this subject. *See* S.A. Tasher, Impact of Environmental Law on Real Estate Transactions (Gov't Insts., Inc. 1986); Bourdeau, *Minimizing Hazardous Waste Liabilities in Real Estate Transactions* (A.B.A. Forum Committee on the Constr. Indus., 2d Annual Meeting, Dallas, Tex., Apr. 17–18, 1986); Bauer, *The Dangers of Hazardous Waste in Real Property Transactions,* 12 A.L.I.-A.B.A. Course Materials J. 95 (Apr. 1988); Newton, *Real Estate Transaction Environmental Considerations,* Pollution Eng'g (Sept. 1988).

[111] AIA Document A201-1987, ¶ 10.2.1.

[112] Note that AIA A201-1987, ¶ 10.2.2 requires the contractor to give "notices" and comply with applicable laws. The contractor is obligated to the owner to provide the "spill" and "facility" notification required by 42 U.S.C. § 9603. However, 42 U.S.C. § 9603 (1982) statutorily obligates the PRPs (such as owners) to provide notification. An owner should comply with the CERCLA notification requirements independent of this obligation on the part of the contractor.

[113] AIA Document A201-1987, ¶¶ 10.2.2, 10.2.3.

[114] Stein, Construction Law § 4.02[3] (Mathew Bender 1988). Cardinal change is a change that goes far beyond the scope of the original contract documents and is an undertaking substantially different than contemplated in the contract.

[115] *See also* Wunderlich Contracting Co. v. United States, 351 F.2d 956, 965 (Ct. Cl. 1965); Luria Bros. & Co. v. United States, 369 F.2d 701 (Ct. Cl. 1966); Nat Harrison Assocs. v. Gulf States Utils. Co., 491 F.2d 578 (5th Cir. 1974); Albert Elia Bldg. Co. v. New York State Urban Dev. Corp., 338 N.Y.S.2d 469 (App. Div. 1977).

Performing CERCLA response activities opens the contractor to a wide range of problems, including additional liability substantially different from a normal construction contract. Under the original construction contract with the owner, the contractor's liability was limited to the parties in privity and others covered under state and common law. If the contractor performs CERCLA response actions, her liability expands to include CERCLA liability and toxic tort liability. Removal and remedial efforts under CERCLA require special work place safety procedures, training, and experience. In addition, the contractor's existing insurance policies are not likely to cover cleanup activities or toxic tort claims. The additional work scope is likely to affect the contractor's surety arrangements.

Unless the contractor is capable of performing removal and remedial action and has done so as part of her regular business, it may not be feasible for the contractor to perform the remedial work. Section 119 of CERCLA[116] addressed some of these problems for contractors who provide response actions pursuant to a contract with the EPA, or under contract with a PRP who is under a CERCLA § 106[117] order or under a CERCLA § 122[118] settlement agreement.[119] CERCLA § 119[120] substitutes the strict liability standard for one of negligence for defined response action contractors. It does not affect any other federal, state, or common law liability.[121] In addition, the EPA may grant indemnification for any response action contractor for negligent acts (except grossly negligent acts or intentional acts) under certain conditions, such as when insurance is not available.[122] Also, CERCLA § 107(d)[123] exempts persons from liability as a result of response action taken (or omitted) under the direction of the EPA on-scene coordinator who is acting in accordance with the NCP.[124]

Despite the statutory relaxation of CERCLA liability for response action contractors, the liability, work methods and procedures, equipment, and experience required to perform some removal or remedial actions are significantly different from that contemplated by contractors when they entered into the contract for construction with the owner. The contractor

---

[116] 42 U.S.C. § 9619 (1982).

[117] *Id.* at § 9606.

[118] *Id.* at § 9622.

[119] *Id.* at § 9619(e)(2) defines response action contractors. These exemptions do not apply to PRPs liable under owner, operator, generator, or transporter liability.

[120] *Id.* at § 9619.

[121] *Id.* at § 9619(a).

[122] *Id.* at § 9607(d).

[123] *Id.* at § 9619(c).

[124] *Id.* at § 9607(d)(1). This exemption does not apply to PRPs liable under owner, operator, generator, or transporter liability.

should seek legal counsel to determine if a cardinal change theory would be appropriate or if other provisions of the contract concerning health and safety would allow the contractor to justifiably refuse to proceed with the work. In the event such a theory is not appropriate and the contractor is obligated under the contract to undertake response action, she should seek the use of the CERCLA § 107(d) liability exemption and the CERCLA § 119 liability indemnification.

§ 6.23   Indemnification Provisions

The AIA Document A201 paragraph 3.18 entitled "Indemnification" allows an owner, architect, and their agents to be indemnified by the contractor for the contractor's negligent acts or failure to act. Included among these acts would be the negligent release of a hazardous substance into the environment, such as, for example, negligently puncturing sealed drums found on-site. Such private party agreements for indemnification and release from liability is allowed under CERCLA.[125] However, all PRPs remain liable to others outside the agreement,[126] the United States, and any other person who incurs response costs due to the release.

In the case study, GCC was not negligent in transferring cut contaminated soil from Site A to Site B because GCC did not have a duty to check for contamination and a reasonably prudent person unaware of the contaminated soil would have acted similarly under the same circumstances. If GCC were found negligent, it would be liable to Ace Developers under the indemnification clause as well as statutorily liable under CERCLA § 107.[127] However, Ace Developers would still be liable to neighboring landowners, the EPA, and any others who may have incurred response costs consistent with the NCP regardless of any indemnification agreement with GCC.

§ 6.24   Site Investigations

The potential liability associated with hazardous waste and hazardous substances is a substantial risk that must be recognized by all parties to a construction project. Examples presented in § 6.1 are based on factual occurrences and are only a sampling of the types of events and risks that are confronting owners, contractors, and architects. Given these risks, it is only prudent that all parties involved in the development process strongly

---

[125] *Id.* at § 9607(e)(1).

[126] *Id. See also* Mardan Corp. v. C.G.C. Music, Ltd., 805 F.2d 1454 (9th Cir. 1986).

[127] 42 U.S.C. § 9607 (1982).

consider performing an environmental site investigation early in the planning process. If possible, this should occur prior to the sale of the land. However, if this is not possible, it should be performed prior to beginning actual site development. In either situation the site investigation will allow a party the opportunity to become more informed about potential problems and risks that may exist at the site.

There are also other reasons for conducting a site investigation. Common-law claims may be brought by third parties such as adjacent property owners if harm to their person or harm to an economic interest (property damage) can be shown to have occurred. For this reason, causes of action based on legal theories of strict liability, negligence, trespass, and nuisance are often brought against property owners in cases in which hazardous wastes are used or have been stored in conjunction with an appropriate CERCLA action.

Several states have also adopted mini-superfund laws fashioned after CERCLA that impose similar liabilities to landowners and in some cases may impose additional liability for personal injury and property damage.

Some states have legislation that requires cleanup prior to sale.[128] Others have legislation that provides for the reporting and cleanup of spills of hazardous substances by the property owner.[129] In this latter situation, the state first incurs the response costs (that is, cleanup costs) and subsequently imposes priority liens on the property on which the spill occurred until costs of cleanup are repaid. In some states, notably New Jersey, the liens are also imposed upon all other property owned by the offending person or company. These liens, however, are lower in priority to existing liens.

§ 6.25 —The Duty of the Owner

It also has become increasingly apparent that the list of parties who might be considered owners and be liable for cleanup is increasing. These include not only the owner but potentially also a lender (mortgagee) who might become an owner by acquiring a site after a foreclosure and thus become liable for cleanup.[130] Lenders, therefore, have been requiring that site investigations be conducted prior to lending money to finance the purchasing of property.

---

[128] N.J. Stat. Ann. § 13:1K; 1985 Conn. Acts 568 (Reg. Sess.).

[129] N.J. Stat. Ann. § 58:10; Conn. Gen. Stat. Ann. § 22a; N.H. Rev. Stat. Ann. § 147-B:10; Tenn. Code Ann. § 68-46-209.

[130] *See* United States v. Maryland Bank & Investment Co., 632 F. Supp. 573 (D. Md. 1986), which held that a bank that acquired the site through foreclosure and held legal title at the time of EPA cleanup was an "owner" within the meaning of CERCLA. *Compare with* United States v. Mirable, 15 Envtl. L. Rep. (Envtl. L. Inst.) 20, 992 (E.D. Pa. 1985).

As discussed in § **6.7**, CERCLA imposes strict liability for cleanup on the present owner, even if the owner had nothing to do with the contamination. The owner may, however, be able to avoid liability by utilizing the third-party defense discussed in § **6.20**, provided that the owner acquired the property after all hazardous substances had been placed at the site and:

1. At the time of the acquisition of the facility, did not know and had no reason to know that any hazardous substances were disposed of on, in or at the property
2. The landowner is a governmental entity that acquired the facility by escheat, other involuntary means, or through the exercise of eminent domain authority, by purchase or condemnation, or
3. The owner acquired the property by inheritance or bequest.[131]

In addition, the present owner must prove by a preponderance of the evidence that it:

1. Exercised due care with respect to the hazardous substances concerned, taking into consideration the characteristics of the hazardous substances, in light of all relevant facts and circumstances, and
2. Took precautions against foreseeable acts or omissions of any third party and the consequences that could foreseeably result from such acts or omissions.[132]

Further, the owner must establish that it has exercised due care and took precautions against foreseeable acts or omissions of third parties. To determine whether the owner had knowledge or reason to know that hazardous substances could be present in the site, the courts have looked at the following factual issues:

1. The relationship of the purchase price to the value of the property if uncontaminated
2. The acquisition of commonly known or reasonably ascertainable information about the property and its prior uses
3. The obviousness of the presence or likely presence of contamination of the property
4. The likelihood of detection of that contamination by appropriate inspection.[133]

---

[131] 42 U.S.C. § 9601(3)(A) (1982).

[132] *Id.* at § 9607(b)(3).

[133] *Id.* at § 9601(35)(B).

§ 6.26   —Performing the Site Investigation

Prudence dictates that the buyer, and in some cases the seller, of property perform a site assessment that will, to the extent practical, identify any potential situations that result in costly cleanup actions. The following briefly outlines the concepts and approaches that may be employed in performing such an investigation. However, the scope of this chapter does not allow for an in-depth discussion of all the activities that should be conducted in such a site investigation. For this reason the reader is directed toward several well-written articles on the subject.[134]

At the outset, it is recommended that any contract for sale of the property include a provision to void the contract in the event a pollution problem is found. This provision should be broadly drafted to allow for extensions of time to fully evaluate the property, because evaluations may take from several weeks to months to perform, depending on the size of the property and the nature and extent of any suspected contamination. Furthermore, this provision should provide an opportunity for the seller to pay for cleanup costs up to an agreed-upon price before the contract is voided.

The hiring of a competent consultant is key to the success of the site evaluation. Such a firm or individual will serve as a guide in the planning and implementation of the program and, should the need arise, provide cost estimates for any cleanup problems which may be useful in further negotiations.

The program for a site evaluation will vary with the site being investigated, but most consultants use a two-phased approach. In the initial phase, a "paper" search is conducted. During this phase, existing records that can best characterize the site's past and present uses are investigated. These include photographs, tax records, land use records, and other approvals. If the site is an existing industrial development, investigation of pertinent environmental records and approvals should also be conducted. This phase is significant for several reasons, even if the property currently appears to be free of hazardous substances. First, investigations may indicate that properties that are currently vacant may have at one time contained facilities that used hazardous materials that may still be stored there. For example, a corner gasoline station may have had its surface facilities removed but not the underground storage tanks, and these may still contain petroleum products. Secondly, other facilities may appear to be innocuous to the uninformed but in reality may have quietly contributed to an existing problem. For example, a lumberyard that appears

---

[134] *See* S.A. Tasher, Impact of Environmental Law on Real Estate Transactions (Gov't Insts., Inc. 1986).

relatively clean may have stored wood preservatives at the site that leaked into the ground, thereby contaminating the soil.

During the second phase, a physical investigation of the site is conducted. The purpose of this investigation is to search for any obvious signs of contamination and, if appropriate, conduct on-site interviews with personnel at the facility and with adjacent property owners. Depending on the results, further investigations may be required to determine if any subsurface (soil or groundwater) contamination exists.

At the initiation of a site investigation, the need for confidentiality should be discussed with the consultant. If required, the site investigation is best conducted under the direction of an attorney so that its results may qualify as privileged under the work product rule. (See § **7.9.**) On this item the following caveat is offered. Some states may require that any party who discovers contamination during the course of business must disclose this information to the proper state authorities. Consultation with counsel on this matter is strongly recommended.

Following completion of the site investigation, all parties associated with the property transaction will be in a position to assess their respective positions. If contamination exists, whether the transaction goes forward will depend on several factors, among which are: (1) the desirability of the property with and without cleanup, (2) the potential that additional contamination will be found, (3) the risks each party is willing to accept following cleanup, (4) what protection against future liabilities (that is, indemnification) any party is willing to grant, and (5) the costs any party is willing to assume.

Each of these considerations has advantages and disadvantages that must be weighed in assessing the risks of proceeding with a project. The reader is directed toward additional reading on the subject for a more in-depth discussion of the entire matter of hazardous waste and real estate transfers.[135]

---

[135] *See* Bourdeau, *Minimizing Hazardous Waste Liabilities in Real Estate Transactions* (A.B.A. Forum Committee on the Constr. Indus., 2d Annual Meeting, Dallas, Tex., Apr. 17–18, 1986). *See also* Baher, *The Dangers of Hazardous Waste in Real Property Transactions,* 12 A.L.I.-A.B.A. Course Materials J. 95 (Apr. 1988); Newton, *Real Estate Transaction Environmental Considerations,* Pollution Eng'g (Sept. 1988).

CHAPTER 7

ENGINEERING METHODOLOGY AND APPROACH FOR STRUCTURAL FAILURE ANALYSIS

George Derbalian*

George Derbalian is the manager of Engineering Mechanics at Failure Analysis Associates, Inc. Dr. Derbalian received his masters and doctorate degrees in Engineering from Stanford University. He specializes in the analysis and reconstruction of structural and mechanical failures and has been a consultant on numerous failure investigations involving structural and mechanical disasters. Dr. Derbalian has extensive publications in the areas of stress analysis and fracture mechanics. His work has had broad applications from investigations of structural collapse to failure analyses of pressure vessels and piping, chemical and power plant components, and off-shore oil platforms; from evaluation of mechanical component failures to studies and analyses of transportation and aerospace systems. He has been lecturer both nationally and internationally on the subjects of failure analysis, stress analysis, and fracture mechanics.

*I wish to acknowledge the invaluable support of my partners and associates who have collaborated with me in the analysis and reconstruction of these and many other failures. Portions reprinted with permission from ASME, Mechanical Engineering, September 1986.

§ 7.1   Introduction

Aside from unforeseen and infrequent acts of God, when a building or a roof collapses or when a structure or mechanical component fractures, catastrophically fails, or burns, some party involved in the architecture, design, fabrication, construction, or maintenance and operation of the system is undoubtedly responsible for the disaster. It is simple for the plaintiff to establish that some party is at fault: the plaintiff has highly convincing evidence—a once-16-story building now lies on ground level. However, determining who among the involved parties singularly or collectively is at fault is frequently a very complex process. Although the burden of proving non-negligence effectively remains on the defendants, it is possible, through rigorous engineering failure analysis and reconstruction, to systematically determine the origin of a failure and the technical contributions to the disaster.

METHODS OF STUDYING THE FAILURE

§ 7.2   Computer Simulations

Analysis of mechanical and structural failures requires a detailed and systematic investigation of the evidence left after an accident. This can be a difficult and complex process. Frequently, the evidence has been partially lost or disturbed by the time the investigation begins, or the accident itself may have destroyed or damaged key components of the failed structure. Absent, incomplete, or distorted evidence is obviously not a promising resource for reconstructing the course of an accident.

   Under these circumstances, it is often necessary to complement the material evidence with data obtained from computer simulations. These can be used to determine mechanical and structural behavior under normal operating conditions and under the extreme conditions that may have induced the failure. Advanced methods can even simulate the failure process itself. When that is the case, the simulated mode of failure can be compared with the material evidence.

§ 7.3   Finite Element Method

Until the advent of modern digital computers and the finite element method, structural analysis was limited to simplified approximations of the actual structure or structural component. Analysts built simplified models based on handbook formulas or closed-form solutions to recreate structural properties and failure conditions. These methods are still used today and can provide valuable insights into the possible mechanics of failure and its causes. However, although designers can offset an approximate analysis result with a safety factor to ensure a safe design, the failure analyst must know more precisely the stress level of a component to determine its failure mechanism. This is where the finite element method provides an invaluable tool.

Structures are usually designed to operate at stress levels below the yield stress;[1] in the design phase, a structure can be analyzed with linear analysis[2] methods and linear finite element programs. When a structure or component fails, however, nonlinear[3] phenomena are usually involved. These include plastic deformation, buckling, and elastic-plastic fracture.

Today's general purpose finite element programs can readily analyze even the most complex structures under a variety of loading conditions. The finite element method is based on the "divide and conquer" concept. Technically, the structure or the configuration to be analyzed is divided into many smaller elements (hence, the name finite element). These elements can be members, sections, patches, areas, or volumes, depending on the type of configuration under study. Deformations are evaluated at discrete locations associated with the finite element nodes.

The finite element programs allow the analyst to assess globally the stress distribution in a structure and to zoom in on critical areas in order to obtain highly accurate predictions of local stress concentrations and possible failure modes. The finite element method is also used to determine a structure's dynamic characteristics, allowing the analyst to assess failures involving excessive vibrations. Finite element heat-transfer and thermal-stress analyses provide vital clues to failures in which temperature plays a role.

---

[1] Yield stress is a material property. For standard structural steel this value is 36,000 pounds per square inch.

[2] Linear analysis means that the response (deformations and stresses) is linearly proportional to loads exerted on the structure.

[3] Nonlinear phenomena are characterized by response that is nonproportional to the loads, with increased deformations in the nonlinear range. These deformations and stresses are partly irreversible. That is, permanent set would occur even if the loads on the structure were relieved.

However, although there are many linear finite element programs, there are only a few programs that can properly perform nonlinear analyses.

§ 7.4   Fracture Mechanics Analysis

No material is immune to the possibility of fracture, even if design stresses are kept below the yield stress of the material. Fractures can be caused by existing flaws that slowly grow until they reach a size of critical instability, severing the structure; they can also be due to reduction of toughness[4] or due to higher-than-designed loads. Although most engineers use the strength of materials approach in their design of structures (that is, they attempt to prevent the design stresses from exceeding the yield stress with an appropriate safety factor), fracture mechanics analysis still remains an infrequent practice among design engineers.

The magnitude of fracture-related failures cannot be underestimated. In 1982, the National Bureau of Standards commissioned a study to determine the cost of fracture to the economy of the United States. This study revealed a staggering cost of some $120 billion (1982 dollars) annually. Included were both direct and imputed costs associated with fracture-related accidents such as repair, unnecessary inspection (due to material variability), and replacement of degraded materials.

Structural failures can be broadly classified as being due to fracture and/or lack of strength. Fracture-related failures are generally caused by one or some combination of the following:

1. Presence of a defect (such as a flaw) or a crack (such as a weld defect or material fabrication flaw)
2. Inadequate toughness
3. Reduction of toughness due to environmental conditions
    a. Temperature (many materials embrittle at colder temperatures)
    b. Radiation embrittlement (this is particularly of concern in nuclear power plant reactor vessels)
4. Stress corrosion cracking—this failure mode requires a combination of the following:
    a. Material that is susceptible to corrosion
    b. Tensile stress (such as tensile residual stresses locked in pipes or vessels)

---

[4] Toughness is a material property that governs fracture. A material with high toughness is ductile and more resistant to cracking, whereas a material with low toughness is brittle and more susceptible to cracking. It is quite different from material strength (or yield stress), encountered earlier. It is entirely possible that a material can have adequate strength (yield stress level) but have low toughness. Generally speaking, these two properties are opposed.

c. Corrosive environment (such as seawater or a high level of oxygen dissolved in the water)

Conversely, the failure of a structure could be caused by exceeding the ultimate strength of the material. This is generally due to inadequate design, either because:

1. The loads are not accounted for in the design and/or are underestimated
2. Material strength or ductility is inadequate.

Although both fracture and material yield will have the same end result (failure), the mode in which the structure fails can lead the investigator to the cause and origin of and, hence, responsibility for the failure. Let us consider a catastrophic sudden fracture. Laboratory examination of the crack surface of the broken part would indicate the presence and size of the flaw and also whether the failure was in a brittle or a ductile mode or whether fatigue (crack growth due to repeated cyclic loading) had occurred. Standard metallurgical tests could also be performed to assess the strength and toughness of the broken piece. Let us assume that a brittle fracture is determined to be the cause. Although this narrows the possible causes, it does not pinpoint one. A sudden brittle fracture could mean that the toughness was inadequate or that a critical crack existed and that, even though the material had adequate toughness, the stress intensity factor (also known as crack driving force) exceeded the toughness. A brittle fracture could also be caused by excessive loads.

§ 7.5 Analyzing the Failure

Regardless of the classification of the failure—whether it is caused by fracture or overload—the human factor cannot be ignored. A Swiss study investigating causes of design and construction failures has concluded that by far the single highest cause of failures, responsible for 60 percent of the failures studied, is lack of experience (see **Figure 7–1**). The next three most significant factors were found to be: negligence (14 percent), lack of education (11 percent), and incompetence (nine percent). Although there is an underlying subjective flavor to these statistics, they nonetheless point to the importance of experience and knowledge in design and construction.

Several failure analysis case histories involving stress analysis (using the finite element method) and fracture mechanics methodologies are examined in §§ **7.6** through **7.10**. In the investigation of each of these failures, the same questions were asked:

1. Did the structure's construction follow the intended design?
2. What were the actual operating loads compared with the intended design loads? Were redundancies built in for critical components?

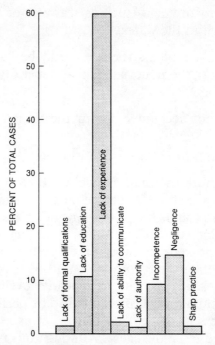

Figure 7–1. Source of fatal weakness in the designer/contractor/user system.

3. Did the design specifications take into account actual environmental circumstances?
4. What were the properties and strengths of the materials used and how did these compare with those called for in the design? Were they adequate to support the design loads?
5. Were any undetected flaws or cracks present that significantly reduced material or structural strength?

CASE STUDIES

§ 7.6 Hyatt Regency Walkway Collapse

A highly publicized accident followed the collapse of walkways at the Hyatt Regency Hotel in Kansas City, Missouri, on July 17, 1981. A picture of the hotel atrium and the offset third-floor walkway which was left standing is shown in **Figure 7–2**. On the floor are remnants of two piled up walkways that collapsed on a multitude of hotel patrons, causing over 100 fatalities. The basic design anomaly in the walkway configuration included a construction change in which the two vertically stacked second and fourth

Plate 1. Kemper Arena roof collapse (1980 in Kansas City).

Plate 2. Model of the D101 tank showing regions of differing materials in the suction-nozzle area.

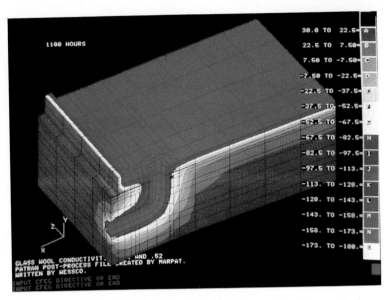

Plate 3. Temperatures in the LNG tank 1100 hours after the cool-down period, as simulated by finite element heat-transfer analysis.

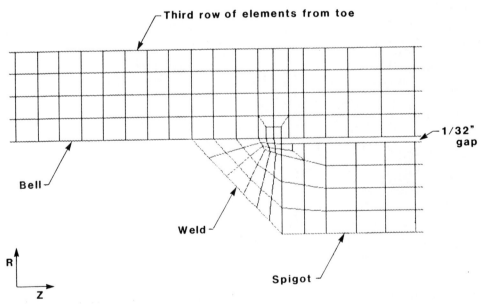

Plate 4. Finite element model of the weld area in the bell-and-spigot joint.

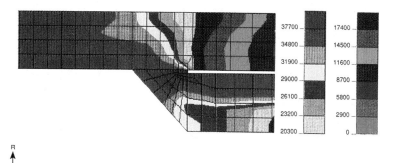

R
→ z

Plate 5. Effective-stress contour plot of the bell-and-spigot area at an applied nominal stress of 18,400 psi.

Plate 6. In-service fatigue caused this connecting rod to fracture despite its considerable size.

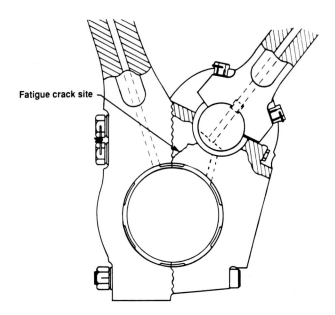

Plate 7. Origin and path of the fatigue crack in the connecting rod.

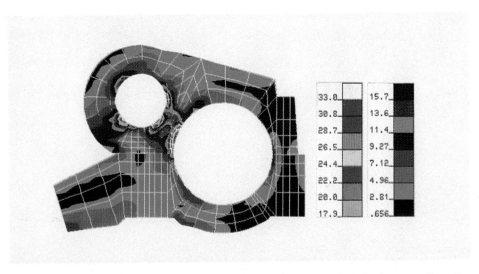

33.0		15.7	
30.8		13.6	
28.7		11.4	
26.5		9.27	
24.4		7.12	
22.2		4.96	
20.0		2.81	
17.9		.656	

Plate 8. This contour plot of the principal cyclic stress was used to predict the origin of the crack in the connecting rods.

Figure 7-2. Hyatt Regency lobby in aftermath of walkway collapse.

floor walkways were suspended by separate suspension rods at the fourth floor walkway crossbeam (**Figure 7–3**). The original design intended that a continuous suspension rod would carry the loads of both walkways. The switch in suspension geometry created a doubling of loads on the upper floor walkway crossbeams, because they had to carry the additional weight of the lower walkway. Moreover, a localized bending moment was introduced in the crossbeam box section because of the offset of the two rods.

In this case, it was determined that the typical walkway crossbeam, rather than being fabricated from an extruded rectangular tube (a structural member that was readily available and certainly cost-effective), was formed as a box section by welding the toe edges of two channel sections together continuously along their flange lengths. The welding was rather poor, particularly given the fact that it was physically impossible to weld along the inside edges of the box beam configuration. Thus, only partial weld penetration resulted at many locations. Under a live load of approximately 90 people, corresponding approximately to the original design load for the structure (not including a factor of safety), the lower nut of the heavier loaded outer suspension rod passed through both bottom flanges of the box beam channels. An examination of the box-beam/suspension rod system, shown in **Figure 7–4**, revealed that the bottom flanges furled upwards, symmetrically, under intense plastic deformation

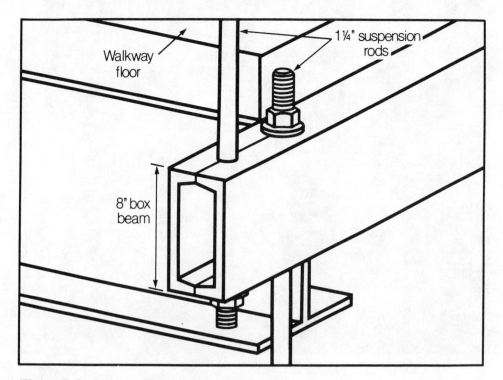

Figure 7–3. Box beam/suspension rod design.

Figure 7–4. Origin of failure in box beam/suspension rod design.

caused by doubled load due to the structural rearrangement, local bending moment, and poor welding of the joint. One of the central crossbeams, having experienced failure, caused the entire walkway to collapse.

§ 7.7 Kemper Arena Roof Collapse

Only a day before the entire roof collapsed, the Kansas City Kemper Arena was in use and crowded by spectators for a cattle show. Luckily, and unlike the Hyatt Regency disaster discussed in **§ 7.6**, on the day of the accident the arena was empty. The failure originated at the roof connection where four type A409F 1 3/8 inch bolts connected the tubular section to horizontal channels.

A finite element analysis, which included the effect of prying action of the bolted joint, indicated that the entire connection could fail if even one bolt failed. The failure would be due to inadequate remaining strength under the live loads. Torrential rains were reported on the day of the accident and, hence, a possibility of ponding, which would increase the load in the center of the roof. Water wave effects could also have contributed to the load. Under these loads, and in spite of the large tubular sections supporting the roof clearly visible after the collapse (see **Plate 1**), the failure of one bolt was sufficient to cause a propagating failure of the entire roof. This example emphasizes the need for redundant systems in critical locations so that should one component fail the structure would still be supported by the remaining connection(s).

§ 7.8   Liquified Natural Gas Tank Failure

In 1983, an analysis was performed of a failed liquified natural gas (LNG) tank on the island of Das in Abu Dhabi. Investigation revealed that the outer-bottom carbon/steel support plates had cracked in a brittle mode, suggesting the prevalence of low temperatures (below the brittle/ductile transition point).

The failed structure is the largest LNG storage tank of its kind, approximately 80 meters in diameter and 30 meters high (**Figure 7–5**). It is of a double-walled design, with an inner shell constructed of nine percent nickel steel to withstand cryogenic temperatures. The inner shell is in contact with the LNG at −160°C. Both the outer shell, which is exposed to the ambient air, and the outer bottom, resting on the soil foundation, are made of lap-welded carbon steel plates. Liquid natural gas is pumped into and drawn from the tank through a suction nozzle located beneath the floor of the tank (**Figure 7–6**). The nozzle is contained in a reinforced concrete box with a carbon steel liner (the suction box).

The designers specified that the carbon steel plates should not be subjected to temperatures below 5°C or they would become brittle. Perlite power insulation was used to maintain the large temperature differential required between the inner and outer tank walls. Perlite concrete blocks and perlite powder provided the insulating barrier between the inner- and outer-bottom plates (**Figure 7–6**). A network of heaters was installed beneath the outer-bottom plate and above the suction box to provide the heat needed to maintain the optimum temperature of the carbon steel. The heaters were controlled by thermocouples located immediately below the outer-bottom plate at the center of the tank. The heaters would go on if the temperature at the thermocouple dropped to 5°C, and off when the temperatures reached 10°C. Unfortunately, the design did not account for the large temperature differential between the suction box area and the center of the tank. Had a thermocouple been placed in the area of the suction box, it would have detected when lower temperatures occurred there.

In March of 1978, frost was observed on the outer shell of the tank, caused by a leak of liquid natural gas. During the subsequent investigation and repair of the tank, a significant number of brittle fractures were discovered in the outer-bottom carbon steel plates. The cracks covered a wide area around the nozzle, extended to the outer shell, and included a six-inch crack on the outer shell itself. It was evident from the brittle nature of the

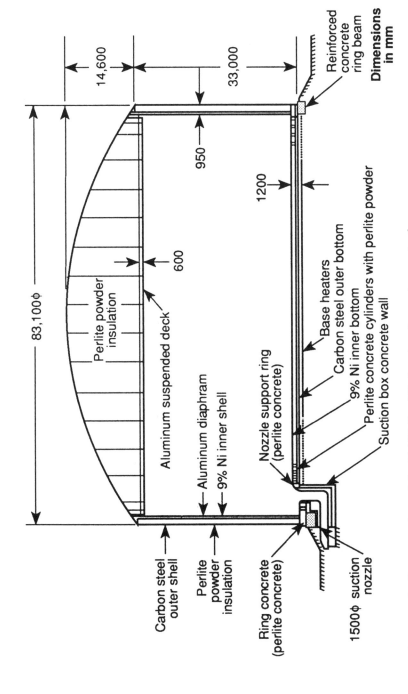

Figure 7–5. Cross section of the D101 liquified natural gas storage tank.

155

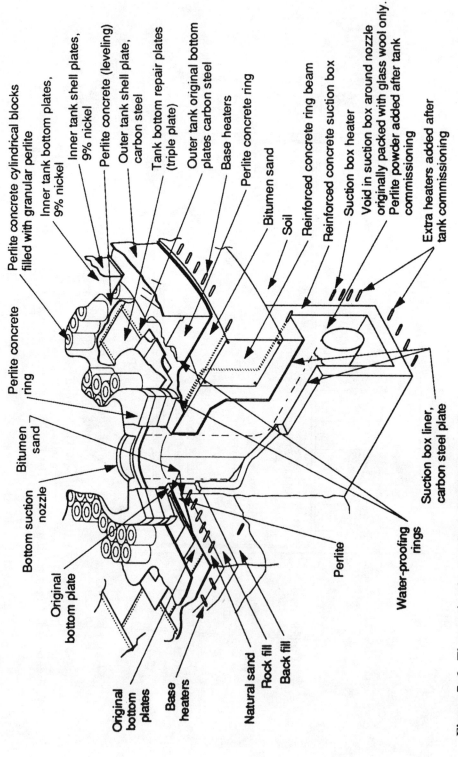

Perlite concrete cylindrical blocks filled with granular perlite

Inner tank bottom plates, 9% nickel

Inner tank shell plates, 9% nickel

Perlite concrete (leveling)

Outer tank shell plate, carbon steel

Tank bottom repair plates (triple plate)

Outer tank original bottom plates carbon steel

Base heaters

Perlite concrete ring

Bitumen sand

Soil

Reinforced concrete ring beam

Reinforced concrete suction box

Suction box heater

Void in suction box around nozzle originally packed with glass wool only. Perlite powder added after tank commissioning

Extra heaters added after tank commissioning

Perlite concrete ring

Bitumen sand

Bottom suction nozzle

Original bottom plate

Base heaters

Natural sand

Rock fill

Back fill

Perlite

Water-proofing rings

Suction box liner, carbon steel plate

Original bottom plates

Figure 7–6. The suction box region of the D101 tank.

cracks that the outer bottom had reached temperatures below the brittle/ductile transition temperature of the outer-bottom steel plates and, in some places, temperatures well below the outer-bottom plate design specification of 5°C.

To determine temperatures at specific locations in the tank, a three-dimensional computer simulation model of the suction nozzle region (**Plate 2**) was developed using interactive graphics mesh-generation techniques. A finite element heat-transfer analysis was conducted. This indicated temperatures on the order of −50°C at the crack initiation site 1100 hours after the tank's cool-down (initial filling) period (**Plate 3**). Temperatures were shown to be gradually decreasing further, and temperatures of −62°C at the initiation site were predicted for 2300 hours after the cool-down period (**Figure 7–7**). At these temperatures, the waterproofing ring, where cracks

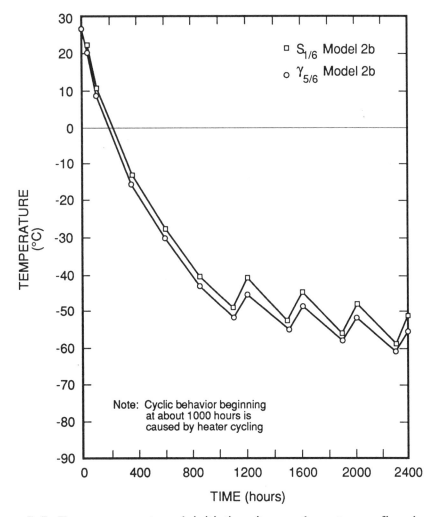

Figure 7–7. Temperatures at crack initiation sites on the waterproofing ring.

began, was as brittle as glass and cracked from thermal stress. The finite element analysis predicted warmer temperatures (of about −15°C) at the crack-arrest points where, in fact, ductile crack arrest was observed. The heat-transfer analysis indicated that the outer-bottom carbon steel plates did not meet the design's temperature requirement, and that the temperatures were well below the safety specification.

This example also demonstrates the complex interdisciplinary engineering activities involved in many failures. In this case, at least six distinct types of expertise were involved to resolve and reconstruct the causes of the failure:

1. Thermodynamics and heat transfer to determine the temperatures in the LNG tank; numerical heat transfer using finite element analysis
2. Stress analysis with thermal/mechanical effects using finite element analysis (to determine stresses in the tank)
3. Soil mechanics/soil settlement (input required in stress analysis)
4. Metallurgy and material engineering to determine toughness and effect of low temperatures on fracture toughness
5. Fracture mechanics to assess crack propagation
6. Risk analysis/statistical analysis/fault tree probabilistic analysis.

An organized team of experts from different disciplines who can and are working in concert toward the final goal is required for analysis and reconstruction of such complex failures as shown in this example. It is crucial that the team communicates with one another about the technical information and engineering discoveries made. Communication can be a problem if the experts are not from the same organization, especially if different conclusions are reached.

§ 7.9   Denver Water Pipe Cracking

A new pipeline designed by the Denver Water Board consisted of 108-inch-diameter steel pipes joined together by bell-and-spigot joints (**Figure 7–8**). The pipeline cracked at several welded joints not long after it was put in service. The pipeline had been constructed in the summer when temperatures reached 100°F. In winter, the pipe cooled down to near freezing temperatures. The large thermal stresses that developed due to the large temperature changes had not been accounted for in the pipeline's design.

A quick analytical calculation of stresses at a failed joint, using combined bending and membrane solutions, indicated that the thermal stresses would exceed the yield strength of the material. The thermal loads (ΔT), combined with internal pressure, produced a nominal stress of 25 kilopounds per square inch (ksi) in the pipe, resulting in much higher local bending stresses at the bell-and-spigot joint.

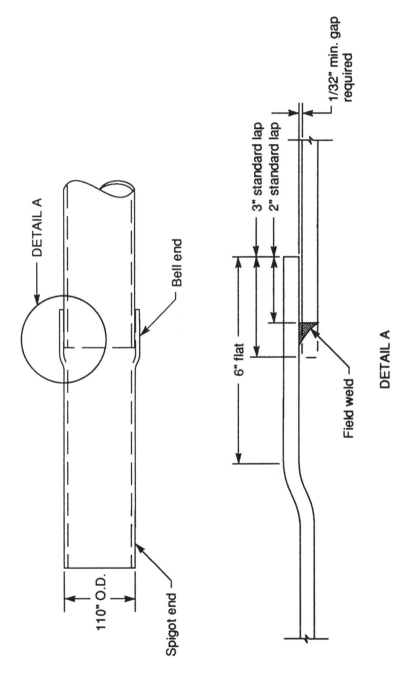

DETAIL A

Figure 7–8. Bell-and-spigot joint in the pipeline.

159

To determine the extent of these local bending stresses, a finite element model of the pipe section was created (**Plate 4**). An elastic-plastic finite element analysis of the bell-and-spigot joint showed that, at 18.4 ksi nominal stress in the pipe (equivalent to the design pressure plus $\Delta T = 59°F$), the entire cross section of the pipe in the bell region had yielded (**Plate 5**). Consequently, elastic-plastic fracture mechanics analysis, using the failure assessment diagram[5] approach and J-integral analysis,[6] showed that, even for upper-bound toughness of the material, the pipe would have failed at the design pressure plus $\Delta T = 42°F$ (**Figure 7–9**).

The temperature differences experienced by the pipeline were well within the expected range for the Denver area and should have been considered by the designers. When the plant was in operation, the internal pressure (not accounting for water hammer) where the failures occurred had been limited to about 70 psi. Had the design pressure of 215 psi prevailed, many more failures would have taken place.

§ 7.10   Connecting Rod Fracture

In a medium-speed, V-configuration diesel engine, the articulated connecting rods underwent in-service fatigue cracking associated with the bolted joint between the master rod and the articulated rod box (**Plates 6** and **7**). These diesel engines are used as standby emergency power generator units in power plants. They are also used as electrical power generators for municipalities and for marine propulsion. Analysis of the entire fracture surface, using fractography and observation of coloration, indicated that the primary source of fatigue was at the root of a thread (**Figure 7–10**). This suggested the possibility of stresses in the bolted joint exceeding the crack initiation limit.

A two-dimensional finite element stress analysis of the connecting rod was performed to investigate this possibility, using plane stress finite element analysis. The model that was created included the lower portion of the master rod and the link-rod-box assembly. The master rod and link-rod box were connected with bolts above and below the crankpin. Bolts below the crankpin extended through the connecting-rod assembly. Any prestressing of these bolts would therefore create compressive stresses in the connecting rod itself. Bolts above the crankpin, however, were threaded directly into the link-rod box, so tightening of the bolts above the crankpin would cause tensile stresses near the threads. In addition to the stresses caused by tightening of the bolts, large cyclic loads were exerted on the

---

[5] The Failure Assessment Diagram is an approach for elastic and elastic-plastic fracture assessment.

[6] J-Integral is a measure of the crack driving force under elastic-plastic conditions. It is analogous to the stress intensity factor K_1 and is related to the stress intensity factor.

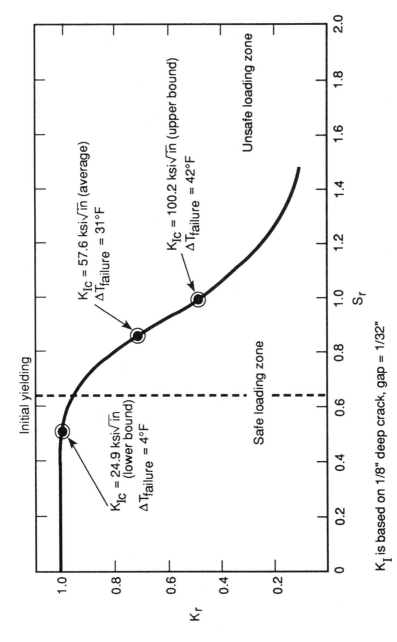

K_I is based on 1/8" deep crack, gap = 1/32"

Figure 7–9. Failure assessment diagram representation of temperature at failure under various operational conditions.

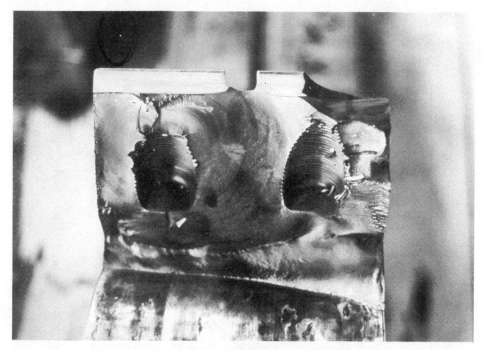

Figure 7–10. Fatigue originated primarily at the root of a thread.

connecting-rod assembly by the gas pressure in the cylinder and by the inertial loads from piston motion.

A separate computer program was written to determine these inertial forces as a function of rank angle, taking into account the gas pressure and the inertial loads of the connecting-rod assembly. A finite element stress analysis of the connecting rod was performed, and the stress results were used to assess crack initiation and propagation from the threaded bolt holes.

The results of the global finite element stress analysis indicated that maximum tensile stresses are produced in the link-rod box when the link rod is near dead center at the top and peak firing pressure occurs. The analysis also determined that tensile stresses in the connecting rod result from loads exerted at the link-pin hole and from the reaction on the crankpin hole. The simulation model predicted that the maximum cyclic stress would occur at the same location where the fatigue failure originated (**Plate 8**). The direction of this stress agreed with the typical direction of the fracture surface.

A modified Goodman diagram[7] was constructed to assess the possibility of fatigue initiation at the bolt hole. The endurance limit is affected by a variety of factors, including surface, size, temperature, and stress

---

[7] A Goodman diagram is a method of assessing whether a crack would initiate under the loading conditions.

concentration. Based on the endurance limit analysis, it was established that fatigue initiation is possible. However, cracks will propagate only if the applied stress intensity factor exceeds the fatigue threshold. The cyclic stress intensity factor, computed using the thread depth as a crack size, approaches the threshold of cyclic stress intensity for fatigue crack propagation.

To prevent future fatigue failures, nondestructive examination was recommended to ensure that the parts were free of flaws. It was recommended that inspections be conducted periodically during operation at full power, based on the number of cycles needed for the growth of a minimum detectable (one-eighth inch) flaw.

A special eddy-current probe was developed to scan the thread roots. This probe can be threaded into the bolt hole, enabling an investigation to be conducted by removing one bolt at a time while the connecting rod remains in the engine.

§ 7.11   Conclusions

The case histories involving structural and mechanical failures presented in §§ 7.6 through 7.10 demonstrate the use of state-of-the-art engineering techniques and tools available to solve complex technical problems involved in failure analysis and reconstruction. Surprisingly, after the evidence is unveiled, it often becomes clear that there were simple ways that the failure could have been avoided. Failures, whether they are design, construction, or manufacturing-related, are frequently the result of simple errors and omissions or some combination thereof. These case studies give clues as to how these failures and similar incidences could have been avoided.

Some lessons are learned. For example, warnings given by the system or structure should not be ignored. Some failures give distress signs before the actual disaster occurs. The Das Island LNG tank discussed in § 7.8 indicated cold temperatures when frost was detected long before extensive outer-bottom steel plate brittle fractures (caused by the cold temperatures) were discovered. During the construction stages of the Denver pipe discussed in § 7.9, tack welds were frequently cracking when overnight temperatures became substantially colder, causing large thermal stresses. The pipe eventually severed due to thermal stresses. There were also incidences of diesel engine component fatigue cracking prior to the failure presented in § 7.10. That there were many other similar engines and designs in operation should have signaled a potential for a generic failure phenomena.

Redundant structural systems are highly desirable. Although the Kemper Arena roof design had a large tubular support system with adequate strength, the connection of those tubular main supports to the roof relied entirely on four 1 3/8-inch-diameter A490F bolts all being intact. The failure of one such bolt implicated that the connection would fail and, subsequently, the roof would collapse. A redundant system would have protected against such a catastrophe by providing additional supports should one component fail.

It is important to perform regular inspection and maintenance of a structure or system, especially after unusual or unexplained behavior is observed. Inspections of critical components by nondestructive evaluation or testing, for example, can reveal the presence of flaws or fatigue cracks that would otherwise grow undetected and eventually cause sudden fractures.

§ 7.12   Courtroom Presentations by a Failure Analyst

Perhaps the most demanding task facing a failure analyst in our legal system is communication and presentation of the complex and often highly technical methodologies used in solving and reconstructing failures to an audience generally untrained in engineering or science and who must become knowledgeable in a particular technical specialty. There are several proven approaches to this need for instant education. Graphics can be a powerful tool to simplify and present complex results. At a minimum, court boards displaying simple, conclusive summaries of analyses performed are effective means of conveying results. Computer graphics, too, are becoming an increasingly powerful tool for presentations. A complex configuration that can be definitively described with computer animation can be understood and "pictured" by the nontechnical audience. Furthermore, a good three-dimensional computer animation has the advantage of locating internal parts and pieces that would be quite difficult if not impossible to present otherwise, even if the actual part was available and could be carried around as evidence. Computer animation can also be used to graphically simulate analytical results, making the abstract concepts more understandable to the nontechnical audience.

Another approach is to relate the technical issues at hand to everyday experiences familiar to the audience. For example, to describe a failure energy of 250,000 foot pounds (which means nothing to a nontechnical person), the analyst could use an equivalent energy scenario that most people can relate to. An example such as "this is equivalent to the effect of a compact Chevy car going 60 miles an hour and hitting a solid wall," gives most people a vivid picture that helps them to understand the level of energy involved.

The audience is not necessarily interested in or capable of understanding technical theory and details. As demonstrated in this chapter, many highly complex technical issues come down to a simple cause and, therefore, can be presented so that most people can understand the issues, even if all the intricacies of the methodologies involved cannot be easily explained. Typically, there is no need for elaborate technical details, complex equations, or a lecture course in engineering.

CHAPTER 8

THE USE OF EXPERTS IN INVESTIGATING A CONSTRUCTION FAILURE

Robert L. Meyers, III, Esquire
Michael F. Albers, Esquire

Robert L. Meyers, III is a partner with Jones, Day, Reavis & Pogue in Dallas, where his practice concentrates on construction documentation and construction litigation and arbitration. He is a member of the Texas and American Bar Associations, and a faculty member for the Practicing Law Institute's construction contracts seminars as well as for numerous other programs, including the ABA's B. Warren Hart Memorial Lecture Series and for the ABA/ASCE on bankruptcy in the construction industry.

A contributing author to various construction law publications, including *A Businessman's Guide to Construction,* Mr. Meyers also wrote "The Contractor in Bankruptcy— Protecting the Interest of the Owner," published in *The Construction Lawyer* (Summer 1984).

Mr. Meyers received both his B.A. and LL.B. degrees from Southern Methodist University.

Michael F. Albers is an attorney with Jones, Day, Reavis & Pogue, having joined the firm in 1981. He received both his B.A. and J.D. from Southern Methodist University in 1976 and 1981, respectively. Mr. Albers concentrates his practice in the areas of construction law and commercial real estate development. His experience includes representing owners, developers, lenders and contractors in construction documentation, dispute resolution procedures, as well as project acquisition, financing and development activities. Mr. Albers has written for and participated in the presentation of a number of programs concerning construction law, including the Practicing Law Institute's Construction Contracts Seminars, the Texas Bar Advanced Real Estate Program, and the ABA/Joint Program on bankruptcy in the construction industry.

§ 8.1   Introduction

Construction projects are by their nature complex undertakings that involve multiple parties. As a result, determining issues of responsibility, liability, causation, and damages poses a confusing and challenging task to the party facing a construction failure. First and foremost in the assessment of any such situation and the formulation of a plan of action are the accumulation and understanding of all available information. Regardless of the particular construction failure or problem at hand, there are five key issues present: (1) the facts, (2) the facts, (3) the facts, (4) the facts, and (5) the facts.[1]

Attorneys, including attorneys experienced in construction matters, are distillers of facts and advocates of positions supported by those facts. The physical investigation of the component parts and systems of a building, its foundation, and subsurface conditions requires a technical skill and expertise with which attorneys are seldom, if ever, blessed. The interpretation and appreciation of mountains of facts contained in diaries, logs, schedules, records, meeting minutes, reports, studies, invoices, drawings, specifications, correspondence, permits, pricing, accounting information, and the other reams of paper upon which construction disputes are built may also require a technical background that lawyers do not possess. The practice of law remains primarily an art, the advances of the computer age

---

[1] This phrase did not originate with the authors. Its creator is unknown, unless (as he claims) it is "the" Overton Currie.

notwithstanding. Construction claims and failure analysis, at the factual level, require the involvement of someone capable of proceeding with some degree of scientific certainty.

The factual inquiry requires the assistance of experts and consultants to evaluate performance problems and actual and potential claims, whether asserted or defended. The term "expert" in this context is something other than an expert witness, although such an expert may also render opinions during trial based on knowledge of the actual facts or on a hypothetical set of circumstances. The expert considered in this chapter may be an engineer in one of many areas of engineering discipline, an architect, an accountant, or a construction consultant. The problem may be of a nature that would require a team of experts. Whatever the expert's specific area, the task is the same: to gather facts, to synthesize and organize information, and from this to provide a concise, understandable history and picture of the events in order that the attorney can present persuasive evidence.

§ 8.2   The Role of Experts and Consultants

Construction problems have been compared to the physical maladies one experiences with the human body.

> As knowledge of the human bone structure, for instance, is within the expertise of the orthopedic surgeon, so knowledge of a steel frame of a building is within the expertise of the structural engineer. Similarly, as a neurosurgeon may be called on to testify about the nature of a nervous disorder, so may an electrical engineer be deemed qualified to testify when the subject matter is an erratic elevator or a defective electrical distribution system. When potential for litigation develops as a result of complaints, engineering specialists are essential to a proper diagnosis, prognosis, and treatment of the problem.[2]

The point is, the type or number of experts required to address complex construction issues depends on the nature and severity of the problem. Subsurface problems require the use of a soils engineer, hydrologist, or geologist; structural problems necessitate the involvement of structural engineers; problems in the timeliness of performance warrant the attention of scheduling experts.

The general litigiousness of the parties to the construction process has given rise to an increasing reliance on experts. The intent and expectation in employing these experts are to establish credibility and support, and to thereby prevail, or at least survive. Although it may sometimes appear that this process has produced an expert for every problem and a problem for

---

[2] M. Schwartz & N.F. Schwartz, Engineering Evidence § 2.01 (1981).

every expert, there are important distinctions between the capabilities and qualifications of different experts that should not be overlooked.

§ 8.3   Types of Experts

There are different types of experts who may be required in an investigation, and each has a particular function to perform.[3]

Civil Engineers.   Civil engineering embraces all studies and activities connected with fixed waterworks, such as those concerning water power, drainage, irrigation, water supply, inland waterways, and harbors. Also included are the designs of foundations, buildings, and bridges and the engineering of sewerage, sewage disposal, and refuse disposal. Civil engineering additionally covers fixed works related to transportation, including railroads, highways, tunnels, and airports.

Soils Engineers.   The primary duty of the soils engineer is to investigate soils for proposed building foundations and site grading for housing, industry, and municipal improvements. The soils engineer is capable of analyzing the presence of ground water and the stability of cuts and fills of earthen structures. The soils engineer may be called in as a consultant to a structural engineer in the design of foundations or to a highway engineer in the design of roadways and bridges. The soils engineer does not investigate for the presence of hazardous materials.

Structural Engineers.   A structural engineer works in the area of force-resisting and load-supporting structural members. These may include foundations, walls, beams, columns, trusses, and other framing portions of buildings and structures.

Architects.   The prime design professional of commercial, residential, and public buildings is the architect. The architect plans and designs buildings, identifies construction problems, and gathers background information. The architect prepares plans, specifications, and other contract documents for the builder and craft workers. In the design and construction process, the architect also coordinates the engineering consultants on the project. Often the architect will monitor the construction of the project for the owner to determine that construction is proceeding in accordance with the plans and specifications. During the construction process, the architect may also be the arbitrator of disputes between owner and contractor. At

---

[3] M. Schwartz & N.F. Schwartz, Engineering Evidence § 2.03 (1981).

the stage of construction claims and failure analysis, however, attorneys take over this central role of directing, coordinating, and monitoring progress of the experts' work.

Mechanical Engineers.   Mechanical engineering deals with the generation, transmission, and utilization of energy in electrical, thermal, and mechanical form. Mechanical engineering also encompasses design relating to production of tools and machinery and has an important function in building and facility design, because it includes responsibility for the planning of heating, ventilation, refrigeration, and plumbing systems. In industrial projects, the mechanical engineer is usually the prime design engineer and is responsible for the major planning of the manufacturing facility.

Electrical Engineers.   Electrical engineers design, develop, and supervise the manufacturing of electrical and electronic equipment as well as prepare plans and specifications for electrical services and wiring in construction projects. This includes areas of illumination, protective devices, instrumentation, controls, electrical machinery, and communication.

Chemical Engineers.   Chemical engineering is that branch of engineering that deals with the industrial uses of chemistry. It relates to the development and application of processes involving chemical or physical changes of materials.

Nuclear Engineers.   In cases based on accidents involving nuclear power plants and equipment, the most qualified engineering expert may be the nuclear engineer. Nuclear engineering relates to the principles of nuclear physics generally and the engineering utilization of nuclear phenomena. Nuclear engineers are concerned with protecting the public from the potential hazards of radiation and radioactive materials, and with the safe design, construction, and operation of the nuclear reaction process.

Metallurgical Engineers.   When the quality of a metal part is in question, or the cause of failure of such a part must be determined, a qualified expert is the metallurgical engineer. Metallurgical engineering is that branch of professional engineering that involves the research, understanding, and application of the principles of the properties and behavior of metals. The field also relates to the stability of metal when exposed to stress, corrosion, and other outside influences.

Quality Engineers.   The engineering discipline dedicated to the maintenance of quality in materials and production methods is known as quality engineering. Quality engineering involves the planning, development, and operation of quality control systems, and the application and analysis of testing and inspection procedures.

Fire Protection Engineers. This is a specialty branch of engineering aimed at safeguarding life and property from fire and fire-related disasters. This area of expertise includes the identification, evaluation, correction, and prevention of present and potential fire and fire-related panic hazards. In addition, this field encompasses the arrangement of fire resistive building materials, fire detection, and extinguishing systems and devices.

Safety Engineers. This specialty is concerned mainly with the engineering principles essential to the identification, elimination, and control of hazards to persons and property. This area of expertise embraces the development, analysis, production, construction, testing, and utilization of systems, products, and procedures to eliminate such hazards.

Certified Public Accountants. These are central figures in construction litigation in terms of cost accounting analysis and contract expenditure reconstruction and in otherwise establishing the measures of damages. The complex and alternative nature of the damages recoverable in construction failures necessitates reliance on the involvement of experts in this field.

Land Surveyors. The acknowledged expert in the field of adjoining property, rights of ways, easements, and other real property problems is the licensed land surveyor. Land surveying includes measuring and locating lines, angles, elevations, and natural and manmade features. Land surveying is the initial part of construction and is central to such activities as staking or monumenting property boundaries, aligning and grading streets or railroads, and establishing corners of buildings.

Testing Laboratories. Laboratories generally fall into categories of physical testing and chemical testing laboratories. Most laboratories specialize in specific areas such as soils, concrete, masonry, bacteriology, chemistry, water quality, air quality, fire resistance, electricity, and electronics. In cases of defective buildings, machinery, or other products, laboratories can determine the extent of fatigue, creep, stress, rupture, chemical deterioration, or other possible cause of failure. Their findings can augment the testimony of the engineering expert, as most engineers lack in-house laboratory equipment facilities. Although engineers rely mainly on mathematical analysis for determining the strength of materials, products, and structures, the use of testing laboratories to support mathematical proof is of great value.

§ 8.4 Criteria for Selecting Experts

Much attention is given in other portions of this book to selecting an expert, and resort to those materials is encouraged prior to making a selection.[4] Typically, the criteria focus on the qualifications, education, experience, and reputation of the person or firm being considered, and there is no substitute for evaluation on this basis.

As a final checklist, one should determine how well the expert grades in a curriculum comprised of "The Seven Cs":

1. *Capability* in dealing with the particular problem at hand
2. Level of *competence* and skill which the expert possesses
3. Actual or potential *conflict* of interests between the expert and those it represents
4. Ability and willingness to *coordinate* its efforts with those of the attorney and other experts
5. *Commitment* of time, resources, and spirit to the task
6. Ability to *communicate,* orally and in writing, in an effective and convincing manner
7. *Cost* of services.

§ 8.5 Consulting the Expert at an Early Stage

Whatever method is employed in finding and selecting an expert, it is important that it be employed early in the process of assessing the construction failure. Potential experts must be interviewed early in the claims and failure analysis process to determine if they can be of service to the claim and failure analysis at hand and to the client's interests. Many of the technical disciplines have various and contradictory schools of thought. There are at least two sides to any dispute, and a competent expert versed in a school of thought inconsistent with the client's interests should be identified early.

If the first expert consulted does not advance the client's position, consider investing in a second opinion. When an expert does not develop a preliminary opinion useful to the client's position, also consider retaining

---

[4] Frequently the construction attorney can recommend experts known through experience or reputation. The American Bar Association's (ABA) Section of Litigation has prepared, through its Committee on Construction Litigation, a *Register of Expert Witnesses in the Construction Industry.* Litigation or construction sections of some state and local bar associations compile similar information.

that expert on an inactive basis as a method of testing or sounding out the analyses and opinions of those selected as testimonial experts.

Like many forms of litigation, construction litigation ultimately becomes a paper case. The primary focus of pretrial and discovery matters is typically the assemblage of materials for expert review, analysis, opinion, and eventual testimony. Failure to engage the necessary experts at the appropriate stage is an error that no competing concerns for time, costs, or other matters can excuse. Only by involving the expert in the early stage of the investigation can the attorney gain the expert's assistance in identifying claims and determining the need for additional experts to substantiate the claims.[5] Retaining experts at the outset also avoids the potential hiring of the preferred expert by other parties to the dispute. Most importantly, early involvement of the expert affords the attorney the benefit of the expert's technical skill and expertise in gathering and evaluating facts, understanding the essence of the construction failure, and preparing the case for recovery or defense.

THE TEAM APPROACH

§ 8.6   The Construction Attorney

The experts employed in the investigation of a construction failure are retained for the specific purpose of determining the cause of the event. They are not asked to proceed in this undertaking in order to satisfy their employer's intellectual curiosity. Their task is to assist the attorney in initiating or defending litigation resulting from the failure, or to render a lawsuit unnecessary by demonstrating a level of knowledge and preparedness that is truly frightening to potential adversaries.

Construction attorneys are included among the experts engaged in this process, although their role is different from the other experts' due to the different nature of their skills. In the investigation of a failure, attorneys must apply their expertise to identifying potential parties, claims, and theories of recovery and selecting the means and methods of best proving them. Given the purpose of the investigation and the likely manner of resolving the resulting disputes, it is the attorney who must be charged with the task of, and given the authority to, captain the team. Purpose, direction, and organization are essential. The construction attorney is the person who must know where the process is going and what it will do when it gets there. The facts give rise to some claims, support others, indict certain parties, and exonerate others. The bottom line is that a

---

[5] M. Schwartz & N.F. Schwartz, Engineering Evidence § 7.01 (1981).

construction failure leaves the injured interests in search of legal remedies, and the significance of the multitude of facts that the experts unearth is measured against their ability to support the pursuit of the remedy. The attorney is not the expert who can discover, identify, explain, or present such facts, but the attorney is the only one who can evaluate them for this purpose.

§ 8.7 Communications between Experts

Careful consideration must be given to how the consultants are to coordinate their efforts. In the design and construction process it may be the architect who is captain of the ship. That traditional role must be avoided in the arena of claims and failure analysis.

Initially, communications should be made directly from the expert to the construction counsel. An expert should not report through another expert to the attorneys. Misinformation, false starts, premature or erroneous opinions, and professional biases being passed from expert to expert are more likely to be avoided by this direct line of communication to the construction attorneys.

There are probably at least two sides for any dispute and an expert for each side. Therefore, when an expert develops a preliminary opinion inconsistent with the client's overall position, it is best that the remainder of the team not be tainted with this position. Furthermore, if the investigation does not proceed in a timely manner, the attorneys are more able to know of this problem early, identify the impediment to completion of the expert's work, and fashion a resolution to the lack of progress.

Direct communication between the experts may be required prior to establishing their respective final analysis and opinions. Depending upon the claim or failure in issue, one or several meetings of the entire team may be warranted, if not required. This meeting of the entire team, however, is best left until the attorneys have a good understanding of each expert's preliminary analysis. Should the attorney have misgraded the expert in the curriculum comprised of The Seven Cs in § 8.4, that team member can be replaced with minimal impact upon the other parties.

§ 8.8 Experts Working as a Team

The importance of having the respective investigating disciplines working together as a team can not be overstated. The effort must be focused and organized. Without guidance, the process readily turns chaotic and nonproductive. **Figure 8–1** depicts the areas of expertise that may be utilized, the specific experts available in each area, and the flow of information.

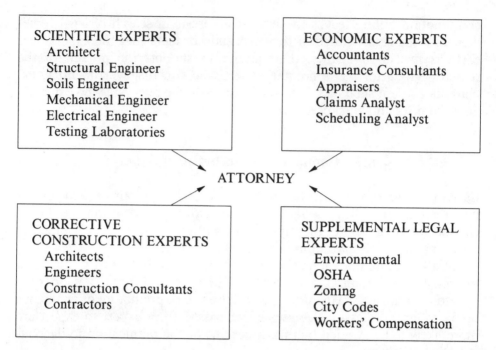

Figure 8–1. The investigation team.

§ 8.9 Hypothetical Failure

In order to understand and appreciate the team approach to construction failure investigation, assume a situation in which the four-story west tower of a connected twin tower project experienced a partial collapse. The collapse was preceded by the connecting pod pulling away from the collapsed west tower. Evidence of ponding roof water, deterioration and tearing of the roof membrane, and penetration along the common wall is present. Additionally, heaving and cracking occurred in the floor slab and along the curtain wall.

The owner of the project is understandably distressed. Although no one was injured, current tenants are facing constructive eviction and future tenants are only encountered in flights of fantasy. Compounding the debacle is the lender's determination that the building is no longer adequate collateral for the loan it secures and the city's designation of the project as unsafe and dangerous to the citizenry and hence subject to condemnation. All the owner knows for sure is that it is one person who had nothing to do with this calamity. Determining who is at fault is your job.

Sections 8.10 through **8.13** comprise a list, admittedly only partial, of the parties potentially liable, the theories of recovery, and the experts who may be involved in substantiating the claims.

§ 8.10   Responsibility of the Architect

Generally, an owner will have claims against the architect in both contract and tort, the latter generally including both negligence and claims under statutory deceptive trade practices or consumer protection acts.[6] Warranty and strict liability claims are not generally available against design professionals.

In the absence of an express contractual provision requiring more, an architect is generally held to the same standard of care, whether the action is based in contract or tort: it must exercise due diligence, skill, and good judgment in accordance with the exercise of the ordinary skill and competence of members of the profession under the same or similar circumstances.[7] The same general standard of care usually governs both negligence and tort claims except in cases of breach of statutory or code requirements where negligence per se may be established.

The process of investigating and establishing liability against the project architect is a particularly futile undertaking without the assistance of another architect as an expert consultant. The review of the drawings and specifications, changes and modifications in design, and the overall design concept must be done with an architect retained for that purpose if any accurate conclusions are to be drawn. Determining whether the project architect properly anticipated and took into account existing conditions in formulating the design and in specifying materials may require the input not only of another architect but also that of a soils engineer who can evaluate such conditions. Experts in construction management procedures may also be called upon to examine the project architect's activities in the administration of the construction contract.

§ 8.11   Responsibility of the General
Contractor and Subcontractors

Contractual and tort theories are available against a general contractor as well as the architect. A contractor also makes certain implied warranties[8] and may make express ones as well. Subcontractors are generally in the same position as the design professionals retained by the architect in that they are not in privity of contract with the owner. However, with

---

[6] *See* Tex. Bus. & Comm. Code Ann. § 17.41 (Vernon 1987).

[7] *See* I.O.I. Sys. v. City of Cleveland, Tex., 615 S.W.2d 786, 790 (Tex. Civ. App. 1980); Coombs v. Beede, 89 Me. 187, 36 A. 104, 105 (1896).

[8] J. Grove & R. Blum, *Suing the Contractor for Construction Defects and Delays,* in Construction Litigation: Representing the Owner 45 (R. Cushman & K. Cushman eds. 1984).

the exception of the express warranty and contract claims, the general contractor and subcontractor occupy very similar legal positions.

Generally, it is preferable for the owner to look to the general contractor, who remains liable on the contract. However, in certain circumstances, such as when the general contractor becomes insolvent, the owner may wish to pursue the subcontractor directly. In those circumstances, because the essential element of privity is lacking, the owner can pursue the subcontractor in contract only if the owner is a third-party beneficiary of the contractor-subcontractor agreement. Generally, owners have been held to be only incidental beneficiaries and therefore unable to recover. However, the agreement may expressly make the owner an intended beneficiary, in which case recovery will be possible.

Although the existence and terms of any express warranty depend upon the specific language of the contract, in the absence of a disclaimer the law implies warranties into the contractor-owner contract. These implied warranties are more in the nature of tort than contractual obligations. For example, courts have imposed an implied warranty to perform the work in a "good and workmanlike manner."[9] The builder also impliedly warrants that it will follow the plans and specifications and use nondefective materials.

Contractors and subcontractors are also responsible for their own negligence, albeit under a different standard than the design professional's. This can be especially important when contract and warranty theories are not available against a subcontractor. The standard for negligence is basically the same as that for the implied warranty of good workmanlike construction.[10]

The investigation of the work of contractors and subcontractors may require any number or combination of architectural, engineering, and accounting experts, depending on the nature of the initial suspicions and the facts disclosed. In the case of the failure described in § **8.9**, an architect would be required to review the initial project design and the as-built structure against that project design. Additionally, a structural engineer would investigate faults in the design, construction, and/or materials used in the building's structural components. Metallurgical engineers and testing laboratories would inspect the structural steel strength at the point of separation and collapse. Testing of the soils conditions in relation to slab

---

[9] Moore v. Werner, 418 S.W.2d at 918 (Tex. Civ. App. 1967). As is true in most jurisdictions, Texas also implies a warranty of habitability in residential construction. Miller v. Spencer, 732 S.W.2d 758, 760 (Tex. Ct. App. 1987) (implied warranty for a particular purpose of U.C.C. rejected in construction contacts). *See also* G-W-L, Inc. v. Robichaux, 643 S.W.2d 392, 394 (Tex. 1984) (rejecting U.C.C. warranties in the construction context generally).

[10] Hartley v. Ballou, 286 N.C. 51, 209 S.E.2d 776, 783 (1974) (work must be performed in accordance with care and skill of an ordinary skilled workman of the area).

damage would be accomplished by a soils engineer, geotechnical expert, and other testing facilities. Other contractors, manufacturers, and construction experts could be called upon to examine the conformance with specifications by the contractor, its subcontractors, and suppliers. These experts and certified public accountants would further analyze the full nature of the damage, the feasible means of repair or reconstruction, and the cost thereof.

§ 8.12   Responsibility of Construction Managers

The use of construction managers has become increasingly prevalent in recent years, especially in fast-track and multiple prime contractor projects. The nature of the owner-construction manager relationship is somewhat hard to define, because there are several variations on the arrangement. In some cases, the role of construction manager is combined with that of the architect, in others with that of the general contractors, and sometimes the construction manager acts only as the agent of the owner. See **Chapters 1** and **3**. Nevertheless, the same general causes of action are available as they are against design professionals and contractors, with some differences.

As was the case with architects and general contractors, the standard of care for construction managers will be substantially the same in contract and tort actions. Precisely what that standard of care will be depends upon the capacity in which the construction manager was acting: whether that of design professional or that of contractor. That capacity may not be readily apparent, however. Although construction managers are not separately licensed, they may be licensed either as an architect or a contractor.[11] This will naturally impact on the standard of care applicable, as well as the sort of indemnity arrangement available. See § **3.20**. Determination of the role of services also affects whether the design professional's errors and omission insurance offers potential coverage or whether the performance bond of a contractor may be available.

Another important issue is the degree of responsibility that the construction manager has for the activities of other parties such as engineers, contractors, and subcontractors. The authority of the construction manager is also important for determining whether the construction manager is treated as an independent contractor or as an agent, although some form contracts address this issue directly. Whether a court will impose an implied warranty of workmanlike performance depends on whether the

---

[11] The traditional view was that construction management falls within the architect's sphere of activity (Lehman, *The Role of the Architect and Contractor in Construction Management,* 6 J. L. Reform 447 (1973)).

construction manager is acting as a design professional or a contractor. In the former case, it is unlikely that the law will imply any such warranty, while in the latter the law generally does.

As previously noted, it is often difficult to distinguish between negligence (tort) and contract standards.[12] When the construction manager is acting as a design professional, it is held to the standard for that profession. But when the services provided are of a nonprofessional nature, the standard will be that of a contractor. Similarly, the duty to supervise construction, to the extent not otherwise regulated by the contract, is one of reasonable care.[13]

Formulating a position or claim vis-à-vis a construction manager requires the use of experts in the same manner as in the cases of the project architect, contractor, and subcontractors. The varying possibilities of the construction manager's role require that it be examined before selecting the appropriate expert. An architect or contractor who has experience as a construction manager is capable of providing the most beneficial assistance and is capable of identifying the need for any other expert consultants.

§ 8.13   Responsibility of Suppliers

Suppliers pose a special problem because the owner seldom contracts directly for the purchase of supplies and materials.[14] Here the Uniform Commercial Code (U.C.C.) warranties enter the picture for the first time, because the business of the materialman is to furnish goods rather than services.

Because an owner seldom purchases construction materials directly from the manufacturer, the owner is only entitled to assert contractural claims if it was a third-party beneficiary of the contractor/materialman contract. This lack of privity creates further problems when the owner wishes to sue the manufacturer for breach of express warranty, unless the warranty or representation regarding it was made directly to the owner. Since the adoption of the U.C.C., it has been held that privity of contract is not required if the manufacturer furnishes samples to a middleman

---

[12] First Nat'l Bank of Akron v. Cann, 503 F. Supp. 419, 438–39 (N.D. Ohio 1980), aff'd, 669 F.2d 415 (6th Cir. 1982); Lee County v. Southern Water Contractors, 298 So. 2d 518, 520 (Fla. Dist. Ct. App. 1974). See J. Tiedar & J. Hoffar, Suing the Construction Manager in Construction Litigation: Representing the Owner 104 (R. Cushman & K. Cushman eds. 1984); Note, Architectural Malpractice: A Contract-Based Approach, 92 Harv. L. Rev. 1075, 1090 (1979).

[13] Lee County v. Southen Water Contractors, Inc., 298 So. 2d at 520.

[14] Brailsford, Suing the Material Supplier, in Construction Litigation: Representing the Owner 123 (R. Cushman & K. Cushman eds. 1984).

with the knowledge that the samples are likely to be submitted to the ultimate buyer in order to induce a sale of the product.[15] A prudent owner requires through the specifications that all manufacturer warranties be extended to the owner, or requires that the contractor and all subcontractors assign all manufacturers' warranties to the owner.[16] In this area it is important to remember that technical specifications often create express warranties.[17]

The U.C.C. also creates implied warranties. The most important of these is the implied warranty of merchantability,[18] and this warranty has been applied to building components.[19]

The other major implied warranty created by the U.C.C. is that of fitness for a particular purpose.[20] This warranty is obviously very important in the construction context when the materials requirements and their intended uses may be described in detail in the plans and specifications.

In negligence actions, the privity of the materialman is not the issue; instead, the key issue is whether the owner is foreseeable as an injured party. Generally, this is not a problem because the laws of most states allow for the assertion of negligence claims against remote parties.

Though similar to, and long intertwined with, the principles underlying implied warranty, strict liability has emerged as a separate theory of liability in tort, independent from sales and contract law. Strict liability has many advantages for the potential plaintiff, specifically in the elimination of the defenses of lack of privity, lack of notice, and disclaimer. However, this cause of action is limited to those products established to be defectively dangerous.

The method of construction failure investigation applicable to the materials of suppliers is similar to that employed for other types of subcontractors; however, the focus is on the quality, integrity, kind, and character of such materials as opposed to labor or other aspects of performance. Nevertheless, the investigation may also include inquiries as to storage, handling, transportation, and other treatment of the material. Returning to the failure described in § 8.9, testing laboratories, metallurgical and

---

[15] Industi-Ri-Chem Laboratory, Inc. v. Par-Pak Co., 602 S.W.2d 282, 287 (Tex. Civ. App. 1980).

[16] Brailsford, *Suing the Material Supplier,* in Construction Litigation: Representing the Owner 124 (R. Cushman & K. Cushman eds. 1984).

[17] S-C Indus. v. American Hydroponics Sys., Inc., 468 F.2d 852, 854–55 (5th Cir. 1972) ("Technical specifications may constitute a warranty, however, even to the extent of displacing the warranties created by inconsistent samples, models, and general language of description.").

[18] U.C.C. § 2-314.

[19] S.C. Indus. v. American Hydroponics Sys., Inc., 468 F.2d 852 at 854; *Tracor Inc. v. Austin Supply & Drywall Co.,* 484 S.W.2d 446 (Tex. Civ. App. 1972).

[20] U.C.C. § 2-315.

soils engineers, and experts in foundation work and concrete would be useful in determining whether and to what extent the structural steel, soil preparation, and compaction materials, concrete materials (components, mix, hydration, and air entrainment), foundation piers and pilings, and re-bar or roofing materials caused or contributed to the collapse.

The investigatory procedure requires physical inspection, testings, analysis, study, and consultation. Feedback and direction are critical to effective use of experts.

§ 8.14   Protecting the Expert

The role of the experts discussed in this chapter has been that of investigator or pretrial consultant, not of expert engaged for the purpose of trial testimony. In order that the construction attorney can effectively captain the team investigating the construction failure, and in order to protect the experts' findings from discovery, the attorney rather than the potential litigant should hire the experts. Proceeding in this manner affords the broadest application of the attorney-client privilege and work product rules (see §§ 7.7 through 7.9); however, discovery is ultimately governed by the Federal Rules of Evidence and comparable state procedures governing discovery and pretrial matters.[21]

There are four categories of experts under the Federal Rules of Evidence: (1) those expected to be called as expert witnesses at trial, (2) those retained in anticipation of litigation or preparation for trial but who are not expected to be called as expert witnesses at trial, (3) those whose information was not acquired in anticipation of litigation or preparation for trial, (4) and those consulted but not retained. The facts known to and opinions held by experts to be called as witnesses are discoverable pursuant to the procedures of Federal Rule of Evidence 26(b)(4)(A)(i), whereas discovery of such matters as they relate to experts not expected to be called as witnesses is restricted.[22] Discovery of the opinions of nontestifying experts is permitted only upon a demonstration of exceptional circumstances, typically that equivalent information is not available from another source.

The protections afforded by these evidentiary rules are appropriate and should be employed. The information obtained and opinions formed by experts investigating the construction failure is often preliminary and forms an integral part of the case being built by the attorney. Consequently, proper classification of the expert is essential in order to avoid premature disclosure of confidential matters.

---

[21] Fed. R. Evid. 26.

[22] Fed. R. Evid. 26(B)(4)(B).

Each expert should be advised that its communications with counsel and its own investigation and analysis are confidential and not to be discussed with anyone other than as directed by counsel. Specifically, publication of the communications and particularly the expert's investigation and analysis at speaking engagements or during casual discussion among professional colleagues is prohibited without the express prior approval of counsel.

CHAPTER 9

GETTING THE INSURANCE COMPANY ON BOARD

Stanley A. Martin, Esquire
James J. Myers, Esquire

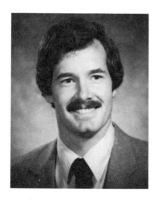

Stanley A. Martin is an associate in the Boston office of the Boston and Washington law firm of Gadsby & Hannah, concentrating in construction law, including architectural and engineering matters and contract negotiation and litigation. Mr. Martin holds a Bachelor of Science degree in Art and Design (Architecture) from the Massachusetts Institute of Technology, and a Juris Doctor degree from Boston College Law School.

Mr. Martin is president of the Massachusetts Construction Industry Council and serves as chairman of the Massachusetts Council of the American Institute of Architects/Boston Society of Architects Legislative Affairs Committee. He has lectured before various trade and industry organizations on construction law matters and is also a lecturer at Northeastern University in the Building Technology Program. Mr. Martin is admitted to practice in Massachusetts and New Hampshire and is a member of the Massachusetts, American, and International Bar Associations.

James J. Myers is a Boston partner in the law firm of Gadsby & Hannah, which has offices in Boston and Washington, D.C. His practice concentrates on all aspects of public and private construction law. He is co-author of the *Manual of Massachusetts Construction Law* and has taught construction, architect, and engineering law to practicing professionals in the construction industry throughout the country and abroad. Mr. Myers is a fellow of the American College of Trial Lawyers and has served for many years as a member of the National Panel of Construction Arbitrators of the American Arbitration Association. He is past chairman of the Public Contract Section of the American Bar Association, and currently serves as chairman of the Construction Contracts Committee of the International Bar Association.

183

§ 9.1 Introduction

When a construction failure occurs, one of the preliminary questions that each party—particularly the designer and the contractor—faces is whether any of the losses or damages are covered by insurance. The first and most obvious step is to locate the insurance policy, and then notify the insurer of the potential claim. There is also a preliminary question as to whether any damages are within the scope of the policy or are excluded from coverage.

This chapter examines the insurer's obligation to defend and the primary exclusions likely to arise in the context of an actual failure. A hypothetical factual outline is presented to first focus on the major issues, and is followed by a discussion of the pertinent policy exclusions. The general scope of the insurer's obligation to defend and its liability for failing to defend the insured are also covered.

§ 9.2 The Hypothetical Cooling Tower Construction Failure

The project was a massive cooling tower to recirculate water for all energy systems at a large university. The cooling tower was framed by structural steel. The water circulation was extremely corrosive on steel.

The contractor entered into a fixed price contract with the construction manager as agent for the University (owner). The contractor's work was to furnish and erect all structural steel and deck, and to coat the steel with a specified black coal tar type coating using a specified spray-on method. The contractor also furnished a performance bond for his work.

The steel was erected in irregular modules in the contractor's plant, and the coal tar coating was applied in the plant under controlled moisture and temperature conditions. The coating was required by the specifications to be sprayed to a thickness of 10 to 15 mils.

Shortly after the contractor had erected some of the steel coated with the specified coal tar coating, the owner's engineer began complaining about runs in the coating and general overspray to thicknesses exceeding the specification limit. As the contractor's crews progressed with the coating operation and the steel erection, they attempted to adjust their equipment, use different nozzles, and try different approaches, but were unable to achieve the 10 to 15 mil thickness specification requirement.

The owner's engineer did not reject the work, but there was a great deal of correspondence from him, particularly throughout the second half of the coating and steel erection operations, notifying the contractor that the coating was being applied too thickly, and that the contractor would be held responsible for any adverse result of the contractor's constant failure to comply with the coating thickness specification.

The contractor's correspondence during the job assured the owner's engineer that the contractor was using only the coal tar coating specified and the specified equipment but that he could not develop a method that would allow the coating to be sprayed as required to a consistent 10 to 15 mil thickness. To achieve that thickness in one location would require a greater thickness in another area. This was particularly true at or near connections in the structural steel, which accounted for most of the steel.

The contractor's letters indicated that he was trying everything, but it appeared that by using the specified coal tar coating with the specified spray equipment, the specified thickness was impossible to attain if full coverage was to be achieved. The engineer made no other recommendations, only requiring that the contractor comply with the specifications.

The contractor completed the work and was paid everything due except for his retainage. The owner began operation of the cooling tower.

About six months after the owner began using the cooling tower, the owner's engineers notified the owner that some scattered areas of the coating had failed and were peeling. The owner notified the contractor to return to the site and correct the peeling areas pursuant to a contract requirement to that effect.

The contractor claimed he had applied the specified coating as required by the specifications and, if the coating failed, it must be due to a defect in the product specified or in the specified method of application. The contractor's personnel inspected the tower and said the peeling was not too severe, however; the contractor estimated that the peeling areas could be repaired and recoated for about one-quarter of the retainage that the owner was still holding.

The contractor arranged with the owner to repair the peeling areas without prejudice or admission that he was responsible for the condition and to brush on the specified coating. After the areas were repaired the owner would pay the contractor his full retainage. The cooling tower was shut down, the repairs were successfully completed, and the contractor was paid his full retainage.

About eight months after the contractor completed the repairs, he was notified in writing by the owner of massive failure and peeling of the coal tar coating on about 70 percent of the surface of the coated steel.

The contractor's personnel again inspected the failed coating on the steel. The steel looked like a jungle. Massive peeling was prevalent throughout. Some hanging peels were eight to 10 feet long. The bare exposed steel under the coating was rapidly rusting.

The owner demanded that the contractor repair the failed coating. This time, the contractor estimated that virtually all the coating would have to be removed by sand blasting and the steel recoated under controlled temperature and moisture conditions in the field. The cost would be three to four times the original contract cost. This time the contractor decided to stand on his position that he was not responsible for the failure and refused to repair the failed coating at his own expense.

At this point, the contractor called his insurance agent and asked whether his insurance policy would cover this situation. The agent replied that the contractor's comprehensive general liability insurance policy did not cover the damage to the contractor's own product.

The owner hired a major national engineering firm to study the problem and advise it. The consulting engineer prescribed a repair procedure and also advised the owner that, if the coating failure was not repaired, it would reduce the useful life of the cooling tower by corrosion and ultimate structural failure from 25 years to seven years. The engineer prescribed an alternate to recoating the steel, which was to add considerable structural steel in the areas where structural failure was predicted to first occur from corrosion.

The owner again requested that the contractor repair the coating according to the consulting engineer's prescribed procedure, or add the additional steel to the structure according to the engineer's alternate structural augmentation plan.

The contractor reestimated both alternatives and found that either alternative would cost at least four times the original coating contract amount. Again the contractor declined the owner's demand that he repair or structurally augment the steel at his own expense.

The owner brought suit against the contractor, alleging that the contractor had failed to comply with the requirements of the specifications and had negligently applied the specified coal tar coating, as a result of which the coating had failed. The owner claimed enormous damages in the amount of either the value of recoating the steel, or alternatively to structurally augment the steel, or for the diminution in value due to the diminished useful life of the cooling tower from 25 years to seven years. The contractor answered by claiming that the specifications were defective. The contractor counterclaimed for the costs of repairs that he had made to the coating, and brought third-party complaints against the engineer for negligently specifying the coal tar coating product and method of application, and against the manufacturer of the coal tar coating for misrepresentation and breach of warranty as to the quality and suitability of the product for the intended use.

After the action was commenced, the contractor reported the suit in writing to his insurer. The insurer replied by letter that, although the comprehensive general liability policy covered damage resulting from the contractor's manufactured product, it did not cover for damage to the contractor's product itself. The insurer then denied coverage.

During the discovery process in the litigation, the contractor learned that the manufacturer had introduced the specified coating to the market only several months prior to the time the specifications were written. The manufacturer's literature, upon which the architect/engineer relied in specifying the product, represented the product as suitable for use on structural steel, but the manufacturer had only tested the material on flat tank surfaces, not on irregular structural steel shapes such as were present here. The contractor also learned that the manufacturer of the coal tar coating had suggested to the specifying engineer the specified application equipment and method of application of the coating.

§ 9.3   The Insurance Policy

The contractor maintained a comprehensive general liability insurance policy covering the entire period from the time the contractor entered into a contract with the owner through the time when the owner notified the contractor of the chipping and peeling of the coal tar coating. The policy covered "occurrences" that took place during the policy period.

Relevant provisions of the policy are quoted in the following discussion. The language in these provisions is typical of, if not identical to, the language in policies issued by insurers.

DETERMINING COVERAGE

§ 9.4   General Scope of the Policy's Coverage

The contractor's policy is typical of comprehensive general liability policies.[1] The policy obligates the insurer to "pay on behalf of the insured all sums which the insured shall become legally obligated to pay as damages because of . . . bodily injury or . . . property damage to which the policy applies, caused by an occurrence." Furthermore an *occurrence* is "an accident, including continuous or repeated exposure to conditions, which results in bodily injury or property damage neither expected nor intended from the standpoint of the insured."

Unless excluded, the coverage section of a comprehensive general liability policy covers the damages the owner in this hypothetical case alleges. A loss is covered unless excluded. Because of the manner in which most such policies are written, the emphasis and primary analysis are on the policy exclusions.

§ 9.5   Exclusions from the Policy's Coverage: Damage to Named Insured's Products

In its letter to the contractor denying coverage, the insurer apparently relied upon a policy exclusion to conclude "there would be no coverage

---

[1] Tinker, *Comprehensive General Liability Insurance Perspective and Overview,* 25 Fed'n of Ins. Couns. Q. 215 (1975).

under products liability with the insurer for damage to the product itself." This exclusion excludes from the policy's coverage "property damage to the named insured's products arising out of such products or any part of such products." *Property damage* is then defined as

> (1) physical injury to or destruction of tangible property which occurs during the policy period including the loss of use thereof at any time resulting therefrom, or (2) loss of use of tangible property which has not been physically injured or destroyed provided such loss of use is caused by an occurrence during the policy period.

Named insured's products, the other operative term in the exclusion, is defined as "goods or products manufactured, sold, handled or distributed by the named insured or by others trading under his name."

The very broad definition of a named insured's products probably includes component parts of an insured's products within the meaning of the exclusion. Though the coating applied by the contractor to the steel was manufactured by a third-party manufacturer, the coating will probably be deemed to be the contractor's own product for purposes of the exclusion. Indeed, the exclusion apparently removes from the policy's coverage any "ultimate product" sold by the contractor to a customer.

Under this exclusion it does not matter whether the product itself is physically damaged or is merely rendered useless in that it does not work properly; in either event the insurer is exculpated from having to pay for the repair or replacement of a product that is incorrectly designed and/or defectively produced. It is also important to realize that when damage to a portion of a product makes the remaining part of the product useless, the exclusion is applicable to the entire product, not just to the part from which the damage arises.

This exclusion must be analyzed in the context of these facts, especially with regard to the contractor's status as a component maker/fabricator. From the standpoint of a component maker, physical damage to the component maker's portion of the overall product that arises from that component would not be covered. Similarly, loss of use of the component maker's product because of physical damage arising from its component would not be covered.

Despite the exclusion, however, the contractor's comprehensive general liability policy would seem to cover loss of use of another's product because of physical damage arising out of the component maker's part, as well as physical damage to another's product arising from a defect of the component maker's product. The distinction here is essentially between property damage confined to the work of the contractor, on the one hand, which would not be covered pursuant to the exclusion, and physical damage to the rest of the project of which the contractor's work forms a part (that is, the steel beams themselves), or physical damage to other property not owned by the contractor stemming from the contractor's allegedly defective coating, for which the contractor would be covered.

§ 9.6   —Court Interpretations of Damage to Insured's Products Exclusion

Most courts have excluded damage to an insured's product from coverage in standard comprehensive general liability insurance policies. The landmark case in this area is *Hauenstein v. Saint Paul-Mercury Indemnity Co.*[2] There, an insured sought indemnification from his insurer for damages caused by the failure of a new type of plaster the insured had distributed. The Minnesota Supreme Court held that "although there is no liability for damage to the plaster itself as a product handled and distributed by the [insured], the insurer is liable under its insurance contract for accidental damage to property caused by the application of the defective plaster."[3]

Other states have followed suit. Massachusetts adopted the *Hauenstein* rule in *Beacon Textiles Corp. v. Employers Mutual Liability Insurance Co.,*[4] in which an insured manufacturer of defective yarn was allowed to recover for damages arising from the knitting of his yarn into sweaters, but not the replacement costs of the yarn itself. Damages in *Hauenstein* (the issue was not reached in *Beacon*) were measured by "the diminution in market value of the building, or the cost of removing the defective plaster and restoring the building to its former condition, plus any loss from deprival of use, whichever is the lesser."[5] Replacement costs for the plaster itself were not covered.

In a few cases, courts have allowed recovery of replacement costs despite the standard "named insured's products" exclusion. These cases turn on the loss of separate identity of an insured's products following sale to a third party. Insurers in such cases have been required to pay replacement costs as well as costs of damages to the third party's property. These cases usually involve component parts. In the leading case, *Pittsburgh Plate Glass Co. v. Fidelity & Casualty Co. of New York,*[6] the court allowed full recovery of replacement costs when an insured's product was "no longer identifiable as a separate entity but [was] intended to and [did] become a part of the finished product."

The Massachusetts Supreme Judicial Court in *Beacon,* however, took a dim view of such logic. It noted "it is true that in the sweaters the yarn

---

[2] 242 Minn. 354, 65 N.W.2d 122 (1954).

[3] *Id.,* 65 N.W.2d at 126.

[4] 355 Mass. 643, 246 N.E.2d 673 (1969).

[5] Hauenstein v. Saint Paul-Mercury Indem. Co., 65 N.W.2d at 125.

[6] 281 F.2d 538 (2d Cir. 1960).

had ceased to have independent significance in a physical product, but it remained yarn, and the dollar effect of the injury thereto is separately ascertainable."[7] A proposition that can be generally applied is the court's observation that the dollar effect of replacement costs is separately ascertainable. Thus, in Massachusetts, it is unlikely that the *Pittsburgh Plate Glass* reasoning will be adopted as an extension of Hauenstein-Beacon. In Massachusetts and in other states following this broader interpretation of the exclusion, the contractor will probably not be allowed recovery of replacement costs of the coating itself.

§ 9.7   —Extent of Coverage under the Exclusion

The only remaining issue arising under the damage to insured's products exclusion of the insurer's policy is the extent of the coverage Hauenstein-Beacon would require the insurer to provide to the contractor. Although another exclusion eliminates from coverage damages "arising from loss of use of tangible property which has not been physically injured or destroyed" as a result of "(1) a delay in or lack of performance by or on behalf of the named insured of any contract or agreement or (2) the failure of the named insured's products . . . to meet the level of performance, quality, fitness or durability warranted or represented by the named insured," under some circumstances the policy may cover loss of use of another's property resulting from deficiencies in the contractor's product. The proper measure of recovery under Hauenstein-Beacon, then, would be the diminution in value of the owner's cooling tower, or the removal and restoration costs arising from replacement of the coating, whichever is less.

§ 9.8   —Damage to Work Performed Exclusion

Even though a "products" hazard under a comprehensive general liability policy is distinct from the so-called "completed operations" hazard, the two are often intertwined. The products hazard deals with

> bodily injury and property damage arising out of the named insured's products or reliance upon a representation or warranty made at any time with respect thereto, but only if the bodily injury or property damage occurs away from premises owned by or rented to the named insured and after physical possession of such products has been relinquished to the others.

---

[7] Beacon Textiles Corp. v. Employers Mut. Liab. Ins. Co., 355 Mass. at 646, 246 N.E.2d at 673.

The completed operations hazard is applicable to

> bodily injury and property damage arising out of operations or reliance upon
> a representation or warranty made at any time with respect thereto, but only
> if the bodily injury or property damage occurs after such operations have
> been completed or abandoned and occurs away from premises owned by or
> rented to the named insured. "Operations" include materials, parts or equip-
> ment furnished in connection therewith.

It is important to realize that, unlike many other forms of insurance,
coverage under a comprehensive general liability policy in this form is not
eliminated merely because a particular activity can be characterized as either a product or completed operations hazard.

Here, any liability on the part of the contractor would seem to arise because of work it performed as a fabricator more than as a handler of the
beams, and hence the completed operations hazard would seem more pertinent to any analysis of coverage than the products hazard. As the completed operations counterpart to the exclusion discussed above, a damage
to work performed exclusion excludes coverage for "property damage to
work performed by or on behalf of the named insured arising out of
the work or any portion thereof, or out of materials, parts or equipment
furnished in connection therewith." Because the heart of the owner's allegations against the contractor deals with improper preparation of the
beams and misapplication of the surface coating, a damage to work performed exclusion rather than a damage to the insured's products exclusion
seems applicable, although the net effect of each would be about the same.
Nevertheless, the insurer's reliance on the former—if incorrect as a technical matter—provides the contractor with a slim reed upon which to partially challenge the insurer's denial.

§ 9.9   —Definition of Property Damage

An issue similar to the exclusion against property damage to the insured's
product itself is also found in the definitions in a comprehensive general
liability policy. *Property damage* is defined in the policy as

> (1) physical injury to or destruction of tangible property which occurs dur-
> ing the policy period, including . . . loss of use . . . resulting therefrom,
> or (2) loss of use of tangible property which has not been physically in-
> jured or destroyed provided such loss of use is caused by an occurrence
> during the policy period.

This definition creates substantial problems when the damage is caused
by defective materials that do not cause physical damage to other parts of

the building. A literal meaning of the definition would lead to the conclusion that if the defective coating did not physically injure other parts of the cooling tower it would not be property damage and would therefore not be covered, unless the sole damage was loss of use.

One line of cases provides the contractor with authority to satisfy this definition with our facts. As previously noted, in the *Hauenstein* case in Minnesota, the court decided that defective plaster that had to be removed after it shrunk and cracked caused physical damage to the remainder of the building within the terms of the general liability policy. The court ruled that: The measure of damages is the diminution of the market value of the building, or the cost of removing the defective product and restoring the building to its former condition, plus any loss from the deprival of use, whichever is the lesser.[8]

Using this reasoning, other courts have subsequently found physical damage to other property after installation of the insured's defective product in cases in which:

1. Defective cement weakened the structural integrity of concrete, requiring that shoring be left in place for an extended time and that it be supplemented with additional shoring[9]

2   Insulating wall panels blistered inside refrigeration rooms, which did not affect their insulating capacity but did cause an unsightly appearance[10]

3. Defective siding was removed from buildings[11]

4. Concrete block with a prefinished exterior presented an unsightly, mottled appearance[12]

5. Defective steel tubing caused a radiant heating system to fail[13]

6. Defective weld wire used in securing the joints of a nuclear submarine had to be ripped out[14]

7. Defective aluminum doors installed in homes had to be replaced.[15]

---

[8] Hauenstein v. Saint Paul-Mercury Indem. Co., 65 N.W.2d at 125.

[9] United States Fidelity & Guar. Co. v. Nevada Cement Co., 93 Nev. 179, 561 P.2d 1335 (1977).

[10] Western Casualty & Sur. Co. v. Polar Panel Co., 457 F.2d 957 (8th Cir. 1972).

[11] Bowman Steel Corp. v. Lumbermens Mut. Casualty Co., 364 F.2d 246 (3d Cir. 1966). *See also* Pittsburgh Plate Glass Co. v. Fidelity & Cas. Co. of N.Y., 281 F.2d 538 (3d Cir. 1960).

[12] Dakota Block Co. v. Western Casualty & Sur. Co., 132 N.W.2d 826 (S.D. 1965).

[13] *See* Bundy Tubing Co. v. Royal Indem. Co., 298 F.2d 151 (6th Cir. 1962).

[14] Arcos Corp. v. American Mut. Liab. Ins. Co., 350 F. Supp. 380 (D.D.C. Pa. 1972).

[15] Geddes & Smith, Inc. v. Saint Paul-Mercury Indem. Co., 63 Cal. 2d 602, 407 P.2d 868, 47 Cal. Rptr. 564 (Cal. 1965). *See also* Eichler Homes, Inc. v. Underwriters at Lloyd's London, 238 Cal. App. 532, 47 Cal. Rptr. 843 (1965).

Most of these cases appear to assume that using defective materials reduces the value of a building, because they do not discuss the evidence on this point. A Massachusetts case has specifically held that diminution in value would constitute property damage. In *Continental Casualty Co. v. Gilbane Building Co.,*[16] the court stated: "There is nothing in the definition [of property damage] requiring physical injury or destruction of property. The guide to determination of coverage is the kind of property rather than the kind of injury. Tangible property rendered useless is injured and hence is covered.

Other courts, however, have rejected this assumption, holding that defective materials cannot diminish the market value of incomplete, nonexistent, or unmarketable structures.[17] For example, in a case in which defective structural supports had to be repaired in place during the construction of a nuclear power plant, the court ruled that the plant had not been diminished in value because it was not yet built.[18]

Several other cases have limited but not entirely rejected the position that comprehensive general liability policies cover diminution in value caused by defective materials. These cases have held that defective components that do not cause damage to other parts of the building do not constitute property damage.[19] Under this rule, there may be coverage under a general liability policy if the defective product becomes so integrated into other tangible property that correcting the defective portion would cause damage to some other part of the building.[20] For example, in a case involving defective studs, the cost of tearing out and putting back other parts of the building to reach the studs was found to be recoverable property damage, but the expense of removing the studs themselves was not recoverable.[21]

---

[16] 391 Mass. 143, 147, 461 N.E.2d 209, 212–13 (1984).

[17] Stone & Webster Eng'g Corp. v. American Motorist Ins. Co., 458 F. Supp. 792 (D.C. Va. 1978); Yakima Cement Prods. Co. v. Great Am. Ins. Co., 93 Wash. 2d 210, 608 P.2d 254 (Wash. 1980). *But see* Weedo v. Stone-E-Brick, Inc., 81 N.J. 233, 405 A.2d 788 (1979).

[18] Stone & Webster Eng'g Corp. v. American Motorist Ins. Co., 458 F. Supp. 792 (E.D. Va. 1978).

[19] St. Paul Fire & Marine Ins. Co. v. Coss, 79 Cal. App. 3d 284, 145 Cal. Rptr. 836 (1978); *see also* Hamilton Die Cast, Inc. v. United States Fidelity & Guar. Co., 508 F.2d 417 (7th Cir. 1975); Dreis & Krump Mfg. v. Phoenix Ins. Co., 548 F.2d 681 (7th Cir. 1977).

[20] St. Paul Fire & Marine Ins. Co. v. Coss, 79 Cal. App. 3d 284, 145 Cal. Rptr. 836 (1978); Vernon Williams & Son Constr., Inc. v. Continental Ins. Co., 591 S.W.2d 760 (Tenn. 1979); St. Paul Fire & Marine Ins. Co. v. Sears, Roebuck & Co., 603 F.2d 780 (9th Cir. 1979).

[21] Wyoming Sawmills, Inc. v. Transportation Ins. Co., 282 Or. 401, 578 P.2d 1253 (Or. 1978); *see also* Hartford Accident & Indem. Co. v. Olson Bros., 187 Neb. 179, 188 N.W.2d 699 (1971); *but see* Fresno Economy Import Used Cars, Inc. v. United States Fidelity & Guar. Co., 76 Cal. App. 3d 272, 142 Cal. Rptr. 681 (1978).

§ 9.10   —Other Possible Exclusions Probably Not Waived by Insurer

In the hypothetical situation posed, the insurer's disclaimer letter did not refer explicitly to any specific provisions of its policy. The letter did, however, observe generally that, although the policy would not cover "damage to the product itself," it would cover "bodily injury or property damage result[ing] from [the contractor's] manufactured product." One can reasonably infer that the insurer relied upon a damage to the insured's products exclusion when making his general observations about the policy's coverages and exclusions. The contractor could argue that the insurer's failure to cite other relevant exclusions in its letter constitutes a waiver of those exclusions. Such an argument, however, may not be successful, because "[w]aiver or estoppel cannot be the basis for creating an original grant of coverage where no such contract previously existed."[22]

§ 9.11   —Failure to Perform Exclusion

The failure to perform exclusion was one such significant exclusion not referred to in the insurer's disclaimer letter. This exclusion eliminates coverage for

> loss of use of tangible property which has not been physically injured or destroyed resulting from (1) . . . lack of performance by . . . the named insured of any contract or agreement, or (2) the failure of the named insured's products or work performed by or on behalf of the named insured to meet the level of performance, quality, fitness or durability warranted or represented by the named insured.

As is evident from this language, this exclusion is unusual in that it applies only to the loss of use of otherwise undamaged tangible property that results from a product's failure to perform as the named insured warrants or represents.

§ 9.12   —Sistership Exclusion

The second exclusion upon which an insurer may rely is the sistership exclusion, which exempts the insurer from paying product recall expenses. It is intended to exclude the cost of the preventive action of withdrawing a

---

[22] Wyoming Sawmills, Inc. v. Transportation Ins. Co., 282 Or. 401, 404, 578 P.2d 1253, 1258 (1978).

product when a danger is apprehended.[23] This exclusion eliminates from coverage "damages claimed for the withdrawal, inspection, repair, replacement, or loss of use [caused by the withdrawal of the insured's product] from the market or from use because of any known or suspected defect or deficiency therein."

Although this exclusion has been used mostly in automobile recall situations, the literal language of the exclusion would seem to exclude coverage of costs the contractor in our hypothetical case might incur in repairing the coating. This is why this exclusion has been raised by insurers of suppliers who are sued by contractors for defective construction products or materials. Most cases have rejected applying this exclusion in such situations, primarily because the claims did not usually involve damages from withdrawing the product from the market, but only from a building.[24] However, except for a 1974 decision by the Court of Appeals of New York holding sistership exclusions inapplicable to third parties,[25] most courts have restricted application of sistership exclusions to actual cases of product recall.[26] Because of the literal wording of the exclusion, however, it seems likely that the sistership exclusion might also be asserted as a defense by the insurer.

§ 9.13 —Pollution Exclusion

Under the factual scenario given in § 9.2, a pollution exclusion would not apply. However, it is one of the exclusions most often argued in environmental or hazardous waste litigation. This pollution exclusion exempts the insurer from paying for damages

> arising out of the discharge, dispersal, release or escape of smoke, vapors, soot, fumes, acids, . . . contaminants or pollutants into or upon land, the atmosphere or any water course or body of water; but this exclusion does not apply if such discharge, dispersal, release or escape is sudden and accidental.

The last clause has been the focus of recent litigation over the scope of the policy, as insureds and insurers have argued over what constitutes "sudden and accidental" discharge. A recent Massachusetts case has stretched the

---

[23] Yakima Cement Prods. Co. v. Great Am. Ins. Co., 93 Wash. 2d 210, 608 P.2d 254 (Wash. 1980).

[24] Wyoming Sawmills, Inc. v. Transportation Ins. Co., 282 Or. 401, 578 P.2d 1253 (Or. 1978); Yakima Cement Prods. Co. v. Great Am. Ins. Co., 93 Wash. 2d 210, 608 P.2d 254 (Wash. 1980); *contra* Commercial Union Assurance Co. v. Glass Lined Pipe Co., 372 S.2d 1305 (Ala. 1978).

[25] Thomas J. Lipton, Inc. v. Liberty Mut. Ins. Co., 357 N.Y.S.2d 705, 34 N.Y.2d 356 (1974).

[26] *See, e.g.,* Arcos Corp. v. American Mut. Liab. Ins. Co., 350 F. Supp. 380 (D.D.C. 1972).

definition on the basis that "sudden and accidental" must be construed with the insured's interest in mind.[27] In that case, the prolonged leakage of gas from an underground tank was considered sudden and accidental from the insured's standpoint, requiring the insurer to provide coverage. Other states, though they may use the same reasoning, may not construe the term quite as liberally.[28]

§ 9.14   —Care, Custody, and Control Exclusion

Another exclusion potentially available to the insurer is the care, custody, and control exclusion, which exempts coverage of damage to "property in the care, custody or control of the insured or as to which the insured is for any purpose exercising physical control." Insurers have attempted to rely on this exclusion for property damage claims when the property was under the control of the contractor during construction, even though the damages occurred after construction.[29]

In the present fact scenario, that same argument is available to the insurer, as the damaged property was at one time under the contractor's care, custody, and control. This exclusion would probably not apply, however, as a number of courts have held it inapplicable after a contractor or subcontractor has completed its work and relinquished control of the materials installed or work performed.[30] A principal reason for this approach is that the exclusion is intended to encourage insured parties to exercise care in ongoing work. The exclusion would thus apply to work being performed by the contractor and his employees but not to work being performed by employees of other companies, even though they might be working for the contractor. In Crane Service & Equipment Corp. v. United States Fidelity & Guaranty Co.,[31] a damaged rented crane was covered by the policy despite the care, custody, and control exclusion, as the crane was only maintained and operated by the rental company and not by the insured general contractor.

---

[27] Shapiro v. Public Serv. Mut. Ins. Co., 19 Mass. App. Ct. 648, 477 N.E.2d 146 (1985). *See* Keeton, Insurance Law § 5.4(a) (1971).

[28] *See, e.g.,* Reliance Ins. Corp. v. Martin, 467 N.E.2d 287, 126 Ill. App. 3d 94, 97–98 (1984); Lansco, Inc. v. Department of Envtl. Protection, 350 A.2d 520, 138 N.J. Sup. 275, 282 (1975); Buckeye Union Ins. Co. v. Liberty Solvents & Chem. Co., 17 Oh. App. 3d 127, 132–33, 477 N.E.2d 1227 (1984); United Pac. Ins. Co. v. Van's Westlake Union, 34 Wash. App. 708, 714–15, 664 P.2d 1262, *review denied*, 100 Wash. 2d 1018 (1983).

[29] Continental Casualty Co. v. Gilbane Bldg. Co., 391 Mass. 143, 147, 461 N.E.2d 209, 212–13 (1984).

[30] Todd Shipyards Corp. v. Turbine Serv., Inc., 674 F.2d 401 (5th Cir. 1982); Continental Cas. Co. v. Gilbane Bldg. Co., 391 Mass. 143, 461 N.E.2d 209 (1984).

[31] 22 Mass. App. Ct. 666, 496 N.E.2d 833 (1986).

Neither the insured nor his employees are required to be present when the damage occurs, however, to be deemed to have care, custody, and control over ongoing work.[32]

§ 9.15   Insurer's Common Law
Obligation to Investigate

The insurer's duty to investigate arises, quite obviously, only upon receipt of notice from the insured. How quickly the insurer must act and investigate, however, is not as clear. There do not appear to be many cases in which the insurer failed to promptly investigate the accident. In a standard comprehensive general liability policy, for example, there is no affirmative obligation on the insurer to immediately or promptly investigate the matter after receiving notice.

Duties arising between the insured and insurer, based upon their fiduciary relationship, include the duty to make a diligent effort to investigate the facts.[33] If the insurer undertakes the defense, it has an obligation to investigate, and its failure to do so may constitute bad faith if the insurer subsequently refuses to settle without having appraised itself of the available information.[34]

The insurer has an obligation to make a diligent investigation, in order to ascertain facts upon which an intelligent settlement can be made.[35]However, simply because the insurer may promptly make a preliminary evaluation of its liability, based upon an investigation, the insurer is not required to immediately settle.[36]

§ 9.16   Obligation to Investigate under Unfair
Insurance Practices Statutes

Some states have enacted statutes requiring insurers to proceed expeditiously with claims investigation. For example, Massachusetts prohibits "unfair claim settlement practices" and includes within the definition of that term:

(b) Failing to acknowledge and act reasonably promptly upon communications with respect to claims arising under insurance policies;

---

[32] Advance Elec., Inc. v. United States Fidelity & Guar. Co., 818 F.2d 378 (5th Cir. 1987).

[33] Warren v. American Family Mut. Ins. Co., 122 Wis. 2d 381, 361 N.W.2d 724 (1984).

[34] 14 Couch on Insurance 2d § 51.56 (rev. ed. 1982).

[35] Glendale v. Farmers, Inc. Exch., 126 Ariz. 118, 613 P.2d 278 (1980).

[36] Smiley v. Manchester Ins. & Indem. Co., 71 Ill. 2d 306, 375 N.E.2d 118, 16 Ill. Dec. 487 (1978).

(c)   Failing to adopt and implement reasonable standards for the prompt investigation of claims arising under insurance policies.[37]

Note, however, that by conducting an investigation, the insurer does not waive any defenses to coverage it may have. In fact, an insurer who promptly conducts an investigation has probably not even waived a defense of lack of timely notice of the claim.[38]

INSURER'S OBLIGATION TO DEFEND

§ 9.17   Coverage for Defense

Two issues exist with respect to the contractor's comprehensive general liability insurance policy with the insurer:

1.   Does the insurance policy cover all or any part of the damages that the owner seeks against the contractor?
2.   Is the insurer required to provide the contractor with a defense in the action by the owner?

§ 9.18   The Duty to Defend

Under the policy, the insurer is required to defend any suit against the contractor in which the allegations seek damages for actions covered by the policy. The policy further obligates the insurer "to defend any suit against the insured seeking damages on account of such bodily injury or property damage, even if any of the allegations of the suit are groundless, false or fraudulent." As a general rule, "the obligation of a liability insurance company under a policy provision requiring it to defend an action brought against the insured by a third party is to be determined by the allegations of the complaint in such action."[39] The insurer is obligated to defend the contractor in any action in which property damage that may fall within the coverage of the policy is alleged. The scope of the inquiry to

---

[37] Mass. Gen. L. ch. 176D, § 9(g) (1986).

[38] Howard Fuel v. Lloyd's Underwriters, 558 F. Supp. 1103 (S.D.N.Y. 1984); Weis v. International Ins. Co., 567 F. Supp. 631 (N.D. Ga. 1983).

[39] Annotation, *Allegations in Third Person's Actions Against Insured as Determining Liability Insurer's Duty to Defend,* 50 A.L.R.2d 458, 465. *See also* Miller v. United States Fidelity & Guar. Co., 291 Mass. 445, 197 N.E. 75 (1935).

decide this issue is based on the allegations in the owner's complaint, even if they are "groundless, false and fraudulent."[40]

The duty to defend is broader than the duty to pay. In order to avoid its obligation to defend, the insurer must show that there is no possible factual or legal basis upon which it might ultimately be held obligated to indemnify the insured. Thus, when one count alleged intentional and malicious acts of the insured (beyond the scope of coverage), but other counts were for reckless or negligent acts (within the scope), the insurer was obligated to defend.[41]

However, no duty to defend arises until a request for defense is made. In a case in which the insurer did not request a defense until after a judgment had been entered, the insurer was not required to pay the cost of defense. Although initial allegations included claims covered by the policy, final determination was on a basis outside of the policy.[42]

In its complaint against the contractor, assume that the owner alleged:

1. The contractor failed to furnish, coat, fabricate, and erect the structural steel for the cooling tower of the University Total Energy Plant in accordance with the terms, conditions, and specifications of the University's agreement with the contractor.

2. The structural steel supplied by the contractor was defectively fabricated and coated and was not suitable for use in the cooling tower of the University Total Energy Plant.

3. As a direct approximate result of the contractor's failure to comply with the terms, conditions, and specifications of the University's contract with the contractor, the University expended substantial amounts of time, at a substantial expense, repairing the defects and structural steel supplied by the contractor, and the useful life of the structural steel in the cooling tower has been substantially diminished.

If there is a possibility that such allegations may give rise to coverage under the policy, any doubts being resolved in the contractor's favor, then the insurer has an obligation to defend.[43]

---

[40] *See* J. D'Amico, Inc. v. Boston, 345 Mass. 218, 186 N.E.2d 716 (1962) in which in a declaratory judgment action the court required the insurer to defend a suit against the insured and made no decision on coverage because the facts were not present as to whether the insurer had defenses against coverage for willfulness.

[41] Nationwide Mut. Fire Ins. Co. v. Burke, 90 App. Div. 2d 626, 456 N.Y.S.2d 223 (3d Dept. 1982).

[42] Washington v. Federal Kemper Ins. Co., 60 Md. App. 288, 482 A.2d 503 (1984).

[43] Appelman on Insurance n.193; County of Munroe v. Travelers Ins. Co., 100 Misc. 2d 417, 419 N.Y.S.2d 410 (1979).

It should also be noted that an insurer may have an obligation to defend even if the allegations in the complaint are not within the policy coverage if the insurer knows or by reasonable investigation should know of facts that would bring the suit within the policy coverage.[44]

§ 9.19   Deductibles

The vast majority of primary insurance policies have a *deductible,* the threshold of the insurer's obligation to indemnify the insured. The deductible, usually stated as a simple amount of money, presents a host of questions. Is the insured obligated to obtain the consent of the insurer for a settlement that will be entirely covered by the deductible? Can the insurer force the insured to accept an offer of compromise within the deductible when the insured believes there is no supportable claim? Are attorneys' fees paid for by the insured included in the calculation to determine whether the deductible has been reached? When are claims aggregated for purposes of the deductible, and when is the amount of the deductible applied to each claim?

There is no defined body of insurance law concerning deductibles or "self-insured retention." Rather, one must look to various aspects of insurance law for answers to these questions, along with, of course, the terms of the policy themselves.

Under the terms of most comprehensive general liability policies, the contractor is obligated to cooperate and assist with settlement of any claims or lawsuits. However, the contractor's consent is not required to the terms of any settlement. The insured's obligation to cooperate has been upheld by various courts, even when there was a dispute between insured and insurer as to whether a settlement should have been negotiated. *Orion Insurance Co. v. General Electric Co.*[45] concerned claims arising from the crash of a DC-10, in which the tires (manufactured by Goodyear) and the engine (manufactured by General Electric) were implicated. General Electric (GE) had $25 million of coverage, with a $5 million deductible. One of GE's insurers also insured Goodyear, which had only a $500,000 deductible. The insurers agreed to settle claims for $13.5 million and to allocate $8 million of that to GE, which did not agree to the settlement. Instead, GE claimed that its insurers had a conflict of interest (the court agreed) and had negotiated and settled in bad faith so that GE ended up paying a large percentage of the settlement. Here the court disagreed. The insurance policy did not require GE's consent to settlement. This was not

---

[44] Woodward v. North Carolina Farm Bureau Mut. Ins. Co., 44 N.C. App. 282, 261 S.E.2d 43 (1979); Aetna Ins. Co. v. Lythgoe, 618 P.2d 1057 (Wyo. 1980).

[45] 493 N.Y.S.2d 397, 129 Misc. 2d 466 (1985).

202 GETTING INSURANCE COMPANY ON BOARD

analogous to potential settlement within the policy when claims are above the policy limits, as that circumstance potentially involves personal assets and interests of the insured. The obligation upon insurers to negotiate and settle in good faith is therefore not viewed in the same fashion when settlement concerns the deductible as when it concerns an amount in excess of coverage.[46]

§ 9.20   Defending under a Reservation of Rights

Insurers typically issue a "reservation of rights" letter when undertaking the defense of the insured. By defending in this fashion, the insurer is preserving its right to determine at a later time that the allegations are not covered by the policy. The insurer's failure to reserve its rights in this manner may constitute a waiver of its right to contest payment for the defense. In *Magoun v. Liberty Mutual Insurance Co.,*[47] the insurer offered to undertake the defense of tort claims under a reservation of rights. The insured declined that offer and undertook its own defense, but with the acquiescence and assistance of the insurer. This letter states that the insurer is going to defend on behalf of the insured, but reserves the right to decide at a later time that the claims it is defending are not covered by its insurance policy. After judgment in favor of the insured, it sought recovery of its defense costs and attorneys' fees. The court held the insurer liable to pay those costs, notwithstanding the possibility that the original claims may have been within an exclusion to the policy, because of the insurer's cooperation in the defense. Thus, there was no effective reservation of rights.

An effective reservation of rights defense will allow the insurer to subsequently disclaim liability.[48]

§ 9.21   Insured's Right to Independent Counsel Paid for by Insurer

Generally, the insurer's duty to defend does not include an obligation to pay attorneys' fees for an attorney consulted by the insured before the insurer provides its own attorney, if the insurer has not received notice of action until after the first attorneys' fees have been earned.[49] Because of

---

[46] *Accord,* American Home Assurance Co. v. Hermann's Warehouse Corp., 215 N.J. Super. 260, 521 A.2d 903 (1987).

[47] 346 Mass. 677, 195 N.E.2d 514 (1964).

[48] Cassidy v. Liberty Mut. Ins. Co., 338 Mass. 139, 154 N.E.2d 253 (1958).

[49] Cobb v. Empire Fire & Marine Ins. Co., 488 So. 2d 349 (La. Ct. App. 1986).

this rule, prompt notice is important to any possible recovery of independent attorneys' fees.

The general rule concerning the right to recover independent counsel fees is based upon the identity (or lack thereof) of interest between the insured and insurer. If the insurer has interests that do not exactly coincide with those of the insured, the insurer may be entitled to reimbursement for its own independent attorneys' fees. In *Allstate Insurance v. Riggin,*[50] the insurer undertook to defend the insured, who had an interest in proving that the consequences of his acts were unintended. The insurer's interest was to show that the acts did not cause the injury, and not that the consequences were unintended. As the insured and the insurer had different and potentially conflicting interests in the way the case was decided, the insurer was thus obligated to pay for the insured's independent defense counsel.

If a conflict of interest has arisen between an insured and his liability carrier, the insured's desire to exclusively control the defense must yield to the obligation to defend, and the latter obligation will extend to costs of independent counsel.[51] This general rule should prevail when a conflict between insurer and insured begins to arise.

§ 9.22 Declaratory Relief for Defense Costs and Coverage

Coverage can be finally determined in many cases only when the facts are fully developed. If the issue of coverage is simply a question of law and not of facts, however, it would appear that coverage could be determined by a court at any time. Coverage is also determined by the actual facts finally asserted by the claimant in the action against the insured and is not necessarily confined to the allegations in the complaint.

In order to determine coverage, the insurer's defenses must also be considered. For example, in *J. D'Amico, Inc. v. Boston,*[52] the complaint alleged trespass and the policy covered only accidental, not intentional, trespass. The court determined that, based on the pure allegations in the complaint, the claim was broad enough to potentially be within the coverage of the policy. The court found that the facts as to whether the trespass was accidental or intentional had not been sufficiently developed to determine coverage, and a determination on coverage had to wait until the action by the claimant against the insured was tried. In the meantime, the insurer was required to defend the insured, however.

---

[50] 125 A.D.2d 515, 509 N.Y.S.2d 594 (1986).

[51] Executive Aviation, Inc. v. National Ins. Underwriters, 16 Cal. App. 3d 799, 94 Cal. Rptr. 347 (1971).

[52] 345 Mass. 218, 186 N.E.2d 716 (1962).

§ 9.23   —Procedure

The issues of defense costs and coverage can be raised in most states as they are raised in Massachusetts,[53] for example, where courts will address the issues separately.[54] However, it would appear that a declaratory judgment action on the issue of defense costs only would open the insurer to a counterclaim for a declaratory judgment on coverage. If the issue of coverage were ripe for decision, the court could address the coverage issue at the same time. Such an issue might not be ripe, based upon the theory that coverage depends upon issues finally presented at trial. See § **9.22.**

Furthermore, the insured may be entitled to recover the costs and attorneys' fees incurred in bringing a successful declaratory judgment action against the insurer to enforce the insurer's duty to defend.[55]

§ 9.24   Bad Faith Refusal to Defend

The insurer's refusal to defend may constitute bad faith if the matters at issue are subsequently determined to be within the scope of the policy. For insurers, there is a substantial risk in deciding whether it is obligated to provide a defense.[56] And the insurer's failure to provide a defense when obligated to do so may be sufficient to sustain a cause of action in tort as well as contract.[57]

The unjustified refusal to defend may bind the insurer to pay a judgment rendered against the insured, or to pay a settlement entered into in good faith.[58] Also, if the insurer negligently rejects a settlement offer, exposing the insured to damages in excess of the policy limit, the insurer may be liable to the insured for those damages.[59]

In sum, there are substantial incentives for insurers to undertake a defense when possibly covered by the policy and significant remedies available to the insured if the insurer unjustifiably refuses to defend.

---

[53] Under the Declaratory Judgment Act, Mass. Gen. L. ch. 231A, §§ 1-9 (1986).

[54] J. D'Amico, Inc. v. Boston, 345 Mass. 218, 186 N.E.2d 716 (1962).

[55] Willoughby Hills v. Cincinnati Ins. Co., 26 Oh. App. 3d 146, 499 N.E.2d 31, 26 Ohio R. 363 (1986).

[56] McGroarty v. Great Am. Ins. Co., 36 N.Y.2d 358, 329 N.E.2d 172, 368 N.Y.S.2d 485 (1975).

[57] Colton v. Swain, 527 F.2d 296 (7th Cir. 1975); Hodges v. State Farm Mut. Auto Ins. Co., 488 F. Supp. 1057 (D.S.C. 1980).

[58] Saragan v. Bousquet, 322 Mass. 14, 75 N.E.2d 649 (1947); Abrams v. Factory Mut. Liab. Ins. Co., 298 Mass. 141, 10 N.E.2d 82 (1937).

[59] Savio v. Travelers Ins. Co., 678 P.2d 549 (Colo. App. 1983).

CHAPTER 10

REPRESENTING THE ARCHITECT/ENGINEER IN A FAILURE OR COLLAPSE

James Eagle Frankel, Esquire*

James Eagle Frankel is the senior partner of the Construction Industry Practice Group of the national law firm of Shea and Gould, and is a recognized specialist and lecturer on construction industry legal issues directed to the architectural and engineering community. He specializes in construction litigation and has represented the many sides of failure and collapse catastrophes, including the engineer of record of the Schoharie Bridge over the New York State Thruway which collapsed in 1987 causing the death of 10 people, as well as one of the structural engineering defendants in the John Hancock glass and superstructure failure in Boston.

A graduate of Ohio University, Mr. Frankel received his J.D. degree from the Albany Law School of Union College and thereafter practiced with the New York State Attorney General's office in its Claims and Litigation Unit which defended all of the state building agencies engaged in the construction of highways, buildings, and other constructed facilities. Mr. Frankel is a member of the American Bar Association; he is General Counsel to the New York Chapter of the American Institute of Architects and is an associate member of the New York State Society of Professional Engineers, the New York Society of Architects, and the Construction Specification Institute.

*The author wishes to express his appreciation for the assistance of Shea & Gould's Construction Industry Practice Group, and in particular Deirdre Byrne, Esquire, for its valuable contribution to this effort.

§ 10.1   Representing the Design Professional

The catastrophic failure or collapse of a constructed facility and its after-math is invariably a time of extreme anxiety for the design professional and her counsel. Both are called upon to insure the preservation of eviden-tiary material to be used in the development of those legal theories neces-sary to the successful avoidance of a claim or in the defense of the design professional. The correct time to protect the design professional from the risk of exposure is during the development of the design professional/owner contract documents.

This chapter addresses procedural and substantive safeguards that should be negotiated prior to the initiation of the design. In addition, it dis-cusses some of the considerations which might be employed by counsel for the design professional after collapse or failure has occurred, recognizing that when the collapse or failure is discovered, counsel must immediately safeguard the architect/engineer from potential liability.

For the purposes of this chapter, a *design professional* is an architect or an engineer whose contractual duties principally involve design and/or su-pervisory work. A design professional is not necessarily an engineer acting as a subconsultant to an architect who has total design responsibility, but is also an engineer with primary design responsibility and a direct contractual relationship with the owner, as is often the case in contracts for bridge and highway design. An *owner* herein refers simply to the party with whom the design professional has contracted to perform services. Therefore, "owner" could refer to another design professional who has secured the architect or engineer's services for a particular project. Finally, for the purposes of this chapter, *failure* means an overall loss of stability and structural integrity but need not be a wholesale collapse.

This chapter guides the reader through some of the important preliminary considerations which must be addressed as soon as a failure/collapse occurs so that the architect/engineer might be saved from the agonizing experience of being named as a defendant in a massive, time-consuming, and expensive litigation. Moreover, early recognition of potential areas of limitation of liability and/or other mechanisms designed to free the architect/engineer from such litigation are also addressed.

Catastrophic failure or collapse usually does not visit the architect/engineer. If it does, rarely would the same architect/engineer suffer more than one such claim in a career. If failure or collapse does occur, however, the inability or failure to act properly in the early hours, days, weeks, and months immediately after the event can bring about the end of the design professional's career and potentially the loss of her firm's equity as well as the individual's own net worth. Proper guidance at this time is invaluable.

DUTIES DURING THE DESIGN PHASE

§ 10.2   Initial Design Phase

If a catastrophic failure or collapse appears to have been the result of a design phase activity, an initial inquiry must be made as to the design professional's duties during the development of the design documents.[1] What is required by the design professional in all phases of her work is usually a function of her contractual obligations to the owner or prime architect/engineer. The design professional's duties may extend, however, to third parties—contractors, laborers, visitors to the jobsite, ultimate users—depending in large part upon the obligations the contract imposes and the standard of care applied to the performance of those obligations. Standard form agreements, published by a number of organizations including the American Institute of Architects (AIA) for the architectural

---

[1] "Design documents" generally refer to the Agreement along with General Conditions, any Addenda thereto, the Plans and Specifications, and the Drawings.

community and the Engineers' Joint Contract Documents Committee[2] (EJCDC) for the engineering community, may have served as a starting point for the drafting and negotiation of the design professional agreements. However, standard forms should be meticulously adapted, modified, and adjusted to suit the needs of the parties. The standard form agreements are dangerous agreements if not carefully used. They will be referenced in this chapter because of their widespread use.

The AIA and the EJCDC separate the design professional's involvement into phases in order to allocate contract tasks. Each phase presents unique duties and possible pitfalls for the design professional. The first phase of architect/engineer involvement is termed the "Schematic Design Phase" by the AIA and the "Study and Report Phase" by the EJCDC. In this first phase, the design professional is given the widest latitude in discretion while working with the client to ascertain how to best fulfill the project's requirements. The owner supplies the design criteria,[3] which form the framework within which the architect/engineer must work in drafting the design documents. The provisions of AIA Document B141[4] require the architect to review with the owner the program and suggest alternative approaches to design and construction. During this phase of the work, a duty is imposed upon the architect to provide the owner with information sufficient to make an informed choice, thus shifting some of the decisionmaking role from the design professional to the owner.

Similarly, the EJCDC Document 1910-1[5] requires the engineer to (1) identify and analyze the requirements of government authorities having jurisdiction and (2) consult with both the owner and the responsible agency to bring the project into conformity with applicable standards.

Whether a standard form document is used or the architect/engineer or her attorney drafts the contract, it is always desirable for the design professional to become actively involved as early as possible in reviewing, commenting upon, and, in appropriate cases, modifying the owner's design criteria. By so doing, the architect/engineer may significantly reduce her risk of potential liability for failure to flag faulty or defective design criteria. Owner expectations must be achievable, and the obligations

---

[2] The Joint Committee documents are issued and published jointly by the National Society of Professional Engineers (NSPE), the American Consulting Engineers Council (ACEC), the American Society of Civil Engineers (ASCE), and the Construction Specifications Institute, Inc.

[3] Design criteria are referred to by the AIA as the "Program," and have been defined as "simply the owner's set of requirements. It should define as specifically as possible what the Owner's needs are. Typically, the program should list functions, area requirements for each function, interrelationships among functions, usage, population, and other data." W. Sabo, *A Legal Guide to AIA Documents* 15, A/E Law News (1987–1988).

[4] (1987).

[5] (1984).

assumed by the design professional must reduce exposure and limit liability whenever possible.

§ 10.3 Design Development Phase

At the end of the first phase of the design process, according to AIA and EJCDC standard documents, the architect/engineer should have a set of designs showing the scale and relationship of project components as well as a calculation that reflects the estimated project cost. The second design phase, termed the "design development phase" by the AIA and the "preliminary design phase" by the EJCDC, focuses and refines the schematic drawings in preparation for the presentation of final plans and specifications. These plans show the location, identification, dimensions, and some coordination of the design components. The specifications describe in detail the materials to be used and the workmanship to be employed.

The completed plans and specifications are not required to be perfect, but must be without substantial defect. The Iowa Supreme Court phrased the design professional's duty as follows:

> A registered practicing architect is duty bound to furnish design [documents] prepared with a reasonable degree of technical skill, such as would produce, if followed and adhered to, a building of the kind called for, without marked defects in character, strength or appearance.[6]

Once a project is in the construction phase, the role of the design professional in most instances is significantly diminished. The lion's share of exposure to liability, then, likely results from errors or omissions that occurred during the design and development of the contract documents. Bearing in mind that the design phase represents a high liability risk for the design professional, after a failure your client faces a number of potential problems that could result from errors in the design phase. As such, in a failure or collapse, the role of the lawyer and the forensic engineer or architectural consultant may be as challenging and difficult as you will ever be required to undertake.

§ 10.4 Course of Action When Presented with Faulty Design

Several dilemmas readily present themselves for discussion at this point. The first arises when the owner furnishes the architect/engineer with defective design criteria.

---

[6] Chrischilles v. Griswold, 260 Iowa 453, 150 N.W.2d 94, 98 (1967).

During the initial design phase, the design professional should review the design criteria and assess any deficiencies or possible deficiencies in them. If your client was given criteria that might subject her or the owner to downstream liability, it is incumbent upon her to make the deficiencies known to the owner when the owner attempts to impose problematic criteria that might enlarge potential design liability.

If the design professional alerts the owner that a problem exists and the owner fails to respond or responds by telling the architect/engineer to proceed, the design professional should put the owner on notice of her objection in writing. Additionally, the design professional should ask the owner for indemnity against claims arising from the particular deficiencies noted and, if she reasonably believes that public safety may be jeopardized, she should seriously consider not participating in the project. The design professional should also report unsafe practices to the appropriate public authority as some building codes mandate.

At the time of failure or collapse you, as the design professional's attorney, should determine whether these steps were taken by your client to protect herself from potential liability and, additionally, you should search your client's files carefully for supporting documentation that would provide evidentiary material to support any indemnity or protective language.

§ 10.5 Protective Contract Provisions

As the foregoing discussion suggests, there are important steps that, as a matter of contract, the design professional should take to limit her potential exposure during the negotiation of the design agreement. Among these are the use of indemnification clauses (also known as "hold harmless" clauses), limitation of liability clauses, insurance requirements, and other clauses appropriately shifting the burden of risk to the owner to approve the architect/engineer's work and narrow the scope of contract services. In commencing your representation of the design professional involved in a design-related failure, you want to determine whether your client's contract contains any such protective provisions and in what manner such provisions might be used most effectively to reduce or limit her potential liability after a failure or collapse.

§ 10.6 —Indemnification Clause

The indemnification clause seeks to shift contractually the burden of potential liability from the architect/engineer at the outset, thereby avoiding procedural maneuvering for the same result once litigation has been commenced. The indemnification clause requires the party bound to indemnify and hold harmless the owner, the design professional, and/or other parties on the project (for example, a lender, construction manager, or consultant) from resulting liability to third parties. By shifting this burden at the contract stage rather than after a problem has developed, the architect/engineer may be spared being named as a defendant or third-party defendant on a claim for which no actual liability exists. In addition, as counsel you need to consider your client's right to tender her defense and indemnity to the indemnifying party.

It is important to note that a number of states will not freely enforce such clauses as a matter of public policy because the clauses seek to absolve a party from the consequences of her own negligence.[7] If you are practicing in such a jurisdiction, you need to advise your architect/engineer client that such a clause will most likely be ineffective as a shield from liability resulting from her acts or omissions. However, a thorough review of all contracts developed to design, construct, and even supply component parts to a facility should be reviewed as early as formal or informal discovery will allow. We have, in the representation of design professionals, found indemnity obligations that have benefited our clients tucked away in sub-consultant and/or trade subcontracts to which we have been able to successfully tender both the defense as well as a fully insured indemnity. A successful tender of the defense and indemnity could be an economic life-saver to your client.

The judiciary has, somewhat inadequately, battled with the question of whether indemnification clauses in owner/contractor contracts should be construed to include the architect/engineer.[8] A cost effective way to avert such a legal tangle is a specific inclusion of the design professional in the indemnification clause to protect her against suits arising from the contractor's work. With respect to safety on the jobsite, for example, an indemnification clause like that shown in **§ 10.7**, can protect the architect/engineer from liability for contractor malfeasance. As a precaution, the design professional should specifically be named in the indemnification provision of the contractor's agreement with the owner. The architect, however, contracts separately with the owner. The architect/ engineer should therefore negotiate with the owner to be specifically included in any indemnification provision in the contractor's agreement as

---

[7] Illinois, for example, will not enforce such clauses. Ill. Rev. Stat., ch. 29, para. 61 (1975) provides:

> With respect to contracts or agreements, either public or private, for the construction, alteration, repair or maintenance of a building, structure, highway bridge, viaduct or other work dealing with construction, or for any moving, demolition or excavation connected therewith, every covenant, promise or agreement to indemnify or hold harmless another person from that person's own negligence is void as against public policy and wholly unenforceable.

[8] N. Coplan, *The Architect as Contractor's Agent,* Progressive Architecture 94 (Dec. 1982).

well as being named as an additional insured under the contractor's insurance policies.

§ 10.7 —Sample Indemnification Agreement

The design professional should negotiate with the owner to be specifically included in the owner/contractor indemnification agreement in terms such as these:

INDEMNITY AND HOLD HARMLESS AGREEMENT

This Agreement made on the _____ day of _____, 1989 in the City, County and State of _____ between _____, located at _____ (hereinafter referred to as the "Contractor") and _____ located at _____ (hereinafter referred to as the "Owner").

WHEREAS, the Contractor for good and valuable consideration, the receipt and sufficiency is hereby acknowledged, hereby agrees to indemnify the Owner upon the terms and conditions and in the manner hereinafter set forth:

1. The Contractor shall indemnify the Owner and all additional parties required by the Contract Documents, upon the terms and conditions and in the manner hereinafter set forth, their officers, agents and employees from any and all loss, expense, damage, costs, and attorneys' fees for any damage whatsoever including, without limitation, personal bodily injury or injury to or destruction of property that may at any time occur with regard to the construction known as [the Project] or out of the performance of the Contractor's Work, or the Work of its subcontractors, agents, or any other persons directly or indirectly employed by the Contractor in connection with its Work on the Project.

2. In the event that any claim(s) made against the Owner or [Architect/Engineer], shareholders, officers, agents or employees by anyone for any matter(s) related to our arising from the performance of the Contractor's Work on the Project, or its subcontractors, agents, or anyone directly or indirectly employed by the Contractor in connection with the Work on the Project, then the Contractor shall defend them and fully answer the claim(s) at its sole expense.

3. This Agreement shall be binding upon, and shall inure to the benefit of, the parties and all persons named herein beneficiaries hereof, their legal representatives, successors, heirs, and assigns.

IN WITNESS WHEREOF, the undersigned, hereby set their hands, the first day written above.

OWNER   CONTRACTOR

By: _____   By: _____

§ 10.8   —Limitation of Liability Clauses

Other than using the broad-form indemnification clauses discussed in § 10.6, actually limiting liability to either the fee earned on the design work or the amount of available insurance coverage may also allocate and reduce effectively the risks of liability. The limitations clause may state with specificity a dollar amount above which the architect/engineer will assume no further liability. This amount may be determined by the design professional's fee or a percentage thereof or by another method of calculation. Alternatively, the limitation may not be a specified amount, but may be tied to the contract's insurance provisions, allowing recovery up to the amount of available and unexhausted insurance coverage as determined at the time a claim is made.

Arguably, the advantage of using limitation of liability methods as opposed to indemnity arrangements is that, given the task of construing them, courts may view them more favorably than indemnity arrangements.[9] Because the potential exposure of a design professional for work on a construction project is likely to be vastly in excess of the fee generated on any given agreement, it is obviously in her best interest to allocate risk in the manner that will best survive judicial scrutiny.

§ 10.9   Standard of Care

No discussion of the design professional's duties during the design phase would be complete without mention of the standard of care. Unlike the duties assumed under the contract, the standard by which the performance of those duties is judged is externally determined. The architect/engineer is not an insurer of her work nor does she contract for perfection. Rather, she must act as a reasonable professional in the administration of her work. As the term "professional" implies, the design professional's performance must conform to the peculiar requirements of each project on an ad hoc basis. As a result, although your client's or her lawyer's careful draftsmanship may be able to fashion an agreement that significantly limits the risk of exposure, performance of the duties thereunder is still subject to this standard of care.

Much recent debate has been focused on the standard of care as applied to the design community. Currently, the American Society of Consulting Engineers (ASCE) and the AIA have engaged in a spirited dialogue concerning the ASCE's use of the term "design professional" in its recent *Quality in the Constructed Project* manual, which is presently

---

[9] D. Hatem, Risk Allocation Through Limitation of Liability: An Effective Liability Control and Management Concept (Aug. 1988) (unpublished manuscript).

published for review purposes only.[10] The publication is under fire for attempting to apply inflexible guidelines to the architect/engineer's duties on a construction project.[11] Although uniformity may be helpful in some aspects, the manual as written may establish an artificial standard, which arguably strips the design professional of the discretion to act pursuant to an individual project's needs. Because of this, the AIA has asked that the broadly interpreted term "design professional" be removed from the text.

Until it is modified to provide a standard that more accurately comports to the realities of the industry, it is unlikely that the manual will be adopted; however, it is believed that it will be utilized in some form by the engineering community to define a more precise formula to judge the standard of care. It will be unfortunate if the manual gains acceptance in substantially its present form, as it may go a long way toward undermining the engineering profession's risk management efforts by creating a new definition of "standard of care" without fully understanding and preparing for the impact that a new definition may bring to the architect/engineer community.

The impact of the manual's use, even in draft form, should be revisited when you are assessing your client's exposure in a failure or collapse.

DUTIES DURING THE CONSTRUCTION PHASE

§ 10.10   Architect/Engineer's Liability during Construction

Absent an agreement with the owner to perform services after the design phase is complete, the architect/engineer has limited obligations during construction of the project. Indeed, once the plans and specifications have

---

[10] American Society of Civil Engineers, Quality in the Constructed Project: A Guideline for Owners, Designers and Constructors (1988).

[11] The abstract to the publication provides, in part:

This book provides guidelines and recommendations for owners, design professionals, and constructors on how to provide quality in constructed projects. *Roles, responsibilities, and limits of authority are clarified and defined for all participants in the constructed project.* (Emphasis supplied).

Be aware, however, that government contracts may impose an entirely different set of duties on the design professional. A supervising architect under contract with the federal government was held to have a duty to the contractor to supervise the project with due care in United States v. Rogers & Rogers, 161 F. Supp. 132 (S.D. Cal. 1958).

been submitted and approved by the owner, the courts have been increasingly reluctant to impose any overall supervisory responsibility upon the design professional.[12]

Thus, as the architect/engineer's counsel, it is important to look to the contract with the owner to see what, if any, duties your client expressly agreed to assume during the construction phase. In addition, it is wise to inquire into what additional duties, if any, the architect/engineer assumed through her course of conduct. To this end, as counsel you should make a detailed review of minutes of meetings in which the progress of the project was discussed as well as the entire correspondence file of the project. In particular, consider whether your client informally agreed to "handle" a problem on the jobsite, or volunteered to "take a look" at work falling outside the skeletal requirements for certification, as discussed in § **10.11**. If she did, you may want to begin to build a defense against a claim that your client, by a course of conduct, expressly assumed obligations in excess of contract obligations.

As a general proposition, however, if the contract between the owner and architect or engineer is one of the standard form agreements discussed in § **10.2**, there is a limitation to the design professional's duty to supervise the work. Paragraph 1.5.4 of AIA Document B141,[13] for example, describes the architect's duties in the traditional case, absent a special arrangement between the owner and the architect:

> The Architect shall visit the site at intervals appropriate to the stage of construction or as otherwise agreed by the Architect in writing to become generally familiar with the progress and quality of the Work and to determine in general if Work is proceeding in accordance with the Contract Documents. *However, the Architect shall not be required to make exhaustive or continuous on-site inspections to check the quality or quantity of the Work.*[14]

Thus, the design professional should at all times limit her ongoing obligations to those expressly assumed by contract, and should guard against volunteering greater service unless given additional compensation for assuming well-defined contractual obligations set forth within a supplemental agreement or change order to the original agreement. In the normal course, the architect/engineer's function is merely to ascertain that the

---

[12] *See, e.g.,* Moundsview Indep. School Dist. No. 621 v. Buetow Assocs., Inc., 253 N.W.2d 836 (1977). In addition, it is worthy of note that the express omission of the term "supervision" in the more recent versions of standard AIA documents regarding architect's duties represents a conscious attempt to limit the architect's role to observation; previous versions contained the term "supervision."

[13] (1977).

[14] Architect's Handbook of Professional Practice 8 (1977) (emphasis added).

work on the project was performed in general conformance with the plans and specifications and, if it is not, to report any deficiencies to the owner.[15]

With respect to the contractor's performance, the architect/engineer usually has no duty to the owner during the construction phase to control the means and methods employed by the contractor throughout progress of the work.[16] At any stage of the construction and at her discretion the design professional can reject work or require inspection or testing.[17] Failure to detect nonconforming work may provide the basis for a successful liability claim, depending upon contract language and the architect/engineer's course of conduct.

§ 10.11   —Certificates of Payment

Although the design professional's obligations during the construction phase are limited, the duties she maintains may nevertheless lead to substantial liability if she does not proceed with caution. One area in which the architect/engineer may be subjected to liability involves participation in the certification of payments to contractors. It is the job of the architect, and the engineer in some instances, to certify that certain progress has been realized and that the contractor should therefore receive a proportionate percentage of the contract price reflective of the work completed to date, less any retainage withheld.[18] This is known as a "progress payment." In certification of project work there exists a natural tension between the interests of the owner and those of the contractor. It is the architect's job to ensure that only the amount of work actually completed, and completed in conformance with the contract documents, is

---

[15] The architect/engineer may be additionally required to notify the owner if he discovers that plans or specifications are flawed during the course of construction. *See, e.g.,* Comptroller of Virginia v. King, 217 Va. 751, 232 S.E.2d 895 (1977).

[16] Paragraph 1.5.5 of AIA Document B141-1977 advises that the architect shall not have control, charge of, or responsibility for construction means, techniques, sequences, or procedures, or for safety precautions or programs in connection with the work.

[17] AIA Document 201-1976, ¶ 2.2.13.

[18] Paragraph 9.4 of AIA Document A201-1987 clearly sets forth the architect's duties and limitations thereupon concerning certification:

The issuance of a Certificate for Payment will constitute a representation by the Architect to the Owner, based upon the Architect's observations at the site and the data comprising the Application for Payment, that the Work has progressed to the point indicated and that to the best of the Architect's knowledge, information and belief, quality of the Work is in accordance with the Contract Documents.

certified and made part of the progress payment.[19] These concerns extend to the issuance of certification for final payment as well.

The exposure that architects and, in rare instances, engineers face with respect to certification of payments poses a serious problem. One possible solution, suggested by Howard G. Goldberg and Ralph L. Arnsdorf, is to "update the language contained in the construction certification" so as to "recognize that the (design professional) is not under a duty to guarantee a perfect result."[20]

If overcertification or miscertification appears to be an issue with regard to your client, look to the actual language in the certification for payment to ascertain what representations were actually made. The implications of a broad form certification might give rise to additional civil liability as well as potential criminal liability in a case of death caused by failure or collapse.

§ 10.12 —Safety of Persons

What liability, if any, may the architect/engineer face for construction site accidents that have not been caused by design failure? Generally the design professional is not an insurer of jobsite safety, nor under normal circumstances does she have any authority to govern the contractors' means and methods. Injured workers, however, precluded from bringing an action against the real malfeasor in most safety related incidents by the workers' compensation bar, have frequently resorted to suit against the design professional. Surprisingly, some courts[21] have allowed plaintiffs to maintain such actions despite the absence of the design professional's duty to provide jobsite safety. More frequently, however, courts focus on the real control conferred by the contract in determining whether the design professional should bear liability of workers' injuries. The inquiry under

---

[19] Paragraph 2.6.10 of AIA Document B141-1977, however, which concerns the architect's certification for payment, in part provides as follows:

> the issuance of a Certificate for Payment shall not be a representation that the Architect has (1) made exhaustive or continuous on-site inspections to check the quality or quantity of the Work, (2) reviewed construction means, methods, techniques, sequences or procedures, (3) reviewed copies of requisitions received from subcontractors and material suppliers and other data requested by the Owner to substantiate the contractor's right to payment or (4) ascertained how or for what purpose the Contractor has used money previously paid on account of the Contract Sum.

[20] H. Goldberg & R. Arnsdorf, *Construction Certification: A Trap for the Unwary Architect,* 6 in The Construction Lawyer (Jan. 1986).

[21] *See, e.g.,* Krieger v. J.E. Griener Co., 282 Md. 50, 382 A.2d 1069 (1977).

this analysis often turns on the ability to stop the work and whether such power was in fact exercised.[22] Finally, a few jurisdictions specifically exclude such claims against the design professional by statute.[23] Depending on the climate in your client's jurisdiction and the nature of the failure or collapse, an inquiry into construction site safety may be in order.

§ 10.13 Architect/Engineer's Responsibility under Design/Build Contracts

An emerging major liability area is worthy of note: design-build contracts. In these contracts, the design professional agrees not only to take on design responsibility but also to build the project; she is responsible not only for the plans and specifications but also for supervision, means, and methods of construction. She therefore wears the hats of both the architect/engineer in the traditional mode and the general contractor or construction manager and is potentially subject to exposure in both roles.

Thus, in addition to liability arising out of negligence in the design phase, the architect/engineer as designer-builder may face potential liability for breach of express warranty, breach of implied warranty, and strict liability in tort. Particularly with respect to express warranties, the courts have imposed a higher standard upon the architect/engineer in a design-build contract than would be imposed on an architect or contractor individually.[24] The courts are unwilling to allow the designer-builder to change hats once construction begins in order to escape liability for defects in design by arguing that as the contractor she is only required to follow the plans, not assure their accuracy. Moreover, a body of thought has emerged urging the imposition of strict liability in tort on design professionals in design-build arrangements.[25] Thus, although these hybrid

---

[22] *See, e.g.,* Reber v. Chandler High School Dist. No. 202, 13 Ariz. App. 133, 474 P.2d 852 (1970); Wheeler & Lewis v. Slifer, 195 Colo. 291, 577 P.2d 1092 (1978).

[23] New York, for example, specifically exempts nonsupervising architects and engineers from liability for job-site safety. Labor Law § 240 (McKinney 1986) provides:

No liability pursuant to this subdivision for the failure to provide protection to a person so employed shall be imposed on professional engineers . . . architects . . . or landscape architects . . . who do not direct or control the work for activities other than planning or design.

[24] *See, e.g.,* First Nat'l Bank of Akron v. Cann, 669 F.2d 415 (6th Cir. 1982) (designer-builder held to express warranty that project would conform to plans) and Lincoln Stone & Supply Co. v. Ludwig, 94 Neb. 722, 144 N.W. 782 (1913) (designer-builder may not hide behind defective plans by arguing that once construction begins her obligation is to follow the plans and not to assure their accuracy).

[25] *See, e.g., The Architect in the Design-Build Model Designing and Building the Case for Strict Liability in Tort,* 33 Case W. L. Rev. 116 (1982).

contracts may appear to be financially lucrative for the design professional, the potential for liability may outweigh the benefits, especially if strict liability is applied to the architect/engineer's work in any particular jurisdiction.

In addition, errors and omissions liability insurance may limit its indemnity obligation to the architect/engineer based upon the proportionate share of the equity she holds in the design-build agreement. Case law is developing with the growth of design-build contracts. As new theories of liability are applied, more and more attention needs to be focused upon contract provisions reflective of the changing liability structure in order to protect the architect/engineer as designer-builder from increasing liability.

LIABILITY CONSIDERATIONS

§ 10.14   Protecting the Design Professional after a Failure

If a failure occurs and your client comes to you for advice, every step should be cautious and governed by the knowledge that litigation may ensue. It is incumbent upon you to proceed as though you are preparing for trial.

The first and most significant task is the retention and organization of your client's documents. Were complete and accurate records kept? Are any important documents missing? Do you have everything you need to effectively defend against a charge that your design professional client was somehow responsible for the failure?

One critical source of evidence necessary to the successful defense of your client is the project itself. An immediate investigation of the failure site will provide photographs and samples that will be invaluable and nonduplicable for use as evidence at trial. Before other parties alter or destroy evidence, either via the investigative process or during rehabilitation and reconstruction, your client must get to the scene and preserve what she needs to protect her interests.

The prospect of litigation calls for the architect/engineer to put together a forensic team that can be mobilized immediately. The team should include a photographer (stills and video), relevant experts, and a team manager. Lawyers experienced in this area can assemble and direct the participants upon short notice based on lessons learned from prior cases. This is not a time for egocentric concern; the prior successful experience of competent counsel marks the difference between being able to mount the kind of defense necessary to protect the architect/engineer's personal and professional assets.

§ 10.15 Architect/Engineer's Participation in Reconstruction

Often, the same design professional who drafted the initial plans and specifications and/or had general observation duties during the construction phase will be asked by the owner to become involved in the project's reconstruction, redesign, or temporary retrofit. This may prove to be a hidden hazard to the architect/engineer, and one that could disadvantage the defense of a claim against her. As one scholar in this area explained:

> A designer of original construction should carefully consider a recommendation for reconstruction of a failed job. If he suggests following the same design and the reconstruction fails, he has helped to prove his own liability for both failures. If he advocates a new design, he impliedly admits that there were deficiencies in the original design.[26]

§ 10.16 Advising the Architect/Engineer after the Failure

Another issue that presents itself almost immediately following a failure concerns which parties should be contacted and which should be avoided. It is always good advice, whether or not a claim (as defined within the insuring agreements) has been made, to report the failure or collapse to the architect/engineer's professional malpractice carrier, because in some instances the carrier will be the one to provide legal and other representation. Conversely, it is usually advisable to avoid the press. The grey areas, however, involve contacting, or allowing contact with, the owner, contractor, or other parties and nonparties. It is the attorney's job to guide the design professional through this process on an ad hoc basis, making only those contacts that may strengthen the architect/engineer's position. Certainly, a way to avoid litigation is to have a decisive plan of action at or near the time of failure that is designed to limit liability.

§ 10.17 Checklist of Information for the Attorney

A checklist of activities to consider at the outset of representing a design professional after a collapse may be of value.

---

[26] B. Fincken, *Defending Against a Claim: An Overview in Architect and Engineer Liability: Claims Against Design Professionals* (1987).

1. **Identify General Nature of Problem**
   - Structural failure
     Steel
     Wood
     Concrete
   - Equipment failure
     Crane collapse
     Rigging failure
   - Architectural failure
     Glass blow outs
   - Electrical failure
     Transformer explosion
   - Mechanical failure
     Explosion at water supply system

2. **Select Team**
   - Your preliminary team members (experts—that is, forensic engineers, the testing lab), should be selected and meeting with you and your client within hours after you are retained—or sooner
   - Get a photographer
   - Identify owner's team hierarchy (they will become important to you)
   - Coordinate your technical team members
   - To the extent possible "select" owner's experts during first hours after collapse

3. **Site Visit**
   - Immediately arrange site access with your team
   - Inform client of your site visit beforehand—her attendance is important
   - Immediately visit site with team
     Assess what is being done with debris (evidentiary material)
     Who is removing debris?
     Who is supervising removal?
       handling
       storage
       marking
     Be prepared to introduce your ideas concerning collection of debris to owner immediately, if appropriate
   - Assess impact of client's visit to site during initial collapse period

4. Daily Activities
   - Keep client informed daily during initial collapse period
   - Damage control: the first hours/days after collapse could direct your client's economic and professional existence
   - Avoid media contact by you and your client
   - Collect all local newspapers daily and subscribe
   - Keep client involved

5. Legal Research
   - Legal research
   Negligence
   Criminally negligent homicide
   Privity
   Statute of limitations
   Statute of repose/limitation
   Intervening cause
   Did client have more than periodic inspection/observation during construction phase?
   Shop drawing review
   - Subconsultants
   Is there a statute of repose?
   Prior general releases

6. Document Research
   - Set up time line to help sharpen focus of all team players; as documents are reviewed, locate key events on the time line
   Historical data
   Design agreement dates
   Construction contract dates, including milestones
   Postconstruction events
   Detail of catastrophic events
   - Review all documents with extreme care
   Look for:
   Corrections
   Erasures
   Notations
   - Retrieve client files
   - Induce owner to set up its files/archives and to allow informal access as soon after failure/collapse as possible

7. Preliminary Strategy Conference
   - Keep client informed and involved
   - Assemble team

- Assess need for additional technical specialists
- Define scope of immediate and long-term tasks
  Surveys
  Samplings
  Tests
- Prepare budgets covering team costs for the performance of anticipated activities on a 30-60-120-day basis
- Review the investigatory programs at site established by others
  Economics of your defense
  Defense costs within policy limits
  Obligation to conserve the indemnity
  What should your technical team be doing at the site—if anything?
- Discuss defense possibilities with client and experts
  Itemize and preliminarily evaluate strengths and weaknesses
  Issue assignments to develop probable causes
- Define need, if any, for additional investigations (people in charge of site may not be doing everything needed)
- Determine when or if to interface with owner/counsel

8. Develop Preliminary Collapse/Catastrophe Scenarios
   - What might have happened? (need for and identification of additional technical experts might emerge at this point)
   - Could it have been prevented?
     How?
     By whom?
   - Contemplate the less obvious possibilities
   - Determine who established the design criteria
   - Was the construction contract executed in accordance with the design plans and specifications?
   - Was the facility modified postconstruction?
   - Maintenance
   - Was other work carried out within relevant vicinity postconstruction that might have impacted the facility?

9. Meeting with Client
   - Review documentation
   - Recollection
   - Damage control: establish guidelines to be strictly followed by client when she interfaces with others postfailure/collapse, for example, the media, the owner.

§ 10.18   Privity of Contract Issues

Of paramount importance in counseling the architect/engineer on liability issues is the trend in the law away from contract privity as a bar to recovery by third parties to the contract. Traditionally, of course, only those bound by a contract could sue on it; nonparties were relegated to causes of action sounding in tort. Beginning in many jurisdictions in limited professions,[27] however, the courts have slowly been replacing the monolith of privity with tort notions of foreseeability in allowing recovery. Thus, rather than inquiring whether a contractor, for example, was either a party to the contract or a third-party beneficiary, the court asks whether it was *reasonably foreseeable* that the contractor would be impacted by the contract. This grafting of tort concepts onto a traditionally purely contract inquiry has a significant impact on architect/engineer liability.

Unfortunately, this movement can potentially greatly expand the design professional's liability in ways against which she has limited ability to guard. As counsel, it will be your task to determine whether your jurisdiction is likely to allow recovery on these quasi tort theories if asserted by noncontracting party plaintiffs.

On the positive side, there are a number of defenses and limitations of liability that affect claims against the design professional. Privity is still one of the most powerful absolute defenses in jurisdictions that have refused to move toward the litmus test of foreseeability.

§ 10.19   Statutes of Limitation and Repose

In addition to general statutes of limitation, many jurisdictions[28] have enacted special statutes for design professionals, and a number of states have

---

[27] In the area of accountants' liability, for example, New York courts, beginning with Ultramares v. Touche, 255 N.Y. 170, 174 N.E. 441 (1931), have carved out an exception to the privity requirement on the rationale that a CPA firm's financial statement used for the purpose of securing financing will reasonably foreseeably impact a third-party creditor such that the firm can be held liable even without the contractual relationship.

[28] Ohio's special statute on Limitations of Actions, Ohio Rev. Code Ann. § 2305.131 (Page 1988), is illustrative:

Limitations of actions against persons involved in improvements to real property, non-application of statute. No action to recover damages for any injury to property, real or personal, or for bodily injury or wrongful death, arising out of the defective and unsafe condition of an improvement to real property, nor any action for contribution or indemnity for damages sustained as a result of said injury, shall be brought against any person performing services for or furnishing the design, planning, supervision of construction, or construction of such improvement to real property, more than ten years after one performance or furnishing of such services and construction.

specific statutes of repose, that terminate any liability at a date certain.[29] Depending upon your client's particular facts and jurisdiction, these statutory devices may preclude a successful claim against the architect/engineer regardless of any actual deficiencies in the design or in her supervision of the project.

---

[29] New Jersey's statute of repose, by way of example, terminates a right of action against a design professional for injury from unsafe condition of improvement to real property to ten years. N.J. Stat. Ann. § 2A:14-1.1 (West 1987) provides, in part, as follows:

No action whether in contract, in tort, or otherwise to recover damages for any deficiency in the design, planning, supervision or construction of an improvement to real property, or for any injury to property, real or personal, or for any injury to the person, or for bodily injury or wrongful death, arising out of the defective and unsafe condition of an improvement to real property, or any action for fee contribution or indemnity for damages sustained on account of such injury, shall be brought against any person performing or furnishing the design, planning, supervision of construction or construction of such improvement to real property, more than 10 years after the performance or furnishing of such services and construction.

PART III

LIABILITY, COMPLETING THE PROJECT, AND TRIAL

CHAPTER 11

THE PROJECT THAT DOESN'T WORK: THE FUNCTIONAL FAILURE AND WHO IS RESPONSIBLE

Donald G. Gavin, Esquire

Robert J. Smith, Esquire

Daniel E. Toomey, Esquire

Donald G. Gavin is a partner in the law firm of Wickwire, Gavin & Gibbs, P.C., in Washington, D.C.; Vienna, Virginia; and Madison, Wisconsin. Mr. Gavin's practice primarily emphasizes public contract law, federal assistance law, and construction and surety matters, and he lectures frequently throughout the country on subjects dealing with grants, construction, and government contracts. Mr. Gavin has authored and coauthored numerous books, articles, and other publications and has served on advisory panels to several federal grantor agencies concerned with construction under federal assistance. Mr. Gavin has been elected a fellow of the American Bar Association and as of August 1989 is the chairman of the Public Contract Law Section of the American Bar Association. He has earned a degree in Economics from the Wharton School, a Juris Doctorate from the University of Pennsylvania School of Law, and a Masters of Law Degree in Government Procurement Law from George Washington University.

Robert J. Smith is a partner in the law firm of Wickwire, Gavin & Gibbs, P.C., in Madison, Wisconsin; Washington, D.C.; and Vienna, Virginia. His practice emphasizes construction contract law, engineering issues, federal assistance law, and surety matters. He is a frequent lecturer throughout the country on subjects dealing with construction contract administration, contract specifications, construction grants, and architect-engineer professional responsibility. Prior to entering into private practice, Mr. Smith was an associate professor of engineering at the University of Wisconsin and also served as chairman of the Wisconsin Transportation Commission. As a Registered Professional Engineer, Mr. Smith is a member of the American Society of Civil Engineers, past chairman of its National Committee on Construction Contract Administration, and chairman of the Engineers-Joint Contract Documents Committee. He earned his civil engineering degree as well as his Juris Doctorate from the University of Wisconsin.

Daniel E. Toomey is a partner in the law firm of Wickwire, Gavin & Gibbs, P.C., in Washington, D.C.; Vienna, Virginia; and Madison, Wisconsin. He previously served as a law clerk to the late chief judge of the District of Columbia Court of Appeals, the Honorable Andrew M. Hood, and as an assistant United States attorney for the District of Columbia, serving in that office's appellate, grand jury, and felony criminal trial sections. Since leaving the United States Attorney's Office in 1972, Mr. Toomey has been engaged in a wide-ranging civil and criminal trial practice and numerous trials and appeals in federal and state courts relating to construction contract litigation and Environmental Protection Agency enforcement proceedings. Mr. Toomey has taught widely in the field of trial advocacy. He is an adjunct professor of construction contract law at Georgetown University Law Center, where he earned a Juris Doctorate.

§ 11.1   Using Litigation as a Remedy for a Project's Malfunction

The public notices when bridges collapse, or buildings significantly settle, or a foundation fails and injury is caused to construction workers or occupants in a building. It complains when highways crack, potholes develop, or vehicles disappear into sinkholes. However, there are more frequent and less publicized occasions of buildings not being capable of reaching a comfortable heating level or a cooling level that will enable the office worker to function efficiently through the summer. Manufacturing plants are built that do not provide the output or functional product sought. Sewage treatment plants are constructed that do not meet the effluent limitations called for in their National Pollutant Discharge Elimination System (NPDES) permits. On a simple level, roofs may leak or pipes may contain construction debris and therefore not carry their projected flow. On the most complex level, only sophisticated engineering or scientific analyses can explain why something fails to function.

When an owner is disappointed with a project that fails to meet design specifications, a careful review is necessary to determine why the project doesn't work, who is responsible, and what remedies are available. The causes for such failure can include a great variety of circumstances, including (1) design deficiencies caused by the negligence of the architects or engineers, (2) failure of a construction contractor to perform in a manner provided for in the plans and specifications, (3) functional deficiencies in major equipment items and systems being furnished by subcontractors and suppliers, and (4) changes in circumstances and conditions. Such changes might include substitutions of raw materials by the owners of the facility, or subjecting a processing facility designed to neutralize or incinerate a toxic substance to hazardous materials for which the facility was not planned or designed and is therefore not capable of handling.

There are, indeed, a host of considerations to be evaluated and analyzed in deciding (1) whether the functional failure is one in which there is a real shortcoming, (2) whether a legal right or remedy is available, (3) the scope of such remedy and whether it is barred by procedural or statutory limitations, and finally (4) the scope of recovery and the possibility of compensation for the cost of pursuing such remedies. In today's world, such considerations are made even more complex by the passage of statutes designed either to protect public owners (particularly when federal dollars are involved) or in other instances to limit the liability of design professionals and those who furnish construction services and materials. Such considerations as warranties and guarantees and latent and patent defects all can become involved in the issues to be assessed and evaluated.

Litigation involving malfunctioning projects is potentially very complex and expensive. Thus, the decision to litigate commits an owner to an onerous expense of time and money, a commitment which should be made only after thorough evaluation of the legal considerations. This chapter discusses the major issues that should be addressed in an evaluation of the case for litigation:

1. Causes of action
2. Parties
3. Defenses
4. Damages
5. Procedures and alternates to litigation.

§ 11.2   Potential Causes of Action

The consequences of a major construction project's failure are legally complex. An owner may have many causes of action against numerous potential defendants. The owner should evaluate the facts to determine the existence of potential claims for breach of contract, negligent design, negligent construction, breach of implied and express warranties, and, possibly, fraud, misrepresentation, and violation of statutes. Keep in mind that unsatisfactory performance, whether manifested by a building's failing to keep a satisfactory temperature or by a manufacturing plant's production problems, does not alone create or establish liability.

§ 11.3   Action for Breach of Contract

A *breach of contract* is an unjustified and unexcused failure to perform a contractual obligation.[1]

A typical construction project has a minimum of two express contractual relationships that need to be examined. The first is the owner's contract with the architect/engineering firm for planning and designing the facilities. (Frequently, the same firm is retained for construction phase services as well, but in some instances there may be a different firm hired for that phase. In other situations, there may be a design firm retained for some services and a construction manager engaged to perform other construction phase services.)

§ 11.4   —Typical Engineer Contract Clauses

Determining the existence of a breach of an engineering contract is not always easy, because by their very nature such contracts contain very general descriptions of the architect's or engineer's services. The following is typical of language in the "boilerplate" of such contracts, here saying the engineer shall

> 1.3.1.   In consultation with OWNER and on the basis of the accepted Study and Report Documents, determine the general scope, extent and character of the Project.
>
> 1.3.2.   Prepare Preliminary Design documents consisting of final design criteria, preliminary drawings, outline specifications and written descriptions of the Project.
>
> 1.4.1.   On the basis of the accepted Preliminary Design documents and the revised opinion of probable Total Project Costs prepare for incorporation in

---

[1] Williston on Contracts § 1290 (Jaeger ed. 3d ed. 1968).

the Contract Documents final drawings to show the general scope, extent and character of the work to be furnished and performed by Contractor(s) (hereinafter called "Drawings") and Specifications (which will be prepared in conformance with the sixteen division format of the Construction Specifications Institute.)[2]

Much of the other boilerplate language in these agreements has evolved over time to generally protect the design professionals from substantial claims founded on contract or warranty. However, the design professional's attorney should carefully scrutinize the project's specific scope of work statement, which is often an appendix or exhibit to the basic contract. These provisions are typically drafted by design professionals who may have unwittingly or unintentionally included some express warranties or explicit representations or conditions.[3] Any specific promises or affirmations in the contract documents should then be compared with actual performance. If they are at variance, the next question is whether the injury and damage that the owner suffered—the improperly functioning construction project—occurred because of the engineer's negligence or failure to perform.[4]

§ 11.5   —Government Contract Clauses

The following policies and procedures are applicable to the acquisition of architect-engineer services by federal executive agencies:

36.608 LIABILITY FOR GOVERNMENT COSTS RESULTING FROM DESIGN ERRORS OR DEFICIENCIES.

Architect-engineer contractors shall be responsible for the professional quality, technical accuracy, and coordination of all services required under their contracts. A firm may be liable for Government costs resulting from errors or deficiencies in designs furnished under its contract. Therefore, when a modification to a construction contract is required because of an error or deficiency in the services provided under an architect-engineer contract, the contracting officer (with the advice of technical personnel and legal counsel) shall consider the extent to which the architect-engineer contractor may be reasonably liable. The contracting officer shall enforce the liability and collect the amount due, if the recoverable cost will exceed the administrative cost involved or is otherwise in the Government's interest. The contracting

---

[2] Engineers Joint Contract Documents Committee (EJCDC) Document 1910-1-1984; *see also* American Institute of Architects (AIA) Document B141-1977, ¶¶ 1.1–1.5.16.

[3] *See* St. Paul Fire & Marine Ins. Co. v. Freeman-White Assocs., 322 N.C. 77, 366 S.E.2d 480 (1988) (waiver of liability clause held to be ambiguous and reversed dismissal of owner's claim against architect).

[4] Gordon T. Gioette v. Press Bar & Cafe, Inc., 413 N.W.2d 854 (Minn. App. 1987); *see also* Grossman v. Sea Air Towers, Ltd., 513 So. 2d 686 (Fla. Dist. Ct. App. 1987).

officer shall include in the contract file a written statement of the reasons for the decision to recover or not to recover the costs from the firm.[5]

36.609-2 REDESIGN RESPONSIBILITY FOR DESIGN ERRORS OR DEFICIENCIES.

(a) *Under architect-engineer contracts, contractors shall be required to make necessary corrections at no cost to the Government when the designs, drawings, specifications, or other items or services furnished contained any errors, deficiencies, or inadequacies.* If, in a given situation, the Government does not require a firm to correct such errors, the contracting officer shall include a written statement of the reasons for that decision in the contract file.[6]

The following clause must be included in fixed-price architect/engineer contracts:

52.236-23 RESPONSIBILITY OF THE ARCHITECT-ENGINEER CONTRACTOR.

(a) The Contractor shall be responsible for the professional quality, technical accuracy, and the coordination of all designs, drawings, specifications, and other services furnished by the Contractor under this contract. The Contractor shall, without additional compensation, correct or revise any errors or deficiencies in its designs, drawings, specifications, and other services.

(b) Neither the Government's review, approval or acceptance of, nor payment for, the services required under this contract shall be construed to operate as a waiver of any rights under the contract or any cause of action arising out of the performance of this contract, and the Contractor shall be and remain liable to the Government in accordance with applicable law for all damages to the Government caused by the Contractor's negligent performance of any of the services furnished under this contract.

(c) The rights and remedies of the Government provided for under this contract are in addition to any other rights and remedies provided by law.

(d) If the Contractor is comprised of more than one legal entity, each such entity shall be jointly and severally liable hereunder.[7]

§ 11.6 —Contracts for EPA Grant Projects

For projects assisted with Environmental Protection Agency (EPA) grants, the following provision (or one substantially similar) must be included in each engineering contract by operation of law:

---

[5] 48 C.F.R. 36.608 (1985) (emphasis added).

[6] Federal Acquisition Circular 84-8, 50 Federal Register 26903, 6/28/85, effective 7/1/85. 48 C.F.R. 36.609.2 (1985) (emphasis added).

[7] 48 C.F.R. 52.236-23 (1985).

(1) The contractor is responsible for the professional quality, technical accuracy, timely completion and coordination of all designs, drawings, specifications, reports and other services furnished by the contractor under this subagreement. If the subagreement involves environmental measurements or data generation, the contractor shall comply with EPA quality assurance requirements in 40 CFR 30.503. The contractor shall, without additional compensation, correct or revise any errors, omissions or other deficiencies in his designs, drawings, specifications, reports and other services.

(2) The contractor shall perform the professional services necessary to accomplish the work specified in this subagreement in accordance with this subagreement and applicable EPA requirements in effect on the date of execution of the assistance agreement for this project.

(3) The owner's or EPA's approval of drawings, designs, specifications, reports and incidental work or materials furnished hereunder shall not in any way relieve the contractor of responsibility for the technical adequacy of his work. Neither the owner's nor EPA's review, approval, acceptance or payment for any of the services shall be construed as a waiver of any rights under this agreement or of any cause for action arising out of the performance of this subagreement.

(4) The contractor shall be, and shall remain, liable in accordance with applicable law for all damages to the owner or EPA caused by the contractor's negligence performance of any of the services furnished under this subagreement, except for errors, omissions or other deficiencies to the extent attributable to the owner, owner-furnished data or any third party. The contractor shall not be responsible for any time delays in the project caused by circumstances beyond the contractor's control.

(5) The contractor's obligations under this clause or in addition to the contractor's other express or implied assurances under this subagreement or State law and in no way diminish any other rights that the owner may have against the contractor for faulty materials, equipment or work.[8]

Comparatively speaking, evaluation of the contractual obligations of the construction contractor(s) and comparison with actual performance are somewhat easier, given the greater detail and specificity of the normal owner's contractor agreement.

In addition, construction contracts assisted with EPA grants awarded since May 12, 1982 are required to include the following clause:

(1) The contractor agrees to perform all work under this subagreement in accordance with this agreement's designs, drawings and specifications.

(2) The contractor guarantees for a period of at least one (1) year from the date of substantial completion of the work that the completed work is free from all defects due to faulty materials, equipment or workmanship and that he shall promptly make whatever adjustments or corrections which may be necessary to cure any defects, including repairs of any damage to other parts

[8] 40 C.F.R. § 33.1030 Subd. 13(a) (1983).

of the system resulting from such defects. The owner shall promptly give notice to the contractor of observed defects. In the event that the contractor
fails to make adjustments, repairs, corrections or other work made necessary by such defects, the owner may do so and charge the contractor the cost
incurred. The performance bond shall remain in full force and effect
through the guarantee period.

(3) The contractor's obligations under this clause are in addition to the
contractor's other express or implied assurances under this subagreement
or State law and no way diminish any other rights that the owner may have
against the contractor for faulty materials, equipment or work.[9]

§ 11.7   —Plans Supplied by Owner

The design professional's attorney must be mindful of the doctrine of the
"implied warranty of specifications" or "defective specifications." Simply
put, this doctrine is based on the proposition that, when an owner provides
plans and specifications of a descriptive or design (materials and methods)
nature, there is an implied warranty that if the specifications are followed a
satisfactory result will be achieved.[10]

If, therefore, a contractor, for example, is able to establish compliance
with plans and specifications for the heating and cooling systems in a hotel
or a specific unit process in a wastewater treatment facility and that temperature or unit process for some reason does not achieve the end results
desired or specified, there is no breach of contract on the contractor's part.
Indeed, if the owner insists on the contractor meeting the performance requirements, this could well create an affirmative claim for additional compensation founded on defective specifications.[11]

As in evaluating performance of the engineering contract, this becomes
a matter of determining whether there are any breaches and, if so, whether
they have contributed to the performance problems.

§ 11.8   —Other Contractual Relationships

There may be other contractual relationships associated with the design
and construction of the project that give the owner certain rights. In some
states, the law may consider the owner to be a third-party beneficiary of
a contractual relationship between a contractor and major equipment

---

[9] *Id.* at Subd. 13(b).

[10] United States v. Spearin, 248 U.S. 132, 39 S. Ct. 59, 63 L. Ed. 166 (1918) (the seminal
case). *See generally* J. Sweet, Legal Aspects of Architecture, Engineering, and the
Construction Process 606-12 (3d ed. 1985).

[11] J. Sweet, Legal Aspects of Architecture, Engineering, and the Construction Process
608-12 n.10 (3d ed. 1985).

supplier.[12] Such a doctrine may be useful when bringing a court action against a party who is a principal actor but is not directly accessible in a breach of contract action.

§ 11.9 Action in Negligence

Negligence is a cause of action not founded on the existence of a contract. *Negligence* is typically defined as a failure to use due care under the circumstances. "One who undertakes to render professional services is under a duty to the person for whom the service is to be performed to exercise such care, skill, and diligence as men in that profession ordinarily exercise *under like circumstances.*"[13]

As a general proposition, a mere mistake or omission does not constitute negligence:

> Architects, doctors, engineers, attorneys, and others deal with somewhat inexact sciences and are continually called upon to exercise their skilled judgment in order to anticipate and provide for random factors which are incapable of precise measurement. The indeterminate nature of these factors makes it impossible for professional services people to gauge them with complete accuracy in every instance. . . . Because of the inescapable possibility of error which inheres in these services, the law has traditionally required, not perfect results, but rather the exercise of that skill and judgment which can be reasonably expected from similarly situated professionals.[14]

But, as with every rule, there is an exception:

> [I]t can be said that certain professionals, such as doctors and lawyers, are not subject to such an implied warranty. However, an architect and an engineer stand in much different posture as to insuring a given result than does a doctor or a lawyer. The work performed by architects and engineers is an exact science: that performed by doctors and lawyers is not. A person who contracts with an architect or engineer for a building of a certain size and elevation has a right to expect an exact result.[15]

A design professional is responsible to the owner of a building or facility for his acts and omissions. Proof of an architect's or engineer's failure

---

[12] *See generally* Annotation, *Third-Party Beneficiaries of Warranties Under U.C.C. § 2-318,* 100 A.L.R.3d 743 (1980).

[13] City of Eveleth v. Ruble, 302 Minn. 249, 253, 225 N.W.2d 521, 524 (1974) (emphasis added).

[14] City of Mounds View v. Walijarvi, 263 N.W.2d 420, 424 (Minn. 1978).

[15] Tamarac Dev. Co. v. Delamater, Freund & Assocs., 234 Kan. 618, 622, 675 P.2d 361, 365 (1984).

to use the degree of care, skill, and prudence normally possessed and applied by members of good standing in the profession, under similar circumstances, can establish liability for negligent design or negligent supervision of construction.[16] Criteria that might be useful in establishing the standard of care can be found in widely recognized design standards or in selected fields. Often there are manuals such as those published by organizations like the American Institute of Steel Construction (AISC), the American Concrete Institute (ACI),[17] the Water Pollution Control Federation (WPCF), and the American Society of Civil Engineers (ASCE).[18]

Courts frequently also look to contracts to help define the standard of care:

> The circumstances to be considered in determining the standard of care, skill, and diligence to be required in this case include *the terms of the employment agreement,* the nature of the problem which the supplier of the service represented himself as being competent to solve, and the effect reasonably to be anticipated from the proposed remedies upon the balance of the system.[19]

For example, the responsibility clause required in direct federal contracts has been held to incorporate the professional negligence standard into a contract.[20]

Proof of negligence generally requires expert testimony.[21] Accordingly, it is prudent for the owner to retain a third-party engineer experienced at offering expert testimony to evaluate the design, construction, and operation of the facility.

In *Clark v. City of Seward,*[22] the Alaska Supreme Court reversed a jury verdict which was for the city because the city failed to introduce expert opinion that the engineers did not use an appropriate professional standard of care in dealing with a comprehensive plan for the sewage treatment plant. The record was void of evidence of what other members of the profession would have done.

---

[16] Roy v. Poquette, 515 A.2d 1072 (Vt. 1986).

[17] Metcalf & Eddy, Wastewater Engineering (1979).

[18] Water Pollution Control Federation and American Society of Civil Engineers, Wastewater Treatment Plant Design (1977).

[19] City of Eveleth v. Ruble, 225 N.W.2d at 524 (emphasis added).

[20] Clovis Heimsath & Assocs., NASA No. 180-1, 83-1 B.C.A. (CCH) ¶ 16,133 (Nov. 16, 1982).

[21] City of Eveleth v. Ruble, 302 Minn. 254 at 255, 225 N.W.2d at 524; Nelson v. Commonwealth of Va., 235 Va. 228, 368 S.E.2d 239 (1988); Tomberlin Assoc. Architects v. Free, 174 Ga. App. 167, 329 S.E.2d 296 (1985).

[22] 659 P.2d 1227 (Alaska 1983).

In some situations, however, experts are not needed to establish breach of duty, such as when a layman is capable of understanding the issues[23] or when the engineer has breached a building code provision.[24] Such occasions will likely be rare, given the complex nature of most major construction projects. In *City of Eveleth v. Ruble*,[25] the city sued the design engineers for negligence and breach of contract in the design of a water treatment facility. The court held that, because it was very apparent that the omission proximately resulted in damage and the damage could be ascertained without the aid of experts, such testimony was not required.

Just as a mistake in design does not necessarily constitute negligence, an error or omission in construction does not necessarily mean that the owner is entitled to recover against the contractor in a negligence action. These are case-by-case decisions. However, negligence can be an appropriate cause of action to allege against a contractor if it is not possible to accurately establish a breach of contract.

§ 11.10   Action for Breach of Warranty

In complex construction failure litigation, grounds for breach of both express and implied warranties may exist against the design professionals, the construction contractor, the subcontractors, and the suppliers of component equipment. The construction contract generally states that the contractor will perform the work in a proper, sound, and workmanlike manner and that the building, facility, or plant will be fit for its intended purpose. Such language creates an express warranty, but the law may also imply a warranty of fitness for the particular purpose of the plant.

The prevailing view would appear to be that contracts for the design and construction are for services, not for goods.[26] Because the Uniform Commercial Code (U.C.C.) is, generally, applicable only to sales of goods and does not deal with service contracts, the warranties contained therein do not normally apply to such contracts. Under the U.C.C., damages for breach of contract can be limited. Moreover, the statute of limitation is generally two years from the delivery of the goods.

Bonebrake v. Cox[27] established the test to determine whether a contract is primarily for goods or is primarily service oriented. The character of the

---

[23] Bartak v. Bell-Galyardt & Wells, Inc., 629 F.2d 523 (8th Cir. 1980).

[24] Huang v. Garner, 157 Cal. App. 3d 404, 203 Cal. Rptr. 800 (1984).

[25] 225 N.W.2d 521.

[26] Allied Properties v. John A. Blume & Assocs., 25 Cal. 3d 848, 102 Cal. Rptr. 259 (1972).

[27] 499 F.2d 951 (8th Cir. 1974).

seller's business, the language used by the parties in the contract, and the intrinsic value of the good apart from its installation should be considered to avoid the U.C.C. if it will bar the plaintiff's claim.

Similarly, to avoid the U.C.C.'s application in an action against a contractor who designs and constructs the entire project, the plaintiff would have to establish that mere goods are not involved.

Omaha Pollution Control Corp. v. Carver-Greenfield Corp.,[28] a leading case in this area, held that the city could recover as a third-party beneficiary for breaches of the implied warranties of merchantability and fitness for a particular purpose under Nebraska's Uniform Commercial Code §§ 2-314(2)(c) and 2-315.[29] To reach this result, the district court found that the plant constituted a product.

The contractor had designed and constructed the facility after investigating and recommending a solution to the city's particular problems. The court found the circumstances analogous to other cases in which a buyer relied on the seller's expertise to examine a problem, make recommendations, prepare the design, and manufacture a product.

The case dealt with two potential bars to the implied warranty theory. First, U.C.C. § 2-316 excludes implied warranties when a conspicuous writing making the exclusions exists. Therefore, a contract should be reviewed for any exclusionary language. Second is the question of whether the U.C.C. precludes a city from third-party beneficiary claims for lack of privity as a "natural person." Relying on the persuasive authority of the official comments and applying a broad reading of the Code, the *Omaha Pollution Control* court found that § 2-318 was not intended to limit *vertical* privity—that is, privity that includes all the parties in the distributive chain from the immediate seller.

The owner of a construction project should be mindful of restrictions that accompany reliance on the U.C.C. Generally, a statute of limitation for breach of a service contract will be longer than the period under the Code. Section 2-725 requires an action to be commenced within four years of the breach or the tender of delivery, whereas a six-year period is often available for breach of contract.

A subcontractor who supplies component segments of the project may argue that U.C.C. § 2-725 bars the case against him as a vendor of goods.[30] In rebuttal, the owner should contend that the circumstances involve a mixed contract of goods and services rather than one for a product alone. Because Article 2 applies to goods only, courts have held that construction contracts for services and goods fall outside the scope of the U.C.C.

---

[28] 413 F. Supp. 1069 (D. Neb. 1976).

[29] 6 Neb. Rev. Stat., U.C.C. § 2-314(2)(c), 2-315 (1980).

[30] Coakley & Williams, Inc. v. Shatterproof Glass Corp., 778 F.2d 196 (4th Cir. 1985).

§ 11.11 Action for Misrepresentation

There may be situations in which the facts will support a claim of misrepresentation against one or more parties. For example, occasionally
during hiring interviews, design professionals make certain representations or promises that are then relied on by owners. In the competitive
atmosphere of trying to land a contract, engineers sometimes overstate
their capabilities, the ability of the planned construction, facility, or
plant, or both.

Additional elements of a basic misrepresentation claim include reliance
on the representations by the owner, and substantial inaccuracy of the representations, all resulting in injury, damage, and loss to the owner.

§ 11.12 Action for Fraud

Fraud is, of course, a very serious claim and one that normally must be
pleaded with specificity. An example of a fraud claim in a complaint
against an engineer follows:

75. On information and belief, Defendant Engineers knew at all times
material to this action that the treatment process as designed and specified
for the District's wastewater treatment plant was defective and required the
use of short term aeration to achieve secondary treatment and EPA 30/30
BOD and SS standards.

76. On information and belief, Defendant Engineers in 1986 were aware
of and knew the contents of Defendant Supplier Bulletin No. ABCD, which
sets out the requirement of aeration as one of the three key elements in the
treatment process to achieve secondary treatment, and Federal EPA 30/30
BOD and SS standards.

77. In spite of this knowledge, Defendant Engineers failed to make any
provision for short term aeration in the plant design before or after the
award of the construction contract.

78. The District reasonably relied upon the representations of Defendant
Engineers as to their experience and ability to ascertain and disclose material design facts, such as the need for aeration, and Defendant Engineers
made said representations as an inducement for the District to enter into
the contracts.

79. On information and belief, Defendant Engineers knowingly, intentionally, and fraudulently concealed from the District the defects and insuffi-
ciencies of the treatment process and of the design prepared by Defendant
Engineers.

80. As a direct and proximate result of such fraudulent conduct, the
District has been materially and substantially prejudiced, injured, and

damaged, and has suffered monetary losses and been deprived of the benefits of the contracts, all in an amount in excess of $4,000,000.00.

WHEREFORE, the District respectfully requests that a judgment be entered in its favor against Defendant Engineers, jointly and severally, in an
amount in excess of $4,000,000.00, and for punitive damages in excess of
$2,000,000.00, together with interest, its costs incurred, and its attorneys'
fees, costs and disbursements, costs of litigation and such other declaratory
and injunctive relief this Honorable Court deems appropriate.

§ 11.13   Actions under Trade Practice Statutes

During the 1970s many states enacted various types of consumer protection statutes.[31] They were generally intended to apply to "deceptive" acts
involving "consumers" in the traditional sense. However, they also have
been applied to commercial transactions between owners and contractors,
subcontractors, and suppliers.[32] Because they frequently impose strict liability and generally lesser problems of proof, and because they also frequently provide for the award of treble damages, they can be powerful
weapons in an owner's arsenal.

§ 11.14   Actions under the False Claims Act

The federal False Claims Act was originally enacted during the Civil War
as a response to meritless claims brought by contractors against the Union
Army. On October 27, 1986, Congress substantially modified the False
Claims Act to make it a more efficient mechanism for stopping fraud
against the federal Treasury.[33] Of key interest to an owner is the fact that
the 1986 revisions make plain that the False Claims Act applies to claims
made against federal grantees.

The False Claims Act defines a claim to include

> any request or demand, whether under a contract or otherwise, for money
> or property which is made to a contractor, grantee, or other recipient if the
> United States Government provides any portion of the money or property
> which is requested or demanded, or if the Government will reimburse such

---

[31] *See, e.g.,* Alaska Stat. § 45.50.471 (1980); Ill. Code ch. 121½ § 261 (Smith-Hurd
1988 Supp.); Mass. Ann. Laws ch. 93A (Law Co-op 1985); Texas Bus. and Com. Code
Ann. § 17.41 (Vernon).

[32] *See, e.g.,* Jim Walter Homes, Inc. v. Castillo, 616 S.W.2d 630 (Tex. Civ. App. 1981).

[33] 31 U.S.C. § 3729 (Supp. IV 1986).

contractor, grantee, or other recipient for any portion of the money or property which is requested or demanded.[34]

Liability for making such claims arises if the claimant:

(1) Knowingly presents, or causes to be presented . . . a false or fraudulent claim for payment or approval;

(2) Knowingly makes, uses, or causes to be made or used, a false record or statement to get a false or fraudulent claim paid or approved by the government;

(3) Conspires to defraud the government by getting a false or fraudulent claim allowed or paid.[35]

Today, many projects are funded in whole or in part with federal assistance such as Federal Highway Administration, Urban Mass Transit Administration, or Environmental Protection Agency construction grants. Sometimes statements or representations regarding the performance capabilities of equipment or processes turn out to be false, and these representations are often coupled with claims or requests for payment for the services or goods furnished to the local governmental owner.

The newly strengthened Qui Tam, or so-called "private attorney general," provisions of the False Claims Act[36] make it possible for a person—such as an owner of a federally funded project like a municipality building or a wastewater treatment plant—to bring an action in the name of the federal government if it supplies the government with a copy of the complaint and written disclosure of substantially all material evidence and information the owner possesses. The complaint remains under seal for 60 days and cannot be served on the defendant until the court orders it. Although the government may obtain an extension beyond the 60 days, before expiration of the 60-day period, the government must decide whether to proceed with the action or decline to take over the action and allow the owner to proceed on its own. The owner is protected under the Qui Tam provisions because once an action is brought under them no person other than the government may intervene or bring a related action.

Proof of a false claim would likely involve actual or presumed knowledge regarding unproven equipment or designs related to requests for payment. Naturally, they would be vigorously contested, and the factual inquiry of "who knew what when" must be detailed, protracted, expensive, and critical.

---

[34] *Id.* at § 3729(c).

[35] *Id.* at § 3729(a).

[36] *Id.* at § 3730(b).

Nevertheless, the serious civil penalties and damages that are available under the act may make it an effective litigation tool. A party found liable under the False Claims Act could be assessed a civil penalty of $5,000 to $10,000, treble damages, and payment of attorneys' fees. A plaintiff needs to prove the existence of a false claim only by a preponderance of the evidence. There is no requirement of proof of specific intent to defraud; proof of "deliberate ignorance and reckless disregard of truth or falsity" will suffice.

An interesting feature of the Qui Tam provisions of the False Claims Act is that a successful action under it brought against an owner on behalf of the federal government could result in the owner or other plaintiff receiving at least 15 percent, but not more than 25 percent of the proceeds of the action, even if the federal government steps in and takes over that aspect of the case. However, if the court finds the successful action was based primarily on disclosures of information not provided to the government by the grantee owner, the court may not award a sum greater than 10 percent. In any event, some of the proceeds of any recovery would be paid to the federal Treasury. If the government does not step in and a false claim is proved, then recovery to the plaintiff shall not be less than 25 percent nor more than 30 percent of the proceeds. Additionally, the provisions permit a grantee owner or other private plaintiff to recover from the defendant reasonable expenses necessarily incurred in pursuing the action including attorneys' fees and costs, if the action is successful in proving a false claim.

§ 11.15 Civil RICO Actions

In 1970, Congress enacted the Racketeer Influenced and Corrupt Organizations Act (RICO)[37] to combat organized crime through governmentally and individually initiated actions. As originally intended, RICO was designed to strip organized crime of the protection and profits it derived by infiltrating legitimate businesses. Because the statute was written in extremely broad terms, however, it recently has gained the favor of litigants outside the organized crime context in so-called "civil RICO" actions.[38]

Under RICO, courts and arbitrators are empowered to hear civil treble damage claims for violations of § 1962, which defines a violation ("prohibited activity") as, among other things, the use of income derived from a "pattern of racketeering activity" to acquire an interest in or to operate an

---

[37] 18 U.S.C. §§ 1961–68 (1968). *See* P. Batista, Civil RICO Practice Manual (1987).

[38] The Supreme Court recently settled any doubt that RICO was a proper subject of arbitration in Shearson/American Express, Inc. v. McMahon, 482 U.S. 220, 1075 S. Ct. 2332, 96 L. Ed.2d 185 (1987).

enterprise engaged in or affecting interstate commerce, or the conduct of or participation in an enterprise's affairs through a "pattern of racketeering activity" by an employee or by one associated with the enterprise.[39]

A *pattern of racketeering activity,* defined in § 1961(5), entails the performance of at least two "predicate" acts of "racketeering activity" since 1970, and within 10 years of each other. (As the U.S. Supreme Court has intimated, two acts, however, may not be sufficient to establish the requisite pattern.[40]) The definition of *racketeering activity,* therefore, is critical. Under § 1961(1)(A), it is defined to include any act "chargeable" under several generically described state criminal laws, any act "indictable" under any of the numerously specified federal criminal provisions, including mail and wire fraud, and any "offense" involving bankruptcy, securities fraud, or drug-related activities. (Mail fraud is the likely possibility in this case.) Lastly, the term *enterprise* is defined as including "any individual, partnership, corporation, association, or other legal entity."

The factual demonstration required to establish a pattern of racketeering activity is currently in a state of flux. The federal circuit courts have crafted variant theories. Some courts focus on the two act requirement,[41] while others focus on the multiple schemes or episodes approach.[42] Other courts apply a hybrid of both approaches.[43] If a defendant commits two or more predicate acts that are not isolated events but are ongoing over an identifiable period of time, and these acts are in furtherance of a single scheme, then the pattern requirement of RICO is seemingly satisfied.[44] Relevant factors to be considered include the number and variety of predicate acts and the length of time over which they were committed, the number of victims, the presence of separate schemes, and the occurrence of distinct injuries.[45]

Within the last few years, RICO actions have been brought by local governments and have arisen within the context of government construction contracting. Its potential application and use by an owner or grantee, therefore, should not be summarily dismissed. The necessary predicate acts, however, must be established, and must satisfy the continuity and relationship requirements. If two or more instances of garden variety mail fraud could be established—for example, intentionally false statements about

---

[39] *See generally* Wickwire, Clearwater & Gitje, *Civil Remedies for Fraud,* Construction Briefings, 87-13 (1987).

[40] Seidma, S.P.R.L. v. Imrex Co., 473 U.S. 479, 105 S. Ct. 3275, 87 L. Ed.2d 346 (1985).

[41] Bank of America Nat'l Trust & Savings Ass'n v. Touche Ross & Co., 782 F.2d 966 (11th Cir. 1986).

[42] Superior Oil Co. v. Kulmer, 785 F.2d 252 (8th Cir. 1986).

[43] Torwest DBC, Inc. v. Dick, 810 F.2d 925 (10th Cir. 1987).

[44] Morgan v. Bank of Waukegan, 804 F.2d 970, 975 (7th Cir. 1986).

[45] *Id.*

performance transmitted through the mail—RICO could possibly be a powerful tool.

§ 11.16   Potential Defendants

It is obvious that the design professionals,[46] prime contractors, and equipment suppliers are potentially parties in an owner's suit. Other potentially liable entities include subcontractors, sureties, insurance companies, plan review agencies, and successor corporations.

§ 11.17   —Sureties

Usually the contractor is required to furnish a performance bond.[47] The surety that issues the bond may be liable if the bond incorporates the plans and specifications of the project and if the contractor, who is the principal on the bond, defaults. However, *City of San Antonio v. Argonaut Insurance Co.*[48] shows that recovery may be difficult in view of short statute of limitation periods for suits on a performance bond. In that case, the action was not commenced within the applicable one-year period; the city had issued a final certificate of acceptance certifying completion of improvements in the project more than three years prior to filing the complaint.

However, because the liability of the surety is co-extensive with that of the contractor, the surety will not be released by issuance of the final certificate and payment if the contractor committed fraud and there is reliance on a fraudulent determination.[49]

§ 11.18   —Insurers

Numerous questions of insurance coverage need to be answered when analyzing any potential litigation for a project that does not perform properly or at all. For example, virtually all architect/engineer errors and omissions insurance is provided on a "claims-made" basis. That is, the insurance

---

[46] *See generally* Toomey, *Design Professional's Liability During Construction,* Construction Briefings, 87-4 (1987).

[47] *See, e.g.,* Miller Act 40 U.S.C. §§ 270a, 270e (1935); the various state "little Miller Acts"; Federally Assisted Wastewater Treatment Construction was governed by 40 C.F.R. § 35.936-22 (1984).

[48] 644 S.W.2d 90 (Tex. Ct. App. 1981).

[49] Metropolitan Sanitary Dist. of Greater Chicago v. A. Pontarelli & Sons, 7 Ill. App. 3d 829, 288 N.E.2d 905 (1972).

policy provides defense and indemnity for only those claims asserted during the period of the policy, regardless of the time of accrual of the cause of action or occurrence of any negligent act.

Another important insurance consideration is the coverage of the construction contractor. Normal exclusionary language eliminates liability coverage for damage to a contractor's own work, and coverage is afforded for only actual property damage, not defective workmanship.[50]

The law of the given jurisdiction must be consulted to determine if the various insurers may or should be specifically named as defendants.

The statute of limitations also affects the obligations of the insurance carriers that may be responsible for damages caused by defective design or construction. In *Zurn v. Eagle Star Insurance Co.,*[51] the court ruled that the policy requirement that suit be brought within 12 months of the "inception of the loss" referred to the point after a physical loss has occurred when the insured has had the opportunity to comply with conditions precedent to suing on the policy. In this case, inception of the loss was the time when the insured reasonably believed that the city's responsibility for loss was countered by the public entity's delayed response that it was not responsible.

§ 11.19 —Federal and State Agencies

An owner of a rail mass transit facility with a computer signal system that shuts down, or a highway bridge with a severely cracked deck, or a malfunctioning municipal wastewater treatment plant may sometimes feel the urge to include the federal grantor agency and the appropriate state agency as defendants, in view of the agencies' roles in plan approval, inspection, or both. Furthermore, defendants may contend that an agency's approval of plans was a contributing cause of the failure. The EPA anticipated the potential for such claims and specifically requires the inclusion of disclaimer language in engineering and construction contracts.[52] Other federal agencies often insist on similar language. The federal government may have other defenses as well, such as the procedural requirements and limitations of the Federal Tort Claims Act[53] and governmental immunity.

Any claims for damages for errors, omissions, or cost of correction against a state agency would presumably be founded on the agency's

---

[50] St. Paul Fire & Marine Ins. Co. v. Murray Plumbing & Heating Corp., 65 Cal. App. 3d 66, 135 Cal. Rptr. 120 (1976).

[51] 61 Cal. App. 3d 493, 132 Cal. Rptr. 206 (1976).

[52] *See, e.g.,* 40 C.F.R. § 33.1030 Subd.2 (1983) & 40 C.F.R. § 35.935-1a (1977).

[53] 28 U.S.C. § 2860 (1982).

negligence in reviewing and approving plans and specifications or in conducting inspections. Such a determination is, of course, going to be dictated by general negligence principles, including the scope of the state agency's duty to a municipality as well as the applicable standard of care. A recent Texas case, *Lake LBJ Municipal Utility District v. Coulson,*[54] addressed the issue at length. The gist of the case was that an engineer sued a municipal owner for his fees and won at the trial level. On appeal, however, the judgment was reversed and the case remanded. The municipality's basis for nonpayment was allegedly substandard work. The engineer contended that, because the plans had been approved by the Texas State Department of Health's Bureau of Sanitary Engineering, his plans had satisfied professional standards. The appellate court founded its reversal of the trial court on an analysis of the contract and its conclusion that

> [n]othing in the contract expressly or in plain words would make the approval of the governmental agency tantamount to determination that the plans and specifications were sufficient to constitute contract performance, notwithstanding however its administrative effect such approval might have for agency purposes.[55]

In spite of the comfort which *Lake LBJ* may give state plan approval agencies, the law in this area does not appear to be well-established. For example, it can be argued that the assertion of authority and assumption of responsibility for plan approval establishes the duty to do so in a nonnegligent fashion.[56] Indeed, the more rigorous the technical review, the greater the probability of liability being found.

Support for the latter line of reasoning can be found in an assortment of cases involving inspection of construction work.[57] In spite of contract language that said inspection and failure to object to defective work did not constitute acceptance, courts have ruled that when such a duty is assumed by a technically knowledgeable person the owner cannot disclaim the

---

[54] 692 S.W.2d 897 (Tex. Ct. App. 1985) (application for writ of error granted).

[55] *Id.* at 905–06.

[56] Clovis Heimsath & Assocs., NASA No. 180-1, 83-1 B.C.A. (CCH) ¶ 16,132 at 80, 133–34 (Nov. 16, 1982). Restatement (Second) of Torts § 323 provides:

> One who undertakes, gratuitously or for consideration, to render services to another which he should recognize as necessary for the protection of the other's person or things, is subject to liability to the other for physical harm resulting from his failure to exercise reasonable care to perform his undertaking, if (a) his failure to exercise such care increases the risk of such harm, or (b) the harm is suffered because of the other's reliance upon the undertaking.

[57] *See, e.g.,* Neal v. Berglund, 646 F.2d 1178 (6th Cir. 1981), *aff'd sub nom.* Block v. Neal, 460 U.S. 289 (1983). *But see* Cash v. United States, 571 F. Supp. 513 (N.D. Ga. 1983) (based on post-Neal regulatory changes).

inspector's actions or inactions.[58] The underlying rationale is that the inspector was put on the project to inspect and take actions to protect the owner.

§ 11.20   —Governmental Immunity

The issue of tort (negligence) liability of engineers employed by a government agency is almost as old as government itself. Although an in depth discussion of the doctrine of governmental immunity is beyond the scope of this work, several general propositions need to be understood in discussing the exposure of government engineers involved in plan review and approval.

The basic concepts of governmental immunity from suit for actions or inactions of an agency or its employees stem from the Anglo-American doctrine of sovereign immunity, loosely translated to mean "the King can do no wrong." That is, an early principle of English jurisprudence was that the sovereign, who established the court system, should not suffer by virtue of his making a remedy forum available to his subjects. The Supreme Court reaffirmed the vitality of this doctrine most recently in *Boyle v. United Technologies Corp.,*[59] extending the doctrine to a government contractor charged with design defects in military equipment.

Other rationales have emerged over time. An important one is the notion of immunity from suit for discretionary acts. Indeed, a provision of the Federal Tort Claims Act[60] and many analogous state laws providing for a limited and specified waiver of immunity, still retain immunity for so-called discretionary acts. The underlying rationale is that, if government employees in policymaking and decisionmaking positions are not insulated from suit, there will be few people willing to assume the responsibilities of government positions. As a general proposition, design related decisions are deemed not ministerial or operational. However, in *Guild v. United States,*[61] the court deemed the planning and design of a dam by the Soil Conservation Service to be an operational, not discretionary, task. Because "the Government engaged in a species of engineering malpractice," the Federal Tort Claims Act was held applicable.

There are many more reported decisions involving allegedly negligent inspection than review and approval of plans. However, at least one recent case addressed the latter issue somewhat squarely. *Gilbert v. Billman*

---

[58] *See, e.g.,* Lester N-Johnson Co. v. City of Spokane, 22 Wash. App. 265, 588 A.2d 1214 (1978).

[59] 108 S. Ct. 2510, 101 L. Ed.2d 442 (1988).

[60] 28 U.S.C. § 2860 (1982).

[61] 685 F.2d 324 (9th Cir. 1982).

Construction Inc.[62] involved an inspector who would not approve the plans for a septic system unless it was built according to a sketch prepared by the inspector and given to the owner. As it turned out, the system built according to the inspector's sketch was incompatible with the site. The Minnesota Supreme Court reasoned that a potential exemption from liability, the public duty doctrine, was not applicable once the county's inspector undertook to design the system. That is, once the public agency assumed responsibility for the design, a special project-specific relationship was created and this in turn gave rise to a duty to the particular plaintiff. The general rule was stated in a 1974 Wisconsin case establishing an architect's liability to a building tenant:

> A defendant's duty is established when it can be said that it was foreseeable that his act or omission to act may cause harm to someone. A party is negligent when he commits an act when some harm to someone is foreseeable. Once negligence is established, the defendant is liable for unforeseeable consequences as well as foreseeable ones. In addition, he is liable to unforeseeable plaintiffs.[63]

Once the "duty" hurdle is surmounted, the question becomes whether in fact there was a failure to use due care: did the professional engineer employed by the agency adhere to professional standards or the state of the art? Typically, this would be the same standard applied to the design engineer, and if the design engineer is negligent by virtue of incorporating features into the design mandated by the review agency, then the review agency should also be held negligent.

The inspection cases are increasingly taking the approach that, even though an inspector is employed by the public and is so employed to protect the public generally, any duty owed to the public is also a duty owed to individual members. For example, in *Coffey v. City of Milwaukee,*[64] the court rejected the distinction between governmental (discretionary) and proprietary (operational) functions. The court found that a suit could proceed against a city if its inspector negligently inspected standpipes, resulting in insufficient water pressure to adequately fight a fire. Furthermore, the inspector was by implication held to have foreseen that his negligence would result in harm to the building occupants and others. This is another example, then, that once an inspector undertakes an inspection he has a duty to exercise reasonable care, and such duty impliedly flows to the foreseeable victims of the negligent conduct.[65]

---

[62] 371 N.W.2d 542 (Minn. 1985).

[63] A.E. Inv. Corp. v. Link Builders, Inc., 62 Wis. 2d 479, 214 N.W.2d 764 (1974).

[64] 74 Wis. 2d 526, 247 N.W.2d 132 (1976).

[65] *See also* Landsfield v. R.J. Smith Contractors, 146 Mich. App. 637, 381 N.W.2d 782 (1985) (denying immunity to government inspectors of a private project).

§ 11.21 —Design Professional Hired by Government Agency

Finally, there is the related question of the liability of an individual engineer employed by a government agency. In many states, the fact that a professional engineer is employed by a corporation does not shield the engineer from personal financial liability for negligent acts.[66] The rationale for this proposition is that professional services are personal in nature and it is against public policy to allow one to escape liability. Thus, it might also be asked whether the various immunities accorded government employees generally are applicable to professional engineering services. For example, limitation of liability, indemnification, and defense costs may be provided by statutory provisions. These are state-specific, and government engineers should seek current information from their counsel.

§ 11.22 Defenses

Defendants to a lawsuit involving functional failure may have a variety of defenses to assert. Agency plan approval, discussed in § **11.19**, is one. The owner's acceptance of the design and construction without objection is another.

Additional defenses that may be asserted against an owner are the doctrine of assumption of the risk and contributory/comparative negligence.

§ 11.23 —Contract Warranties

Frequently, after the warranty period established under the contract documents for the construction contractor has expired, the owner encounters a failure of a particular piece of equipment or process and looks to the construction contractor for correction. The first inquiry of the construction contractor should be: what does the contract provide? A typical example of relevant contract language might be as follows:

Remedy of defects: Notwithstanding the making be Owner of final inspection and payment, the Contractor shall, at his own expense, remedy all defects in the Work due to:

(a) Failure to comply with Contract Documents or with applicable laws, ordinances, codes, rules, regulations or restrictions;

---

[66] *See, e.g.,* Jabczenski v. Southern Pac. Memorial Hosps., Inc., 579 P.2d 53 (Ariz. 1978); L.B. Indus., Inc. v. Smith, 817 F.2d 69 (9th Cir. 1987); Bischofshausen, Vasbinder & Luckie v. D.W. Jaquays Mining & Equip. Contractors Co., 700 P.2d 902 (Ariz. 1985).

(b) Faulty materials, equipment, appliances or other items supplied by him or supplied by subcontractor's or

(c) Faulty workmanship, whether his own, his employees', or subcontractors';

and shall pay for all damage resulting therefrom which shall appear within a period as may be allowed by law or by the terms of any applicable special warranty required by the Contract Documents. The Owner shall give notice of observed defects within reasonable promptness.

This type of provision must be read together with any "warranty" language that may specify the warranty period. An example of a typical warranty might be:

WARRANTY

The Contractor shall secure and furnish to the Owner all written guarantees and warranties called for in the Contract Documents. Said guarantees and warranties shall be executed in favor of the Owner. Guarantees and warranties on all products shall begin upon Final Acceptance and shall run for one full calendar year thereafter. The Contractor shall require that each manufacturer or supplier that furnishes material and equipment for this project shall agree in writing on his quotation for such material and equipment to furnish and provide the specified guarantees and warranties called for in the Contract Documents on behalf of the Owner and Contractor.[67]

The relevant question that arises given such contract language is when was there substantial completion so as to start the commencement of the warranty period? Most often, the contractor will look to the certificate of final or substantial completion normally issued by a construction owner after final acceptance, usually at some time well after the date of substantial completion. In some states there may be a state statute that will actually dictate the date upon which warranties commence to run, as in Indiana which mandates as a matter of law that warranties will begin not later than the date of substantial completion.[68]

In order for a contractor to respond to a warranty claim, the owner must have a given notice of an observed defect with reasonable promptness.[69] If the owner failed to give such notice within the warranty period, then the contractor should assert that the obligation to provide such warranty work has not arisen.

---

[67] *Note:* in order for there to be a waiver of implied warranties, such as merchantability, or fitness for use intended, they must be specifically and conspicuously disclaimed in the contract. *See* Steele v. Gold Kist, Inc., 186 Ga. App. 569, 368 S.E.2d 196 (1988).

[68] Ind. Code § 36-1-12-14(f) (1981 Cum. Supp.).

[69] *See, e.g.,* Catalytic Eng'g & Mfg. Corp., ASBCA No. 15257, 72-1 B.C.A. (CCH) ¶ 9342; U.C.C. § 2-608(2).

§ 11.24   —Latent Defects

When timely notice of a defect after completion has not been given, the owner may assert that the functional failure encountered is a *latent defect*. The contractor may well then assert that during the period of time that the facility or plant was in operation the contractor was not responsible for and had no knowledge of any repair, maintenance, replacement, or modification that may have taken place which could have affected the performance or condition of the facility or unit or element that has functionally failed. The contractor will undoubtedly argue that the inference that the problem is a latent defect is thus very questionable. The contractor will likewise infer that the problem may have arisen from poor maintenance of the facility or repairs by the maintenance staff of the owner or abuses in the manner in which the equipment or facility has been used.

The basic issue concerning latent defects is whether the contract makes the contractor responsible for their correction. If the contract places responsibility upon the contractor only for correction of deficiencies for a stated warranty period and that period expired before the owner gave notice of a deficiency or problem to the contractor, then the contractor may not have any further liability. Acceptance can be final and conclusive. The Federal Acquisition Regulations grant the federal government the contractual right to rescind final acceptance of a contractor's work in the event of latent defects, fraud, or gross mistake amounting to fraud, as well as providing the government with the right to rescind final acceptance when the contractor's work fails to comply with any warranty or guaranty.[70] Most public owners and even federal grantor agencies have never required in their contracts language similar to that utilized by the federal government.

In most states there may not be a common-law obligation to correct latent defects. For instance, in the case of *Capitol Builders, Inc. v. Shipley*,[71] the principle of latent defects was discussed. The court held that if a latent defect in material purchased from another was unknown to the contractor and not discoverable in the exercise of ordinary care, and such materials were purchased by the contractor from a reputable dealer, the contractor was not responsible for correcting any latent defects. It is to be expected that, in states having case law similar to the *Capitol Builders* decision, the contractor charged with responsibility for a latent defect will assert the necessary elements recited in the case law to absolve the contractor of

---

[70] *See* 48 C.F.R. § 52.246-12(i) (1987), which contains express and clear language to be included in direct federal construction contracts.

[71] 439 N.E.2d 217 (Ind. Ct. App. 1982).

further responsibility. Therefore, absent clear and express contract language, a latent defect argument made by an owner against a construction contractor could be difficult to sustain.

§ 11.25   —Acceptance by Owner

Defendants to functional failure suits should raise the defense of waiver of defects by virtue of an owner's acceptance of the design and construction. The acceptance defense may be mitigated by a latent defects doctrine or express contract language that the owner's rights survive acceptance. Moreover, experiences such as that which occurred in *Chet J. Castille v. 3-D Chemicals, Inc.*[72] can overcome the defense of acceptance. In that case, nonconforming grain storage bins were accepted because they were needed immediately to store the owner's harvest. As a result, the owner was not barred from asserting breach of contract despite his acceptance.

§ 11.26   —Assumption of Risk and Comparative Negligence

Defenses of assumption of the risk and contributory or comparative negligence can be asserted against an owner's claims for defects. *Contributory negligence* is the failure on the part of someone asserting a claim to exercise reasonable care for his own person or property. If his negligence contributes, in whole or in part, to the damages claimed, it is a complete defense to recovery in some jurisdictions.[73] *Comparative negligence* seeks to ameliorate this harsh doctrine by allocating and apportioning responsibility for the damages.[74]

Assumption of the risk is the voluntary acceptance of a risk attendant to an obvious, appreciable damage. If proved, this is also a bar to recovery. In one case, an owner was deprived of any recovery against an engineer when the owner had been informed that a revision of plans and specifications for pilings would increase the chances of soil settlement.[75] The owner elected to save money on pilings, the building settled, and the claims against the engineer were barred.

---

[72] 520 So. 2d 1022 (La. Ct. App. 1987).

[73] Bell v. Jones, 523 A.2d 982 (D.C. Ct. App. 1986).

[74] Clovis Heimsath & Assocs., NASA No. 180-1, 83-1 B.C.A. (CCH) ¶ 16,132 (Nov. 16, 1982) apportioned the damages 50% each to the two parties.

[75] Bowman v. Coursey, 433 So. 2d 251 (La. App. 1983); *see also* Greenhaven Corp. v. Hutchcraft & Assocs., 463 N.E.2d 283 (Ind. App. 1984).

§ 11.27 —Statutes of Limitation

A very formidable defense against an owner's claims may be statutes of limitation. Because many construction projects and facilities are sized for future growth, a plant's inability to produce a result stated at initial design levels may not be apparent until some years after completion of the facility.

In any given situation there will probably be several statutes that are applicable. They need to be carefully analyzed, and the latest case law in the given state should be reviewed.

Speaking generically, most breach of contract claims are deemed to have accrued at the time of the breach, which is, of course, going to be during the performance of either the engineer or the contractor. Thus, the number of years stated in the contract's statute of limitations clause will be measured from that point. Some states, however, apply the "continuous treatment" or "last treatment" doctrine, which assumes that the breach occurred on the last day of more or less continuous performance by the engineer or contractor or that the statutory period is revived by the last occasion that professional services are rendered.[76]

Tort (negligence, misrepresentation, and fraud) claims are governed by the discovery rule in most states. That is, the time for commencing an action begins on the date when the owner discovered and reasonably could have discovered the negligent act or the resulting injury.[77]

Widespread adoption of the discovery rule in the 1960s resulted in suits against a number of design professionals for negligent acts that occurred dozens of years prior to the commencement of the lawsuits. Accordingly, the design professions launched a generally successful effort to enact special statutes of repose, which essentially created a "cap" or limit on the time allowed for bringing an action, measured from the date of substantial completion.[78] (*Substantial completion* may be defined by contract or common law; it is generally the time at which the facility is usable for its intended purpose.[79]) Because of the special protection these statutes provide to the members of the construction team and because they sometimes tend to deprive owners of their day in court, such statutes have been determined to be unconstitutional in many of the states in which they have been enacted.[80]

---

[76] Piracci Constr. Co. v. Skidmore, Owings & Merrill, 490 F. Supp. 314 (S.D.N.Y. 1980). *Compare:* City of Midland v. Helger Constr. Co., 157 Mich. App. 736, 403 N.W.2d 218 (1987) and Hilliard & Bartko v. Fedco Sys., 309 Md. 147, 522 A.2d 961 (1987) (both courts refused to adopt either theory to extend the statutory periods).

[77] Ehrenhaft v. Malcolm Price, Inc., 483 A.2d 1192 (D.C. 1984).

[78] *See generally* J. Sweet, Legal Aspects of Architecture, Engineering, and the Construction Process, § 27.03(G) n.10.

[79] *See, e.g.,* JCDC Doc. 1910-8-1984 at 1 n.2.

[80] McClanahan v. American Gilsonite Co., 494 F. Supp. 1334 (D. Colo. 1980); State Farm & Casualty Co. v. All Elec., Inc., 660 P.2d 995 (Nev. 1983); Phillips v. ABC Builders, Inc.,

Finally, there are a few states in which either the common law or statutes essentially exempt municipal entities from, or ameliorate the effects of, the restrictions of statutes of limitation when the municipalities are plaintiffs in lawsuits to enforce public rights.[81]

§ 11.28   —Improper Operation and Maintenance

Another major family of defenses that should be anticipated is based on allegations of improper or inadequate operation and maintenance by the owner. Whether phrased to support claims of contributory negligence, misuse, or some other doctrine, improper operation and maintenance is inevitably an issue. A thorough review of other practices and careful attention to the quality and quantity of operation and maintenance effort will be very helpful. The skills, training, commitment, and attitude of the operation and maintenance personnel should be reviewed and documented. Likewise, it should be confirmed that the budget and staffing are consistent with the design engineer's recommendations.

§ 11.29   Types and Measures of Damages

The ultimate objective of construction litigation by an owner in the event of a functional failure is to obtain the necessary funds to bring the facility into compliance with whatever requirements or standards are required by safety, design, or usage standards.

§ 11.30   —Cost of Correction versus
Diminution in Value

A contract measure of damages appears to be the most appropriate and straightforward way to bring the project into compliance. It is hornbook law that damages for breach of contract are intended to put the nonbreaching party in the position it would have been in if the contract had been

---

611 P.2d 821 (Wyo. 1980); Broome v. Truluck, 241 S.E.2d 739 (S.C. 1978); Kallas Millwork Corp. v. Square D Co., 225 N.W.2d 454 (Wis. 1976) (all finding statute of repose unconstitutional). *Note: People Who Live in Glass Houses Should Not Build in Vermont: The Need for A Statute of Limitations for Architects,* 9 Vt. L. Rev. 101 (1984). *Compare* Britt v. Schindler Elevator Corp., 637 F. Supp. 734 (D.D.C. 1986) upholding a ten-year statute of repose *with* Turner Constr. Co. v. Scales, 752 P.2d 467 (Alaska 1988) (finding a similar statute unconstitutional).

[81] *See, e.g.,* Alaska Stat. § 09.10.120 (1962); Bellevue School Dist. 405 v. Brazier Constr., 100 Wash. 2d 776, 691 P.2d 178 (1984) (*en banc*).

properly and completely performed.[82] The question then becomes what nonperformance needs to be cured in order to have a properly performing facility. Analysis of all relevant contracts is critical.

It is likewise fundamental to contract law that the preferred measure of damages for defective construction is the cost of correction. However, the plaintiff-owner should be prepared to deal with the contention that, when the cost of correction is enormous as compared to the diminution in value, then the owner is entitled only to diminution in value.[83] An interesting issue arises also when the project that is damaged has no fair market value, such as a bridge or other public property. In such a case one court has held that the cost of replacement or repair was the appropriate measure of damages.[84]

§ 11.31 —Betterment

There is also the question of payment for items that were simply omitted in the original design. Some cases take the view that when an omission from plans and specifications causes an owner to expend extra dollars, the owner should not receive a windfall of added value to a facility through an award of damages against an engineer. One such case involved the owner of a garage who hired a design professional to do plans and specifications and field supervision of a heating system.[85] The heating system was to be sufficient in size and design to keep the building heated to 70 degrees Fahrenheit. After construction, it was found that the building was inadequately heated, which was traced to an error in design. The architect prepared additional plans calling for some new heaters and the relocation of other heaters. The owner accepted these plans and authorized the contractor to do the work they called for at an additional cost of $1,403. The owner then sued the architect for this sum, less a balance due the architect.

The court found that, had the plans been correctly drawn in the first place, the original cost to the owner would have been $183.30 less than the final cost of the original heaters plus the added heaters. (The increment was due to an increase in costs of materials and labor between the dates of the original and final installations.) The owner was only entitled to the lower sum.

---

[82] Williston on Contracts § 1363 (Jaeger 3d ed. 1968).

[83] *See generally* J. Sweet, § 26.06 n.10; Annotation, *Modern Status of Rule as to Whether Cost of Correction or Difference in Value of Structures is Proper Measure of Damages for Breach of Construction Contract,* 41 A.L.R.4th 131 (1985).

[84] Commonwealth Dep't of Transp. v. Estate of Crea, 92 Pa. Commw. 242, 483 A.2d 996 (1977).

[85] Henry J. Robb, Inc. v. Urdahl, 78 A.2d 387 (D.C. App. 1951).

Another case on this issue involved a hospital.[86] The architect failed to comply with a contractual obligation to specify materials meeting building code standards. Accordingly, a certain wall paneling with an unacceptably high flame spread rating was installed and the hospital was therefore denied its operating license. In the ensuing lawsuit, the hospital sued the architect, the contractor, and the paneling supplier. The hospital received a jury award of $300,000 for removing the original paneling and replacing it with code-complying paneling, along with $20,000 for additional architectural services.

On appeal, the court noted that, if the architect had complied with the requirement to specify the proper wall paneling in the first place, the original construction contract price would have been substantially higher. The court then looked at evidence that showed the proper paneling had an installed price of $186,000 and the improper paneling had an installed price of $91,000. The court held that the original overall judgment should have been reduced by the difference of $95,000, for to do otherwise would give a windfall to the owner; if the proper paneling had been specified originally, the original construction contract price would have been $95,000 more.

The recent case of *Zontelli & Sons v. City of Nashwauk*[87] suggests that in certain circumstances the betterment defense may be avoided. In that case, the engineer failed to discover certain subsurface conditions that substantially increased the costs of construction. Had the owner known of the condition before beginning construction, it would not have undertaken the project, so it was permitted to recover for the increased costs.

§ 11.32   —Restitution

Before payment is due a contractor, there must be substantial performance. Failure of substantial performance entitles a contractor to no recovery and is grounds for restitution. What constitutes substantial performance is a jury question and is not subject to a precise definition. As long as there is evidence on which reasonable minds could differ, a court will not disturb a finding of failure of substantial performance.

In a city's action seeking restitution of money paid the contractor for a water and sewer system, the central issue was whether there was substantial performance by the contractor.[88] The court refused to overturn the jury's decision of failure of substantial performance. The evidence adduced at trial, that one-and-one-half percent of the entire sewer and water system

---

[86] St. Joseph Hosp. v. Corbetta Constr. Co., 21 Ill. App. 3d 925, 316 N.E.2d 5 (Ill. App. 1974).

[87] 373 N.W.2d 744 (Minn. 1985); *but see* Gagne v. Bertron, 275 P.2d 15 (Cal. 1954).

[88] Nordin Constr. Co. v. City of Nome, 489 P.2d 455 (Alaska 1971).

needed rebuilding, was such that the jury could reasonably infer that the entire system contained similar defects. Evidence that had a bearing on substantial completion included: the original contract and specifications; testimony regarding materials found on site, including failed materials and materials in deviation with the specifications; testimony regarding the facilities' present condition; and expert opinion regarding the system's future, as well as the cost of rebuilding.

§ 11.33 —Consequential and Economic Loss Damages

Fines and penalties resulting from a facility's noncompliance arguably could be characterized as consequential damages and are potentially recoverable if the breaching party could have foreseen them at the time of contracting.[89]

Economic loss damages in most jurisdictions are generally recoverable.[90] Other jurisdictions require that, when the defect has caused no personal injuries, the owner seeking recovery for economic loss must be in privity of contract (that is, have a direct contractual relationship) with the party charged,[91] or the defect alleged must have been hazardous in itself.[92]

§ 11.34 —Treble and Punitive Damages

Just as economic loss damages are in some instances not recoverable in tort actions, punitive damages are generally not recoverable in breach of contract actions. The conduct necessary for supporting a claim of punitive or exemplary damages is defined by state law. In a recent case in South Carolina, for example, a court found that when a supplier of wastewater treatment equipment knew that its product was defective and failed to disclose this information, the supplier was subject to both replacement costs and punitive damages.[93] In most instances a fraud claim can be coupled with a demand for punitive damages.

---

[89] *See generally* United States v. City of Twin Falls, 806 F.2d 862 (9th Cir. 1986), *cert. denied,* 1078 S. Ct. 3185 (1987).

[90] *See* Bacco Constr. Co. v. American Colloid Co., 148 Mich. App. 397, 384 N.W.2d 427 (1986).

[91] Blake Constr. Co. v. Alley, 303 S.E.2d 724 (Va. 1987).

[92] Pennsylvania Glass & Sand Corp. v. Caterpillar Tractor Co., 652 F.2d 1165 (3d Cir. 1981).

[93] Aiken County v. B.S.P. Div. of Envirotech Corp., 657 F. Supp. 1339 (D.S.C. 1986).

And, as mentioned in §§ **11.13** and **11.15**, consumer protection and RICO statutes may allow the award of treble damages. (See §§ **11.26** and **11.27**.)

An important caveat should be added here with respect to punitive and treble damages. Because of their devastating financial impact, they generally carry a stricter standard of pleading and proof. In addition, rarely will such damages be covered by any sort of insurance policy.

§ 11.35   —Attorneys' Fees

The cost of litigating a major project failure can be substantial, easily running into the hundreds of thousands and sometimes over a million dollars. The numerous parties, the tens of thousands of documents and facts, the number of witnesses, and the amount of time over which a facility was planned, designed, constructed, and ultimately operated all tend to increase the cost. This may be far more than leaky roof or cracked wall litigation. However, with few exceptions, the plaintiff and defendants are all going to be paying their own fees and expenses. The exceptions occur in those states where statute or court rule expressly provides for an award of attorney fees to the prevailing party, and those circumstances in which the parties have by contract agreed to indemnify the prevailing party in any litigation for its legal fees and expenses.

There may, however, be a possibility of obtaining technical and financial assistance from the EPA on EPA grant funded projects.[94]

§ 11.36   Procedural Considerations

The residence of the various potential defendants vis-à-vis the plaintiff generally dictates the availability of the federal courts as a forum. Factors such as backlog, physical location, and discovery rules should be considered in evaluating federal versus state courts. The advantage of having a hometown jury of taxpayers evaluating the engineer and contractor defendant should not be overlooked. Indeed, some owners have included provisions in their contracts regarding where actions must be brought. The Supreme Court in *Breman v. Zapata Offshore Co.*[95] held that "forum selection clauses should control absent a strong showing that it should be set aside."[96]

---

[94] *See, e.g.,* 40 C.F.R. § 35.2350 (1986).

[95] 407 U.S. 1 (1972).

[96] *Id.* at 15.

With the liberal Audit and Access to Records language that is incorporated into federal and many grant-assisted contracts by operation of law,[97] a prospective plaintiff may demand access to all of the engineer's and contractor's records for the project prior to commencing suit.

Care must be taken before suit is filed to ensure that there is a valid basis for bringing the lawsuit. Indeed, in California, at the time of bringing lawsuits against design professionals, attorneys must certify that they have consulted with another professional who has become familiar with the facts and that there is "reasonable and meritorious cause" for the suit.[98] More importantly, under Rule 11 of the Federal Rules of Civil Procedure, the bringing of a suit without proper investigation and the later dismissal of that cause of action as not well founded in law or fact may subject both the attorney and his client to reimbursing their opponents for reasonable costs and attorneys' fees.[99]

Assuming a valid basis for bringing the suit, soon after commencement of the action, an initial wave of discovery should be conducted. This would typically include written interrogatories and a request for production of documents, followed by the scheduling of oral depositions. On larger cases it is recommended that the *Manual For Complex Litigation*[100] be consulted to help control the oftentimes staggering cost of discovery.

§ 11.37   Alternate Dispute Resolution

In light of the complexity of these cases and their attendant costs and attorneys' fees, owners are increasingly giving careful consideration to the possibility of employing other, less expensive and quicker means for resolving their disputes. This, of course, has spawned a revolution in *alternate dispute resolution,*[101] a generic term for "any alternative to full-scale litigation."[102]

In the main, alternate dispute resolution techniques are voluntary efforts on the part of litigants to devise less costly ways of fact-finding,

---

[97] In direct federal contracts audit access is provided primarily under 10 U.S.C. § 2306(f) (1986) and 10 U.S.C. § 2313(a) (19___) and as implemented by 48 C.F.R. § 52.215-2 (1987). For an example of Access to Records language in a federally assisted contract *see* 40 C.F.R. § 33.1030 Subp. 9 (1983).

[98] Cal. Civ. Proc. Code § 411.35 (West Supp. 1988). *Note:* this provision will be repealed on January 1, 1992, unless extended by the legislature.

[99] Johnson, Cassaday & Edward, *Frivolous Lawsuits and Defensive Responses to Them,* 36 Ala. L. Rev. 927, 944 (1985).

[100] (Clark Boardman & Co. 1986.)

[101] Edwards, *Alternate Disputes Resolution: Panacea or Anathema,* 99 Harv. L. Rev. 668 (1986).

[102] Annual Judicial Conference, Second Circuit, 115 F.R.D. 349, 377 (1987).

negotiating, mediating, and resolving disputes. Importantly, these techniques need not be employed in lieu of litigation but can also serve as an adjunct thereto, such as when impasses are reached and need to be overcome in order for negotiations to proceed. One of the most commonly utilized alternate dispute resolution techniques is the so-called "mini-trial." This has been described as follows:

> Senior executives of the parties hear abbreviated presentations by opposing attorneys of the best of both cases, often in the presence, but not always in the presence, of a neutral adviser who may keep order. He may render an advising opinion, he may assist in mediating or he may do both of the above. Following the presentations, the executives meet to negotiate settlement which, in most mini-trials, has entailed a creative, materially advantageous business solution.[103]

It is interesting to note that the Kansas City Hyatt-Regency collapse case employed these alternate dispute resolution techniques in its resolution.[104] These techniques are as varied as lawyers' imaginations, and most worthy of consideration.

---

[103] *Id.* at 378.
[104] *Id.* at 381–86.

CHAPTER 12

LIABILITY OF THE DESIGN PROFESSIONAL FOR CONSTRUCTION FAILURES

Kenneth I. Levin, Esquire

Kenneth I. Levin is a partner in the law firm of Pepper, Hamilton & Scheetz in Philadelphia, Pennsylvania, and specializes in construction and surety litigation. He is Pennsylvania State Chairman of the American Bar Association's Section of Public Contract Law and a member of the ABA's Section of Litigation, Construction Litigation Committee, Section of Torts and Insurance Practice, Fidelity and Surety Committee, and Forum Committee on the Construction Industry.

Mr. Levin coauthored *Construction Contracts 1987: Rights and Responsibilities of the General Contractor, Sub-Contractor and Material Supplier,* and is also a coauthor of chapters on design professional liabilities in *Construction Litigation: Representing the Contractor* and *Architect and Engineer Liability: Claims Against Design Professionals.*

Mr. Levin received his undergraduate degree from Cornell University and graduated magna cum laude from Villanova Law School.

BASIS AND PROOF OF LIABILITY

§ 12.1   The Basis of Liability

In the absence of express contractual warranties or stipulations imposing a different standard of care, proof of negligence has traditionally been required as a basis for the imposition of liability in damages upon design professionals. The basic rule has been stated as follows:

> Plaintiff was an engineer and was employed as such. In performing the work which he undertook, it was his duty to exercise such care, skill and diligence as men engaged in that profession ordinarily exercise under like circumstances. He was not an insurer that the contractors would perform their work properly in all respects; but it was his duty to exercise reasonable care to see that they did so.[1]

Although the doctrines of implied warranty and strict liability (liability without fault) are widely applied as a basis for imposing liability upon manufacturers of defective products, the courts, for the most part, have rejected these doctrines in assessing the liability of design professionals.[2]

---

[1] Pastorelli v. Associated Eng'rs, Inc., 176 F. Supp. 159, 166 (D.R.I. 1959) (quoting Cowles v. City of Minneapolis, 128 Minn. 452, 151 N.W. 184, 185 (1915)).

[2] Del Mar Beach Club Owners Ass'n v. Imperial Contracting Co., 123 Cal. App. 3d 898, 176 Cal. Rptr. 886 (1981); Castaldo v. Pittsburgh-Des Moines Steel Co., 376 A.2d 88 (Del. 1977); Borman's, Inc. v. Lake State Dev. Co., 60 Mich. App. 175, 230 N.W.2d 363 (1975); City of Mounds View v. Walijarvi, 263 N.W.2d 420 (Minn. 1978); Board of Trustees v. Kennerly, Slomanson & Smith, 167 N.J. Super. 311, 400 A.2d 850 (Law Div. 1979); Sears, Roebuck & Co. v. Enco Assocs., 43 N.Y.2d 389, 372 N.E.2d 555, 401 N.Y.S.2d 767 (1977). *Contra,* Federal Mogul Corp. v. Universal Constr. Co., 376 So. 2d 716 (Ala. Civ. App. 1979) (dicta); Broyles v. Brown Eng'g Co., 275 Ala. 35, 151 So. 2d 767 (1963) (limited to provision of routine services); Bloomsburg Mills, Inc. v. Sardoni

The rationale for refusing to impose strict liability upon design profession-als was articulated in *City of Mounds View v. Walijarvi*,[3] in which the court observed:

> Architects, doctors, engineers, attorneys, and others deal in somewhat inex-act sciences and are continually called upon to exercise their skilled judg-ment in order to anticipate and provide for random factors which are incapable of precise measurement. The indeterminate nature of these factors makes it impossible for professional service people to gauge them with com-plete accuracy in every instance. Thus, doctors cannot promise that every operation will be successful; a lawyer can never be certain that a contract he drafts is without latent ambiguity; and an architect cannot be certain that a structural design will interact with natural forces as anticipated. Because of the inescapable possibility of error which inheres in these services, the law has traditionally required, not perfect results, but rather the exercise of that skill and judgment which can be reasonably expected from similarly situ-ated professionals.
>
> [Further], while it is undoubtedly fair to impose strict liability on manu-facturers who have had ample opportunity to test their products for defects before marketing them, the same cannot be said of architects. Normally, an architect has but a single chance to create a design for a client which will produce a defect free structure. Accordingly, we do not think it just that architects should be forced to bear the same burden of liability for their products as that which has been imposed on manufacturers generally.[4]

It is, however, possible for a design professional to contract to a higher standard of care, as was illustrated in *Arkansas Rice Growers Cooperative Association v. Alchemy Industries, Inc.*,[5] which arose out of a project to construct an experimental plant for the combustion of rice hulls. When the plant did not perform as anticipated, the owner sued the designer.

The designer had agreed to provide

> the necessary engineering plant layout and equipment design and the on-site engineering supervision and start-up engineering services necessary for the

---

Constr. Co., 401 Pa. 358, 164 A.2d 201 (1960) (warranty of fitness). *See also* Doundoulakis v. Town of Hempstead, 42 N.Y.2d 440, 368 N.E.2d 24, 398 N.Y.S.2d 401 (1977) (holding that strict liability could apply when design is for a project which in itself constitutes an abnormally dangerous activity as defined in Restatement (Sec-ond) of Torts § 520 (1976)).

[3] 263 N.W.2d 420 (Minn. 1978).

[4] *Id.* at 424, 425. This formulation is consistent with the professional standard of care articulated in the Restatement (Second) of Torts § 299A (1965):

> Unless he represents that he has greater or less skill or knowledge, one who undertakes to render services in the practice of a profession or trade is required to exercise the skill and knowledge normally possessed by members of that pro-fession or trade in good standing in similar situation.

[5] 797 F.2d 565 (8th Cir. 1986).

construction of a hull by-product facility capable of reducing a minimum of seven and one-half tons of rice hulls per hour to ash and producing a minimum of 48 million BTUs per hour of steam at 200 lbs. pressure.[6]

Both the trial and appellate courts concluded that this provision amounted to an express warranty of the design. Accordingly, proof that the plant failed to perform as anticipated because the furnace system, as designed, could not perform properly when the outside temperature was less than 50 degrees Fahrenheit was sufficient to establish the owner's case. Additional proof of professional negligence was not required.[7]

As *Arkansas Rice Growers* demonstrates, a design professional may by contract agree to a more rigorous standard of care, but it has also been held that the benefit of such higher standard runs solely to those in privity and not to third-party tort claimants.[8]

§ 12.2 Proof of Design Professional Negligence

To establish a design professional's liability for professional negligence, the plaintiff must present evidence (1) establishing the applicable standard of care, (2) demonstrating a violation of the standard, and (3) demonstrating the causal relationship between the violation and the alleged harm.[9]

Ordinarily, proof of design professional negligence must be established by expert testimony. The standard of care must be determined from the testimony of experts unless the conduct involved is within the common knowledge of laymen.[10] Depending on the jurisdiction in which the claim

---

[6] *Id.* at 566.

[7] However, although it might be tempting for an owner to contract a professional to a higher standard of care, as in *Arkansas Rice Growers,* this benefit might prove illusory, as the provision of a special warranty may impair or exceed the scope of coverage afforded by the professional's errors and omissions insurance policy.

[8] *See* Peter Kiewit Sons' Co. v. Iowa S. Utils. Co., 355 F. Supp. 376, 394 (S.D. Iowa 1973).

[9] *Bell v. Jones,* 523 A.2d 982, 987 (D.C. App. 1987).

[10] *See* Allied Properties v. John A. Blume & Assocs., Eng'rs, 25 Cal. App. 3d 848, 102 Cal. Rptr. 259 (1972); Paxton v. County of Alameda, 119 Cal. App. 2d 393, 259 P.2d 934 (1953); Overland Constructors, Inc. v. Millard School Dist., 220 Neb. 220, 369 N.W.2d 69, 76 (1985); R.G. Wood & Assocs., 85-1 B.C.A. (CCH) ¶ 17,898 (PSBCA 1985). *See generally* Annotation, *Products Liability: Manufacturer's Responsibility for Defective Component Supplied by Another and Incorporated in Product,* 3 A.L.R.4th 1023 (1981).

In Milton J. Womack, Inc. v. House of Representatives, 509 So. 2d 62, 67 (La. Ct. App.), *cert denied,* 513 So. 2d 1208, *cert. denied,* 513 So. 2d 1211 (1987), the court held that the failure of an architect who drew plans for the renovation of a state capital building to discover a metal x-brace within an interior basement wall scheduled for

arises, the design professional's conduct may be measured by a national, rather than a local or regional, standard of care.[11] Although the standard of care is determined with reference to ordinary practices, nevertheless, it has been urged that a failure to adopt new and available technology might constitute design professional negligence even though its utilization is not yet customary in the profession.[12]

It has been held that proof of a violation of a municipal building code constitutes evidence of negligence,[13] as may violation of private safety standards.[14]

§ 12.3 Design Professional Negligence in Design Preparation

A design professional may be held liable for negligent acts or omissions committed either in the preparation of plans and specifications or in the administration or inspection of the work of construction contractors. A review of several relevant cases will be useful to illustrate the general contours of the duty of care owed by design professionals.

---

demolition was an omission from which laymen could infer negligence without the necessity of expert testimony. The existence of the x-brace was shown in the original blueprints for the capital, which were available on microfilm. The court stated:

> It is "common sense" to conclude that it is the duty of an architect to use reasonable skill and care to determine the location of important structural elements before he completes his plans and authorizes work to begin in accordance with those plans.

[11] *See* Bell v. Jones, 523 A.2d 982, 988 (D.C. App. 1987).

[12] *See,* Peck & Hoch, *Engineer's Liability: State of the Art Consideration in Defining Standard of Care,* 30 Villanova L. Rev. 403, 422–33 (1985) (citing, inter alia, The T.J. Hooper, 60 F.2d 737, 739–40 (2d Cir.), *cert. denied,* 287 U.S. 662 (1932)). Judge Learned Hand stated:

> There are, no doubt, cases where courts seem to make the general practice of the calling the standard of proper diligence. . . . Indeed in most cases reasonable prudence is in fact common prudence; but strictly it is never its measure; a whole calling may have unduly lagged in the adoption of new and available devices. . . . There are precautions so imperative that even their universal disregard will not excuse their omission.

[13] Johnson v. Salem Title Co., 246 Or. 409, 425 P.2d 519 (1967) (Uniform Building Code). Indeed, in Burran v. Dambold, 422 F.2d 133, 135 (10th Cir. 1970), it was held that a failure to design in accordance with a state building code constituted negligence per se.

[14] Evans v. Howard R. Green Co., 231 N.W.2d 907 (Iowa 1975) ("Ten-State Standards" promulgated by Great Lakes-Upper Mississippi River Board of State Sanitary Engineers). *But see* Hackley v. Waldorf-Hoerner Paper Prods. Co., 149 Mont. 286, 425 P.2d 712 (1967) (advisory codes or standards of safety without force of law not admissible in evidence).

Reasonable precision is required in the drafting of plans and specifications for the work. In *Eggers Partnership,*[15] an architect was held negligent for specifying that installation of a particular roofing material should be in accordance with the manufacturer's installation manual, when project conditions, in fact, required a special application technique. It was improper for the architect to rely upon the contractor to ascertain that special application techniques were required.

A design professional is not entitled simply to rely upon the assurances of manufacturers or the advice of their consultants. In *Scott v. Potomac Insurance Co.,*[16] an architect was held to be negligent in substituting tin-plated steel tubing for copper tubing in a radiant heating system without changing the method of installation to allow for differing expansion characteristics of the steel tubing. Reliance upon the manufacturer's statement that the steel tubing would be a suitable substitute and a heating consultant's approval of the substitution was not sufficient to satisfy the architect's duty of care. The court held that the architect had an obligation independently to ascertain the true suitability of the substitute material and to determine if it could be safely installed in the manner originally prescribed for the copper tubing. The court stated: "It ill-behooves a man professing professional skill to say I know nothing of an article which I am called upon to use in the practice of my profession."[17]

The design professional's duty of care and design extends to the development of solutions to problems arising during the course of construction. In *Clemens v. Benzinger,*[18] the original plans for the erection of steel columns called for the columns to be attached to anchor bolts embedded in concrete floors. However, the concrete contractor neglected to embed the anchor bolts in several locations when the floor was originally poured. The engineer therefore directed the contractor to drill holes for the installation of the omitted anchors and then to grout around the bolts with cement. Although the strength of those bolts as supports for the columns was then entirely dependent on the resistance of the cement around the bolts, the engineer thereafter failed to warn the steel erector that the grout was not fully cured. An employee of the erection contractor was killed when anchor bolts to which columns were then attached pulled up out of the floors because the cement grout had not fully hardened. The court stated:

> When the [concrete contractor] deviated from the original plans, a new situation arose which required a new plan, or at least a new direction to the contractors in place of the original plan. The duty to take care of the situation which had then arisen rested on the defendant [engineer], and it

---

[15] 82-1 B.C.A. (CCH) ¶ 15,630 (IBCA 1982).

[16] 217 Or. 323, 341 P.2d 1083 (1959).

[17] 341 P.2d at 1088.

[18] 211 A.D. 586, 207 N.Y.S. 539 (1925).

recognized such duty and took steps in accordance with it. The superintendent of that company gave direction as to how the problem was to be met. Negligence in this act is the same as negligence in respect to the original plans, and gives rise similarly to a cause of action in favor of one who receives injury therefrom.[19]

§ 12.4   Design Professional Negligence in Construction Supervision

In general, the courts have rejected efforts to impose "clerk of the works"-type supervisory or inspection responsibilities upon design professionals which would, in effect, make them guarantors of the quality of construction. In *Weill Construction Co. v. Thibodeaux,*[20] an architectural firm was sued by the owner of a roller skating facility. After completion of the facility, water seeped through the concrete slab and damaged the hardwood floor of the rink. The trial court found that the general contractor for the project had poured the slab improperly so as to create a horizontal cold joint through which the seepage had occurred.

The owner's claim for negligent supervision of the construction by the architectural firm was rejected by both the trial and appellate courts, which held that the architect had no duty to supervise the construction of the slab floors. The appeals court relied on testimony that the architect's fee for the project was five percent of the construction costs, whereas a fee of six or seven percent would have been required if it had contracted to supervise the work of the general contractor. Similarly, the court concluded that the language of the general conditions of the contract for construction tended to negate, rather than create, a duty of supervision. The contract provided:

The Architect will make periodic visits to the site to familiarize himself generally with the progress and quality of the work to determine if the work is proceeding in accordance with the Contract Documents. On the basis of his on-site observations as an Architect, he will keep the Owner informed of the progress of the work, and will endeavor to guard the Owner against defects and deficiencies in the work of the Contractor. The Architect will not be required to make exhaustive or continuous on-site inspections to check the quality or quantity of the work. The Architect will not be responsible for the construction site, means, methods, techniques, sequences or procedures, or for safety precautions and programs in connection with the work, and he will not be responsible for the Contractor's failure to carry out the work in accordance with the Contract Documents. The undertakings of periodic visits and observations by the Architect or his associates shall not be construed as superintendence of actual construction. Neither

---

[19] 207 N.Y.S. at 543.
[20] 491 So. 2d 166 (La. Ct. App. 1986).

the provisions of this paragraph nor their failure specifically to exclude other liability shall extend in any way the liability of the Architect to any person whomsoever.

However, even though, as in *Thibodeaux,* an architect has not contracted to provide continuous on-site inspection, the cases demonstrate that she still owes a duty of care when making such periodic observations or inspections as she does make.[21] It has been held that, when making periodic inspections or observations, an architect has a duty to specifically inspect those aspects of the construction likely to create safety hazards if installation is improper. In *Pastorelli v. Associated Engineers, Inc.,*[22] after completion of construction, an employee of the owner was injured by a falling heating duct. The duct, which was 20 feet long and weighed 500 pounds, was suspended from hangers attached by nails to a ceiling of seven-eighths inch sheathing. In view of the weight of the duct, good installation practice would have required securing the hangers to the roof joists or the roof itself with lag screws. The evidence showed that the architect was not aware of the defective manner of installation of the hangers. He had not been present while the duct was being installed and had made no effort afterwards to determine how it was installed. The court held that, because it was apparent that the safety of persons in the structure required that the ducts be securely fastened, the architect's failure to take steps to ascertain how they were affixed constituted negligence.

§ 12.5   Liability for Errors and Omissions of Consultants

The risks are substantial that a design professional will be held responsible for the errors or omissions of a consultant whom he engages. However, the courts are not uniform in the theories they apply in these cases. For example, design professionals have been held liable for such errors on the theory that their consultants are their agents.[23] In *Johnson v. Salem Title Co.,*[24] on the other hand, the court characterized an engineering consultant whom an architect had engaged to design a masonry wall as an independent

---

[21] *See* Dickerson Constr. Co. v. Process Eng'g Co., 341 So. 2d 646 (Miss. 1977). *But compare* Moundsview Indep. School Dist. No. 621 v. Buetow & Assocs., Inc., 253 N.W.2d 836 (Minn. 1977) (architect did not observe deficiencies in installation of roof on periodic visits that it did make, summary judgment in favor of architect was appropriate; court would not give owner benefit of clerk of the works-type inspection when owner paid for less).

[22] 176 F. Supp. 159 (D.R.I. 1959).

[23] *See* Scott v. Potomac Ins. Co., 217 Or. 323, 341 P.2d 1083 (1959); Bayuk v. Edson, 236 Cal. App. 2d 309, 46 Cal. Rptr. 49 (1965).

[24] 246 Or. 409, 425 P.2d 519 (1967).

contractor. However, the architect was held vicariously liable for the engineer's failure to design the wall to conform with a city building code, because the code was construed to impose upon the architect a nondelegable duty intended to protect the public. Therefore, the architect was held vicariously liable in spite of the consulting engineer's independent contractor status. Moreover, even if a consultant should be regarded as an independent contractor, an architect/engineer still could be held liable for negligence in the selection of the consultant or for negligent failure to ascertain deficiencies in her work.

In a case in which a design professional has been subjected to liability as a result of an error by her consultant, it would appear that she would have a right against her for indemnity.[25]

§ 12.6 Proximate Cause

It is fundamental that for liability to be imposed upon a design professional her negligence must be a causal factor in bringing about the injury for which a recovery is sought. *Bayne v. Everham*[26] is illustrative. A wrongful death action was brought against the designer of a system of reinforced concrete construction for a parking garage after the structure collapsed. There was evidence of negligence in design: the system did not conform to the applicable building code. However, uncontradicted evidence showed that the contractor had deviated from the plans in several respects pertinent to the cause of the failure. The court ruled the designer could not be held liable under the circumstances. It stated:

> [W]here the variance is not disputed, and involves the integrity of the mode of construction of the affected part, and is so far material that it may have been the direct cause of the injury for which the [plaintiff] seeks to hold the architect responsible, it must be held, we think, that the plaintiff has failed to establish the cause of action upon which he relies.[27]

However, a design professional will not be relieved of liability merely because the negligence of the contractor is a cause concurrent with the design professional's own negligence in bringing about the harm.[28]

---

[25] *See, e.g.,* Grossman v. Sea Air Towers, Ltd., 513 So. 2d 686, 689 (Fla. Dist. Ct. App. 1987).

[26] 197 Mich. 181, 163 N.W. 1002 (1917).

[27] 163 N.W. at 1007 (quoting Lake v. McElfatrick, 139 N.Y. 349, 34 N.E. 922, 925 (1893)). *See also* Goette v. Press Bar & Cafe, 413 N.W.2d 854, 855–56 (Minn. App. 1987) (architect not liable for injuries resulting from collapse of wall which resulted from contractor's deviation from plans when owner-architect agreement imposed no obligation of supervision on architect).

[28] Palmer v. Brown, 127 Cal. App. 2d 44, 273 P.2d 306 (1954).

POTENTIAL PARTIES

§ 12.7　Direct Actions by the Owner

A significant area of controversy in actions by owners is the scope of damages recoverable. In *Pearce & Pearce, Inc. v. Kroh Bros. Development Co.,*[29] the architectural firm that drew up the plans and specifications for a medical office complex was sued by the owner when the building suffered damage due to interior water leakage. The trial court concluded that the architect's failure to include flashings in the specifications constituted negligent design and was the major contributor to the leaks experienced on the project. The trial court awarded the owner, who had sold the project prior to trial, damages of $198,000 based upon a "cost of repairs" measure. The value of the building as established at trial was $4.9 million. On appeal, the architectural firm raised, inter alia, the contention that the proper measure of damages should have been the "diminution in value" caused by the water leakage. However, the appellate court held that either diminution in value or the cost of repairs was a proper measure of damages for breach of a construction contract, absent evidence of economic waste. The court then held that the cost of repairs could not be characterized as unreasonable economic waste in relation to the total value of the building in this case.

The architect suggested that cost of repair damages was also inappropriate because the owner had sold the building prior to trial and had not, in fact, made any repairs. The architect argued that the owner should not be able to recover costs that it would never incur. The appellate court rejected this argument, however, stating, "[W]e do not believe that [the owner's] sale of the subject property prior to trial affects appellee's right to recover damages for a breach of construction contract which occurred prior to sale. *See,* Subsection 346(1)(a), Restatement (First) of Contracts (1932)."[30] It noted that there is no requirement that a plaintiff spend any recovery it may receive to make the repairs and added that it could be logically presumed, without specific proof on the issue, that the defective condition of the building was reflected in the purchase price the owner received on sale.

In *Fairfax County Redevelopment & Housing Authority v. Hurst & Associates Consulting Engineers, Inc.,*[31] the owner of an apartment project sued its consulting engineer for breach of contract. The engineering firm had specified replacement air conditioning units, which would not fit into the

---

[29] 474 So. 2d 369 (Fla. Dist. Ct. App. 1985).

[30] *Id.* at 371.

[31] 231 Va. 164, 343 S.E.2d 294 (1986).

apartment mechanical rooms and also required heavier wiring than was available in the project.

The jury returned a verdict for the housing authority, but the trial court had excluded evidence of the expense to the authority of repairing the old units and of storing the new units pending a resolution. The court of appeals held that merely because such damages were "consequential" did not mean they were unrecoverable. Rather, the issue was whether the losses claimed were within the contemplation of the parties at the time of contracting, an issue on which there was sufficient evidence to go to the jury.[32]

In *Grossman v. Sea Air Towers, Ltd.,*[33] a concrete deck open to service vehicles collapsed because it was underdesigned to support the traffic load. Although the design was sufficient for the originally contemplated use of the deck, the architect and its structural consultant negligently failed to advise the owner of the need for an increased structural capacity after the traffic pattern was redesigned to accommodate heavy service vehicles. However, the damages for which the professionals were liable were limited to the costs of restoring the deck to its original condition plus related losses occasioned by the interruption of or adverse effect on business operations. They were not liable for costs incurred in increasing the load capacity of the deck because that "would have been the owners' responsibility even if there had been no negligence on the part of the defendants."[34]

Design professionals may also be liable to owners on theories of express or implied indemnity for liabilities to contractors resulting from design errors and omissions.[35]

§ 12.8 Erosion of the Concept of Privity

Traditionally, the scope of a design professional's liability was limited by the doctrine of privity. A design professional could only be sued by the person with whom she had contracted: her client. Although the contract

[32] 343 S.E.2d at 295–96. In *Kishwaukee Community Health Serv. Center v. Hospital Bldg. & Equip. Co.,* 638 F. Supp. 1492, 1504 (N.D. Ill. 1986), the district court, applying Illinois law, held that an owner could not sue a design professional in tort when he had an adequate contract remedy available against the design professional. This holding might have significance if an owner seeks to recover for unforeseen consequential damages not recoverable in contract.

[33] 513 So. 2d 686 (Fla. Dist. Ct. App. 1987).

[34] *Id.* at 688.

[35] *See* United States v. Skidmore, Owings & Merrill, 505 F. Supp. 1101 (S.D.N.Y. 1981) (express indemnity); Miller v. City of Broken Arrow, 660 F.2d 450 (10th Cir. 1981) (implied indemnity); Fairbanks N. Star Borough v. Roen Design Assocs., 727 P.2d 758 (Alaska 1986) (implied indemnity).

for architectural or engineering services still remains the basic measure of the scope of the duties that the professional has undertaken for a particular project, her liability for breach of those duties has in many cases (see §§ 12.8 through 12.10) been held to extend to third persons with whom she is not in contractual privity.

Increasingly, the scope of the architect's or engineer's liability is determined by applying tort concepts of foreseeability rather than contractual concepts of privity. The concept of foreseeability has been explained by one court in the following manner:

> Under the existing status of the law, an architect who plans and supervises construction work, as an independent contractor, is under a duty to exercise ordinary care in the course thereof for the protection of any person who foreseeably and with reasonable certainty may be injured by his failure to do so.[36]

A design professional is now generally subject to suit by employees of contractors or users of facilities who have been injured as a result of her negligence in design or in the inspection of construction.[37] The courts, however, are divided on whether design professionals are liable for economic losses claimed by tenants or subsequent buyers of facilities that they have designed.[38]

In *A.E. Investment Corp. v. Link Builders, Inc.,*[39] the court held that a tenant, the operator of a supermarket, could sue an architect for damages consisting of loss of profits, loss of fixtures, equipment, and merchandise, and loss of reputation and good will under its claim that the architect's design negligence had resulted in floor subsidence that made the leased structure untenantable. The court stated:

> A defendant's duty is established when it can be said that it was foreseeable that his act or omission to act may cause harm to someone. A party is

---

[36] Montijo v. Swift, 219 Cal. App. 2d 351, 353, 33 Cal. Rptr. 133, 134–35 (1963).

[37] *See, e.g., id.* (customer of owner); Hiatt v. Brown, 422 N.E.2d 736 (Ind. Ct. App. 1981) (passenger injured on airport ramp); Evans v. Howard R. Green Co., 231 N.W.2d 907 (Iowa 1975) (employee of contractor); Inman v. Binghamton Hous. Auth., 3 N.Y.2d 137, 164 N.Y.S.2d 699, 143 N.E.2d 895 (1957) (owner's tenant); Clemens v. Benzinger, 211 A.D. 586, 207 N.Y.S. 539 (1925) (contractor's employee); *Johnson v. Salem Title Co.,* 246 Or. 409, 425 P.2d 519 (1967) (pedestrian injured by falling wall); Pastorelli v. Associated Eng'rs, Inc., 176 F. Supp. 159 (D.R.I. 1959) (employee of owner).

[38] Cooper v. Jevne, 56 Cal. App. 3d 860, 128 Cal. Rptr. 724 (1976) (purchasers of condominium units could sue for purely economic losses); San Francisco Real Estate Investors v. J.A. Jones Constr. Co., 524 F. Supp. 768 (S.D. Ohio 1981), *aff'd,* 703 F.2d 976 (6th Cir. 1983) (subsequent purchaser of structure may not sue architect).

[39] 62 Wis. 2d 479, 214 N.W.2d 764 (1974).

negligent when he commits an act when some harm to someone is foreseeable. Once negligence is established, the defendant is liable for unforeseeable consequences as well as foreseeable ones. In addition, he is liable to unforeseeable plaintiffs.[40]

The court, however, ruled that the architect would, at trial, be permitted to present evidence on whether public policy considerations should in that particular case preclude an award of damages for such economic losses.[41]

Finally, as will be discussed in detail in § 12.11, the courts have also divided on whether a contractor may sue an architect or engineer for damages for economic harm resulting from professional negligence.

§ 12.9   Injured Construction Employee's Right of Action

It is established that a design professional will be held responsible for the injury to or death of a construction contractor's employee resulting from the professional's negligence in design or in providing improper directions in the course of construction.[42] However, the courts have divided on the issue of the architect/engineer's liability for injuries resulting from unsafe construction methods or procedures employed by a contractor. Some courts respect provisions of the architect-owner agreement limiting the professional's obligation to observe or inspect in terms of both frequency and scope (to guard the owner against deviations from the plans and specifications) and disclaimers of responsibility for the construction procedures of contractors. Nevertheless, other courts have inferred from provisions vesting a professional with the right to stop the work a corresponding duty to exercise care to prevent contractors from employing unsafe procedures.[43]

The genesis of the present-day standard form American Institute of Architects (AIA) agreements reflects a history of efforts to eliminate those provisions that have been held to impose duties on design professionals with respect to job-site safety and performance. For example, architects

---

[40] 214 N.W.2d at 766.

[41] *Id.* at 770.

[42] *See* Evans v. Howard R. Green Co., 231 N.W.2d 907 (Iowa 1975) (negligent design); Clemens v. Benzinger, 211 A.D. 586, 207 N.Y.S. 539 (1925) (negligent design and failure to warn).

[43] *Compare* Miller v. DeWitt, 37 Ill. 2d 273, 226 N.E.2d 630 (1967) (duty imposed), *with* Krieger v. J.E. Greiner Co., 282 Md. 50, 382 A.2d 1069 (1978) (duty rejected). *See generally* Annotation, *Liability to One Injured in Course of Construction, Based upon Architect's Alleged Failure to Carry Out Supervisory Responsibilities,* 59 A.L.R.3d 869 (1974).

no longer "inspect," they just "observe." Whether the most recent revisions that disclaim an independent authority to stop the work will prove successful remains to be fully tested in the courts. In some cases such provisions have resulted in the conclusion that an engineering firm could not be held liable for a contractor's unsafe construction practices resulting in injury to an employee.[44]

LIABILITY TO CONTRACTORS

§ 12.10   Contractor's Right of Action

The recognition of the contractor's right of action against the design professional, though no longer a novelty, is still a relatively recent development. Moreover, although it appears that the right has been sanctioned by the majority of jurisdictions that have considered it in recent years, acceptance has neither been universal nor unqualified.

The 1958 decision in *United States ex rel. Los Angeles Testing Laboratory v. Rogers & Rogers*[45] marked the beginning of a new era in the law of architectural malpractice. Before *Rogers,* the defense of privity had effectively insulated the design professional from malpractice liability for economic losses to all members of the contracting group except her client, the owner. In *Rogers,* a prime contractor sued a project architect. The architect had, as required by the owner-architect agreement, reviewed tests performed on concrete supplied by the plaintiff's subcontractor, and had authorized the incorporation of the concrete in the building under construction. Upon later inspection, a state agency refused to pass the structural members in which the concrete had been incorporated and the architect stopped the work while corrective measures were taken. The prime contractor sued the architect to recover costs incurred in compensating for the defects and resulting from the ensuing delay on the theory that the architect had been negligent in interpreting the test reports.

The architect moved for summary judgment, asserting that because he was not in contractual privity with the contractor he owed no duty of care to the contractor (as opposed to the owner) in interpreting the test reports. However, the court held that the architect owed a duty to the contractor to supervise the project with due care under the circumstances alleged, even though his sole contractual relationship was with the owner. The court said that whether the absence of privity should bar a right of action was a

---

[44] Swartz v. Ford, Bacon & Davis Constr. Corp., 469 So. 2d 232 (Fla. Dist. Ct. App. 1985).

[45] 161 F. Supp. 132 (S.D. Cal. 1958).

matter of policy that involved a balancing of factors, which it identified as follows:

the extent to which the transaction was intended to affect the plaintiff, the foreseeability of harm to him, the degree of certainty that the plaintiff suffered injury, the closeness of the connection between the defendant's conduct and the injury suffered, the moral blame attached to the defendant's conduct, and the policy of preventing future harm.[46]

Weighing these factors, the court concluded that a right of action should exist, stating:

Considerations of reason and policy impel the conclusion that the position and authority of a supervising architect are such that he ought to labor under a duty to the prime contractor to supervise the project with due care under the circumstances, even though his sole contractual relationship is with the owner, here the United States. Altogether too much control over the contractor necessarily rests in the hands of the supervising architect for him not to be placed under a duty imposed by law to perform without negligence his functions as they affect the contractor. The power of the architect to stop the work alone is tantamount to a power of economic life or death over the contractor. It is only just that such authority, exercised in such a relationship, carry commensurate legal responsibility.[47]

The *Rogers* decision has been criticized, not so much because it rejected the defense of privity as an absolute bar to a contractor's right of action for professional negligence, but because of the way in which it stated the test for liability. One commentator has observed that the characterization of the design professional as an all powerful "master builder" with independent authority to stop the work is no longer universally accurate. The language of the standard form owner-design professional agreements has in recent years been modified to divest the design professional of the independent authority to stop the work. Further, the design professional's supervisory, quality control, administrative, and coordination functions are now often shared with a separate construction manager. Therefore, the commentator argues, it is inappropriate to impose a liability upon the design professional simply on the basis of assumptions regarding her status and powers. Rather, whether she owes a duty to the contractor should depend upon (1) the scope of the design professional's obligations under the owner-design professional agreement (or otherwise assumed by the design professional apart from that agreement) and (2) whether the contractor's reliance upon the design professional's careful performance of such

---

[46] *Id.* at 135 (citations omitted).
[47] *Id.* at 135–36.

obligations was reasonably foreseeable.[48] In fact, it appears that considerations of scope of duty and foreseeability of reliance have been implicitly,
if not explicitly, operative in the cases that have followed *Rogers*. And it
seems appropriate that such considerations should be the primary focus of
inquiry.[49]

In *Rogers's* wake, numerous decisions have recognized the contractor's
right of action in negligence against the design professional.[50] However,

---

[48] See Note, *Architectural Malpractice: A Contract-Based Approach*, 92 Harv. L. Rev.
1076, 1084–85 (1979).

[49] However, it is important to note that a design professional may by its conduct assume
duties beyond the scope of the limitations of its contract with the owner. Hence, in
Seattle W. Indus. v. David A. Mowat Co., 110 Wash. 2d 1, 750 P.2d 245, 251 (1988), the
court refused to give an instruction that the scope of an engineer's duty to a contractor
was defined by its contract with the owner. The court stated:

> The scope of an engineer's common law duty of care extends at least as far as the
> duties assumed by him in the contract with the owner. . . . It is not true, however,
> that the scope of the duty is always limited thereby. Additional duties might be
> assumed by affirmative conduct. . . . There was sufficient evidence to raise a
> jury question regarding such additional duties in this case. (Citations omitted).

[50] *See, e.g.,* E.C. Ernst, Inc. v. Manhattan Constr. Co., 551 F.2d 1026 (5th Cir. 1977), *cert.
denied,* 434 U.S. 1067 (1978) (applying Alabama law); Donnelly Constr. Co. v. Oberg/
Hunt/Gilleland, 139 Ariz. 184, 677 P.2d 1292 (1984); A.R. Moyer, Inc. v. Graham, 285
So. 2d 397 (Fla. 1973); Gateway Erectors Div. of Imoco-Gateway Corp. v. Lutheran
Gen. Hosp., 102 Ill. App. 3d 300, 430 N.E.2d 20 (1981) (actually involving construction manager); W. H. Lyman Constr. Co. v. Village of Gurnee, 84 Ill. App. 3d 28, 403
N.E.2d 1325 (1980); Normoyle-Berg & Assocs. v. Village of Deer Creek, 39 Ill. App. 3d
744, 350 N.E.2d 559 (1976); Peter Kiewit Sons' Co. v. Iowa S. Utils. Co., 355 F. Supp.
376 (S.D. Iowa 1973); Gurtler, Hebert & Co. v. Weyland Mach. Shop, Inc., 405 So. 2d
660 (1981), *cert. denied,* 410 So. 2d 1130 (La. Ct. App. 1982); City of Columbus v.
Clark-Dietz & Assocs. Eng'rs, Inc., 550 F. Supp. 610 (N.D. Miss. 1982); Owen v. Dodd,
431 F. Supp. 1239 (N.D. Miss. 1977); Lane v. Geiger-Berger Assocs., 608 F.2d 1148
(8th Cir. 1979) (applying Missouri law); Conforti & Eisele, Inc. v. John C. Morris
Assocs., 175 N.J. Super. 341, 418 A.2d 1290 (Law Div. 1980); Shoffner Indus., Inc. v.
W.B. Lloyd Constr. Co., 42 N.C. App. 259, 257 S.E.2d 50, *cert. denied,* 298 N.C. 296,
259 S.E.2d 301 (1979); Davidson & Jones, Inc. v. County of New Hanover, 41 N.C.
App. 661, 255 S.E.2d 580, *cert. denied,* 298 N.C. 295, 259 S.E.2d 911 (1979); Detweiler
Bros. v. John Graham & Co., 412 F. Supp. 416 (E.D. Wash. 1976); Forte Bros., Inc. v.
National Amusements, Inc., 525 A.2d 1301 (R.I. 1987); Milton J. Womack, Inc. v.
House of Representatives, 509 So. 2d 62, *cert. denied,* 513 So. 2d 1208, *cert. denied,*
513 So. 2d 1211 (La. Ct. App. 1987); United States *ex rel.* Seminole Sheet Metal Co. v.
SCI, Inc., 828 F.2d 671 (11th Cir. 1987); Prihard Bros. v. Brady Co., 428 N.W.2d 391
(Minn. 1988); Seattle W. Indus., Inc. v. David A. Mowat Co., 110 Wash. 2d 1, 750 P.2d
245 (1988). *See also* COAC, Inc. v. Kennedy Eng'rs, 67 Cal. App. 3d 916, 136 Cal.
Rptr. 890 (1977) (holding contractor to be third-party beneficiary of engineer's duty
under owner-engineer agreement); John E. Green Plumbing & Heating Co. v. Turner
Constr. Co., 742 F.2d 965 (6th Cir. 1984), *cert. denied,* 471 U.S. 1102 (1985) (applying
Michigan law) (holding that construction manager owes duty to contractor on third-
party beneficiary theory); James McKinney & Son, Inc. v. Lake Placid 1980 Olympic

the cases have not been unanimous.[51] Not all of those that have refused
to permit a right of action have turned upon the bar of privity. Some
have questioned a contractor's ability to recover in tort for purely economic losses.[52]

§ 12.11   —Economic Loss Limitation

The rationale for the economic loss limitation in the context of the
contractor-design professional relationship has not been explored to any
substantial extent in the cases that have relied on it. One of the principle
arguments presented by design professionals for such a limitation is that it
is consistent with the general rule applied in the law of torts that there
may be no recovery in actions for negligence if a plaintiff's losses are entirely economic in character.[53] Design professionals also argue that the allocation of liabilities among members of the contracting group should be
purely a matter of contract.

A contractor could be expected to present the following counter-
arguments against the arguments for an economic loss limitation. Regarding the rule of no recovery for purely economic losses in an action
based solely upon negligence: The rationale for requiring physical injury
to property or person as a predicate to recovery for economic losses is
that a "bright line" rule is necessary to protect against a virtually limit-
less scope of liability for negligence in terms of dollar magnitude and

---

Games, Inc., 92 A.D.2d 991, 461 N.Y.S.2d 483 (1983), *modified on other grounds,*
61 N.Y.2d 836, 462 N.E.2d 137, 473 N.Y.S.2d 960 (1984) (holding that responsibilities of project/construction manager were such as to establish duty in tort to subcontractor).

[51] *See, e.g.,* Bryant Elec. Co. v. City of Fredericksburg, 762 F.2d 1192 (4th Cir. 1985)
(applying Virginia law); Peyronnin Constr. Co. v. Weiss, 137 Ind. App. 417, 208 N.E.2d
489 (1965); Hogan v. Postin, 695 P.2d 1042 (Wyo. 1985); Bernard Johnson, Inc. v.
Continental Constructors, Inc., 630 S.W.2d 365 (Tex. Ct. App. 1982).

[52] *See, e.g.,* Bernard Johnson, Inc. v. Continental Constructors, Inc., 630 S.W.2d 365
(Tex. Ct. App. 1982); Bryant Elec. Co. v. City of Fredericksburg, 762 F.2d 1192 (4th
Cir. 1985); Bates & Rogers Constr. Corp. v. North Shore Sanitary Dist., 128 Ill. App.
3d 962, 471 N.E.2d 915 (1984), *aff'd on other grounds sub nom.* Bates & Rogers Constr. Corp. v. Greeley & Hansen, 109 Ill. 2d 225, 486 N.E.2d 902 (1985); Waldinger
Corp. v. Ashbrook-Simon-Hartley, Inc., 564 F. Supp. 970 (C.D. Ill. 1983), *aff'd in part
and remanded in part sub nom.* Waldinger Corp. v. CRS Group Eng'rs, Inc., 775 F.2d
781 (7th Cir. 1985).

[53] *See, e.g.,* Restatement (Second) of Torts § 766C (1977) (providing, among other
things, that as a general rule there is no liability in tort for negligence which interferes
with another's performance of his contract or makes the performance more expensive
or burdensome); East River S.S. Corp. v. Transamerica Deelaval, 476 U.S. 858
(1986).

number of potential plaintiffs.[54] However, a contractor might argue that this rationale should be inoperative when it is possible to confine the right of action to a narrow and readily identifiable group whose reliance upon the performance of a duty with care is reasonably foreseeable. For example, the *Restatement (Second) of Torts* notes that the general bar to an action for negligent interference with contract does not apply when the plaintiff stands in a special relationship to the tortfeasor:

> e. *Duty of care to prevent pecuniary loss.* Outside the scope of this Section are certain cases in which the actor renders a service or has some other contractual relationship in which he owes a duty to use reasonable care to avoid a risk of pecuniary loss to the person with whom he is directly dealing, *and that same duty is held to extend to another person whom he knows to be pecuniarily affected by the service rendered.* Most of the cases coming within this category are covered by § 552, involving information negligently supplied for the guidance of others. Other cases, involving other services than the supplying of information, may not fall within the exact provisions of § 552 but are covered by the general principle underlying it.[55]

Similarly, the illustration of the *Restatement* dealing with the scope of liability for negligent misrepresentation could support an argument that members of the contracting group are a sufficiently confined group as to invest in them a right to be free of economic loss resulting from a design professional's malpractice. Illustration 9 provides:

> 9. The City of A is about to ask for bids for work on a sewer tunnel. It hires B Company, a firm of engineers, to make boring tests and provide a report showing the rock and soil conditions to be encountered. It notifies B Company that the report will be made available to bidders as a basis for their bids and that it is expected to be used by the successful bidder in doing the work. Without knowing the identity of any of the contractors bidding on the work, B Company negligently prepares and delivers to the City an inaccurate report, containing false and misleading information. On the basis of the report C makes a successful bid, and also on the basis of the report D, a subcontractor, contracts with C to do a part of the work. By reason of the inaccuracy of the report, C and D suffer pecuniary loss in performing their contracts. B Company is subject to liability to B [sic C] and to D.[56]

---

[54] *See, e.g.,* Louisiana *ex rel.* Guste v. M/V Testbank, 752 F.2d 1019 (5th Cir. 1985), *cert. denied,* 477 U.S. 903 (1986). For example, as a matter of policy, it would be inappropriate for an individual who negligently caused an automobile collision during the morning rush hour to be held liable for lost wages to all commuters who were delayed on their way to work. As a matter of policy, the law has drawn lines short of the broader limits of foreseeability in such circumstances.

[55] Restatement (Second) of Torts § 766C comment e (1979) (emphasis added).

[56] Restatement (Second) of Torts § 552 illustration 9, at 135 (1977).

In short, it appears that the issue of whether the contractor's right of action against the design professional should be circumscribed by an economic loss limitation remains to an extent in flux. It remains to be seen how all of the courts will resolve this issue; however, it appears that the majority of courts that have followed to date *Rogers* have done so without regard to an economic loss limitation. This is not, however, to say that the imposition of such a limitation is inappropriate in cases in which claims are brought by members of the public outside the contracting group and not standing in any special relationship to the design professional.[57]

§ 12.12   Cases in Which Liabilities of Design Professionals to Contractors Have Been Considered

Against this background, it is appropriate to consider in more detail representative cases that have considered the design professional's liabilities and duties to contractors. The courts have evaluated the liabilities of design professionals to contractors for errors or omissions in the areas of (1) design, (2) supervision and inspection, (3) administration (including review of submittals, consideration of substitutes, and reaction to unanticipated conditions), and (4) scheduling and coordination. The cases demonstrate that, in assessing such liabilities, the courts have been attentive to the scope of the design professional's responsibilities as set forth in the owner-design professional agreement or as otherwise established by the design professional's conduct during the project, to the foreseeability of the contractor's reliance on the design professional's performance of such duties, and to evidence of the design professional's compliance or noncompliance with prevailing standards of care.

§ 12.13   —Liability for Defective Design

City of Columbus v. Clark-Dietz & Associates, Engineers, Inc.[58] arose out of the construction of a wastewater treatment plant and, more particularly, the failure of a protective levee surrounding the construction site when the project was nearly complete. As a result of the failure the site was inundated, causing extensive damage and delay in the completion of the facility. The owner brought suit against the contractor and the engineer for

---

[57] *Cf.* Moore v. Pavex, Inc., 356 Pa. Super. 50, 514 A.2d 137 (1986) (owner and contractors on construction project could not be held liable to class consisting of entire business community of City of Harrisburg for purely economic losses resulting from puncture of water main).

[58] 550 F. Supp. 610 (N.D. Miss. 1982).

damages resulting from the failure, and the contractor both counter-claimed against the city and crossclaimed against the engineer to recover for extra construction expenses resulting from negligent design. The court concluded that the failure of the levee was due to negligent design on the part of the engineer, that the contractor had a right of action in tort against the engineer for negligence, and that the owner and the engineer were therefore jointly and severally liable to the contractor for the damages resulting from the failure.

The parties agreed that the levee failure had occurred at the point where pipes encased by concrete seepage collars penetrated a slurry wall. They also agreed that the failure occurred as a result of water seepage and consequent "piping" through the wall at the level of the pipes, which eventually permitted the water to surge through and cause the wall to collapse. The contractor claimed that the failure was due to the design professional's negligence and defective design. The engineer claimed that the failure was a result of defective construction.

The original design had called for pipes to be placed through the levee with a slurry wall then to be placed around the pipes. When the necessary pipes were unavailable at the outset of the slurry wall construction, the engineer decided that the slurry wall construction could proceed without the pipes in place and that cuts could be made in the wall for later installation of pipe. The engineer's representatives determined that seepage collars would be adequate to restore the cuts in the slurry wall necessitated by the delayed pipe installation.

During the course of installation of the pipes and collars, a disagreement arose as to the method of installation of the collars. The contractor maintained that the collars should be encased with clay to seal the concrete, thus eliminating direct contact between the slurry and the collar itself. The engineer, however, insisted that the collar be keyed directly into the slurry.

Based upon expert testimony presented by the contractor, the court ultimately concluded that vastly differing deformability characteristics of the concrete collar and the cement-bentonite slurry in the wall were the primary cause of the seepage and piping that led to the failure of the levee. The court also concluded that the engineer's conduct with respect to the placement of the collars constituted professional negligence in that the engineering personnel who made the design decisions (1) did not have sufficient experience with cement-bentonite slurry to provide them with a basis for evaluating the sufficiency of the collar design, (2) did not consult a report available to them from which the compressive strength of the slurry could have been computed, (3) did not run tests to compute the strength of the slurry, and (4) indeed made no effort to determine the suitability of the collar design through consultation either with slurry experts or with specialty engineers in-house at their own firm. The court therefore concluded that the engineer was liable to the contractor for the losses resulting from the levee failure.[59]

The significance, then, of the *Columbus* case is that it establishes that the design professional's liability to the contractor for defective design requires proof not only of a design deficiency, but also that the deficiency was a result of the design professional's negligence.

§ 12.14 —Liability for Negligence in Supervision

Also at issue in the *Columbus* case were the relative responsibilities of the contractor and the engineer for deficiencies in other areas of the levee that had not failed, but which nevertheless required correction. Although these deficiencies were found, in part, to be a result of deficiencies in construction work as opposed to design, the contractor argued that the engineer should bear full responsibility because of his supervisory responsibilities on the project. Given that the owner-engineer agreement, however, did not impose upon the engineer a duty of continuous and exhaustive inspection, the court held that the engineer owed no duty of supervision to the contractor other than to exercise reasonable care when providing instructions and test results at the job site. Upon analysis of the design professional's contract with the owner, the court concluded:

> These paragraphs unambiguously limit Clark-Dietz' duty for supervising construction to an obligation to observe the general progress of the work, and not to make continuous and exhaustive inspections. We hold that Clark-Dietz performed this contractual duty by generally overseeing construction and conducting soil tests with reasonable care. . . . The language in the Clark-Dietz-City contract clearly does not create a requirement for Clark-Dietz to inspect and verify every step of Basic's work. In the absence of an active undertaking to guarantee the contractor's work, courts have ordinarily held that similar language absolves the architect of any liability for the contractor's poor workmanship. . . . Thus, we hold that Clark-Dietz owed

---

[59] Closely related to the concept of liability for negligent design is liability for negligent misrepresentation. For example, in Davidson & Jones, Inc. v. County of New Hanover, 41 N.C. App. 661, 255 S.E.2d 580, *cert. denied,* 298 N.C. 295, 259 S.E.2d 911 (1979), the court held that a contractor could maintain an action against the owner's soils consultant for negligent misrepresentation of subsurface conditions. This right in tort was held to exist notwithstanding provisions of an exculpatory character contained in the owner-contractor agreement. Similarly, in Lane v. Geiger-Berger Assocs., 608 F.2d 1148 (8th Cir. 1979), the court held that a subcontractor's reliance upon the design professional's representation as to the character of fill which would be permitted on a project would provide a basis for a claim by the subcontractor against the professional. *See also* Gulf Contracting v. Bibb County, 795 F.2d 980 (11th Cir. 1986) (applying Georgia law).

no duty of supervision to Basic other than to exercise reasonable care when it provided instructions and test results at the job site. Having found that Clark-Dietz was not negligent in these respects, Basic must bear responsibility for the unacceptable soil material found in the embankment except for sand seams directly above the slurry wall, and is liable to the City for damages resulting therefrom.[60]

Although *Columbus* absolves the design professional of a duty of continuous inspection, it does reaffirm the design professional's responsibilities for specific approvals as did the *Rogers* case discussed in § **12.10**. Similarly, in *Shoffner Industries v. W.B. Lloyd Construction Co.,*[61] the court held that a contractor had a right of action against the design professional for negligence in approving the work of his supplier. The case arose out of the collapse of a roof structure as a result of defective trusses supplied by the contractor's supplier. The contractor claimed that the architect had inspected and approved the trusses before they had been incorporated in the roof structure, and that the contractor had relied on that approval. The allegations were held adequate to state a cause of action against the professional.[62]

§ 12.15 —Liability for Negligent or Intentional Interference in Contract Administration

E.C. Ernst, Inc. v. Manhattan Construction Co.[63] deals primarily with the issue of the design professional's liability to the contractor for negligence in the performance of the design professional's obligations of project administration. In *Ernst,* an electrical subcontractor on a hospital construction project sued to recover damages for delays from the owner, the general contractor, the architect, and a supplier. Following a lengthy bench trial, the district court denied the subcontractor's claims for damages. The subcontractor appealed.

On appeal, the court concluded that a no-damage-for-delay clause in the subcontract barred Ernst's claims against the general contractor. The court also concluded that the subcontractor could not recover directly from the owner because it was not a third-party beneficiary of the owner-general contractor agreement. Nevertheless, the court concluded that the subcontractor did have a viable right of action in tort against the architect.

---

[60] 550 F. Supp. at 627.

[61] 42 N.C. App. 259, 257 S.E.2d 50, *cert. denied,* 298 N.C. 296, 259 S.E.2d 301 (1979).

[62] In connection with the holding in *Columbus,* it should be noted that, even though an architect has not contracted to provide continuous on-site inspection, she still owes a duty of care in making such periodic observations or inspections as she does make.

[63] 551 F.2d 1026 (5th Cir. 1977), *cert. denied,* 434 U.S. 1067 (1978).

Ernst's claims against the architect were predicated upon claims that the architect had been negligent in refusing to approve a particular bed light fixture application and, with respect to an emergency generator system, in drawing faulty specifications and failing to act promptly on submittals. The court of appeals held that the architect's procrastination and inconsistency in acting on generator submittals constituted negligence as a matter of law, for which the subcontractor could recover damages. It also remanded to the district court for further consideration the issues of whether the architect had been negligent in his actions upon the bed light submittals and in drafting the plans and specifications for the emergency generator system.

The pattern of action with respect to the emergency generator submittals, which the court concluded amounted to professional negligence as a matter of law, was marked by an initial approval ("providing that the requirements of the plans and specifications [would be] met"), followed by a series of criticisms based initially upon claims of foreign manufacture and later upon claims that the submitted generator was not a standard product and failed to meet horsepower requirements. The architect initially urged resubmittals, then suggested that he would accept the generator subject to tests, then refused to permit tests, and ultimately disapproved the system. During the process, which spanned more than a year, the architect consistently failed to list his reasons for disapprovals in a manner that might have resolved the impasse. Reviewing the history of this process, the court concluded:

> [The architect's] activities regarding its arbitral responsibilities on the emergency generator submittals . . . represent a pattern of procrastination which, in view of the interdependence of effort so vital on a construction project, falls below the standard of care required in this situation for professional architects.[64]

In *Waldor Pump & Equipment Co. v. Orr-Schelen Mayeron & Associates, Inc.,*[65] a subcontractor on a wastewater treatment plant sued the owner's engineer for negligence in preparing and drafting the plans and specifications. The subcontractor had agreed to supply eight Wilden sludge pumps to the successful bidder for the prime contract. The subcontract provided that, if the engineer should reject the Wilden pumps, the sub would provide

---

[64] 551 F.2d at 1032. Significant, also, was the court of appeals' conclusion that the professional could not use the traditional defense of arbitral immunity based upon his status under the owner-contractor agreement as resolver of disputes between owner and contractor and as interpreter of the contract documents. The court concluded that the architect's pattern of delay and of tentative, incongruous, and inconsistent action deprived him of the benefit of this defense. *Id.* at 1033–34.

[65] 386 N.W.2d 375 (Minn. Ct. App. 1986).

conforming pumps at no additional cost. When the engineer rejected the Wilden pumps, the subcontractor was required to supply more expensive Dorr-Oliver pumps. The subcontractor sued the engineer on a variety of theories, including negligence in drafting and interpreting the specifications. The subcontractor presented evidence at the trial to show that the Wilden pumps satisfied the salient performance requirements of the specifications and that the engineer had unreasonably relied on a design, rather than performance, feature in rejecting the pumps. The jury found that the engineer had been negligent and awarded the subcontractor the increased costs of supplying the replacement pumps.

On appeal, the engineer argued that it could have no liability for negligence to the subcontractor, because the subcontractor was not in privity of contract with it. The court, however, held that "[t]he reasonable skill and judgment expected of professionals must be rendered to those who foreseeably rely upon the services."[66]

Relying on decisions in other jurisdictions, the court further held it foreseeable that this subcontractor and others who were bound to follow the specifications prepared by the engineer could be harmed by the engineer's negligent drafting or interpretation of the specifications, and that the engineer therefore owed a duty to the subcontractor to reasonably draft and interpret the specifications. The appellate court also rejected the engineer's contention that the subcontractor could not recover for losses because they were purely economic losses for which a recovery would not apply under a negligence theory. The court held that "economic losses are those resulting from the failure of a product to perform to the level expected by the buyer. . . . We do not read [the rule limiting recovery for economic losses] to limit the legal remedies of individuals economically injured by the negligent rendition of professional services."[67]

Other cases have also considered other conduct of design professionals in their administrative functions that may give rise to liability to a contractor on tort theories. For example, in *Detweiler Brothers v. John Graham & Co.,*[68] the court held that an engineer could incur liability to a contractor for reversing a decision upon which the contractor had relied to its detriment. In *Detweiler,* a cause of action in negligence was stated by allegations that an engineer had first approved a mechanical subcontractor's submittal to substitute grooved piping for welded or threaded

---

[66] *Id.* at 377.

[67] *Id.* at 377–78. *See also* Waldinger Corp. v. Ashbrook-Simon-Hartley, Inc., 564 F. Supp. 970 (C.D. Ill. 1983), *aff'd in part and remanded in part sub nom.* Waldinger Corp. v. CRS Group Eng'rs, Inc., 775 F.2d 781 (7th Cir. 1985); Craviolini v. Scholer & Fuller Assoc'd Architects, 89 Ariz. 24, 357 P.2d 611 (1961) (imposing liability upon a professional for intentional interference with contract).

[68] 412 F. Supp. 416 (E.D. Wash. 1976).

pipe and then later ordered the contractor to stop work and replace the grooved pipe with welded pipe.

Similarly, in *W.H. Lyman Construction Co. v. Village of Gurnee,*[69] the court held that, although an engineer had no liability to a contractor for an alleged failure to disclose a subsurface water condition, the engineer could be liable in tort to the contractor for delay in devising a design solution to the problem. In *Gurtler, Hebert & Co. v. Weyland Machine Shop, Inc.,*[70] the court held that allegations that an architect had delayed in the approval of shop drawing submittals were adequate to support a claim in tort against the architect.

§ 12.16   —Scheduling and Coordination Liabilities

Peter Kiewit Sons' Co. v. Iowa Southern Utilities Co.[71] involved a contractor's claim against an engineer for alleged negligence in scheduling and coordinating the construction of a power plant project. Although the contractor's claim was ultimately denied, the decision is significant because (1) it holds that an engineer with scheduling and coordination functions does owe a duty of care to a contractor in the performance of those functions and (2) it illustrates the manner in which the performance of those functions will be evaluated.

The work for the construction of the project was let on a multiple prime, modified fast-track basis. Both the contract for engineering services and the various prime contracts contained provisions requiring completion by May 1, 1968. Completion by that date was essential because the owner's contracts for outside power were to expire then. The engineer's contract with the owner required the engineer to coordinate and expedite the work on the project, and the various prime contracts also contained provisions pertaining to the engineer's authority in coordination and scheduling.

The claim in *Kiewit* was brought by the prime contractor for general construction. Delays in precedent work under the structural steel fabrication and erection contract and the boiler fabrication and erection contract (which were determined to have occurred essentially without the fault of either contractor) considerably impacted the general construction contractor in its ability to proceed with its work in a productive fashion. In particular, the delays affected the contractor's sequencing and scheduling of concrete slab pours. The contractor's work was further adversely impacted when efforts to bring the project back on schedule after the initial delays

---

[69] 84 Ill. App. 3d 28, 403 N.E.2d 1325 (1980).

[70] 405 So. 2d 660 (La. Ct. App. 1981), *cert. denied,* 410 So. 2d 1130 (1982).

[71] 355 F. Supp. 376 (S.D. Iowa 1973).

led to congestion and further disruption of its activities. The general contractor sought to recover damages resulting from the disruption and loss of productivity from the engineer on a theory of negligent scheduling and coordination.

Initially, the court held that, despite provisions in the owner-contractor agreement that gave the engineer broad discretion in the planning and management of the project, the engineer's discretion was tempered by a duty of care owed to the contractor.[72] Ultimately, however, the court concluded that the engineer did not breach the duty of care that it owed to the contractor, stating:

> There is no evidence that Black & Veatch failed to provide adequate and competent personnel to administer the contract documents on the job site. . . . [T]he evidence is that Black & Veatch handled the site supervision very efficiently, by coping with potentially disastrous set backs and yet completing the job substantially on time. . . . There is no evidence that Black & Veatch administered the contract in any manner other than that accepted by the trade. . . . Under the circumstances, the Engineer adhered, and caused the work to proceed, as closely to [the original schedule] as was possible. As the Court has concluded . . . [that schedule] was not absolutely binding on the Owner. Deviations were anticipated by the parties, depending upon the circumstances. All contractors were bound by [that schedule], or schedules closely approximating it. The circumstances on the site caused the Engineer to order substantial deviations, in some instances, from [that schedule]. The Engineer's actions in this regard, however, were reasonable and were within the contemplation of the contracts of all parties involved.[73]

The factors identified in the findings of fact that appeared to lend support to the conclusion that the engineer had not breached his duty of care to the contractor were:

Preparation of Shop Drawings.   When it appeared that the project might be delayed by default in the preparation of shop drawings by the structural steel contractor, the engineer actively worked to assist the contractor in the preparation of shop drawings, and also assigned additional staff to the review of such drawings, thus avoiding a delay in that regard.

Longer Day Shifts.   When delays did unavoidably occur in the steel erection work due to delays in material deliveries, the engineer required the erection contractor to run longer day shifts at premium time in order to speed up the work. Other alternatives, such as night shift work, were

---

[72] *Id.* at 394.
[73] *Id.* at 395–96.

considered but rejected because of concerns about safety and the lack of qualified ironworkers to man such a shift.

Relaxed Specifications.   The engineer relaxed specifications and sequencing requirements affecting the general construction contractor's work in order to assist in maintaining productivity.

Alleviate Safety Hazards.   The engineer actively worked to alleviate safety hazards created by other contractors to the general contractor's performance and also to mitigate damage caused by other contractors to the general contractor's work.

Critical Path Method.   When it became apparent that the project was falling behind schedule, the engineer adopted a monthly Critical Path Method update process not called for in the original contract documents, and often made daily field scheduling adjustments to accommodate events as they occurred on the project.

On-Site Staffing.   The engineer provided adequate and competent staffing on-site, and the project was never delayed for want of such staffing.

No Hindrance.   There was no hindrance of the general construction contractor's work due to defects in plans and specifications.

No Favoritism.   The general construction contractor conceded that there had been no favoritism in the engineer's scheduling decisions and it appeared that the engineer had considered the economic impact upon various contractors and the overall goal of the May 1, 1968, completion date as prime considerations in making scheduling decisions.

Therefore, although the *Kiewit* case denied a recovery to the contractor, the case also supports the proposition that an engineer with scheduling and coordination responsibilities can be held liable to a contractor on a negligence theory if the engineer (1) fails promptly to address, acknowledge, or respond to delays that are occurring on the project, (2) fails to consider available alternatives for bringing the project on schedule, (3) fails to properly update or adjust schedules, (4) shows favoritism in scheduling or coordination decisions, or (5) provides inadequate or incompetent staffing to perform the scheduling and coordination functions.

CHAPTER 13

COMPLETING CONSTRUCTION PROJECTS WHEN THERE HAS BEEN A MAJOR FAILURE

Irvin E. Richter, Esquire
William J. Doyle
S. Leonard DiDonato

Irvin E. Richter is chairman and chief executive officer of HILL Group, Inc., a 2,300-person engineering, consulting, and environmental science firm headquartered in Willingboro, New Jersey, with 26 offices worldwide.

A graduate of Rutgers University Law School and Wesleyan University, Mr. Richter is a noted construction claims expert, arbitrator, and author. He has written *International Construction Claims: Avoiding and Resolving Disputes,* coauthored the *Handbook of Construction Law and Claims,* and contributed chapters to a number of other works and numerous articles in his field.

Mr. Richter is a member of the New Jersey and Pennsylvania Bars, the Philadelphia Chapter of the Young President's Organization, and the Construction Industry Presidents Forum.

William J. Doyle, president and chief operating officer of Hill International, has more than 35 years of experience in the construction management, contract administration, and claims management of major construction projects throughout the country.

Prior to joining Hill, Mr. Doyle was chairman of the board of General Energy Resources, Inc., which grew to be the largest power piping and mechanical contracting firm in the United States during his tenure.

Mr. Doyle currently is principal-in-charge of many of Hill's projects. In this capacity, he has assisted major utilities with the contract management procedures utilized in the construction of power plants throughout the country and supervised Hill's project team in the completion of the Tropicana Hotel and Casino in Atlantic City and the Denver RTD Transitway Mall, as well as numerous other major projects.

S. Leonard DiDonato, senior vice president for special projects for Hill International, is an expert in contract administration, construction management, and claim settlement. He has more than 35 years of experience in the design/construction industry and has been involved in all aspects of industrial, commercial, and institutional development and construction.

Mr. DiDonato is a member of the Panel of Arbitrators of the American Arbitration Association, a member of the Construction Specifications Institute and the Construction Management Association of America and an associate member of The American Institute of Architects.

§ 13.1   Introduction

Construction failures and disasters present special problems to the various parties in the construction process. Aside from the immediate concerns that are generated by the failure (repairing physical damage, defending allegations of negligence, and so on), certain longer-range issues invariably follow. Paramount among them are how the project will be completed, by whom, at what cost, and within what time frame.

In most cases, construction failures and disasters either signal the beginning of a troubled project or are symptoms of a project already in significant trouble. Once failure occurs, focus immediately shifts to resolving the problem. Resources may be reallocated from day-to-day construction functions to investigate, evaluate, and correct the problem. In other circumstances, the party responsible for the failure may be unable to complete his responsibilities on the project. In addition, the morale of the project participants may be destroyed and productivity may fall precipitously. These and countless other results of construction failure will significantly affect the cost and schedule of the remaining work unless effective steps are implemented to mitigate their continued impact on the project.

When a project is already in trouble, schedules may have slipped, trades may be stacking, and sequencing may have disintegrated into chaos. Mistakes are being made and shortcuts are being taken to try to get the job back on schedule and the cost more in line with the budget. If these and other symptoms of a troubled project had been identified earlier, the failure or disaster might have been averted.

The primary objective of this chapter is to help the participants in a construction project recognize the symptoms of a troubled project early enough to avoid a disaster. But, once a disaster has occurred, the second objective is to provide practical insights into how best to get the project back on track and minimize the failure's impact on cost, time, and quality.

§ 13.2   Early Recognition: The Warning Signs

The key to preventing a troubled project is acknowledgment of the early warning signs. What are those signs? An example of an actual construction project will highlight the early warning signs.

A national hotel chain was constructing a $22 million luxury hotel in a major northeastern city and had signed a guaranteed maximum cost contract with a single local general contractor that called for the completion of the facility within 20 months. They were in the 30th month of construction, had already approved and paid approximately $1.5 million in change orders, and were deeply concerned because the general contractor had just delivered a claim bound in nine volumes that totaled $9.6 million. The owner had tried to redesign the hotel from an economy to a luxury facility while construction was underway. The result was an 18-month delay and $3 million in delay damages.

Several other examples come to mind, but the story is almost always the same. The real question is why didn't these owners know that they were headed for disaster? The answer is that they ignored some of the most obvious warning signs that can trigger early recognition of trouble.

Five obvious signs should serve as a warning that a project is heading for trouble. They are:

1. Delays
2. Change Order Requests and Claims
3. Failed Project Communication
4. Slippage in the Quality of the Work
5. Complaints from Subcontractors and Vendors.

Each of these early warning signs deserves a closer look.

§ 13.3 —Project Delays

When the progress of the work begins to be delayed, trouble is brewing on your project. The following may indicate this is occurring:

1. Schedule Time Overruns. The periodic review of the schedule, whether it be a Critical Path Method or a simple bar chart, may first reveal that delays are occurring.
2. Requests for Time Extensions. Contractors ask for extensions of time in writing or they announce at job meetings that they are incurring delays and will provide notification in a more formal manner once they determine the extent of the delays.
3. Work Force Reductions. During the first two-thirds of the project, the total number of the work force should continue to grow month by month. If that pattern of growth stops or if there are reductions in the number of workmen on site, problems are occurring that are causing a change in the normal pattern.
4. Disorderly Construction Site. Disorder in the storage of materials, the maintenance of equipment and tools, and the organization of the

work force, indicates trouble. A sloppy, disorganized work site is not only a symptom but also a cause of a troubled project.

§ 13.4   —Change Order Requests and Claims

All projects have their share of change orders and minor claims resulting from disputes over interpretations of the contract documents. However, a substantial increase in the submission of change order requests or claims is a clear sign of trouble. In addition, a substantial backlog in the number and dollar value of change orders in process is not only a symptom of a troubled project but also can contribute to its cause. Look to the following as trouble indicators:

1. Change Order Backlog.   The backlog of unapproved change orders will usually be in one of three categories:
    a. Undisputed: those which are undisputed but, because of poor administration or lack of funding, have not been approved and issued
    b. Cost Disputed: those in which the nature of the change is not in dispute, but the value of the cost is in dispute and is delaying approval and payment
    c. Eligibility Disputed: the nature and cause of the work performed is in dispute as to its eligibility under the contract.
2. Disputed Claims.   Claims for time extensions and delay damages usually involve:
    a. Added Work Cost: the cost of added work performed because of delays
    b. Acceleration Cost: added costs for labor arising from acceleration in order to maintain schedule
    c. Lost Productivity: the added costs of labor due to productivity losses even when there is no acceleration
    d. Extended Overhead Cost: added costs such as extended home office and field office costs, loss of business, and so on.

§ 13.5   —Project Communications

Failing project communications is a symptom as well as a cause of a troubled project. These failures usually fall into the following categories:

1. Field Communications.   The day-to-day flow of field communications is crucial to the successful conduct of a project. One troubled

project site had a row of trailers each about ten feet apart. The first was for the construction manager, the second for the project engineer, and the third was for the general contractor. Instead of walking to each other's trailers or calling each other on the telephone, each of the three participants mailed each other letters through the U.S. mail.

2. **Owner to/from Contractor.** Most of the correspondence on a project between the owner and the contractor is between the owner's representatives on site and the contractor's field superintendent at the field office. When the flow of correspondence to and from the home office of both the owner and the contractor increases, trouble is on its way.

3. **Architect/Engineer to/from Contractor.** Crucial to the success of a project is the constant productive communication flow between the contractors and the architect/engineer or construction manager who is administering the project for the owner. When that flow of communication becomes adversarial and more formal in nature, expect trouble.

4. **Attorneys and Surety.** When attorneys representing one or more of the parties begin to send letters on behalf of their clients, or when letters are addressed or copied to attorneys or bonding companies, again expect trouble.

§ 13.6 —Quality of Work

The continued high quality of work in place is the sign of a healthy project. Therefore, look for:

1. **Substitutions.** When a Contractor or his subcontractor begins to submit an abnormal number of requests for material and equipment substitutions, something is wrong.

2. **Design Problems.** When the number of Requests for Information from a contractor or his subcontractors and material/equipment suppliers begins to increase, the contractors are either in trouble or there are major problems with the design documents.

3. **Careless Subcontractors.** When the nature of the operations of subcontractors and the quality of their workmanship and materials begin to deteriorate, they have problems under their subcontracts with the prime.

4. **Deteriorating Supervision.** When there is a deterioration of quality control and supervision by the prime contractors, or if there is a major change in the attitude of the owner's representatives toward

being more strict or less observant, once again, it means trouble or it will become the cause of trouble.

§ 13.7 —Complaining Subcontractors or Vendors

If either by reading mail or walking around the site you begin to notice problems with subcontractors and/or materials and equipment vendors, watch for the following:

1. **Subcontractor/Vendor Stopwork.** If a subcontractor stops work and abandons the site, or if a manufacturer delays the shipment of equipment and material, there has to be a problem.
2. **Payments and Liens.** When the owner begins to receive liens or notices that liens have been filed against the property, or payment demands are made directly to the owner, the prime is usually in the midst of financial problems.
3. **Business Failures.** When subcontractors repeatedly fail financially, it usually means they are experiencing a cash flow problem. When a subcontractor tells you during a walk around the site that he has not been paid for several months, suspect that he is about ready to leave.
4. **Supplies and Equipment.** When manufacturers of equipment and material suppliers begin to send their products on a cash-on-delivery basis or if they demand payment before shipment, you can bet they are afraid they will not be paid.

§ 13.8 Evaluating the Troubled Project

To summarize, those of us who have spent most of our careers in construction on site develop a distinct talent for reading the condition of a project from what we see and hear while visiting that site for a few hours. Subcontractors, foremen, and even individual workmen are always ready to say exactly what they see as a problem on a project site. Most of them will also be just as quick to say what a good job it is, if in fact the project is moving along in good fashion. Those with experience can maintain a feel for a project by reading key correspondence and the job meeting minutes, reviewing financial documents, and conducting periodic visits to a site. However, those without that kind of experience have to obtain the services of an independent source of information either within their organization or from without.

I am frequently asked what appears to be the principle cause of troubled projects based on my experience. Occasionally, contractors, either because of their inexperience or poor financial status, have taken on more responsibility than they can handle. However, most troubled projects have experienced substantial design changes by the owner during the construction process, or serious design errors or omissions by the architect/engineer. There are other causes, of course, but these two happen far more than any of the others. Moreover, on most troubled projects the participants have lost credibility; the owner no longer knows whom to believe or trust, and the contractor may have resorted to overstating his claims in order to get the owner's attention. Finally, the scheduling has usually been in the control of the contractor, which has made it more difficult for the owner to monitor and determine the cause of the delays.

§ 13.9   Assessing Revival Alternatives

Two of the most important issues on any construction project are time and money. These issues are even more important on a project that has experienced a construction failure. Time is important because it means obtaining use and occupancy of the facility. Money is important because a construction failure means that the planned budget may be exceeded or the project participants may be exposed to substantial consequential damages that are not directly related to the failure.

Depending upon the nature of the project, the impact of time and money can vary substantially. Hence, the incentive to invest in a revival plan and the choice of a revival alternative will vary depending upon the anticipated loss resulting from the project failure.

Three major courses of action are available to revive a troubled project. The first alternative is to terminate the contractor(s) whose acts or omissions represent or are responsible for the project's failure. After termination, the project must be completed by a replacement contractor hired by the owner or contractor's surety. A second alternative is to terminate the contractor and have the owner manage the completion of the work with the existing subcontractors and/or selected replacement subcontractors. The third alternative is to negotiate with the contractor responsible for the failure and attempt to manage the completion of the project in the most timely and cost-effective manner possible.

Obviously, the most drastic and risky course of action is the decision to terminate the contractor. A decision to terminate must first be based upon the examination of several legal issues that are beyond the scope of this chapter. However, even if a legally defensible termination for default can be proven, there are several practical effects that must be considered.

Because the primary thrust of this chapter is to discuss the options for getting the project back on track, the focus will be on the options for revival through the eyes of the owner, who is generally the one having the greatest stake in a troubled project. Obviously, the construction manager, general contractor, subcontractors, or other project participants may have the same incentive to revive the project. However, their primary motivation may be to settle their claims as a precondition to participating in the revival program.

§ 13.10   Deciding Whether to Terminate a Contract

The first issue to be examined when deciding whether to terminate a contractor's agreement is the nature of the disputes on the project. Typically on a troubled project, the nonperformance of a contractor is not the only issue that must be dealt with in implementing the revival program. For this reason, it is often difficult to determine from a factual standpoint whether the contractor may have legitimate defenses to a default termination, such as owner interferences, changed conditions, or acts of God. Consequently, the decision to terminate is risky.

§ 13.11   Possible Contractor Defenses

Only when the contractor has exhibited either the technical or financial inability to perform or has wrongfully abandoned the project does the termination option usually become the clear choice. But even in these circumstances there are exceptions to the rule.

The nature of the contractor's failure to perform can run the gamut from failing to submit shop drawings on time to failing to meet the project's completion date. However, only certain acts as defined in the termination provision of the contract or a material breach of the contract are sufficient to justify a termination.

Often the troubled project is plagued by the owner's acts or omissions that may have precipitated or aggravated the performance failure of the contractor. A prime example of this type of interference is the owner who issues changes right up to the completion date of the project. Other examples of interferences by the owner or his agents include:

1. Defects in the plans and specifications
2. Changes in the method or manner of performance
3. Failure to coordinate the work
4. Improper inspection or rejection
5. Nondisclosure by the owner of material information.

The point is that, even when there has been a performance failure by the contractor, it is important to analyze the project in order to identify other circumstances that may have precipitated the failure. Any plan for revival must include a remedy not only the specific performance failure but also for the other conditions that may be less visible but are just as important to successful completion of the project.

A changed condition, such as a differing site condition, may also be the cause for the performance failure, rather than the mismanagement or incompetence of the contractor. In such cases the primary focus of the revival should be on 1) determining whether in fact a changed condition existed, 2) determining the cost and time impact of the changed condition, and 3) determining the remedial measures to be implemented.

Sometimes the construction failure may not be the fault of any of the parties and can be considered an act of God. We were recently involved in an airport project in which the paving contractor had been terminated for deficiencies in the embankment for the main runway. After remedial work was completed by a replacement contractor, a sink hole developed in the main runway, further delaying the project. After a thorough investigation, it was determined that the sink hole was not the result of a design defect or deficient construction practices, and it was therefore considered an act of God.

§ 13.12   The Nature of the Contract

The construction contract(s) may take many forms. The nature of those contracts should be taken into consideration when assessing the various alternatives for reviving a troubled or failed project. The contracts might be:

1. Public or Private
2. Single or Multiple
3. Lump Sum or Unit Cost.

§ 13.13   —Public versus Private Contracts

On a public project, the decision to terminate a contractor may have far-reaching consequences. First, because of the public bidding laws, a public body or agency is generally precluded from entering into a contract with a successor contractor without advertising for bids. Hence, unless the surety is willing to contract directly with the successor contractor (which a surety is often unwilling to do), a long delay could ensue while obtaining a successor contractor. This not only adds to the delay in getting the project back on track but also results in additional fees and expenses from the architect/engineer.

If the public project is funded by a federal agency such as the Environmental Protection Agency (EPA), the funding could be in jeopardy. If there is a dispute concerning the basis for the termination and the contractor has claims against the owner, the funding agency may conclude that there has been grantee mismanagement and limit the funding available for the completion contract.

With a private contract, the owner does not have any legal restrictions on his ability to hire a replacement contractor. However, a private owner may have more economic constraints, because a termination may entail completion costs that are two to three times the remaining contract balance. In addition, the delays in replacing a terminated contractor and the resulting loss of use of the facility typically have a much greater economic impact on the private owner.

§ 13.14   —Single versus Multiprime Contracts

With a single prime contract in which the majority of the work has been subcontracted, it may be difficult to maintain the same subcontractors on the project after the prime contractor has been terminated. If the prime has mismanaged the project and not paid the subcontractors, the subcontractors may have filed substantial claims and liens against the project.

With a multiprime project, it is generally easier to terminate one of the primes without having a major impact on the entire project if the work is recontracted in a timely manner.

§ 13.15   —Lump Sum versus Unit Cost Contracts

With a lump sum contract, a default termination results in inadequate funds to complete the project. Contract balances and retainage are likely to be substantially less than the cost to finish the project because of (1) front-end loading by the contractor, (2) payments for material and equipment that may not be recoverable, and (3) the contingency typically required by the replacement contractor.

With a unit cost contract, such as a pipeline project, it is much easier to establish the physical status of completion. It is less likely that the contractor has been overpaid for the work in place.

§ 13.16   —Attitude of Major Subcontractors

The attitude of the major subcontractors (mechanical and electrical) may have a substantial impact on the ability to complete the project. If the subcontractors are aligned with the terminated prime contractor, they may refuse to perform or be unwilling to release major pieces of equipment, like switchgear or chillers. Conversely, if the subcontractors have not been paid or have been otherwise damaged by the prime contractor, they may cooperate with the owner. Typically, such cooperation has a price.

§ 13.17   Status of the Project

After a troubled project has been recognized, the most important task is to determine the completion status of the project. This is important not only in deciding whether to default the contractor or negotiate with him, but it also dictates the various actions that might be taken to get the project back on track, such as accelerating and resequencing of activities.

The primary indication of a project's status is the percentage of completion reflected in the payment applications approved by the architect/engineer or construction manager. When there has been a performance failure in the early stages of a project (less than 25 percent completed), it is typically less disruptive to terminate and replace the contractor. Furthermore, if the contractor exhibits the financial or technical inability to perform at an early stage, it may foreshadow greater problems if the contractor is allowed to continue. Conversely, in the later stages of a project (over 50 percent completed), the impact of replacing a contractor is much greater because of his familiarity with the project and the stage of construction. In addition, it is much more difficult and costly to find a suitable replacement contractor because of uncertainties regarding the adequacy of the installed work and the scope of the remaining work.

Access to key pieces of equipment and material is an important factor to be considered if termination is one of the options for revival. If the equipment or material is stored on site, it is a simple matter to take possession. Obtaining possession may be more difficult if the equipment is stored off site or at the manufacturer's facility. Securing equipment such as switchgear or chillers is extremely important because of the long lead time required to obtain the equipment.

One of the most important status considerations in deciding upon a course of action for reviving a project is the owner's occupancy requirements. A good illustration of the importance of obtaining occupancy in a timely fashion is the revamping of an Atlantic City casino/hotel. In this case, the casino operator was faced with the loss of his temporary license to operate if the casino did not open by the end of the year, and he would have been required to go through the entire licensing process a second time. This could have meant a delay of up to one year before he could be relicensed and operating. Because of a variety of project delays, the casino had missed the summer season in Atlantic City. In addition, the casino was in danger of losing the substantial gaming revenues that peak between the Thanksgiving and New Year's weekends. After significant acceleration efforts of key trades, the Certificate of Occupancy was obtained and the casino opened the weekend before Thanksgiving. The gross revenues for gaming between Thanksgiving and the end of the year totaled millions of dollars.

Another case was a corporate headquarters building in Connecticut that was to house thousands of employees to be relocated from 15 different locations in Manhattan. The failure to obtain timely occupancy of this facility by the owner would have resulted in enormous logistical problems and substantial additional costs.

In both these cases termination was not a viable alternative because of the consequences of delaying occupancy that would result from bringing in a replacement contractor.

Another important status consideration in deciding whether to terminate a contractor is whether the owner would have sufficient financing if the surety should refuse to perform. On public projects funded by EPA grants this becomes a particularly difficult problem. Long delays can interfere with obtaining additional grant funding to complete a project. For example, on a recent airport project the construction of the facility was financed by revenue bonds. Because of an inadequate original estimate and costs expended to remedy defective work, the owner was required to issue additional revenue bonds at a substantially higher interest rate and also absorb the underwriting fee for the bond.

§ 13.18   Position of Surety

Once a termination for default has been issued, the surety must investigate the project to determine whether it is obligated to perform under the performance bond. If the surety determines that it does not have any defenses to the termination, it must choose one of the following options:

1. Complete the project with its principal
2. Tender a new contractor to complete the work under a contract between the owner and the new contractor
3. Tender a new contractor to complete the work under a contract between the surety and the new contractor
4. Allow the owner to directly obtain a new contractor to complete the work, with the surety then responsible for paying the cost of completion in excess of the contract balance at the time of the default up to the penal sum of the bond.

If the surety determines that its principal has been wrongfully terminated or that there are other defenses, such as overpayment, the owner may be left to its own resources to complete the project and proceed to recover the damages through litigation with the surety. This risk must be factored into the evaluation of whether to terminate. If there is a chance that the surety will not come in on the bond, the owner must have the financial resources to complete the project on its own and also be prepared to litigate with the surety and the terminated contractor to recover its losses.

§ 13.19   Pros and Cons of Revival Alternatives

The advantages and disadvantages of each of the revival alternatives are summarized below.

1. Terminate and Rebid (Owner and Surety)
   a. Advantages
      (1) Obtain contractor with financial/technical ability to perform
      (2) Minimize loss (early stage)
   b. Disadvantages
      (1) Increased costs
      (2) Delay in completion
      (3) Risk of surety refusing to honor bond
      (4) Difficulty in obtaining equipment and material
      (5) Cost of litigation
2. Terminate and Manage (Owner or Surety)
   a. Advantages
      (1) Avoids delay in replacing contractor
      (2) Minimizes loss
   b. Disadvantages
      (1) Increased costs
      (2) Requires expertise
      (3) Subcontractors may not cooperate
      (4) Surety may refuse to honor bond
3. Negotiate with Present Contractors
   a. Advantages
      (1) Cost effective
      (2) Expeditious

    (3) Performance can be dictated as requirement for settlement

    (4) Limitation on future claims exposure

  b. Disadvantages

    (1) Requires expertise

    (2) Potential for overpayment on claims and changes.

§ 13.20   Implementing the Revival Plan

Once the early warning signs of a troubled project have been recognized and the revival alternatives have been assessed, the next action must be to implement the revival plan by using several proven steps.

§ 13.21   —Select and Organize a Revival Team

The most important step in turning around a failed construction project is to organize the core revival team. In selecting a team it is vital to choose a project leader who is a strong, competent manager, and who truly understands the construction industry. There can be only one leader, and his authority and responsibilities must be established very quickly. The project leader selected must also have a personality that allows him to be rational and reasonable during the heat of the crisis caused by a failed construction project. Throughout the extremely stressful turnaround process, all the parties to the project must have the confidence that rational but prompt decisions in the revival process will not be overlooked or underestimated. The leader must be equipped to handle all issues calmly and decisively.

The importance of selecting the members of the revival task force is second only to that of selecting the project leader. It is important to select the best people available. The team must include someone from every major discipline of construction. The project revival team needs to give its undivided attention to turning the project around; therefore, team members must be free of all other assignments until the revival is complete.

§ 13.22   —Identify and Understand the Problems

The first item on the revival team's agenda must be to identify the project's problems. Many of the problems will have already been identified during the problem identification phase discussed in § 13.2. However, additional problems usually surface upon a more in-depth analysis. It is important for the team to understand fully each of the problems identified through their interviews and walk-throughs.

It is imperative that each identified problem be clearly defined by the team. The common wisdom of "you can't solve a problem until you understand what the problem is and why it is there" has never been truer than during a troubled project. The problems that may be uncovered could include site/water/rock conditions, delayed materials and equipment, or shortages of tools and equipment. There may also be problems involving the architect and engineer, including errors and omissions, timely approval of drawings, and inept or slow decision making.

These issues are often very sensitive. They must be addressed and resolved as soon as possible.

The problems uncovered may go beyond site conditions, materials, or drawings. In a failed construction project there can be significant problems in the area of overall management of the project, including the supervision. Often problems occur when supervisory levels are stronger than management. Problems may exist with labor. Frequently labor is given the blame for a failure, although in many instances it was the owner himself who posed the greatest threat to the project, by making excessive changes, for example.

§ 13.23 —Define and Manage the Objectives

For the revival to be successful, it has to be managed by clear, concise, and realistic objectives. Having clearly identified the problems, the team members must recognize, even with all the chaos around them, that they must take the planning time required to set the objectives. The need for adequate planning time cannot be overstated. The project team must be available to work long hours in order to find timely solutions to the problems. While planning, the team must also strategize the methods, procedures, and personnel resources required to reach the objectives.

The objectives should include:

1. Determining the earliest, realistic completion date.
2. Providing the owner with the best possible estimate of the final completion cost.
3. Identifying the resources, including the owner, management, supervision, and labor, at the earliest possible time. This may require the replacement of some or all of the top members of the construction team. It can be done—although it is difficult—with everyone staying in place if the leader is strong enough and the purpose and benefits from reviving the project are clearly defined and set.
4. Constantly and consistently coordinating communications with all the parties to the construction project. This communication is needed

from the top management of the company or agency building the project to the laborers who will be removing the last load of trash from the site. It is extremely important to keep all the regulatory and licensing officials informed as well. The best scheduling plans can be destroyed if the people who must provide the ability to use the project do not cooperate.

5.   Determining exactly where the project stands and what remains to be done. It is absolutely necessary that the work remaining within each contract discipline be estimated in units of work left to complete. This will permit the determination of what has to be done on a daily, weekly, monthly, and overall basis in order to reach realistic time and cost objectives.

6.   Creating geographical work plans so that the resources that have been designated are utilized both effectively and efficiently.

7.   Keeping morale upbeat. One effective way to accomplish this is to make every conceivable party to the project a part of a task force that is responsible for a major element of the revival plan. Also, there has to be some reward in it for everyone which goes beyond just the pride of having been a part of completing the project.

Once the objectives have been identified, they must be managed to turn the failed project around. The revival team must review its adherence to the objectives on a daily, weekly, and monthly basis. Before closing shop each night, the daily objectives for the next day must be set. In addition, there should be goal setting for every member of the task force as well as each member of the team, including the architect/engineer, the contractors, the vendors, labor and, most importantly, the owner.

§ 13.24   —Conduct Key Meetings

One cannot overstate the importance of key meetings to review and monitor all the objectives. These meetings, of necessity, must be formal, regularly scheduled, completely organized, and start and finish on time. In a troubled project, key review and coordination meetings are often disorganized, are not held on a regular basis, and do not have established starting times, agendas, or finishing times. As a result, either people do not come to the meetings or they send people to the meetings who cannot make the decisions required. It is beneficial to schedule certain people at specific intervals to avoid wasting the valuable time of many people who must listen to reports or objectives that, although meaningful to them, they cannot effect.

§ 13.25   —Adhere to Schedules and Costs

There must be a schedule that is realistic for and understandable by all the parties. This schedule should identify each important milestone and be consistently updated so that task force members know exactly where they are at all times. There must be plans to work around any potential deviations and it is absolutely necessary to eliminate all or most of the obstacles to achieving time and cost objectives. With proper planning, proper resources, and the cooperation of all the parties, it is a rare obstacle that cannot be eliminated.

Perhaps most important is that all changes must stop. There can be little deviation from the planned procedure. If changes must be made, they should be made after the project is on line, even if it costs a few more dollars. In a troubled situation, changes may provide the contractors with an excuse as to why it will cost more or take more time. In theory, the contractor may allege that it was the change, not his performance, that was responsible for exacerbating an already bad situation. The team should constantly be striving to accelerate the critical path activities because obstacles will show up that require prompt attention. In rare cases, there will be some obstacles that cannot be so easily overcome. Therefore, the importance of trying to compress critical path activities wherever possible is clear.

§ 13.26   —Changes and Claims

In most troubled or failed projects, the one thing that is sure to emerge is disagreement on change orders and claims. Therefore, these issues have to be addressed very rapidly and aggressively so that decisions reached allow the contractors to build the project and not build claims. Most important, the revival team must obtain the trust of all parties. It must be credible, objective, and immediately address this very dangerous area. The team should make a complete list of all outstanding and potential change orders and claims, set priorities based on what needs to be done on the project, and then begin to immediately:

1. Assess the individual damages (both hard and soft cost), and determine in an objective manner what is equitable for the parties.

2. Overcome "pride and suffering" damages. Very often, the crux of the inability to settle some of these issues is based more on personality and emotion than on fact. The team leader must find a way to zero in on the factual circumstances and steer away from emotionalism. Once having reviewed the situations and made equitable determinations, the owner's team must react with prompt decisions—the

luxury of procrastination cannot be afforded in this highly volatile area. The entire team must get back to building the project and not chase counterproductive claims.

Three constant objectives must always be kept in the forefront of the minds of all the members of the revival task force. They are:

1. Time. The importance of the schedule
2. Cost. It ain't the money—it's the money
3. Pride. Getting everyone involved in the project and proud of what is happening.

Note that, if all the above had been done from the start of the project, there would not have been a project failure in the first place.

CHAPTER 14

FIXING THE FAILURE AND SETTLING THE DISPUTE

William J. Postner, Esquire

Robert A. Rubin, Esquire

Lisa A. Banick, Esquire*

William J. Postner is a partner in the law firm of Postner & Rubin, New York, New York. He received a Bachelor of Arts Degree from Fordham University and a Bachelor of Laws Degree from New York University. A member of the New York Bar, Mr. Postner is also admitted to practice before the United States Supreme Court and various federal courts.

He has been involved in many phases of construction contract law, representing owners, contractors, construction managers, subcontractors, architects, engineers, and sureties. He has negotiated and drafted contracts on behalf of those parties, has prepared and negotiated claims and has prosecuted and defended suits before arbitration tribunals, administrative agencies, and state and federal courts.

He serves as a Special Master in the Supreme Court of the State of New York, and is a member of the American Judges Association, the Construction Arbitration Panel of the American Arbitration Association, the Defense Research Institute, the New York County Lawyers' Association, the New York State Bar Association, and the American Bar Association.

Robert A. Rubin is a partner in the law firm of Postner & Rubin, New York, New York. He received a Bachelor of Civil Engineering from Cornell University and a Juris Doctor from Columbia University. Since entering the practice of law in 1964, his practice has been limited to construction matters, principally in the litigation and arbitration of complex construction disputes.

Mr. Rubin is coauthor of *Construction Claims: Analysis, Presentation, Defense* and author of chapters in *Construction Contracts, Construction Litigation, Risk Management, Consulting Engineer, The Construction Lawyer, The McGraw-Hill Construction Business Handbook,* and coauthor of chapters in *Public Contract Law Journal, Using Experts in*

*The authors gratefully acknowledge the assistance of James W. Glassen and Jeffrey R. Cruz in the preparation of this chapter.

313

Civil Cases, Public Contract Law Journal, and *The Construction Lawyer.*

He is a member of the Management of Construction Programs Committee, the National Academy of Sciences (1979–82), and the Building Futures Council (1983–present). In 1984 he served as court appointed mini-trial referee in the Gilbane-Nemours Foundation Litigation, U.S. District Court, District of Delaware.

Mr. Rubin is a member of the New York State Bar and is a licensed Professional Engineer in the State of New York. He is a member of the Construction Industry Arbitration Panel of the American Arbitration Association; a Fellow of the American Society of Civil Engineers, a member of The Moles, New York County Lawyers Association, Association of the Bar of the City of New York (Construction Law Committee), New York State and American Bar Associations (Member: Litigation, Public Contract Law, and Torts and Insurance Practice Sections and the Forum Committee on the Construction Industry, Chairman, Dispute Avoidance and Resolution Division (1983–86)), and International Bar Association (International Construction Contracts Committee).

Lisa A. Banick is a partner in the law firm of Postner & Rubin, New York, New York. She received a Bachelor of Science, Civil Engineering, from the University of Virginia and a Juris Doctor, Magna Cum Laude, from New York Law School.

Ms. Banick is coauthor of "The Hyatt Regency Decision—One View," *The Construction Lawyer,* "The Lawyer's Role in Improving Contracting Practices in Underground Construction," *RETC Proceedings,* and "The Resident Engineer's Position Regarding Claims," 1985 ASCE Specialty Conference Proceedings.

Ms. Banick is a member of the New York and New Jersey Bars. She is an associate member of the American Society of Civil Engineers and a member of the New York County Lawyers' Association, the New York Bar Association, the New Jersey Bar Association, and the American Bar Association.

---

§ 14.1 Introduction

A construction failure creates disputes on many fronts. It can delay or even completely halt the work. Moreover, a construction failure creates some measure of potential liability for virtually every party who contributes to the construction process: owner, architect, engineer, contractor, subcontractor, materialman, surety, and insurer. Settling such a dispute presents many options in both form and method. This chapter examines various options for settling the complex multi-party litigation that attends a construction failure and the methods for structuring a successful settlement.

When representing a potentially liable party in this situation, the initial step is to evaluate that party's possible degree of fault. Was the failure caused by improper design, deviation from the plans, defective materials, a combination of these, or something else? Only after this evaluation is made can the possibilities of reaching an equitable, if not advantageous, settlement be examined.

Thus, before any settlement discussions ensue, the implicated parties must ascertain the possible causes of the failure, the potential liability of the responsible parties, and the cost to correct the failure. A settlement offer made without proper preparation can be neither reasonable nor persuasive.

The advantages, disadvantages, and effects of each settlement device should be understood in order to tailor the settlement agreement to the particular facts at hand. This chapter is not intended to explore every possible form of settlement or present every option but rather to discuss in general the kinds of analyses and considerations involved. Following an introduction to the available forms of settlement, two case histories will demonstrate how different fact patterns affect the decision to choose one form of settlement over another.

§ 14.2   Settlement of Multi-Party Disputes

Construction failures, like any multi-party dispute, can present problems when fewer than all the potentially liable parties wish to settle. The absence of one or more parties makes it difficult to properly apportion the degree of fault among the parties. This problem arises particularly when the causes of the failure have not been or cannot be clearly ascertained. It can also arise when one or more parties is financially unable to contribute to a settlement or is unwilling to concede any degree of fault for the failure. Therefore, the absence of one or more parties from the settlement discussions will be an important factor when choosing the legal form and negotiating the terms of any settlement.

When approaching settlement negotiations, it is important to keep in mind the position that each party will take. It may be possible for one party to structure a successful settlement around the positions of the other potentially liable parties, present or not.

Generally, an owner views a potential settlement with a single party as an opportunity to ensure some measure of recovery while preserving rights to continue the action against the other parties. From the perspective of the other parties, a settlement represents a means either to limit liability or to remove oneself from litigation altogether on terms more favorable than defending to conclusion.

Once a settlement is reached, it is necessary to take care to draft the correct form of settlement agreement. In the haste of completing negotiations, careless draftsmanship can render an agreement unforeseeable under applicable law or subject to collateral attack from co-defendants.

§ 14.3   Legal Concepts

An understanding of certain legal concepts that prevailed under common law is necessary as a background to a discussion on settling a multi-party dispute.

Joint and several liability.   Under the common-law concept of joint and several liability, an injured party is entitled to recover the full amount of its damage from any one of two or more joint tortfeasors. Thus, although its degree of negligence may be small in relation to the negligence of the other tortfeasors, a joint tortfeasor can be compelled to pay the full amount of the injured party's damage. Of course, the injured party can only recover the amount of its damage once, but it may elect how much to collect from any one or more of the joint tortfeasors. Moreover, the joint tortfeasor paying a disproportionate amount of the injured party's damage may not collect any of the amount paid from the other tortfeasors (see "Contribution" below).

Contributory negligence.   Under the common-law concept of contributory negligence, if an injured party's negligence contributed in any degree to its injury, it is not entitled to recover any damages, even though the negligence of others contributed to the injury to a much greater degree than the injured party's own negligence did. This concept naturally follows from the concept of joint and several liability in that the injured party is considered to be a joint tortfeasor and, as such, is responsible for the full amount of its own damage.

Contribution.   Sometimes referred to as "apportionment of damages," contribution permits the joint tortfeasor paying a disproportionate amount of the injured party's damage to collect the excess paid over and above its equitable share from the other tortfeasors. It does not affect the injured party's right to recover the full amount of its damage from any one of the joint tortfeasors (see "Joint and several liability" above).

Contribution was not permitted under common law. Under the common law, if one of two or more joint tortfeasors is required to pay a disproportionate amount of the injured party's damage, it is not entitled to recover any amount from the other tortfeasors whose degree of negligence is greater. Thus, if a tortfeasor's negligence contributed only one percent to the injured party's injury and that tortfeasor paid the full amount of the injured party's damage (as it could be required to do under the concept of joint and several liability), it could not recover the 99 percent overpayment from the other joint tortfeasors whose negligence contributed 99 percent to the injured party's injury.

Indemnification.   Under the concept of common-law indemnification, "where one is held liable solely on account of the negligence of another . . . the entire liability [is shifted] to the one who was negligent."[1] The concept of indemnification ameliorates the inequity of the common-law prescription against contribution (which, as noted above, prevents one joint tortfeasor who paid a disproportionate amount of the injured party's damage from recovering the excess from the other tortfeasors) by "allowing one who was compelled to pay for the wrong of another to recover from the wrongdoer the damages paid to the injured party."[2] Under the

---

[1] D'Ambrosio v. City, 55 N.Y.2d 454, 461, 450 N.Y.S.2d 149, 151, 435 N.E.2d 366, 369 (1982).

[2] *Id.* at 460, 450 N.Y.S.2d at 151, 435 N.E.2d at 369.

common law, indemnification was permitted even though contribution was not because the party indemnified did nothing wrong. The party indemnified was compelled to pay the injured party's damage only because of its relationship with the tortfeasor—for example, the owner of a vehicle, not itself negligent, was entitled to be indemnified by the negligent driver. The party seeking indemnification was seeking to recover the full amount paid the injured party, whereas the party seeking contribution was seeking to recover only the excess above its equitable share.

Release. Under the common-law concept of release, if the injured party releases one of two or more joint tortfeasors, the nonreleased tortfeasors are also released. Again, this concept is based upon the concept of joint and several liability. As the released tortfeasor is liable for the full amount of the injured party's damage regardless of its degree of fault, the injured party, by releasing it, has accepted payment of the full amount of its damage.

Privity of contract. Under the common-law concept of privity of contract, one could be liable for breaching a contract only to the other party to the contract. Thus, when an owner contracts with an architect to design a structure and the architect, in turn, contracts with an engineer to design the foundation, the owner cannot maintain an action against the engineer for an improperly designed foundation because the owner has no contract with the engineer. The owner's action is solely against the architect who may seek indemnification from the engineer. But if the architect has no assets, the owner is left without a remedy because the engineer is not directly liable to the owner; the engineer's only liability is to reimburse the architect for the amount actually paid the owner (zero if the architect has no assets).

These concepts have been changed, to varying degrees, in divergent ways, in different states, by statute, court-made case law, or a combination of statute and case law. Thus, it is of paramount importance to determine the applicable law before considering how to structure a settlement.

§ 14.4 Settlement Considerations

Obviously, some of the common-law concepts discussed in § 14.3 seem inequitable, inhibit settlement, and may constitute a trap for the unwary. It is not surprising, therefore, that changes have occurred in them. However, changes made to ameliorate concepts perceived to be inequitable can result in further complicating settlement. For example, permitting contribution among joint tortfeasors seems fairer than the common-law prohibition of contribution but, as a result, a tortfeasor settling with the injured party must now protect itself against contribution claims by its joint tortfeasors. It can no longer settle with the injured party and walk away from the litigation; it is still as much a party to the litigation to defend the contribution claims as if it had never settled with the injured party.

The following settlement devices made it easier for the injured party to settle with some, but not all, tortfeasors; however, the benefit to the settling tortfeasor was questionable.

§ 14.5 The Common-Law Release

As noted in § 14.3, under the common law the release of one joint tortfeasor or joint obligor worked to release all others.[3] Thus, the common-law release inhibited settlement of multi-party litigation because, unless all tortfeasors agreed to settle and agreed to an apportionment of the fault, the injured party could not settle with one party for less than full recovery without precluding further recovery. The harshness of this rule affecting an injured party wishing to settle with a single party, however, was mitigated to some degree by the development of case law allowing the intent of the parties to govern the effect of the release on the litigation—that is, if the injured party, in its release in favor of the settling tortfeasor, specifically reserved its rights against the nonsettling tortfeasors, courts would permit the action to continue against the nonsettling tortfeasors.[4] The law in most jurisdictions now allows an injured party to relinquish a portion of its claim against one joint tortfeasor in exchange for a stated consideration while preserving its right to proceed against the nonsettling joint tortfeasors.[5]

§ 14.6 The Covenant Not to Sue

In those jurisdictions following the common law of release, an alternative settlement device is a covenant not to sue. In fact, some courts would ameliorate the harshness of the common-law concept by equating a release in favor of one joint tortfeasor to a covenant not to sue by finding in the

---

[3] Restatement (Second) of Torts § 885 (1965); Restatement (Second) of Contracts § 294 comment a (1981).

[4] 47 Am. Jur. 2d *Judgments* § 989 at 85 (1969). *See also* 4 Corbin on Contracts §§ 931, 933 (1952).

[5] *But see* Prosser on Torts § 49 at 302–03 (4th ed. 1971): "[T]he only states which continue to cling to the old rule, and make it impossible to settle with one tortfeasor without releasing another, are Washington and Virginia." *Id.* at 302 (citing Rust v. Schaitzer, 175 Wash. 331, 27 P.2d 571 (1933)); Haney v. Cheatam, 8 Wash. 2d 310, 111

release an intent to release only one joint tortfeasor and allowing the injured party to proceed against the nonsettling tortfeasors.[6]

The covenant not to sue is a contract in which the injured party promises not to enforce a cause of action against a settling defendant.[7] For example, an owner who has a cause of action against a contractor for defective performance promises, in exchange for a stipulated sum, not to enforce that cause of action. The covenant not to sue has been construed not to forfeit the injured party's cause of action against the nonsettling tortfeasors as a release would under the common law.

However effective this type of release is between the injured party and the settling tortfeasor, the covenant not to sue is not without its drawbacks. The injured party in such a situation risks reducing its recovery at trial. Eliminating a single tortfeasor from trial allows the remaining tortfeasors the opportunity to reduce their liability, and the amount of a jury verdict, by arguing the greater liability of the absent tortfeasor. From the settling tortfeasor's point of view, because such a covenant does not extinguish the injured party's cause of action against the nonsettling tortfeasors, the settling tortfeasor may still be a party to the lawsuit and remain exposed to subsequent claims for contribution from the other tortfeasors.

It is always crucial to consult the joint-tortfeasor rules of the applicable jurisdiction. For example, in some states, it is presumed that a release of one tortfeasor releases all tortfeasors, unless the injured party expressly reserves its rights to proceed against the nonsettling tortfeasors.[8] In other jurisdictions, the presumption cuts the other way: the release of one does not release the others unless there is express language to that effect.[9]

§ 14.7 The Covenant Not to Execute on the Judgment

Some of the problems arising under a covenant not to sue can be solved by a covenant not to execute on the judgment. This settlement device, usually

---

P.2d 1003 (1941); Richardson v. Pacific Power & Light Co., 11 Wash. 2d 288, 118 P.2d 985 (1941) (suggesting a change in Wash. law); Bland v. Warwickshire Corp., 160 Va. 131, 168 S.E. 443 (1933); Goldstein v. Gilbert, 125 W. Va. 250, 23 S.E.2d 606 (1942).

[6] Community School Dist. of Potsville in Counties of Allmakee v. Gordon N. Peterson, Inc., 176 N.W.2d 169 (Iowa 1970); United Pacific Ins. Co. v. Lundstrom, 77 Wash. 2d 162, 459 P.2d 930 (1969); Mills v. Standard Titles Ins. Co., 39 Colo. App. 261, 568 P.2d 79 (1977).

[7] See Penza v. Neckles, 340 So. 2d 1210 (Fla. Dist. Ct. App. 1976); Allen v. Ouachita Marine & Indus. Corp., 606 P.2d 607 (Okla. 1979).

[8] See Restatement (Second) of Torts § 885 (1965).

[9] See Unif. Contribution among Tortfeasors Act (U.C.A.T.A.) § 4 (1955):

When a release or a covenant not to sue or not to enforce a judgment is given in good faith to one of two or more persons liable in tort for the same injury or the same wrongful death:

used following a verdict on the issue of liability at trial and a finding of the relative degrees of fault of the joint and several tortfeasors, but prior to an assessment of the amount of the injured party's damage, enables the settling tortfeasor to assess its position with respect to the contribution issues. Once the apportionment of fault has been determined at trial, however, the motivation of the injured party to settle may be limited to immediate financial considerations or potential issues for appeal.

For example, suppose an injured party sued a contractor and subcontractor in negligence and obtains a verdict against both with a finding that each is 50 percent at fault. At this point, the subcontractor knows that it will be responsible for at least 50 percent of the injured party's damage, whatever that may be, under several possible scenarios:

1. The injured party may elect to collect 100 percent of its damage from the subcontractor but the subcontractor may not be able to recover the contractor's proportionate share due to the contractor's shaky financial condition.

2. If the contractor is required to pay more than its 50 percent share, the subcontractor is liable to it in contribution.

The subcontractor and the injured party then settle.

The injured party would promise that it will not enforce the judgment against the subcontractor, thus solving the problem presented by the first scenario, and, in return, the injured party would receive cash up front from the subcontractor. The subcontractor stays in the lawsuit to attempt to make sure that the amount of the injured party's damage does not exceed twice the settlement amount, thus attempting to solve the problem presented by the second scenario.

§ 14.8 The High-Low Agreement

Another settlement device is commonly known as a high-low agreement.[10] Under this form of settlement, a plaintiff and defendant agree to a minimum and maximum amount the defendant will pay after judgment, notwithstanding the verdict. For example, suppose an injured party sued an architect and various other defendants for damages totalling $100,000. The injured party and the defendant architect could

---

(a) It does not discharge any of the other tortfeasors from liability for the injury or wrongful death unless its terms so provide; but it reduces the claim against the others to the extent of any amount stipulated by the release or the covenant, or in the amount of the consideration paid for it, whichever is the greater; and,

(b) It discharges the tortfeasor to whom it is given from all liability for contribution to any other tortfeasor.

[10] 27th Ave. Gulf Serv. Center v. Smellie, 510 So. 2d 996 (Fla. Dist. Ct. App. 1987).

agree that, no matter what the amount of the verdict is, the injured party's recovery from the architect would be limited to no less than $10,000 and no more than $25,000. If the verdict against the architect is between $10,000 and $25,000, the architect will be responsible for that sum. But if the verdict against the architect is $2,000, she still must pay the minimum $10,000 she agreed to pay. Likewise, if the verdict against the architect is $50,000, she only pays $25,000.

The parties may also structure their high-low agreement in terms of apportionment. They can agree that the architect will be responsible for not less than 10 percent and not more than 25 percent of the verdict.

This type of agreement, similar to a Mary Carter agreement (see § 14.15), has the advantages of flexibility of terms, retaining the defendant through trial, and limiting the plaintiff's recovery. Again, a defendant should assess possible issues of contribution and collateral attack by codefendants before entering into such an agreement.

The following changes to the common law made it easier for one of the several joint tortfeasors to settle with the injured party.

§ 14.9 Contribution

When choosing any method or form of settlement, the defendant must consider the possibility that the nonsettling defendants who go to trial may seek contribution or indemnification from her. The laws among the jurisdictions vary with respect to joint and several liability, contribution, and indemnity issues. While keeping in mind that each jurisdiction has different rules with respect to contribution and indemnification, an attempt will be made to point out those areas of particular concern when negotiating a settlement.

Generally, contribution issues are addressed by the 1939 Uniform Contribution among Tortfeasors Act (U.C.A.T.A.) or the 1955 U.C.A.T.A.[11] Also, some jurisdictions determine liability under a comparative fault theory.[12]

§ 14.10 —The 1939 Uniform Contribution among Tortfeasors Act

The 1939 U.C.A.T.A., adopted in eight jurisdictions,[13] handles partial settlements in one of two manners,[14] both of which are determined by the terms of the settlement agreement.

---

[11] U.C.A.T.A. (1939), 9 U.L.A. 233 (1957); U.C.A.T.A. (1955), 12 U.L.A. 63 (1975).

[12] See, e.g., Bielski v. Schulze, 16 Wis. 2d 1, 114 N.W.2d 105, 107 (1962).

[13] The substance of the 1939 U.C.A.T.A. is retained in Arkansas, Delaware, Hawaii, Maryland, New Mexico, Pennsylvania, Rhode Island, and South Dakota.

[14] See U.C.A.T.A. § 4 (1939).

Under the first method, the plaintiff, upon settlement with one of the co-defendants, can proceed against the nonsettling defendants for the full amount of its claim. The nonsettling defendants are required to pay the full amount of the verdict reduced by the amount which the settling defendant paid in settlement, but they retain the right to seek pro rata contribution from the settling defendant (pro rata contribution means that the plaintiff's damage award is divided equally by the number of defendants held liable). This method is attractive to the plaintiff because, despite the settlement, she still recovers the full amount of the verdict, but is unattractive to the settling defendant because its liability is not capped by the amount paid in settlement.

Assume that there are four defendants, that the plaintiff settles with one for $10,000 and obtains a verdict against the remaining three for $100,000. The $100,000 verdict is reduced by the $10,000 paid in settlement to $90,000. Each of the three nonsettling defendant's pro rata share is then $30,000. However, if the plaintiff had not settled with one defendant, each of the four defendant's pro rata share would have been only $25,000. The plaintiff still recovers her $100,000: $10,000 from the settling defendant and $30,000 from each of the three nonsettling defendants. However, the settling defendant is still liable to each of the three nonsettling defendants for the $5,000 they paid to the plaintiff over their pro rata share of $25,000. Thus, the settling defendant gained nothing by having settled, other than the cost of continued litigation if the settling defendant chooses not to defend further: its liability is still $25,000 ($10,000 paid to the plaintiff plus $5,000 to each of the three nonsettling defendants), exactly what it would have been had it not settled (25 percent of the $100,000 verdict).

The only way in which the settling defendant can assure that its liability is capped by the $10,000 settlement is to remain in the action to contest the amount of the plaintiff's damages. If the plaintiff's verdict is only $40,000 instead of $100,000, each of the three nonsettling defendant's pro rata share is then only $10,000 after the $40,000 verdict is reduced to $30,000 by the $10,000 paid in settlement, exactly what it would have been had there been no settlement (25 percent of $40,000). Thus, none of the nonsettling defendants has paid more than its pro rata share, the settling defendant is not liable to them and it has successfully capped its liability at the $10,000 paid in settlement.

Of course, if the settling defendant, by remaining in the action, is able to reduce the plaintiff's verdict to less than $40,000, it benefits the nonsettling defendants but not itself. A $25,000 verdict reduced to $15,000 by the $10,000 paid in settlement results in the pro rata share of each of the three nonsettling defendants being only $5,000 but the settling defendant has paid the $10,000 settlement amount.

Under the second method, the 1939 Act permits the plaintiff to credit the nonsettling defendants with the pro rata share of the settling party's settlement amount. The second approach is more attractive to the settling defendant but represents a danger to the plaintiff in settling for less than what she may recover by a verdict.[15]

Again, assume that there are four defendants, that the plaintiff settles with one for $10,000 and that the plaintiff obtains a verdict against the remaining three of $100,000. The $100,000 verdict is reduced to $75,000 by the settling defendant's $25,000 pro rata share and the plaintiff recovers only $85,000 ($75,000 under the verdict as reduced and the $10,000 settlement amount).

§ 14.11   —The 1955 Uniform Contribution among Tortfeasors Act

Under the 1955-revised U.C.A.T.A., adopted in 10 jurisdictions,[16] the plaintiff's claim against the nonsettling defendants would be reduced by the amount of the settling defendant and provided that the settlement agreement was entered into in good faith,[17] the settling defendant would not be liable to the nonsettling defendants for contribution.[18]

This may seem to solve many of the problems impeding an equitable settlement because the plaintiff is not prejudiced by having settled and the settling defendant's liability is capped by the amount paid in settlement.

Again, assume that there are four defendants, that the plaintiff settles with one for $10,000 and that the plaintiff obtains a verdict against the remaining three of $100,000. The $100,000 verdict is reduced by the $10,000 paid in settlement to $90,000. The plaintiff still recovers her $100,000: $10,000 from the settling defendant and $90,000 from the nonsettling defendants. However, the nonsettling defendants are not entitled to any

---

[15] See U.C.A.T.A. Commissioners' Comment § 4(b) (1955). The effect of this provision of the 1939 Act

> has been to discourage settlements in joint tort cases, by making it impossible for one tortfeasor alone to take a release and close the file. Plaintiff's attorneys are said to refuse to accept any release which contains the provision "to the extent of the pro rata share of the released tortfeasor," because they have no way of knowing what they are giving up. The "pro rata share" cannot be determined in advance of judgment against the other tortfeasors.

[16] Alaska, Arizona, Colorado, Florida, Massachusetts, Nevada, North Carolina, North Dakota, Ohio, and Tennessee.

[17] See Commissioners' Comment § 4(b): "The requirement that the release or covenant be given in good faith gives the Court occasion to determine whether the transaction was collusive, and if so there is no discharge."

[18] See U.C.A.T.A. § 4(a) n.6 (1955). See also generally Harris, The Modified Pro Tanto Credit and the Reasonableness Hearing Requirement, 20 Gonzaga L. Rev. 69 (1984).

contribution from the settling defendant unless they can prove that the $10,000 settlement was not a good faith settlement. If the nonsettling defendants cannot prove that the $10,000 settlement was not made in good faith, the settling defendant's liability is "capped" at the $10,000 paid in settlement and each of the nonsettling defendants is "penalized" for not having settled by being required to pay $30,000, $5,000 more than its pro rata share of $25,000. Thus, by protecting settling defendants from contribution claims to the detriment of nonsettling defendants, the 1955 Act encourages defendants to settle and, by assuring that plaintiffs will recover the full amount of their verdicts despite a settlement with some but not all defendants, it encourages plaintiffs to settle.

§ 14.12   Comparative Fault

In comparative fault jurisdictions, liability is apportioned based upon fault and the plaintiff's judgment is reduced by an amount proportionate to the settling defendant's degree of fault.[19] "Pro rata" shares refer to the concept that, if there are four tortfeasors, then each is responsible for one-fourth of the judgment. See § 14.10. Thus, if the injured party sues three defendants and recovers $120,000, each is responsible for $40,000. Suppose that there is a fourth party who was also responsible for the wrong but was not named in the lawsuit. Under the applicable laws, the three defendants can seek contribution from the fourth defendant, reduce their own shares to $30,000, and recover the difference from the fourth defendant.

In a comparative fault jurisdiction, however, a defendant's portion of responsibility for the injured party's damages is proportionate to her degree of fault in causing the damage. Thus, the jury must decide not only the questions of liability and damages, but also must calculate each defendant's degree of fault. So, if the three defendants in the above example wish to obtain contribution from the fourth defendant, they can only recover an amount proportionate to that fourth defendant's degree of fault.

In comparative contribution jurisdictions, the plaintiff would want the settling defendant to remain at trial, thus obviating the nonsettling defendants' ability to diminish their own liability by arguing the settling defendant's fault was greater. However, comparative fault jurisdictions represent the best situation for a settling defendant who wishes to cap her liability at a predetermined amount.

---

[19] *See* Bielski v. Schulze, 16 Wis. 2d 1, 114 N.W.2d 105 (1962); Mitchell v. Branch, 45 Haw. 128, 363 P.2d 969 (1961); Little v. Miles, 213 Ark. 725, 212 S.W.2d 935 (1948).

§ 14.13 Indemnification

Contribution is not the same as indemnification. Contribution divides the injured party's loss among the responsible tortfeasors by requiring each to pay its proportionate share. Indemnification shifts the burden of the entire loss from one tortfeasor who has been found liable to the shoulders of another who should bear it instead.[20] The right to indemnification can arise from agreement between the parties or from rights created at common law or by statute.

It is common practice for a contractor who builds for an owner to contractually agree to indemnify that owner against claims by subcontractors and others. This means that, if anyone should recover a judgment against the owner, the contractor agrees to pay the amount of that judgment to the owner.[21] This is contractual indemnification.

The right to indemnification can also arise by statute. For example, a municipality might be required by statute to indemnify the operators of municipally owned vehicles with respect to negligence claims.[22]

§ 14.14 Modern Settlement Techniques

There are three other techniques that potentially represent the most creative methods of settling multi-party disputes that should be considered in negotiating the settlement of construction failures. These techniques hold the hope of avoiding some of the difficulties discussed above. These three techniques—the Mary Carter Agreement, the Loan Receipt Agreement, and the Pierringer Release—represent methods by which a defendant may limit its liability yet meet the needs of the injured party in assuring a full recovery at trial.

---

[20] *See* Prosser on Torts § 51 at 310 (4th ed. 1971).

[21] The American Institute of Architects (AIA) standard form General Conditions (AIA Document A201 (14th ed. 1987)) provides in pertinent part:

> 3.18.1 To the fullest extent permitted by law, the Contractor shall indemnify and hold harmless the Owner, Architect, Architect's consultants, and agents and employees of any of them from and against claims, damages, losses, and expenses, including but not limited to attorney's fees, arising out of or resulting from performance of the Work, provided that such claim, damage, loss, or expense is attributable to bodily injury, sickness, disease or death, or to injury or destruction of tangible property (other than the Work itself) including loss of use resulting therefrom, but only to the extent caused in whole or in part by negligent acts or omissions of the Contractor, a Subcontractor, anyone directly or indirectly employed by them or anyone for whose acts they may be liable, regardless of whether or not such claim, damage, loss, or expense is caused in part by a party indemnified hereunder.

[22] *See* N.Y. Gen. Mun. Law § 50-b (McKinney 1986).

Because of the contractual nature of construction disputes and the fact that documentary and physical evidence are often available for inspection, each party must investigate the potential causes of the failure, determine whether it is at fault and whether any of the other parties may also be at fault, and assess the degrees of responsibility of each of the parties for the specific failure. Further, the failure may have been fixed and the injured party's damage thereby liquidated, or reasonable estimates can be obtained to determine the cost of the repair. Although such favorable circumstances encourage settlement, rational approaches to settlement can be frustrated by the nature of the failure or by the responsible parties' ability or inability to contribute to any settlement. The three techniques discussed in §§ **14.15** through **14.17** enable a single defendant to effect a settlement while allowing the injured party the opportunity to proceed to court for a full recovery.

§ 14.15   —Mary Carter Agreements

Broadly defined, a *Mary Carter Agreement*[23] is an agreement between the plaintiff and one of two or more defendants exposed to joint liability to limit the recovery from the settling defendant notwithstanding the amount of the verdict.[24] This has an effect similar to a covenant not to execute. The Mary Carter Agreement addresses most of the problems raised in each of the earlier forms of settlement in that it ensures a recovery to the plaintiff without reducing the potential liability of the other defendants. Under the agreement, the settling defendant remains in the action, preventing other defendants from laying all blame upon an absent defendant and allowing the owner to concentrate on the issues of liability of the remaining defendants.

A distinguishing feature of many Mary Carter Agreements is a sliding scale provision that allows the settling defendant's liability to be decreased, depending upon the total amount of recovery by the injured party. Generally, however, the Mary Carter Agreement includes a guaranteed recovery clause to the plaintiff under any circumstances. Also, these agreements have historically been intended to remain secret between the settling parties. Therefore, the basic features of a Mary Carter Agreement include:

1. the settling defendant guarantees a certain amount to the plaintiff, regardless of the outcome at trial

---

[23] Booth v. Mary Carter Paint Co., 202 So. 2d 8 (Fla. Dist. Ct. App. 1967).

[24] Maule Indus., Inc. v. Rountree, 264 So. 2d 445 (Fla. Dist. Ct. App. 1972).

2. the settling defendant remains in the action to its conclusion

3. the agreement is secret.[25]

The sliding scale aspect of a Mary Carter Agreement is best exemplified by California's statutory equivalent to the Mary Carter Agreement, providing for a sliding scale recovery.

> [A]n agreement or covenant between a plaintiff or plaintiffs and one or more, but not all, alleged tortfeasor defendants, where the agreement limits the liability of the agreeing tortfeasor defendants to an amount which is dependent upon the amount of recovery which the plaintiff is able to recover from the non-agreeing defendant or defendants. This includes, but is not limited to, agreements within the scope of Section 877, and agreements in the form of a loan from the agreeing tortfeasor defendant to plaintiff or plaintiffs which is repayable in whole or in part from the recovery against the non-agreeing tortfeasor defendant.[26]

This type of provision, potentially decreasing the settling defendant's liability based upon the plaintiff's amount of recovery from co-defendants, has the apparent effect of joining the interests of the owner and the settling defendant at trial. This had led to criticism of Mary Carter Agreements as being void based upon principles of public policy, champerty, ethics, and trial fairness.[27]

The champerty, and its corollary maintenance, issue arises under the theory that one without an interest in the litigation may not maintain or assist in the prosecution of the case. The party assisting the maintenance

---

[25] Eubanks & Cocchiarella, *In Defense of "Mary Carter,"* For the Defense (Feb. 1984).

[26] Cal. Civ. Proc. Code § 887.5(b) (West 1980). Section 877 reads:

> Where a release, dismissal with or without prejudice, or a covenant not to sue or not to enforce judgment is given in good faith before verdict or judgment to one or more of a number of tortfeasors claimed to be liable for the same tort, or to one or more other co-obligors mutually subject to contribution rights, it shall have the following effect:
>
> (a) It shall not discharge any other such party from liability unless its terms so provide, but it shall reduce the claims against the others in the amount stipulated by the release, the dismissal or the covenant, or in the amount of the consideration paid for it whichever is the greater.
>
> (b) It shall discharge the party to whom it is given from all liability for any contribution to any other parties.
>
> (c) This section shall not apply to co-obligors who have expressly agreed in writing to an apportionment of liability for losses or claims among themselves.
>
> (d) This section shall not apply to a release, dismissal with or without prejudice, or a covenant not to sue or not to enforce a judgment given to a co-obligor on an alleged contract debt where the contract was made prior to January 1, 1988.

[27] *See* Entman, *Mary Carter Agreements: An Assessment of Attempted Solutions,* 38 U. Fla. L. Rev. 522 (1986).

of the action benefits under champerty, by the profit or compensation derived from the lawsuit.[28] The leading case holding a Mary Carter Agreement void is *Lum v. Stinnet.*[29] In that case the Nevada Supreme Court held that the settling defendant insurers, by entering into a Mary Carter-type agreement, were strangers to the litigation and construed the insurers' actions as maintenance, continuing the litigation, and thereby profiting from the terms of the Mary Carter Agreement. Other courts have also rejected this argument, finding that the settling defendant did indeed have an interest in the lawsuit.[30] Challenges to Mary Carter Agreements on the bases of champerty and maintenance have not been universally successful, however.[31] Thus, these issues may not be significant enough to deter use of this device in settlement in a given jurisdiction.[32]

However, the ethical problems resulting from the realignment of the true interests at trial remain troublesome.[33] They include the joining of the owner and settling defendant's interests at trial giving rise to the potential for perjury. Some of these issues have been resolved by requiring disclosure of the Mary Carter Agreement to the jurors at trial.[34] Once the terms of agreement have been disclosed, the court can address the potential problems of determining the real parties in interest and the potential for perjury at trial. Some jurisdictions, by either statute or case law, require automatic disclosure of such settlement agreements.[35] Further, if a proper procedural inquiry by the nonsettling defendants is made, disclosure may be required in some jurisdictions. Regardless of whether the agreement is to be disclosed under case or statutory law, an argument can be made under Federal Rule of Civil Procedure 26(b), or comparable state rules for disclosure, that the agreement is a matter relevant to the litigation and not protected by privilege.

---

[28] 14 C.J.S. *Champerty & Maintenance* §§ 1, 2 (1939).

[29] 87 Nev. 402, 488 P.2d 347 (1971).

[30] *See* Wright v. Commercial Union Ins. Co., 63 N.C. App. 465, 305 S.E.2d 190 (1983); Lahocki v. Contee Sand & Gravel Co., 41 Md. App. 579, 398 A.2d 490 (1979), *rev'd sub nom.* General Motors Corp. v. Lahocki, 286 Md. 714, 410 A.2d 1039 (1980).

[31] *See id.; see also* Cullen v. Atchison, Topeka & Santa Fe Ry., 211 Kan. 368, 507 P.2d 353 (1973).

[32] Lahocki v. Contee Sand & Gravel Co., 41 Md. App. 579, 398 A.2d 490 (Ct. Spec. App. 1979), *rev'd sub nom.* General Motors Corp. v. Lahocki, 286 Md. 714, 410 A.2d. 1039 (1980); Wright v. Commercial Union Ins. Co., 63 N.C. App. 465, 305 S.E.2d 190 (1983).

[33] Entman, *Mary Carter Agreements: An Assessment of Attempted Solutions,* 38 U. Fla. L. Rev. 537 n.16 (1986).

[34] *Id.* at 561.

[35] Cal. Civ. Proc. Code § 877.5(a)(1) (West 1980); Wash. Rev. Code § 4.22.060(1); Or. Rev. Stat. § 18.455 (1983); State *ex rel.* Vapor Corp. v. Narick, 320 S.E.2d 345, 348 (W. Va. 1984); Johnson v. Moberg, 334 N.W.2d 411, 415 (Minn. 1983); Gatto v. Walgreen Drug Co., 61 Ill. 2d 356, 337 N.E.2d 23, 28 (Ill. 1975).

The secrecy of the Mary Carter Agreement has also come under attack as being a violation of the Model Code of Professional Responsibility.[36] These arguments question the ethics of parties who have settled their dispute but remain at trial. Some commentators have also raised the issue of the potential for perjury resulting from the realignment of the real parties in interest. Although disclosure addresses some of these issues, questions regarding the jury's understanding of the issues, once informed of such an agreement, create the danger of prejudice against the nonsettling parties.

In large measure, the facts and circumstances of a particular case must guide the structure of a settlement agreement. A Mary Carter Agreement, however, fails to address and resolve some of the weaknesses inherent in some of the other forms of settlement.

As a practical matter, when drafting a Mary Carter Agreement, attention should be paid to the language used in the agreement and options available under applicable law regarding the terms of settlement.[37] For example, it may be useful to include statements regarding the nonsettling defendants when case disclosure of the agreement is made to a jury. Such statements may include the fault of the nonsettling defendants in the action, their irresponsibility in failing to negotiate a settlement in good faith, or other matters that support the position of the injured party and the settling defendant. The court might not allow such self-serving statements to be heard by the jury, but the statements, if admissible, may help to educate the jury regarding the facts and circumstances leading up to settlement.

It should be noted that the use of Mary Carter Agreements is not restricted to bargaining on dollar terms alone and may include other matters helpful to the position of the settling parties. The exchange of otherwise privileged (undiscoverable) technical reports, engineering studies, or other discovery information may be a basis to settle a dispute. Also, terms regarding trial tactics or discretionary matters reserved to the parties, such as juror selection, may be a basis for exchange. Therefore, as a negotiating position, any matter potentially useful to the settling parties may be included as terms in the agreement.

For a sample Mary Carter Agreement based on a hypothetical failure, see § **14.22.**

§ 14.16 —The Pierringer Release

A settlement device for use in a comparative negligence jurisdiction, used to cap liability and avoid the dangers to settling defendants from collateral

---

[36] Entman, *Mary Carter Agreements: An Assessment of Attempted Solutions,* 38 U. Fla. L. Rev. 537 (1986).

[37] *See generally Negotiation and Settlement: Mary Carter Agreements,* 51 Civil Trial Manual (BNA) 641, 643 (1988).

attacks, is the Pierringer Release.[38] The plaintiff and the settling defendant execute a covenant not to sue coupled with an agreement to credit the settling defendant's portion of liability under contribution to the remaining defendants after judgment.[39] The plaintiff's right to proceed against the nonsettling defendants is reserved under the terms of the agreement. The contribution issues are resolved by virtue of the plaintiff's promise to credit any amount for which the settling defendant is determined to be liable against the judgment ultimately recovered.[40] Therefore, in return for an insured recovery from one party, the owner agrees that its recovery will be limited to the amount of the judgment against the nonsettling defendants. The nonsettling defendants remain liable only for their portion of the judgment as a result of the action. Therefore, the settlement agreement may provide that the plaintiff could receive less than the amount the settling defendant might be liable for under theories of comparative negligence and contribution had the case proceeded to trial.

Assume that the jurisdiction is one in which the jury is instructed to apportion degrees of fault among the liable joint tortfeasors. The injured party sues two defendants and settles with one. The injured party releases the settling defendant for $10,000 and agrees that the nonsettling defendant's share of the damages will be reduced by the settling defendant's proportionate share. In the case of this agreement, the injured party presupposes that its damages are in the neighborhood of $100,000 and the settling defendant is about 10 percent responsible.

Two intriguing scenarios emerge. First, suppose that the jury finds that the injured party damages are $100,000. If the jury decides that the nonsettling defendant is 100 percent liable, then the injured party recovers $110,000 ($10,000 in settlement from the settling defendant and a $100,000 verdict against the nonsettling defendant). Here, the settling defendant has misjudged her portion of the liability.

Second, if the jury decides that the nonsettling defendant was 15 percent liable and the settling defendant 85 percent liable for the damages, the injured party recovers only $25,000 ($10,000 from the settling defendant and 15 percent of the $100,000 verdict from the nonsettling defendant). Here, the settling defendant has bought $90,000 worth of liability for $10,000. Under a Pierringer Release the trial becomes one of apportioning liability among the nonsettling defendants because the settling defendant and plaintiff have already "bought" their peace.

Ethical problems arising from the sliding scale recovery under a Mary Carter Agreement do not exist with a Pierringer Release because the settlement is for a lump sum amount and is final between the parties. The

---

[38] Shantz v. Richview, Inc., 311 N.W.2d 155 (Minn. 1980); Frey v. Snelgrove, 269 N.W.2d 918, 920–922 (Minn. 1978).

[39] Pierringer v. Milwaukee Gas Light Co., 21 Wis. 2d 182, 124 N.W.2d 106 (1963).

[40] 124 N.W.2d at 111.

potential for perjury is lessened because the settling defendant has no financial interest in the outcome at trial. Further potential prejudice can be avoided by disclosure to the jury of the settlement, omitting any terms that may be troublesome to all parties, such as the amount paid by the settling defendant. Contribution among defendants is determined by the percentages of fault found in the judgment.

Thus, the theory behind a Pierringer Release[41] is that in a comparative negligence jurisdiction it allows a single defendant to settle with the aggrieved plaintiff, while the plaintiff reserves its right to proceed against the other nonsettling defendants. This allows a resolution of the concerns of the settling defendant regarding contribution claims by nonsettling defendants.

§ 14.17   The Hypothetical Irreparable Failure

The following two hypothetical cases will serve to illustrate how the techniques just discussed can be applied to structuring practical settlement agreements.[42]

In the first case, in 1983, under a contract with a designer, a subdesigner performed hydraulic model tests and other studies in connection with the design of a rubble mound breakwater. The designer was under a contract with the city. The design called for many large-sized rocks. By early 1984, the subdesigner completed its services and was paid in full by the designer.

In the spring of 1984, a competitively bid contract was let by the city to a contractor for the construction of the 2,000-foot-long breakwater, based upon plans and specifications prepared by the designer. The city retained the designer as construction manager to supervise the contractor's work and verify that the breakwater was being constructed in accordance with the plans and specifications. The subdesigner was to perform no further services in connection with the construction.

In June 1984, the contractor reported to the designer and the city that it had encountered "changed conditions" and would not be able to construct the breakwater as it had been designed and specified by the designer. The changed conditions involved the unavailability in the local quarry of the specified large-sized rocks.

The designer contacted the subdesigner to inquire whether the breakwater might be redesigned to dispense with the large-sized rocks and

---

[41] *See* Swanigan v. State Farm Ins. Co., 99 Wis. 2d 179, 299 N.W.2d 234 (1980) for a sample Pierringer Release.

[42] These are based on actual cases in which the authors have been involved. Facts have been altered, however, for purposes of discussion.

be constructed instead from smaller-sized rocks. The subdesigner recommended using an innovative design which did not require the larger-sized rocks specified in the original design.

From June through August, 1984, the designer and subdesigner conferred with each other to develop the redesign. The subdesigner undertook hydraulic model tests to determine the stability of the breakwater.

At the same time that the designer and subdesigner were working out the details of the breakwater redesign, the designer, contractor, and city were involved in separate discussions involving the following:

1. The contractor was threatening to walk off the job unless it received some relief as a result of the alleged "changed conditions."
2. The designer feared potential liability to the city arising from the "changed conditions" issue.
3. The incumbent city government officials expressed a need for the breakwater to be completed by October because they feared suspension of construction would imperil state funding for the breakwater project.

In August, 1984, the contractor and the city agreed that a change order would be issued to the contractor for the construction of the breakwater according to the redesign. As the contractor proceeded, the construction was fraught with continuing problems. The designer's representatives were dissatisfied with the contractor's construction methods and voiced frequent complaints that the redesign plans and specifications were not being followed and that undersized rocks and other contaminates were being placed in the breakwater. The contractor completed the breakwater in October.

Two severe winter storms, one in November and the other in December, progressively damaged the breakwater to such a degree that it represented a "failure" of the breakwater. As would be expected in such a situation, recriminations and finger-pointing ensued among all the parties. Did the failure occur because the redesign was inadequate or because the construction was deficient or both?

Following the failure, the city elected to rebuild the breakwater at a cost of $5 million using the original design but a different construction manager and contractor. Faced with correcting the failure itself, the city looked to the parties involved in the failure for compensation. The contractor held a $3 million surety bond on the project but, beyond that, had no assets to cover the loss or contribute to any eventual recovery. The designer/construction manager held a $1 million professional liability insurance policy and the subdesigner $2 million in professional insurance coverage.

§ 14.18   Considerations in Determining Settlement Methods

In this case, there was a total failure of the breakwater, so no opportunity existed for the responsible party or parties to repair the damage. Because remedial measures are therefore precluded as a settlement tactic, it becomes important to analyze the potential theories of liability and the possible opportunities for settlement within that framework.

The city is faced with two inconsistent theories of liability. Should it pursue the contractor and surety under a theory of deficient construction or the designer and subdesigner under a theory of defective design? The merits of the various possible actions will depend on the operative facts regarding the failure, the city's own acts and omissions, and the possible defenses each party may have to liability.

The contractor's liability is covered by its surety bond. The surety bonded the contractor for the construction of a rubble mound breakwater. The change in design that occurred during construction may represent a "material change" that could absolve the surety of liability on the bond. On the other hand, as the city assesses the designer and subdesigner's liabilities, it must first consider the fact that it has no direct contractual relationship with the subdesigner and the law of the jurisdiction does not yet recognize a cause of action by an owner, such as the city, against the subdesigner in the absence of privity.

The city is in the position of realizing a potential recovery limited to the aggregate of the bond and insurance policy, or $4 million. Taking into consideration the problems associated with pursuing the subdesigner, the city elects to settle the matter with the designer and subdesigner as to their respective portions of the liability. The city's negotiating posture is bolstered by the possible negligence of the designer in failing to supervise the construction as it progressed and of the subdesigner in providing a defective design.

§ 14.19   Settling with the Designer

In its settlement discussions, the city recites the facts and theories establishing its potential causes of action against the designer and subdesigner. It then offers to cap the joint potential liability between the two at $2 million. Included in the $2 million liability cap is the city's offer to split any settlement from the contractor and surety. The city will retain the first $1 million of recovery and the city and the designer and subdesigner will then split any remainder.

Under these proposed circumstances, the city would receive $2 million from the designer and subdesigner, the first $1 million from any recovery against the contractor, and potentially recover another $1 million from the contractor's $3 million surety bond, for a total of $4 million. The designer and subdesigner would cap their liability at $2 million total and potentially be reimbursed $1 million of that amount from the city's recovery from the surety. By this form of settlement, the city is assured of the designer and subdesigner's interest in recovery against the contractor and the surety. The proposed settlement could be effected by a covenant not to sue, as there would be no need to have either party in a subsequent action.

For the city's strategy to work, a complete settlement with the designer and subdesigner is essential. The designer, recognizing her precarious position and anxious to settle on these terms, proposes splitting the $2 million liability with the subdesigner. The subdesigner, in a relatively stronger position, determines its direct liability to be minimal; moreover, the potential for any recovery from the contractor and its surety may be limited by the fact that the change in design could represent a material change, negating the surety's obligation. The subdesigner, however, recognizes that the potential legal fees could be substantial and offers $250,000 to any potential settlement, representing the amount the subdesigner believes it would spend to defend the suit. Furthermore, the subdesigner believes the designer to be wholly at fault and to have the resources to make up the difference. Rejecting this apportionment, the designer decides to pursue its own strategy with the city.

In later discussions with the city, the designer raises the problems with the city's case. Representatives from the city were on site each day and observed the contractor's work. Also, the city was involved in the decisionmaking as the project progressed. The designer, acting as construction manager, points out all of this and, reminding the city of the political pressure to produce an acceptable project prior to elections, suggests that the city is not without fault. The designer, seeking to remove herself from the case entirely, offers to finance the cost of any lawsuit by paying $250,000 to the city in exchange for a covenant not to sue. It is understood that in exchange for the release from the suit the designer will suffer from a "poor memory" as to those matters that would not be helpful to the city's position.

The city now recognizes its options are limited. First, the rift between the designer and subdesigner complicates its case against the contractor and the surety. Second, the city needs the designer as an ally in any subsequent suit. The designer has the necessary engineering expertise and records to argue the fault of the contractor. Also, the city cannot run the risk of having the designer reveal to the other parties the city's culpable actions during construction. Third, the city also needs the designer in the suit as a defendant. But, fourth, the city wants to guarantee some amount of recovery from the failure, particularly from the designer, as the facts tend to show that the designer was liable for the failure because it had responsibility for both the design and supervision of construction.

Considering all of these matters, the city decides upon an offer to the designer consisting of (1) accepting the $250,000 to finance a lawsuit against the designer and contractor's surety and (2) capping the designer's liability at the $1 million represented by its insurance coverage, and in a sliding-scale agreement, reducing the designer's liability by a sum equal to 50 percent times the amount determined to be the liability of the contractor's surety. Thus, should the city recover $1 million from the designer and $1.2 million from the contractor's surety, the designer's liability to the city would be reduced to $400,000, that is, $1 million or (50 percent) ($1.2 million).

The designer accepts this proposal and at that point negotiations end with those terms agreed to by the parties.

What are the effects of the agreement? The designer will be a defendant throughout the trial. The amount of settlement is determined on a sliding scale dependent upon the city's recovery against the contractor's surety. The interests of the parties have been joined by the agreement, a fact that necessarily must remain a secret. The advance of the litigation fees may, in fact, turn out to be a loan, but this agreement is a type of Mary Carter Agreement.

§ 14.20   —Effect of Agreement

Clearly, from the discussion of Mary Carter Agreements in § 14.15, this form of settlement would not withstand attack by the contractor's surety, if it learns of the agreement. From an objective viewpoint, the agreement was dictated by an assessment of the maximum amount of recovery from each party rather than by an accurate reflection of the potential liability of the parties. Aside from the obvious ethical and legal problems with the agreement, should a judgment be rendered against the designer for any amount, it would be hard to argue that the agreement was made in good faith when, potentially, the designer was relieved from its liability without any payment for its portion of liability determined at trial.

In defending against such a situation, the contractor's surety would want early enough in the litigation to use the appropriate discovery devices to unearth any agreements or understandings of this nature. By discovering the agreement early, it can be attacked and defeated, thus strengthening the contractor's surety position in settlement or trial. In the event that the agreement is upheld, a remedy such as disclosure of the agreement to the trier of fact can be fashioned to diminish the potential impact of this secret agreement.

However onerous the Mary Carter Agreement may appear to be to nonsettling defendants, especially under these circumstances, it remains a useful settlement tool in jurisdictions permitting such agreements. In situations in which a dispute is fairly settled for an amount reasonably close to the potential liability figure and steps are taken by all parties to avoid the prejudice that may result, it is an option the practitioner cannot avoid considering.

§ 14.21   Alternative Methods of Settlement

If the negotiations had progressed differently or the facts changed, other opportunities to settle may have presented themselves. When approaching potential settlement options, it should be apparent that the variety of methods used to reach an agreement is limited only by the ingenuity of counsel and the constraints imposed by applicable law.

§ 14.22   The Hypothetical Failure That Can Be Repaired

An alternate approach to resolving the issue of responsibility for a construction failure among multiple parties involves actual repair of the failure. One of the potentially responsible parties must perform the necessary remedial work, and issues of liability that may remain can later be resolved at trial. As with any attempted settlement, the parties must first assess the cause of the construction failure, responsibility for the failure, and the cost of the remedial work. Although other factors may influence the negotiating positions of the parties, a determination of these variables is crucial to an effective settlement.

In this second hypothetical case, the contractor entered into a lump sum contract with the owner to build a dam with a contract price of $20 million. The design called for the use of roller compacted concrete, a relatively new technology in dam construction. Roller compacted concrete is a concrete that can be transported, placed, and compacted using earth and rockfill construction equipment. It contains coarse aggregate and develops properties similar to conventionally placed concrete. It was developed as a result of efforts to design more economical concrete dams that can be constructed rapidly.

After the contractor began performance, the engineers made many changes that appeared to be motivated by a concern for the adequacy of the original design. For some changes, the contractor was given change orders, but many of the field directives were issued under the guise of "clarification of the specifications" and the engineers refused to issue change orders. The engineers also refused to recognize and approve impact damages, even though hundreds of changes were being made. The engineers were responsible for daily inspection. They had some complaints about the workmanship, but they never rejected any of the contractor's work.

The final cost to complete the dam was $28 million. The contractor completed the dam six months after the adjusted scheduled completion date and filed an $8 million claim with the owner, alleging a cardinal change and material breaches of the contract.

As soon as water was placed behind the dam, the dam began to leak. The dam is located in a heavily populated area and serious concern arose about the stability of the dam. The engineers claimed that their design was proper and that the dam was improperly constructed. They recommended a grouting program that would cost approximately $2 million and had a good chance of stopping the leaks. An independent impermeable wall on the upstream side of the dam would have a 100 percent chance of stopping the leaks, but would cost $5 million.

As a result of work on this project, the contractor has cash flow problems and might default on other bonded work. The engineers have $1 million coverage in error and omissions insurance and essentially no other assets.

§ 14.23 Considerations in Determining Settlement Methods

Not having accepted the work under the contract, the owner has several options. The first is to effect a remedy through the provisions of the contract and then pursue the engineers and contractor for the cost of the repair. Completing the project is of paramount importance to the owner; litigation of the responsibility issue becomes a secondary consideration. In this case, the methods to be used in correcting the failure have been identified and the cost to effect those methods established. The task now facing the owner is to construct a settlement to achieve the objectives of obtaining a working dam and resolving questions of liability in the process.

Standard construction contract provisions[43] allow the owner to direct the contractor to perform work necessary to complete the project. Claims by the contractor against the owner for issuing an improper directive can be reserved until later. The contractor's failure to comply with the directive issued can be deemed a material breach of the contract, even if a court should later find that the owner's directive was improper. This would give the owner the right to find the contractor in default, terminate the contract, and proceed against the contractor's surety bond.

By pursing this strategy, the owner can realize its objective of completing the project without further delay. Any litigation that arises from later claims will take time to conclude. The owner will have avoided being put

---

[43] *See* AIA Document A201-1987, General Conditions ¶¶ 2.4, 12.2.4.

in the position of having to pour more money into the project. The contractor's surety is the only potentially liable party with funds to effect completion of the dam without contribution by the owner. Therefore, pursuing the contract liability strategy represents a viable solution to the situation presented.

Before approaching the parties, the owner must consider the contractor's claim and current financial difficulties that could impact upon the negotiations. There appears to be some merit to the contractor's $8 million claim and through a settlement of that claim the contractor's financial difficulties may be eased. Also, the owner recognizes that the engineers' limited insurance coverage restricts their ability to pay any claims.

Depending on the strategy the owner chooses, the engineers can be either the owner's ally or opponent. Should the owner issue the work directive to the contractor, the owner will need to hide behind the engineers when the time comes to defend the claim the contractor has against it. But to accomplish the objective of completing the project, the owner must rely on the contractor and surety, thus diminishing its ability to argue the design was correct.

In resolving this dilemma, the owner must evaluate the contractor's and surety's available defenses. The owner could expect the contractor to argue that the original design was inadequate, because the engineers supervised and approved the work without complaining of defective work. The contractor could also argue that there was a cardinal change from the original plans and the repair as directed could be a cardinal change itself, giving rise to a claim of betterment—that is, a claim that the dam, as fixed, is a better and more expensive dam than designed and contractor for.

Whatever strategy the owner chooses in negotiations, it must consider the continuing liability for the integrity of the dam. Should it choose to correct the failure, it may be exposed to liability should the dam later fail.

As a negotiating strategy, the owner also realizes that if it issues a directive and the surety disclaims liability under the bond, it can claim bad faith against the surety. Therefore, the owner's objectives in approaching a potential settlement are completing the project first and limiting liability for potential claims in the process.

§ 14.24 Settling with the Contractor and Surety

Having analyzed the situation, the owner decides to approach the contractor and surety with its demand. The owner plainly states its position: It wants a dam that doesn't leak and expects the contractor and surety to do whatever is necessary to get the job done. Otherwise, the owner will (1) issue a directive under the contract to correct the failure, (2) claim default and terminate the contract if the contractor and surety do not comply with the directive, and (3) claim bad faith against the surety if it does not comply with the directive and complete the work under the bond. The owner, attempting to resolve the outstanding claims against it by the contractor, offers to assign the claim the owner has against the engineers and the claim for the cost of the repair to the contractor and surety.

Presented with this offer, the surety recognizes its potential liability from the owner's position. The surety also considers the time and expense of litigation in contesting the directive and the cost of funds in financing the repair.

As a counteroffer, the surety suggests paying $1 million in settlement of the entire dispute. However, should the owner be successful in recovering from the engineers, the $1 million would be returned in a Loan Receipt Agreement settlement. Although the owner expresses some interest in the proposal, the surety must convince the contractor of the terms. Understandably, the contractor finds these terms unacceptable and rejects the surety's suggestion.

The impermeable wall, estimated to cost $5 million, represents expenses of $3 million in labor and material and $2 million in equipment. As the contractor is already on the site, should it perform the remedial work it will bear the cost of labor and materials but, if the contractor cannot use the equipment on another job, there is no additional equipment cost to the contractor. The surety suggests a settlement of the claim for the $3 million. In this manner the surety would be relieved of liability, the owner would receive a completed project, and the claim would be settled. The contractor rejects this proposal by the surety. A $3 million settlement of the outstanding claim, which will be spent in correcting the failure, does not represent an adequate settlement of the contractor's $8 million claim.

As the party in the middle, the surety recognizes that the only reasonable settlement approach is to join with the contractor and negotiate from a united position. The strength of the owner's negotiating position resulted from playing the exposure of the surety against the financial weakness of the contractor. Therefore, they agree to approach the owner with a joint proposal.

In essence, the contractor and surety accept the first offer of the owner. They offer to perform the remedial work necessary, reserve the contractor's $8 million claim and, in addition, claim for the work under the directive as a betterment. They expect the owner to direct the method of the repair, thus shifting the liability for the adequacy of the repair to the owner.

The owner is now faced with the situation of achieving its first objective of completing the dam but faces continuing exposure itself to the contractor's claims as well as responsibility for the repair. Clearly, under these circumstances, the owner is not going to receive what it originally bargained for, a completed dam at the contract price. Realizing this, in an attempt to shift the liability for the repair, the owner now offers to settle the claim with a $6 million payment to the contractor and an assignment of the owner's claim against the engineers in exchange for a 10-year guarantee on the integrity of the dam.

The contractor and surety finally accept this proposal but refuse to guarantee the integrity of the dam. By settling on these terms, the contractor is relieved of its financial difficulties, the owner is free from potential claims under the contract, the surety remains whole, and the dam is fixed. The question of the integrity of the dam remains open and dependent upon the repair as designed. The contractor is free to pursue the owner's claim against the engineer with the potential of increasing its recovery from $6 million to $7 million.

§ 15.1   Introduction

Litigation costs surrounding complex, multi-district construction-related disasters have increased substantially in the past few years. In the event of a major construction-related disaster in which many people are killed and injured, complex, expensive litigation will ensue. In the last few years disasters such as the tragic fire at the MGM Grand Hotel in Las Vegas and the collapse of two skywalks at the Hyatt Regency Hotel in Kansas City, Missouri, have amply demonstrated this.[1]

The victims of such disasters are often from many different states and even countries. In the recent past the trend has been that many of these

---

[1] *In re* MGM Grand Hotel Fire Litig., Multi-Dist. Litig. No. 453 (1981); *In re* Federal Skywalk Cases, 93 F.R.D. 415 (W.D. Mo.), *vacated* 680 F.2d 1175 (8th Cir.), *cert. denied*, 459 U.S. 988 (1982).

plaintiffs immediately retain premier plaintiffs' attorneys who file complaints as early as the day of or within a few days after the disaster itself in numerous state and federal courts, retain acknowledged experts in relevant disciplines (often people well-known to government agency investigating personnel in order to facilitate access to the site and access to information on the progress of the governmental agency investigation), and seek injunctive relief in order to permit their experts to conduct site investigations and preserve evidence prior to any site deterioration or alteration. Such plaintiffs increasingly are being well represented.

Meanwhile, the target defendants—the owner, architect, construction manager, general contractor, subcontractors, and suppliers who constructed the project years before and who often are located in other geographic regions—must struggle to deal both with the immediate psychological and potential economic impact of such a disaster upon their companies, their personnel, and their clients. Each of these defendants probably will end up asserting crossclaims and counterclaims against each other and implead numerous third-party defendants who, in turn, will assert crossclaims and counterclaims against each other and implead fourth-party defendants. Thus, inevitably, such a construction-related disaster leads to complex, multi-district, expensive litigation.

Although many kinds of litigation are complex and may involve multi-district litigation, such as, for example, air crash, antitrust, construction claims, product liability, and toxic tort litigation, construction-related disaster litigation is, perhaps, unique in that it requires litigation expertise and experience in at least one complex procedural area and three complex substantive areas. The procedural area is the handling of complex, multi-district litigation. The substantive areas are: (1) complex contract law, construction claims; (2) complex tort law, both negligence and products liability; and (3) an amalgam of the first two, insurance law, particularly the rights and duties of the insured and of primary and excess insurers. Additionally, unlike, for example, most antitrust litigation, in most construction-related disaster litigation parties assert and vigorously prosecute claims against one another, thus eliminating many of the cost economies of careful defense coordination.

Anyone who has been involved with such litigation knows that no matter how much expertise or experience a client, insurer, expert or attorney has, the litigation is certain to be expensive. In fact, those who have such experience have struggled hard with the task of containing costs. There is no panacea nor definitive solution to cost containment in construction-related disaster litigation. Additionally, in view of the proliferation of legal literature with respect to law firm and litigation management in general, this chapter does not discuss the common, albeit important, concepts of such legal management tools as in-house computer programs for briefs and research and the use of legal assistants. Rather, the purpose of this chapter

data retrieval litigation support systems. They have also researched many of the traditional procedural and substantive legal issues that arise—for example, procedural motions to shape the contours of the litigation, and substantive research on issues like the constitutionality of statutes of repose with respect to the design and construction of buildings and the liability of owners.

In retaining counsel it is critical to recognize that ultimately the success of the litigation effort in general and the cost containment effort in particular will be directly proportionate to the professional stature, intelligence, creativity, integrity, and persuasive abilities of the counsel. Counsel's ability to effectively assume control of and shape the contours of the litigation including, most importantly, obtaining the implementation of cost containing procedures, is, perhaps, the single most important factor in cost containment. Moreover, in such litigation it is critical to retain counsel with disaster litigation expertise and experience at the commencement of litigation. The failure in the first instance to effectively assume control of the litigation often makes it extremely difficult to effectively contain costs during the course of the litigation. Much like a space launch, seemingly small individual miscalculations at the early strategical and tactical stages result in missing goals two years later by thousands of miles and, with respect to cost containment, by thousands of dollars.

Although the insurer probably will have the exclusive right to appoint counsel, in construction disaster litigation the insured has greater reason to have some input into the retention of counsel and has additional leverage in making the choice. First, along with compensatory damages, plaintiffs often seek punitive damages. Because the insured's liability insurance policy usually does not cover punitive damages, the insured has an increased interest in making sure that it receives a full and competent defense. In fact, the insured may well consider retaining additional counsel to protect it with regard to the assertion of punitive damages. Second, the insurer owes the insured a full and competent defense, as if there were no policy limits. Indeed, should the insurer breach, negligently perform, or perform in bad faith its duty to provide a full and competent defense, the insurer could be liable for its insured's loss without regard to its policy limits.[6] In construction disaster litigation that is probably the single greatest potential exposure for the insurer. Thus, realistically, the insured and the insurer have a joint interest in providing the most cost-effective, full, and competent defense available. Therefore, it may well be best that any issues with respect to the retention of counsel be discussed candidly and agreed to by the insurer and the insured at the commencement of such litigation.

---

[6] *See, e.g.,* Continental Casualty Co. v. United States Fidelity & Guar. Co., 516 F. Supp. 384 (N.D. Cal. 1981); D. Dey, Rights and Duties of Primary and Excess Insurance Carriers 1 (Defense Research Institute Monograph No. 1, 1984).

Once a decision has been reached as to whether the insurer is going to appoint counsel experienced in construction disaster litigation, the insurer and/or the insured should interview several possible firms, to the extent time permits and consistent with a prompt initial case analysis and site investigation. Among other things, the interviews should attempt to determine the firm's expertise and experience in construction-related or other complex, multi-district litigation, the firm's experience with litigating under the *Manual for Complex Litigation Second,* the firm's experience in negotiating with microfilm, microfiche and computer support vendors, the firm's ability to staff the case with appropriate levels of partners, associates, legal assistants, and other support personnel who actually have construction disaster expertise and experience, the firm's proposal of how to manage the case, the firm's willingness to discuss and develop a disaster litigation budget, and the firm's willingness to consider various fee structures. Although each of these factors is important, perhaps the most important is the firm's ability to handle the case with appropriate staff who have the actual construction disaster litigation experience. In significant part, that is the expertise that will contain costs. It is not cost-effective to retain a firm that has such expertise and experience if it staffs the case with partners, associates, legal assistants, or other people who are new to the area. To the extent possible, the core management team the firm will commit to the case should be identified and agreed upon in advance.

One of the advantages in retaining a firm that has construction disaster litigation expertise and experience is that it often has detailed knowledge of and experience with the premier plaintiffs' attorneys and experts from prior cases. Immediately after a construction disaster occurs there is usually keen competition to retain those experts who are considered to be the best available in particular areas—for example, with respect to our hypothetical, fire, and construction experts.

§ 15.5   —Experts Who Have Worked with Agencies

In any construction disaster, various federal and state government agencies immediately will commence detailed investigations. In our hypothetical, for example, the National Fire Protection Association and various county and city government agencies would no doubt conduct independent investigations and produce reports purporting to establish the cause and origin of the fire. Such agencies, with or without the consent of the owner of the project, often in effect control access to critical areas of the site. It is extremely helpful to have as one of the client's experts, therefore, a person who has worked with one of these agencies. Although it is recognized that the expert has been retained by one of the parties and has gained access to the site by, for example, court order, often that

archives of the architect, construction manager, general contractor, or others, the change documents often are located at the project itself. If necessary, the legal team should seek injunctive relief to locate and preserve this latter category of documents, particularly if they may be destroyed or seriously damaged at the site during the disaster, the rescue efforts, or the demolition and cleanup.

As the initial site investigations are completed, the client, the legal and expert teams, and the insurer should proceed to the next critical step in cost containment: litigation management and budgeting.

LITIGATION MANAGEMENT AND BUDGETING

§ 15.8   The Legal Team

First, aside from the lead partner, a more junior partner should be selected to manage the case—a managing partner.[8] The managing partner is responsible for all case decisions on a daily basis, and must devote a substantial portion, if not all, of his time to the case.[9]

Second, the lead and managing partners must determine the composition of the legal team.[10] The critical task is to decide in advance what the minimum or core noncrisis composition of the legal team will be in terms of partners, senior and junior associates, senior and junior legal assistants, and document clerks.[11]

In the event the client has an in-house legal staff or outside corporate counsel, an important decision will be whether and to what extent to utilize the services of those attorneys. In-house staff can be most useful for gaining the trust and confidence of the client, understanding the client's business and corporate policies and goals, and assisting in understanding and organizing the client's documents for analysis and discovery purposes. Additionally, as the legal team conducts comprehensive, detailed interviews with the client's directors, officers, and personnel who have knowledge of the project, the in-house staff also can prove invaluable in facilitating the implementation of such an investigation.

---

[8] J. Baughman, R. Cushman, & I. Richter, *Cost Containment in Construction Litigation*, in Construction Litigation: Representing the Owner 323 n.9 (R. Cushman & K. Cushman eds., John Wiley & Sons, 1984).

[9] *Id.*

[10] *Id.* at 323–24.

[11] *Id.*

Outside corporate counsel can be best utilized initially to obtain a corporate history of the client and to assist the legal team in understanding the client's business and corporate policies and goals. To the extent the client consists of various related corporations and the plaintiffs attempt to pierce them, and to the extent the plaintiffs allege punitive damages, again, outside corporate counsel can be utilized effectively to develop the factual bases for defending such claims.

The lead and managing partners must develop a preliminary schedule of tasks to be accomplished and staff those tasks with the lowest cost personnel capable of performing the tasks efficiently. Such staffing decisions must, however, be made intelligently. In the case of preparing for and taking depositions, for example, it is often more cost effective to utilize mid- or junior level partners than senior or middle level associates. Such partners' hourly rates often are only a few dollars per hour higher, but they bring to the task the kind of experience and confidence that permits them to execute it more cost efficiently and with better results.

As the legal team begins to develop a solid sense of the case issues, the lead and managing partners should be responsible for devising the litigation themes, a litigation plan, and a case outline. Once these are developed they will be the basis for organizing documents to be microfilmed or microfiched, and, eventually, to be placed on computer support systems either by the indexing or full text method. Additionally, the litigation plan and case outline will be utilized to develop legal subteams with respect to pursuing claims and defenses on specific issues.

§ 15.9   The Experts Team

The next critical cost containment issue is whether and the extent to which to use experts.[12] Experts may be nontestifying or testifying experts. It is imperative to retain acknowledged, premier testifying experts and competent nontestifying experts. The testifying experts should be retained as soon as possible and utilized during the site investigation. They might not be utilized again, however, until much later in the case in order to prepare them to testify.[13] Nontestifying experts may be utilized both during the site investigation and during the entire preparation of the case to assist the client and the legal team in developing the client's claims and defenses.[14] The principal cost savings of utilizing nontestifying experts is to make sure the legal team does not waste time developing claims and

---

[12] *Id.* at 325.

[13] *Id.*

[14] *Id.*

§ 15.11   Analysis of the Client's Claims and
Defenses: The Litigation Themes

Although seemingly obvious, an important predicate to cost containment is an extremely early and thorough understanding of the client's business, its corporate policies and goals, and its claims and defenses. Early in the litigation, an intensive effort must be made to understand and organize all of the client's relevant documents, with particular emphasis upon the original contract documents, including the plans and specifications. After all, the client is the best and foremost source for the development of its claims and defenses.

At the commencement of this process, the lead and managing partners should introduce to the client and the client's personnel who will be working with the legal and expert teams all of their members. From a psychological standpoint, it is important for both the client and the litigation teams to generate a spirit of camaraderie and team cooperation that will be necessary to survive the stressful periods of any such litigation. Such a solid relationship provides the basis for good communication, which is a prerequisite to cost containment in any litigation.

In short, the client and the legal and expert teams cannot be afraid of or mistrust each other. In too many cases, because of a variety of factors, attorneys often direct their primary effort to discovering their client's case from other parties in the litigation. Not only may this be strategically and tactically unwise, but it can prove very expensive.

As the legal team develops the client's claims and defenses, the litigation plan, and the case outline, the lead and managing partners should be responsible for generating the essential litigation themes. The litigation plan, the case outline, and these themes will be the principles upon which the case is developed and discovery pursued.

With respect to the hypothetical case, for example, suppose the client is the general contractor and, except for the concrete work, did no actual, physical construction work; rather, he was responsible for supervising the actual construction work performed by the subcontractors. Suppose further that he has very favorable indemnity provisions in each of his subcontracts. Thus, for various specific issues on the case outline, a principal litigation theme will be that the subcontractors were primarily responsible for performing their work in accordance with the architect's plans and specifications, and the general contractor was only secondarily responsible for determining that the work was in conformance with the plans and specifications. A set of litigation themes such as this makes the conduct of discovery easier and, consequently, less expensive.

Once the litigation plan, case outline, and litigation themes have been developed, they should be distributed to the legal team members and thoroughly discussed and understood. The time spent carefully analyzing and developing such items is probably the most cost-effective time ever spent in construction disaster litigation. It is upon this work product that the strategical and tactical decisions during the litigation will be based.

ACTUAL LITIGATION

§ 15.12   Contours of the Litigation

With respect to the hypothetical fact situation, the plaintiffs probably would file suits in various federal and state courts. Usually, in construction disaster litigation the plaintiffs will not file class actions; however, there are exceptions.[20] The next critical step in cost containment is to attempt to shape the contours of the litigation so that the client does not have to respond to pleadings, undertake discovery, and conduct other pretrial activities in each of the individual actions in a variety of forums. This is probably the first juncture at which the legal team will contact attorneys for other defendants and schedule the defendants' first coordination meeting. Hopefully, the attorneys for the respective defendants will have the requisite expertise, experience, and confidence to recognize the advantages that can be gained from appropriate coordination efforts.

One of the best devices to shape the contours of the litigation is to have the federal cases consolidated for all pretrial and discovery activities by the judicial panel on multi-district litigation.[21] In short, once complex, multi-district litigation is identified, all federal cases should be assigned in their entirety to one judge for all pretrial proceedings. Once that is accomplished, generally speaking, the federal cases will proceed in accordance with the *Manual for Complex Litigation Second* (*Manual*).

Conducting litigation in accordance with the *Manual* is one of the best methods of containing costs. It was designed as a guide to the prompt, fair, and cost-efficient disposition of otherwise protracted, complex, multi-district litigation. The *Manual* sets forth basic principles that characterize the fair and efficient resolution of complex litigation, and describes certain procedures that have been successfully utilized to accomplish those goals

---

[20] *Compare In re* MGM Grand Hotel Fire Litig., Multi-District Litig. No. 453 (1981) *with In re* Federal Skywalk Cases, 93 F.R.D. 415 (W.D. Mo.), *vacated,* 680 F.2d 1175 (8th Cir.), *cert. denied,* 459 U.S. 988 (1982).

[21] The Judicial Panel on Multi-district Litigation was created in 1968 by Act of Congress, Pub. L. No. 90-296, § 1, 28 U.S.C. § 1407 as a result of the federal judiciary's experience in the electrical equipment antitrust litigation and other multi-district litigation. *See, e.g.,* Cahn, *A Look at the Judicial Panel on Multi-district Litigation,* 72 F.R.D. 211 (1976).

§ 15.15   —Document Control

The production, control, and use of documents at trial is probably the single most difficult cost to control effectively in any construction disaster litigation. A relatively small number of documents among hundreds of thousands will end up being critical to the success or failure of each parties' case. The task is to make sure that those documents are discovered, retained, and effectively utilized during pretrial activities and at trial. It is not within the scope of this chapter to discuss in any detail the production, control, and use of documents in such litigation. Nevertheless, a few comments are warranted.

First, a decision must be made with respect to whether to attempt to work with documents in their "hard" copy form or whether to utilize microfilming and/or microfiche support systems. In any case involving over approximately 20,000 documents, which includes virtually every construction disaster case, either microfilming or microfiching should probably be utilized. It saves space, is cheaper than duplicating, is easy to index, and numbering can be done automatically.[33] Second, a decision must be made as to whether to use a computer-based litigation support system and, if so, whether it will be done in-house or outside. Litigation computer support system vendors are sophisticated and excellent sales people. Generally, they recommend using computers when the number of documents is five to 10 thousand.[34] With the advent of increasingly sophisticated mini and micro computer systems and good software, although as many as approximately 50,000 documents can be handled manually, as few as 5,000 documents can be handled cost-effectively in an appropriate computer data base. Probably most cases, however, will require the use of a litigation computer support system. If done by either the client or the legal team, one must make certain that they possess the technical ability to accomplish the goals of the computerization including quality control and training within the required time. The client and legal team will have enormous challenges in litigating any construction disaster litigation without the added burden of being responsible for designing and implementing an effective computerized litigation support system. If done outside, suffice it to say that careful negotiations are required with respect to vendors of litigation support systems. Contract provisions should carefully delineate the client's and legal

[33] M. Gowen, Computerized Litigation Support, Legal Assistants 623 (Practising Law Inst. 1982).

[34] J. Baughman, R. Cushman, & I. Richter, *Cost Containment in Construction Litigation,* in Construction Litigation: Representing the Owner 330 n.9 (R. Cushman & K. Cushman eds., John Wiley & Sons, 1984); Sherman & Kinnard, *The Development, Discovery and Use of Computer Support Systems in Achieving Efficiency in Litigation,* 79 Colum. L. Rev. 267 (1979).

team's expectations in terms of the system performance, the quality of the data base, the training for users, and the technical assistance that will be provided if problems arise. Increasingly, many clients and lawyers are turning to consultants with expertise in all aspects of computerized litigation support systems to develop for them a request for proposals for a particularly complex litigation, solicit bids from the principal vendors, evaluate the bids, negotiate and enter the contract, and then monitor the vendor's performance. Certainly, these are decisions in which the client and insurer should be intimately involved.

Once it is decided to use a litigation computer support system, the next decision is whether to use a full text or an index method. There are advantages and disadvantages to each method.[35] Under the full text method, the text of each document is coded into the data base. Thus, the principle advantage is that each word can serve to identify a relevant document. The principle disadvantages are the cost and time of putting the entire text into the computer. The index method involves a preselection of documents for relevance and only certain key words are coded into the computer data base, for example from the case outline. The principle advantage is that the preselection results in a more precise and cost-effective generation of the data base. The principle disadvantage is that it requires an early assessment of the relevance of a document before knowing what may eventually become the critical legal issues. Generally speaking, the index method is probably preferable with respect to cost containment. But with increasingly sophisticated hardware and software many litigation support systems now effectively combine full text and index methods. Additionally, to the extent information exists in electronic form, it can often be used effectively in a full text system at minimal cost.

§ 15.16   —Discovery from Prior Litigation

One additional point should be made with respect to document discovery. In many cases, the project at issue was the subject of prior litigations during construction. In our hypothetical, for example, four prior litigations occurred involving the project. It is imperative that early in the litigation the legal team obtain from each such prior litigation any and all statements under oath or representations by counsel with respect to the client, its directors, officers, and employees. Needless to say, during the course of those prior litigations, strategies and tactics were most likely devised without any regard to a potential disaster years later. Thus, positions may have been taken that will bear directly upon the case outline and the litigation

---

[35] Sherman & Kinnard, *The Development, Discovery and Use of Computer Support Systems in Achieving Efficiency in Litigation,* 79 Colum. L. Rev. 267–71 n.38 (1979).

to commit to a statement of their allegations with respect to how the project varied from relevant plans and specifications and applicable building codes. To the extent that this results in the disclosure of the identity and proposed testimony of experts, the disclosure should be required. Without such a statement by the plaintiffs, after a generous but reasonable period of time, the defendants are forced to expend an inordinate amount of time and resources guessing at what will be the plaintiffs' technical claims. This can be very expensive and a most inefficient manner in which to litigate the case. On the other hand, once the plaintiffs have made such a disclosure, the defendants should then have a reasonable period of time in which to make their response. At that juncture, the depositions of all expert witnesses should be permitted. Such depositions often promote settlement or at least a narrowing of the real claims at issue, and thus often prove very cost-effective.

§ 15.21   —Appointment of a Master

Finally, §§ 21.52 and 21.53 of the *Manual* provide for the appointment of a master or magistrate to supervise discovery and other special assignments. In many complex, multi-district litigations, a regular weekly or monthly discovery conference is held before such a master or magistrate to resolve all pretrial discovery matters. This has met with mixed success. Sometimes it is better for the judge to conduct all such conferences.

Perhaps more importantly, a magistrate or special master may be appointed to conduct special assignments. One of the most productive special assignments is to engage a special master to develop and implement a program designed to lead to settlement of the case. The pace and complexity of construction disaster litigation often leaves no time for the litigants and court to develop and implement an effective settlement program. A special master's sole purpose can be to accomplish this task. By way of example, such a special master might meet individually with each plaintiff's and defendant's counsel to establish the parameters of damages for each of the respective plaintiffs' cases. Additionally, the special master might be charged with generating a detailed memorandum of law outlining the structure of a settlement.

An excellent example of the use of such a special master occurred in the Agent Orange litigation. There, Chief Judge Weinstein appointed two special masters to attempt to structure a settlement.[36] The special masters drafted a memorandum that provided a way for the defendant chemical companies to allocate the costs of any settlement among them and recommended how a settlement fund could be administered and who would be

---

[36] More, *Long Road Ends in Agent Orange Pact,* Legal Times 1, May 14, 1984.

eligible for the benefits.[37] According to one article, both plaintiff and defense lawyers applauded Chief Judge Weinstein's use of the two masters, and the efforts of the masters themselves which were deemed to have resulted in that unique settlement.[38]

Finally, the key to cost containment of discovery is the client and the legal team's joint cost benefit analysis with respect to each step in the discovery process.

§ 15.22 Pretrial Motions

Generally speaking, many pretrial motions are not successful and therefore are not warranted from the cost containment perspective. Other than with respect to certain determinative defenses such as statute of repose defenses, only certain pretrial procedural motions accomplish worthwhile results. Motions which themselves relate to cost containment in discovery, for example, are often helpful. One might move for the establishment of a document depository (see § 15.19). Similarly, certain pretrial procedural motions with respect to the conduct of the trial can be extremely useful. In view of recent United States Supreme Court decisions, however, motions for summary judgment may now be more successful and extremely useful.[39] The *Manual* specifically addresses summary judgment motions and the role they may play in complex litigation in § 21.34.

One type of motion is particularly worth noting, however, because of the difficulty of the issue, in spite of two decisions. In construction disaster litigation, often the plaintiffs assert punitive damages against the defendants. In an excellent article, an author suggests that in appropriate circumstances, a class action may provide the best means of resolving the numerous problems presented by punitive damage claims in mass tort litigation.[40] In two decisions, however, the Ninth and Tenth Circuit Courts of Appeals have vacated district court decisions certifying such classes.[41] Despite these two decisions, the law is evolving in this area and the class action device may well be not only the best, but one of the only, methods

---

[37] *Id.* at 6.

[38] *Id.*

[39] *See, e.g.,* Celotex Corp. v. Catrett, 477 U.S. 317 (1986); Anderson v. Liberty Lobby, Inc., 477 U.S. 242 (1986); Matsushita Elec. Indus. Co. v. Zenith Radio Corp., 475 U.S. 574 (1986).

[40] Seltzer, *Punitive Damages in Mass Tort Litigation: Addressing the Problems of Fairness, Efficiency and Control,* 52 Fordham L. Rev. 37 (1983).

[41] *In re* Northern Dist. of Cal. "Dalkon Shield" IUD Prods. Liab. Litig., 526 F. Supp. 887 (N.D. Cal. 1981), *vacated,* 693 F.2d 847 (9th Cir. 1982), *cert. denied,* 459 U.S. 1171 (1983); *In re* Federal Skywalk Cases, 93 F.R.D. 415 (W.D. Mo.), *vacated,* 680 F.2d 1175 (8th Cir.), *cert. denied,* 459 U.S. 988 (1982).

CHAPTER 16

POSTFAILURE ACCOUNTING SYSTEMS AND METHODS OF PRICING DAMAGES

James T. Schmid*

James T. Schmid is a director with Coopers & Lybrand in their San Francisco office. He is responsible for providing operations consulting and litigation support services to contractors, owners, bonding companies, and other entities involved in construction projects. Mr. Schmid earned an MBA degree from the University of Michigan and a BS in engineering from Oakland University. He is a coauthor of *Construction Industry Forms* and *Construction Litigation: Representing the Contractor* (John Wiley & Sons 1987 and 1988). During his career, Mr. Schmid has worked as an industrial engineer and has performed consulting assignments involving almost every aspect of construction project control and claims analysis. He has acted as an arbitrator for the American Arbitration Association and has provided expert testimony for general business litigation and construction disputes.

*The author would like to thank the following people for their insights in the area of controlling problem construction projects: Mr. John McGinnity, senior vice president of American Real Estate Group, Richard D. Warren, Esquire, partner at Landels Ripley & Diamond, and Deborah K. Miller, Esquire, partner at Landels Ripley & Diamond.

postfailure phase they will accumulate data that correlates specific project activities with the underlying factors that made these activities necessary. Additionally, these systems should be adapted to enhance management's control by improving the timeliness of cost and activity information, and by ensuring that an approved method of payment has been established for each area of work and that these methods of payment do not overlap. Finally, these systems should be adapted to ensure that the information collected will support the variety of analyses that might be necessary to determine damages if a dispute develops among the parties. This is particularly important if there is a potential for claims involving either delay, acceleration, or disruption; analysis of these types of claims can be extremely difficult, particularly if appropriate data is not collected from the field while the problem is occurring.

§ 16.3   Contracting Approach

Ideally, the postfailure phase of a troubled project should be controlled by the original contractor's lump sum contract (assuming the original contractor can complete the project), or by a lump sum contract with a successor contractor. To be successful, this form of contract should include a reliable, well-defined change order control procedure that is supported by a timely method of reporting on the scope of work being performed and the cost of ongoing work. Additionally, the contract should include well-defined notification requirements that specify the method and maximum time period allowed for a contractor to submit a claim.

Frequently, the completion of a troubled project cannot be bid on a lump sum basis. This may be due to the number of uncertainties associated with the work in place or the need to start work before the scope of work can be fully defined. In this situation, a time-and-material approach is typically used. This approach requires greater participation by the owner in order to be successful, particularly in the areas of cost and activity reporting.

A major risk associated with using a time-and-material approach is that the owner assumes greater responsibility for controlling the productivity of the contractor. To reduce this risk, the owner must either dedicate extra staff with sufficient expertise to interface with the contractor on a detailed level or contract with a construction manager or program manager to fulfill this role.

Another contracting method often used during the postfailure phase of a troubled project is a hybrid of the lump sum and time-and-material approaches. This involves using a time-and-material contract to control work immediately after the disaster and then bidding the remaining postfailure work on a lump sum basis after the scope of this work can be sufficiently defined.

§ 16.4 The Postfailure Disaster Management Team

When a construction disaster occurs, the parties involved must first focus all efforts on eliminating any physical dangers that might still exist. After accomplishing this, the parties must focus on organizing their respective teams, assessing the status of the project, and planning for the project's completion.

The management team should be made up of professionals who are experienced in completing failed projects. In addition, if a new (successor) contractor has been selected to complete the project, then the owner and/or successor contractor should consider hiring key individuals who were previously employed by the predecessor contractor, if possible. These individuals may possess unique insights that might prove indispensable in reducing transition problems and in analyzing claims.

Two key positions on the contractor's or owner's management team are the project manager and the information director. The project manager will be responsible for completing the project and interfacing with the counterpart in the owner's (or contractor's) organization. Although the project manager will be responsible for taking a longer-term view of the project, much of the focus will be on resolving the immediate problems associated with completing the work. Consequently, the information director is needed to assume responsibility for the project's information systems. This position is critical because of the long-term importance of information on a troubled project and because project managers typically cannot give sufficient priority to the information and documentation needs of a troubled project.

§ 16.5 Interim Information Systems

The first task of the information director is to secure the project records generated prior to the disaster. This includes making sure that access to the records is controlled and minimized, and that they are safe from water or other environmental hazards. Once secure, the records may be organized and cataloged as time permits.

Another important early task of the information director is to establish interim procedures that maximize the detailed cost and activity information that is generated in the field. These interim procedures are needed so that critical data are not lost during the time required to develop and

§ 16.6   —Supervisor's Daily Activity Report

W.P. TAYLOR CONSTRUCTION COMPANY   Page ___ of ___

SUPERVISOR'S DAILY ACTIVITY REPORT

Record No.:_____

Project Number: Project Name: Date:

Supervisor's Signature: Date: Reviewer's Signature: Date:

Weather Conditions: Temperature:

Pay-Point Code	Pay-Point Description (Activity Description)	Approx. Crew Size	Hrs	Units Placed	Est. Percent Complete	Est. Days to Complete
	TOTAL					

Major Owned and Rented Equipment Used:

_____

_____

_____

Subcontractors Under Supervision	General Description Of Work Performed	Work Location	Aprox. Crew

Description of Problems or Unique Situations:

_____

_____

_____

_____

_____

_____

Note: Be sure to consider:
- Material:
  o Availability
  o Quality
- Access
- Interference
- Delays
- Design problems
- Equip. problems
- Subcontractors
- Unanticipated conditions
- Changes

§ 16.7 —Daily Subcontractor Report

W.P. TAYLOR CONSTRUCTION COMPANY   Page ___ of ___

DAILY SUBCONTRACTOR REPORT

Record No.:_____

Project Number: Project Name: Date:

Subcontract No.:   Subcontractor Name:

Authorized Sub. Signature: Date: Authorized G.C. Signature: Date:

General Description of Work Performed:

P.P. Code (Location & Work Category)	Pay-Point Description	Crew Size	Units Placed	Est. Percent Complete	Est. Days to Complete
	TOTAL				

Major Owned and Rented Equipment Used:

Comments:

§ 16.8   —Field Work Order

W.P. TAYLOR CONSTRUCTION COMPANY

FIELD WORK ORDER   FWO No: 45678

Project Number: Project Name: Date:

Contract Number: Subcontractor Name:

Prepared By (signature):   Authorized By (signature):

This Field Work Order authorizes the subcontractor listed above
to proceed with the work described below in addition to the work
authorized in their contract and approved change orders.   Bills
for the work authorized by this Order must be accompanied by
signed Force Account Forms (FAF).   One FAF must be completed for
each day that work is performed under this Order.

Work performed under this Field Work Order should be Charged to
Pay-Point Code number (location & Work Category): _____

Description of Work to be Performed:
_____
_____
_____
_____
_____
_____
_____
_____
_____
_____
_____
_____
_____
_____
_____

§ 16.9 —Force Account Form

W.P. TAYLOR CONSTRUCTION COMPANY

```
                                            Record No.:___
                    FORCE ACCOUNT FORM

   Project Name:        Project Name:


   Field Work Order              Pay-Point Code to
   authorizing this             be charged for
   work.............            this work........

   Contract Number:    Subcontractor Name:
```

This form must be completed for each Field Work Order and signed by an authorized field representative of WPT Construction Company each day work is performed on a Field Work Order. Payments will not be made to a subcontractor for Field Work Order work unless this form has been properly completed and submitted as support for the amount billed.

General Description of Work Performed:

Work Task Description	Man Hours Required	Units Placed	Estimated Mandays To Comp.
TOTAL......		XXXXXXXXX	

Major Owned and Rented Equipment Used:

Direct Materials Used:

Authorized Signatures:

_____ , _____   _____ , _____
Subcontractor Rep.   Date   WPT Const. Co. Rep.   Date

§ 16.10   Risk Assessment

Once the interim information gathering procedures are implemented, the information director should work with other members of the management team to develop the documentation needed to define:

1.   The project's state of completion at the time of the failure
2.   The remedial work required to correct problems caused by the disaster (for example, removal of collapsed structure)
3.   Any repair work needed to correct poor workmanship of a predecessor contractor (for example, reinforce steel connections).

The information director should also begin developing a long-term plan for the information needs of the project by developing an understanding of the challenges facing the postfailure construction effort and any unique risks that the organization faces.

Critical risks that must be assessed include:

1.   The likelihood that work already performed will require extensive repairs
2.   The likelihood that completion work will be significantly disrupted
3.   The likelihood that the other parties involved in the project will be able to function adequately. For example:
     a.   From the owner's perspective:
          i.   Can the contractor produce a quality product?
          ii.   Will the contractor be able to control the subcontractors?
          iii. Will the contractor be able to control and efficiently process change order documentation?
          iv.   Will the contractor be able to control change orders in the field?
          v.   Will the contractor be able to control work performed on a time-and-material basis?
          vi.   Will the contractor be able to maintain accurate cost and activity records?
     b.   From the contractor's perspective:
          i.   Will the owner be able to approve change orders on a timely basis?
          ii.   Does the owner have the capacity to pay for the completion work?
          iii. Can the architect provide quality designs in a timely manner?

Once the status of the project is documented and the risks faced during the completion phase are understood, the information director can develop necessary modifications to the cost, schedule, change order, and other control systems.

§ 16.11   Project Accounting Systems

The accounting systems controlling a construction project can be divided into two primary components, the project cost accounting system and the home office accounting system. The project cost accounting system is used to accumulate and report the direct costs of the construction project, such as site overhead, craft labor, materials, and subcontractor costs. This system is critical to controlling the progress of a project and when analyzing direct cost claims such as acceleration, disruption, changes in conditions, and changes in scope.

Most of the source documents used by the project cost accounting system (for example, time cards, purchase orders, and draw requests) must be prepared by the staff at the project site. Reports generated by the project cost accounting system, such as the job cost report, are critical to the management of the project.

The project cost accounting system will play an important role in both the management of the postfailure work and in resolving any disputes that might occur as a result of the failure. This is because during the postfailure phase the costs on a troubled project often differ significantly from standard or planned costs. As a result, project management cannot rely on "normal" cost as a benchmark for monitoring progress, pricing change orders, or negotiating claims.

Costs on troubled projects often vary significantly from what is normal because of the many disruptions that are likely to occur, including:

1. Scheduling work out of sequence
2. Inability to plan work effectively
3. Numerous changes caused by the discovery of latent defects
4. Difficulty in coordinating material orders and delivery with workflow
5. Low worker morale due to extensive repair and rework.

§ 16.12   —Role of the System

Because of the increased risk of disruption on a troubled project, it is critical that the project cost accounting system have the ability to fulfill two key roles.

The project cost accounting system must first provide timely feedback to the project management team on the cost of work so that problem areas can be identified and corrected before they incur excessive costs. This is particularly important if some activities are being billed on a time-and-material basis or if some activities are proceeding in an inefficient manner due to disruption.

The second key role of the project cost accounting system is to provide the cost and activity data needed to resolve potential disputes. The contractor is usually in a much better position to implement a comprehensive project cost accounting system than the owner. Consequently, owners sometimes specify in their contracts critical elements of the contractor's project cost accounting system and certain management reports. In some situations in which this is not done, the owner may have to implement extensive inspection procedures to collect cost and production information from the field in order to obtain timely information needed to negotiate changes or claims. Owners frequently turn to a construction or program manager for assistance with this type of problem.

§ 16.13   The Chart of Accounts

The Chart of Accounts (see § 16.14) is the backbone of the project cost accounting system. It defines the coding system and cost categories into which costs will be recorded. These categories then become the most detailed level upon which the system can report. Additionally, the cost categories defined in the Chart of Accounts should have a logical relationship with the activities defined in the scheduling system and the change order control system if cost/schedule or change order cost reports are required.

A comprehensive Chart of Accounts should incorporate the following basic categories of information into the logic of the numbering system:

1. Physical location, such as east wing, third floor, and basement
2. General work category, such as sitework, electrical, mechanical, and general requirements
3. Detailed work category, such as pilings, shoring, paving, and forms
4. Cost type, such as labor, material, subcontractor, and equipment
5. Work authorization, such as base contract, change order number, and field work order number.

The more detailed the Chart of Accounts, the greater the capability of the contractor, subcontractor, or owner to determine the actual cost of a specific work area. This is particularly important if the work area in question has a high likelihood of becoming involved in a dispute. If the level of detail in the Chart of Accounts is not sufficient to isolate a disputed activity, then the parties may be forced to use a less accurate method of pricing such as the total cost approach or an engineering estimate.

It is also helpful to establish units of production for the detailed work categories defined in the Chart of Accounts. Example units of production are listed in **Table 16-1**.

The number of units actually produced or placed should be obtained from the field on a daily basis. These data can be estimated by the supervisor or subcontractor responsible for the activity and then recorded on either the Supervisor's Daily Activity Report, the Daily Subcontractor Report, or the Force Account Form.

Units of production are often difficult to define and data on the units produced can be difficult to obtain, particularly for repair or remedial work. Nevertheless, these data are critical if management hopes to monitor performance in the field during the postfailure phase of work. In addition, production statistics provide data that will prove invaluable if a dispute arises related to delay, acceleration, or disruption.

Modifications to the Chart of Accounts during the course of a project should be minimized if possible. Modifications can create problems in compatibility of cost data between the pre- and postfailure phases of the project. In addition, certain modifications may be hard to implement and may therefore result in generating unreliable data. In spite of these risks, changes in the Chart of Accounts should be implemented in situations in which the prefailure account structure cannot support the postfailure phase of work. The account structure might require modification if:

1. The system does not designate location of work
2. The system does not distinguish work done on change orders or field work orders, or if these costs are not broken into their work-area components
3. The system does not designate units of production.

When modifications to the Chart of Accounts are required, a detailed cross reference table should be prepared so that it is clear how the old system maps into the new system and vice versa.

Table 16-1

EXAMPLES OF UNITS OF PRODUCTION

Detailed Work Category	Unit of Production
Excavation	Cubic yards of material removed
Steel erection	Tons of steel installed
Interior demolition	Square feet of wall removed
Install HVAC duct	Feet of duct work installed
Rough plumbing	Feet of pipe installed
Finish plumbing	Number of fixtures installed
Rough electrical	Feet of wire installed
Finish electrical	Number of outlets installed
Painting	Square feet of surface painted

§ 16.14   —Chart of Accounts Form

W.P. TAYLOR CONSTRUCTION COMPANY

CHART OF ACCOUNTS

Project Number: Project Name:

Prepared By: Date: Reviewed By: Date:

LOCATION; 2 DIGITS; (WING, FLOOR, ETC.)
GENERAL WORK CATEGORY; 2 DIGITS; (ELECT, MECH, GEN REQ'S, ETC.)
DETAILED WORK CAT.; 3 DIGITS; (PILING, SHORING, PAVING, ETC.)
COST TYPE; 3 DIGITS; (LABOR, MAT, SUB, EQUIP, ETC.)

				ACCOUNT DESCRIPTION:	UNITS:

§ 16.15   Home Office Accounting Systems

Both the contractor and owner have home office operations that may be affected by a troubled project. The home office accounting system will be relied upon to determine the extent of the project's impact on home office costs. This system is used to accumulate overhead costs at the home office, and to summarize the results of individual projects. It generates the company's overall financial reports as well as detailed reports needed to control home office overhead expenses. Generally, home office overhead information is not needed to monitor a project's status or to guide decisions related to project activities. Data from the home office accounting system will, however, be needed to analyze contractor or owner disruption and/or delay claims. On a troubled project, an owner or contractor may have to increase the level of home office support and/or incur extended home office costs if the project is delayed. Pricing home office costs for change orders or construction claims is frequently a major area of dispute. Generally, home office costs are priced using one of the following methods:

1. For change orders or disputes that do not affect the project's schedule: price home office overhead using a percentage mark-up obtained from the contract, industry average, company historical average, or other similar source
2. For delay claims: price home office overhead using either an allocation technique such as the Eichleay Formula or a direct costing technique such as one that charges home office costs directly to the project that received the benefit.

Using the direct costing method to determine home office costs related to a troubled project requires that data are collected that document whether the costs incurred were a result of a specific project (that is, the troubled project or some other project), or as a result of a nonproject activity (for example, sales or marketing). This type of data collection usually focuses on labor data and usually involves charging the hours worked by home office workers to the benefiting project or to a nonproject classification if no single project benefited.

§ 16.16   Scheduling System

The construction schedule is key to the success of the postfailure effort on a troubled construction project. Ideally, the schedule should use the Critical Path Method (CPM), which controls activities according to their duration, preceding activities and successor activities. The schedule should be as detailed as reasonably possible, particularly with regard to defining any remedial work that is required because of the failure. The schedule should be updated weekly, if possible, and distributed to owner and contractor personnel who are involved in the management of the project. All supervisors should also receive a copy of the schedule sections affecting their work area and be required to comment in writing on both favorable and unfavorable variances. Changes in the schedule should be highlighted and explained, especially if they affect the critical path of the project.

In complex projects it is very important that the activities defined in the construction schedule be coordinated with the cost categories defined in the Chart of Accounts. Ideally, the schedule activities and the cost categories should tie on a one-to-one basis. At a minimum the cost categories should be more detailed than the schedule activities, and no cost category should be applicable to more than one schedule activity. This structure allows the cost categories to roll into the schedule categories and greatly increases the usefulness of both the cost and the schedule systems in analyzing performance and claims.

§ 16.17   Change Order Control Systems

The postfailure phase of a troubled construction project will place extraordinary pressure on the change order control system. The volume of change orders will increase due to changes in design and the discovery of latent defects. Additionally, change orders will probably become more difficult to price during the postfailure phase for several reasons, including:

1. Disruptions such as changes in sequence may cause costs to differ significantly from standard costs or industry averages.
2. The volume of changes may be so great that it is difficult for the contractor or subcontractors to prepare and submit quotes before the work is completed.
3. Change orders for demolition or exploratory work will be difficult to price because the scope of work may not be known until the work is complete.
4. Contract deductions for work scope that is eliminated from the base contract or from approved change orders may be significant and may become difficult to negotiate.

Because of the problems associated with pricing change orders on a troubled project, there will probably be some change orders that have to be billed on a time-and-material basis. If this occurs, the time-and-material work must be easily distinguished from the work being billed on a lump sum basis, otherwise the parties face the risk of a dispute over whether costs incurred for lump sum work have been commingled with costs that were included in the time-and-material billing. Consequently, it is important to maintain accurate cost records on all change orders if the work cannot be adequately segregated and if there is a high risk that the parties may enter into a dispute. The most effective method of monitoring change order cost is to structure the Chart of Accounts so that it has a field available for coding the change order number in addition to the fields that designate location, work area, and cost type (see § **16.14**).

Special attention should be given to the procedures used to process change orders on a troubled project. Many times on problem projects the change order processing procedures become overloaded and significantly out of phase with actual construction. When this occurs, the owner may commit the project to costs that exceed expectations and maybe even the owner's ability to pay.

A bottleneck in the change order processing procedures will also slow cash flow to the contractor because there will not be a routine basis for paying for a large portion of the work performed. Stopgap measures, such as issuing advances, may have to be implemented by the owner. Advances, if not properly documented, can eventually become yet another area of disagreement on a troubled project, particularly if they are to be applied to a work area involving more than one subcontractor.

In addition, if change order pricing lags significantly behind actual construction, the price eventually negotiated will probably be equal to or greater than the contractor's actual cost. As a result, the owner will have lost the advantage of having a fixed price incentive to motivate the contractor to control productivity on the changed work.

Several actions that might be considered in order to improve the capability of the change order control system include:

1. Establish a clear definition of how the change order processing system is supposed to work. Include a system flowchart, procedure description, and illustrations of all of the forms to be used by the owner, architect/engineer, general contractor, and subcontractors. Also establish processing time guidelines for each activity defined in the procedure.
2. Prepare periodic reports that show:
    a. The status of each pending change order, including the current estimate of change order price (see § **16.18**, Change Order Control Log).
    b. The number of change orders issued to, and processed by, the owner, contractor, and architect/engineer (see § **16.19**, Change Order Processing Status Summary).

3. Initiate follow-up procedures to eliminate bottlenecks identified in the periodic change order reports.

4. Implement a force account system (see **§§ 16.8** and **16.9**) to document the actual cost for all change orders that do not have a fixed price. Summarize the information from the Force Account form on a periodic basis to determine the current cost of unpriced change orders (see **§ 16.20**, Estimated Cost of Unpriced Commitments).

§ 16.18 —Change Order Control Log

W.P TAYLOR CONSTRUCTION COMPANY

CHANGE ORDER CONTROL LOG

Page _____

Project Number: _____

Project Name: _____

Change Order Number	Description	Owner OK Work Startup On T&M Basis	Under-lying N.P.C No.'s	Key Dates:				Cost Data:				Cost Code (1)
				Orig-inated	Sub Quotes Req'ed	Quoted To Owner	Owner Sign-Off	A/E's Est.	Est'ed By Sub's	Quoted By Sub's	Final Agreed Amount	

Footnote: 1) Specify only Location and Work Category (i.e., Sitework, Mech., Elec.) portion of cost codes only.

§ 16.19   —Change Order Processing

CHANGE ORDER PROCESSING STATUS

MONTH ENDING

PROJECT NUMBER

PROJECT NAME

NUMBER OF CHANGE ORDERS AT EACH C/O
PROCESSING STEP:

CHANGE ORDER PROCESSING STEP	RECEIVED	IN - PROCESS	ISSUED	RETURNED FOR REQUOTE
OWNER:				
New Changes				X X X X X X
Quoted by Gen. Contractor; To be Approved				
ARCHITECT:				
New Changes	X X X X X			X X X X X X
Quoted by Gen. Contractor; To be Approved				
GENERAL CONTRACTOR:				
Process and submit to Subs for Quote				X X X X X X
At Subs being Quoted		X X X X	X X X	X X X X X X
Quoted by Subs; Consolidate and Issue				
Owner Approved; Obtain Sub Sign-Off				X X X X X X X′

§ 16.20 —Estimated Cost of Unpriced Commitments

```
          ESTIMATED COST OF UNPRICED COMMITMENTS

              MONTH ENDING: [        ]

  PROJECT NUMBER [        ]    PROJECT NAME [        ]
```

FIELD WORK ORDER NO.	DESCRIPTION	COST TO DATE (1)	EST. % COMPLETE (2)	TOTAL INDICATED COST

TOTAL

(1) From Force Account Forms

(2) Engineer's Estimate

§ 16.21   Progress Reporting

The ability to control a troubled construction project depends greatly on the ability of management to monitor progress and to identify and respond to problems before they have a chance to grow. To accomplish this, management must rely on progress reports that are accurate, detailed, and timely. Three areas of control are particularly important on a troubled construction project: (1) cost-schedule status, (2) labor productivity, and (3) change order system control. Following are the key reports that should be helpful in controlling these dimensions of a troubled construction project:

1.   Cost and schedule status
    a.   Weekly Cost Report (§ **16.22**)
    b.   Weekly Schedule Status Report (§ **16.23**)
    c.   Cost-schedule Budget Report (§ **16.24**)
2.   Labor productivity
    a.   Weekly Productivity Report (§ **16.29**)
3.   Change order system status
    a.   Change Order Control Log (§ **16.18**)
    b.   Change Order Processing Status Summary (§ **16.19**)
    c.   Estimated Cost of Unpriced Commitments (§ **16.20**).

These reports also provide valuable historical data that can be used to analyze construction disputes, particularly those based on delay and disruption. Refer to Wiley Law Publications' *Construction Industry Forms*[1] for other project management forms which might be helpful in controlling a troubled construction project.

---

[1] (Cushman & Blick eds. 1987).

§ 16.22 —Weekly Cost Report

W.P. TAYLOR CONSTRUCTION COMPANY

WEEKLY COST REPORT

Project Number: _____

Project Name: _____

Week Ending: _____

Cost Code	Description	Units		Cost		Percent Complete	Total Indicated Cost	Budget	Budget Variance
		To Date	Est. Total	To Date	This Week				

§ 16.23 —Weekly Schedule Status Report

W.P. TAYLOR CONSTRUCTION COMPANY

Page ___ of ___

WEEKLY SCHEDULE STATUS REPORT

Project Number:

Project Name:

Week Ending:

Pay-Point Code (Location & Work Category)	Pay-Point Description	Pay-Point Completion:		Days Ahead (Behind)	Comment:
		Scheduled	Expected		

§ 16.24 —Cost-Schedule Budget Report

W.P. TAYLOR CONSTRUCTION COMPANY

COST – SCHEDULE BUDGET REPORT

Page ___ of ___

Project Number: _____

Project Name: _____

Date: _____

Pay-Point: - Number - Name	Current Period: Budgeted Cost: Work Scheduled	Work Done	Actual Cost of Work Done	Variance: Schedule	Cost	Cumulative Performance To Date: Budgeted Cost: Work Scheduled	Work Done	Actual Cost of Work Done	Variance: Schedule	Cost	At Completion: Budgeted	Latest Estimate	Variance
No.: _____													
No.: _____													
No.: _____													
No.: _____													
No.: _____													
No.: _____													
No.: _____													
No.: _____													
No.: _____													
No.: _____													
No.: _____													
No.: _____													
PAGE TOTAL....													
TOTAL PROJECT													

§ 16.25   —Weekly Productivity Report

W.P. TAYLOR CONSTRUCTION COMPANY

WEEKLY PRODUCTIVITY REPORT

Project Number: _____   Project Name: _____   Week Ending: _____

Pay-Point Code (Location & work Category)	Pay-Point Description	Earned Units:			Labor Hours per Unit:			Total Labor Hours:		
		To Date	This Week	To Go	Budget	To Date	This Week	Budgeted	Pro-jected	Variance Under (Over)
TOTAL; THIS PAGE........										
TOTAL; THIS REPORT......										

§ 16.26   Types of Damages

There are three primary types of damage that might be asserted by an owner or a contractor on a troubled construction project: extra work, disruption and acceleration, and delay. Other types of damage exist such as lost opportunity; however, analysis of these damages depends on the unique nature of the business involved and are beyond the scope of this chapter.

§ 16.27   Calculating Extra Work Claims

Extra work claims are based on the assertion that the cost of extra work should be borne by the entity that benefits from the extra work or, in the absence of a benefiting party, by the entity that created the need for the extra work. For example, owners should not be required to pay for the cost of rebuilding a wall that was originally formed with contaminated concrete, nor should contractors be charged for work that is beyond the scope of their original contract such as increasing the size of a building.

Generally, extra work claims involve claims by contractors against owners. However, in a troubled construction project, an owner might have to pay a successor contractor to repair a predecessor's work and then sue the predecessor for reimbursement. In this situation, it is imperative that the successor contractor and the owner's site representative coordinate their efforts to ensure that the repair costs are identified and adequately segregated.

Damages associated with extra work claims should be relatively easy to calculate if management maintained detailed cost reporting procedures during the course of the project. Ideally, a unique code will have been established in the project cost accounting system's chart of accounts when the repair or "overscope" work was being performed. In this situation, the direct damages can be priced directly from the project's cost reports and then adjusted for site and home office overhead as appropriate.

If the actual costs of the extra work were not accumulated under a distinct cost code in the project cost accounting system, then the extra work claim will have to be based on an estimate. One approach to estimating the extra work cost is to analyze the Supervisor's Daily Reports and estimate the amount of labor and material required based on the task descriptions, location of work, time period in which the work was performed, and other information that can be extracted from the reporting systems. Another approach is to perform an engineering estimate based on the drawings and specifications and adjusted for known impacts that affected the work.

§ 16.28   Calculating Disruption and Acceleration Claims

Disruption-based claims are claims for extra direct costs that result when a contractor is prevented from performing work efficiently and in a manner consistent with reasonable expectations under the contract. Disruption claims involve productivity-related costs. Contractors incur disruption costs when they must commit extra direct resources to a project to overcome a problem.

Disruption claims can occur for a variety of reasons, including interfering work crews, excessive changes, nonsequential work patterns, poor site access, or schedule acceleration.

Owners generally do not incur disruption-based costs on construction projects. However, on troubled construction projects an owner may have to pay a successor contractor for excess costs caused by disruptive factors introduced by the predecessor contractor. For example, if the predecessor's latent defects are not discovered until halfway through the postfailure phase, and if the repair of these defects disrupted the successor contractor, then the predecessor may be responsible for both the repair costs and the related disruption costs. The approach to calculating disruption costs is basically the same for an owner's claim against a predecessor contractor as it is for a contractor's claim against an owner.

There are three basic approaches to calculating disruption costs:

1. Comparing the costs of a disrupted work area with an undisrupted work area: This approach requires that a basis for comparison exists. The basis is usually a similar work area (for example, floor, wing, or building) that was not disrupted. The actual cost of the undisrupted "basis" is used to determine the expected cost in the disrupted work area. The "Disruption Cost Estimate Worksheet— Comparable Work Area Approach" (§ 16.29) provides an illustration of the methodology that might be applied in this type of cost analysis.

2. Analyze the trends in labor productivity and compare them with the productivity achieved in the disrupted work area: This approach uses the trends in labor productivity achieved in undisrupted work areas as a basis for determining the expected productivity in the disrupted work area. Data obtained from the Weekly Productivity Report (§ 16.25), sorted by location and time, can be used to quantify both the expected and the actual productivity in the disrupted area. The expected productivity is then compared to the actual productivity achieved in the disrupted area to estimate the labor hours lost due to the disruption. The "Disruption Cost Estimate Worksheet—

Productivity Trend Approach" (§ **16.30**) can be used for this type of cost analysis.

3. Collect productivity-related statistics from the field during the period of disruption: This approach uses actual "lost time" data as the base element for determining disruption costs. The success of this approach often depends on the ability to recognize that a disruptive event is taking place and to develop and implement a method for collecting meaningful information regarding its occurrence and magnitude. Examples of data that might be collected to determine disruption include time lost traveling to and from a remote work area, time lost moving tools and setting up in a new work area, or time lost loading materials by hand instead of with a crane or high-low. This lost time approach provides a very strong basis for determining the cost of disruption, particularly if the lost-time data is obtained from the field during the time of the disruption. Refer to the "Disruption Cost Estimate Worksheet—Lost Time Approach" (§ **16.31**) for an illustration of the methodology that might be applied in this type of cost analysis.

Acceleration claims are very similar to disruption claims. They are based on the assertion that work was performed less productively than it should have been because the time available for performance was compacted. Examples of how schedule compaction might affect productivity (output per unit labor) include excessive crew sizes and excessive overtime.

In order to establish liability for acceleration damages a plaintiff must perform a schedule analysis to ascertain whose actions caused the available time to be reduced for the work in dispute. Acceleration damages consist primarily of direct labor costs which are based on the difference between the but-for and the actual labor hours required to accomplish the work. Calculating the direct labor damages in an acceleration claim should follow the same basic methodologies as those described earlier in this section for calculating disruption cost. Frequently acceleration damages also include the cost of overtime or the cost of expediting construction materials. These costs may be asserted if they resulted from compaction in the project's schedule.

If the acceleration also reduced the overall time required to complete the project, then the damage calculation might have to be adjusted in order to reflect any savings in fixed costs (costs which are a function of time). For example, if as a result of the acceleration, the project incurred less expense for site trailer rental, then this savings might have to be deducted from the plaintiff's claim.

§ 16.29   —Disruption Cost Estimate Worksheet: Comparable Work Area Approach

DISRUPTION COST ESTIMATE WORKSHEET
COMPARABLE WORK AREA APPROACH

ANALYSIS:

DIRECT COST CATEGORY:	UNDISRUPTED, COMPARABLE WORK:			DISRUPTED WORK:			ESTIMATED COST OF DISRUPTION
	TOTAL COST	UNITS PLACED	COST PER UNIT	UNITS PLACED	EST. COST "WITHOUT" DISRUPTION	ACTUAL COST	
algebraic operation ⟹	A	B	C = A/B	D	E = C * D	F	G = F − E
Labor Costs:							
Mechanical							
Electrical							
Carpentry							
Maintenance							
General							
Other Labor:							
Subcontracts:							
Other Costs:							
TOTAL							

RATIONALE:

DESCRIPTION OF UNDERLYING FACTORS CAUSING DISRUPTION:

DIRECT COST CATEGORY:
Labor Costs:
Mechanical
Electrical
Carpentry
Maintenance
General
Other Labor:
Subcontracts:
Other Costs:

Footnotes: 1) This form is to be used to estimate disruption costs, a more detailed analysis may be required to calculate the exact amount.

§ 16.30 —Disruption Cost Estimate Worksheet: Productivity Trend Approach

DISRUPTION COST ESTIMATE WORKSHEET
PRODUCTIVITY TREND APPROACH

ANALYSIS:

DIRECT COST CATEGORY:	PROJECTED COST PER UNIT BASED ON TREND ANALYSIS	DISRUPTED WORK:			ESTIMATED COST OF DISRUPTION
		UNITS PLACED	EST. COST "WITHOUT" DISRUPTION	ACTUAL COST	
	A	B	C = A * B	D	E = D − C
algebraic operation ⟹					
Labor Costs:					
Mechanical					
Electrical					
Carpentry					
Maintenance					
General					
Other Labor:					
Subcontracts:					
Other Costs:					
TOTAL					

RATIONALE:

DESCRIPTION OF UNDERLYING FACTORS CAUSING DISRUPTION:

| DIRECT COST CATEGORY: |
| Labor Costs: |
| Mechanical |
| Electrical |
| Carpentry |
| Maintenance |
| General |
| Other Labor: |
| Subcontracts: |
| Other Costs: |

Footnotes: 1) This form is to be used to estimate disruption costs, a more detailed analysis may be required to calculate the exact amount.

§ 16.31   —Disruption Cost Estimate Worksheet: Lost Time Approach

DISRUPTION COST ESTIMATE WORKSHEET
LOST TIME APPROACH

ANALYSIS:

WORK TASKS WHICH WERE DISRUPTED	DATA FROM TIME STUDY: LABOR HOURS REQUIRED TO COMPLETE ONE CYCLE (TASK OR WORK UNIT) WHEN CREW IS:		DIFFERENCE IN CREW'S LABOR HOURS	AVERAGE COST PER LABOR HOUR	NUMBER OF CYCLES PERFORMED DURING THE PERIOD OF DISRUPTION	ESTIMATED COST OF DISRUPTION
	DISRUPTED	NOT DISRUPTED				
algebraic operation ===>	A	B	C = A - B	D	E	F = C*D*E
Nonsequential Work Sequence (i.e., crew location changes)						
Site Access						
Material Access						
Excessive Inspection						
Equipment Access						
Equipment Breakdowns						
Interfering Work Crews						
Unprotected Work Spaces						
Other:						
					TOTAL ...	

RATIONALE:

DESCRIPTION OF UNDERLYING FACTORS CAUSING DISRUPTION:

DIRECT COST CATEGORY:	
Nonsequential Work Sequence (i.e. crew location changes)	
Site Access	
Material Access	
Excessive Inspection	
Equipment Access	
Equipment Breakdowns	
Interfering Work Crews	
Unprotected Work Spaces	
Other:	

Footnotes: 1) This form is to be used to estimate disruption costs, a more detailed analysis may be required to calculate the exact amount.

§ 16.32   Calculating Delay Claims

Delay occurs when the contractor's normal, as-planned progress is interrupted in some fashion. This might involve the interruption of all project activities or the delay of only a few activities that are on the project's critical path.

Delay claims typically include assertions for extended home office overhead costs. Frequently these claims use the Eichleay Formula (§ 16.34) as an approach to estimating these costs. The Eichleay Formula is a cost allocation technique involving three basic steps:

1. Determine the number of delay days: compare the as-planned and as-build CPM schedules.
2. Determine the project's portion of home office cost: multiply the corporation's total home office costs times the percent of total sales generated by the troubled project.
3. Determine the home office cost applicable to the delay: multiply the project's portion of home office cost times the percent of total project days that were delayed.

The Eichleay approach and other allocation techniques are frequently challenged because they do not provide a direct linkage between the home office costs and the troubled project. Consequently, to be successful these approaches must be supplemented with additional rationale and related documentation supporting this linkage, such as the inability to do other projects because of the staff requirements of the troubled project or the inability to finance other projects due to the working capital needs of the troubled project.

Another approach for determining home office costs uses home office labor data to assign overhead costs to the project. This approach requires that the home office personnel keep track of the hours they work according to three basic categories:

1. Hours worked on the troubled project
2. Hours worked on other projects
3. Hours worked that cannot be associated with a specific project.

These data are then used to determine the percentage of direct home office labor hours that are applicable to the troubled project. This percentage is then weighed based on actual salaries and used to allocate home office costs to the troubled project. Once the actual home office costs have been determined for the project, they can be compared to the planned (or average) home office costs to determine the excess overhead costs, or they can be allocated to a delay period to determine extended overhead costs. This approach may be applicable to claims initiated by either an owner or a contractor.

§ 16.33   —Eichleay Formula Worksheet

```
                    DELAY COST ESTIMATE WORKSHEET
                    EICHLEAY FORMULA WORKSHEET


STEP #1: CALCULATE THE DELAY DAYS:


   As-Built Dates:   Stop [          ] - Start [          ] = Days [  +  ]

   As-Planned Dates: Stop [          ] - Start [          ] = Days [  -  ]

   Noncompensable Delay Days ...................................  [  -  ]

   Compensable Delay Days .....................................  [  =  ]


STEP #2: CALCULATE THE TOTAL OVERHEAD "ALLOCATABLE" TO THE PROJECT IN DISPUTE:


   Revenue from the Project in Dispute .........  [  +        ]

   Total Company Revenue (during the term of
   the Project) ................................  [  /        ]

       Percent of Home Office Overhead
       Applicable to the Project in Dispute ......  [  =        ]

   Total Home Office Overhead (during the term
   of the Project) ............................  [  X        ]

       Total Home Office Overhead Applicable to
       the Project in Dispute ...................  [  = $      ]


STEP #3: CALCULATE THE HOME OFFICE OVERHEAD APPLICABLE TO THE PERIOD OF DELAY:


   Total Home Office Overhead Applicable to
   the Project in Dispute .....................  [  +        ]

   As-Built Project Days ......................  [  /        ]

       Daily Home Office Overhead Rate for
       Project in Dispute ......................  [  = $      ]  PER DAY

   Compensable Delay Days .....................  [  X        ]

       Home Office Delay Cost ..................  [  = $      ]
```

Footnote: 1) This form is to be used to estimate home office delay cost, a more
detailed analysis may be required to calculate the exact amount.

CHAPTER 17

SPECIAL ISSUES INVOLVED IN THE TRIAL OF A CONSTRUCTION FAILURE AND DISASTER CASE

Jesse B. Grove, III, Esquire

Jesse B. Grove, III is a trial lawyer with substantial experience in all phases of construction claims on major projects such as dams, tunnels, powerhouses, wastewater treatment plants, highways, bridges, and municipal, industrial, and highrise buildings; antitrust claims involving predatory pricing, tying, attempted monopolization, price discrimination, and mergers; and insurance disputes, including builder's risk and computer lease indemnity claims.

§ 17.1 Introduction

Many of the special issues that accompany the trial of a failure case deserve, and have received in this work, separate chapters of their own. This chapter will discuss some additional concerns.

A failure case will not ordinarily get to trial. Liability is too obvious and, unless there was personal injury, damages are often fairly easy to ascertain. So, when a failure case is tried it is because there is already something special about it. Let us consider what those things may be and the problems they present.

§ 17.2 Opposed Defendants

When the dam goes downstream during construction, the contractor will find fault with the engineering of it, while the engineer will be convinced there were construction deficiencies. When the owner sues both, each on the strength of the other's allegations, the fact that the plaintiff is bound to win will not have its normal settlement-inducing effect. Each defendant will instead strive to insure that responsibility for the entire loss falls on the other. It is also common for each defendant to implead his consultants and subcontractors into the fray in order to spread the threatened loss. At trial, a jury may accept the versions of both defendants and hold both liable. It is excruciating to watch the plaintiff's counsel smirk his way through one of these donnybrooks.

One of the ways out of this situation for a defendant is the so-called *Mary Carter settlement* (see §§ 14.5 and 17.3–17.6). This is an arrangement in which one of the defendants settles with the plaintiff on a sliding scale basis, usually within a range defined by a floor figure and a ceiling figure. It presumes that the case will be tried against the other defendant and the ultimate payment by the settling defendant will depend on the size of the verdict against the nonsettling defendants. Success at trial means only the floor amount will be paid. "Success" is defined as a verdict in a certain dollar amount, and a verdict for less calls for an increased contribution by the settling defendant.

The only other way out of the finger-pointing spectacle is for the defendants to make some sort of arrangement with each other. This could be a percentage-based liability-sharing agreement but that is possible only when the defendants agree on their relative exposure. When that occurs, the case will more likely be settled with each defendant contributing according to the agreed proportion of exposure.

Another form of arrangement between defendants is an agreement to link arms in defense against the plaintiff (that is, both defendants, for purposes of the proceeding, will agree that neither erred) while reserving rights to accuse each other in a subsequent proceeding. The ideas are, of course, to avoid helping the plaintiff win, to in fact cause the plaintiff to lose and thereby obviate the subsequent proceeding, and to guard against the possibility that the entire responsibility will be assessed against the wrong (in the opinion of each) defendant. Such agreements require consideration of statutes of limitation and principles of res judicata and collateral estoppel. If the reservations of rights are to be complete, there should be no possibility of preclusion, merger, or bar. The main disadvantage of this type of arrangement is the possibility that the dispute between defendants can go on for twice as long at twice the cost. This risk must be carefully weighed against the likelihood that the strategy will produce victory against, or minimized loss to, the plaintiff.

It is not uncommon, therefore, for opposed defendant cases to go to trial. The defendants may try not to go after each other at the start. They could both, for example, hope that a common defense, such as an act of God, will work. Both counsel will be evaluating the case constantly. Whenever it appears likely to one of them that the case is lost, he will turn on the other. In any event, both will be attempting to hedge their bets in every way possible. This kind of trial does wonders for sphincter muscle tone.

§ 17.3 Mary Carter Agreements

Defendants in construction failure cases involving multiple parties have powerful motivations to settle and settle early. In addition to those described in § 17.2, the fear of ruinous legal fees, fees not reimbursable from insurance, other limitations on insurance coverage, and the existence of something to hide often militate against trial. Plaintiffs may have motivations of their own: a perceived need for case simplification, insufficient funds in the "war chest," the elimination of aggressive opposing counsel, and fear of a total defense verdict are among them. All trials are gambles; only the odds vary. Mary Carter agreements hedge the bets for both sides.

A *Mary Carter* agreement is a pretrial contract between the plaintiff and less than all of the defendants in which the parties establish the ultimate recovery amount against the agreeing defendants according to a formula.

The formula normally includes a maximum amount, or *ceiling.* This ceiling provides the agreeing defendants with assurance of a fixed exposure that is usually much less than the maximum potential exposure and is perhaps within the limits of available insurance coverage. It also amounts to a minimum or *floor* recovery for plaintiffs, usually insuring that the continued investment of fees and costs to pursue other defendants will be worth it. There may also be a floor amount that defendants will have to pay no matter how the ultimate trial comes out.

The formula will then work from either the defendants' floor or ceiling by providing, for example, that the ceiling amount will be reduced in some inverse ratio to the amount of recovery against the nonagreeing defendants; the more the holdouts have to pay, the less the burden on settling defendants.

There are, of course, many variations on these basic themes. The pro rata reduction feature may be on a more (rarely) or less (often) than dollar-for-dollar basis. All or part of the minimum settlement amount may be payable at once, after trial, or on other terms. Frequently some amount of pretrial payment is crucial to the deal because of the plaintiff's need to fund the war chest. The trigger point for the application of the reduction formula may also be negotiated so that it does not apply, or applies in different ways, to first dollars or dollars above a certain level of recovery against the holdouts.

To illustrate, assume that an adjoining property owner has sued the owner and contractor because of a shoring failure that caused injury to the adjoining property. The contractor contends that the owner is responsible due to inadequate soils investigation, while the owner points to inadequate shoring design by the contractor. Both defendants have brought in their professional advisers and subcontractors as cross-defendants. Because the repair work performed by the plaintiff is controversial, there is a wide range of potential damages, between one and five million dollars.

When the plaintiff settles with the owner and his group of cross-defendants, the Mary Carter agreement could have the following features:

1. The owner's group will immediately pay $500,000.
2. The owner's group will pay another $500,000 unless the recovery against the contractor exceeds one million dollars.
3. If and to the extent that the recovery against the contractor exceeds one million dollars but is less than three million dollars, the owner's group will pay 50 cents for every four dollars paid by the contractor.
4. If the recovery against the contractor exceeds three million dollars, the owner's group shall receive back $250,000 of the immediate payment and shall have no further obligation.
5. If the recovery against the contractor exceeds five million dollars, the owner's group shall receive back its entire immediate payment with interest and have no further obligation.

The structuring opportunities are endless but all have the common features of a sliding scale within a range.

The effect of all such deals is to change the orientation of the settling defendant from that of a party with an incentive to cause the plaintiff to lose to that of a party who now wants the plaintiff to win, and win big.

This effect raises a host of troublesome questions. Should the parties be permitted to keep the deal secret from the court or the jury? Should the settling defendant be permitted to continue as a party in the case? Are ethical considerations implicated? If a secret deal of this sort is accompanied by sub rosa cooperation through continued participation, the result can be so obviously devastating to the nonsettling defendant that most courts have felt concern. On the other hand, virtually all courts promote settlements (read "reduce court load") above all other policy considerations.

§ 17.4 —Judicial and Statutory Precedents

The lawyer considering such arrangements is well advised to research carefully the cases in his jurisdiction and elsewhere because courts' reactions have varied.[1] There is now a substantial body of case law, notably in Florida and the western states, that provides guidance, starting, of course, with the namesake case, *Booth v. Mary Carter Paint Co.*[2] It is fair to generalize that such arrangements can be, and have often been, found to be judicially acceptable. However, the Canons of Professional Ethics provide against representing conflicting interests, taking technical advantage of opposing counsel, and stirring up strife and litigation, and require candor and fairness.[3]

Most of the existing case law involving Mary Carter agreements relates solely to tort law; that is, the cases present only tort issues and the law of cotortfeasors (notably equitable contribution principles) is drawn into play. The most obvious point to be made in this type of case is that care must be taken not to effect a release or set-off opportunity for the nonsettling defendant under the law of the relevant jurisdiction. Ironically, this usually means that the settling defendant must stay in the case, which increases the possibility of an unfair trial.

Under California law, a judicial determination that the Mary Carter settlement was entered into in good faith bars any other joint tortfeasor or co-obligor on a contract debt from further claims against the settling defendant for equitable comparative contribution, or partial comparative indemnity on the basis of comparative negligence or comparative fault.[4] The statute has been held to bar all forms of equitable indemnity claims against

---

[1] *See generally* Annotation, *Agreement Limiting Cotortfeasor's Liability,* 65 A.L.R.3d 602 (1975 & Supp. 1988).

[2] 202 So. 2d 8 (Fla. 1967).

[3] Canons of Professional Ethics Canons 6, 22, 25, 28 (1967). For a discussion of why Mary Carter agreements implicate these canons, *see* Lum v. Stinnett, 87 Nev. 402, 488 P.2d 347 (1971).

[4] Cal. Civ. Proc. Code § 877.6 (Deering 1988).

the settling tortfeasor.[5] There is a split in authority among the appellate
courts with respect to whether the statutory provision also creates a bar to
claims for implied contractual indemnity,[6] but the issue is presented in a
case currently pending before the California Supreme Court.[7]

Complicated analytical issues arise when both contract and tort causes
of action exist against one, but perhaps not all, of the codefendants. Under
contract law principles, the purpose of awarding damages to the injured
party is to put that party in as good, but no better, a position as he would
have been in had the contract been performed.[8] The collateral source rule
that, under certain circumstances, may allow a party injured by the tortious conduct of another to recover in excess of the amount of his injury,[9]
does not apply in an ordinary breach of contract case.[10] As a result, one
injured by a breach of contract can only recover for uncompensated injury.

A California statute explicitly provides that, when a plaintiff settles
with less than all of the defendants who are cotortfeasors or co-obligors
on a contract debt, claims against the nonsettling defendants shall be
reduced by the amount of such a settlement.[11] What, then, is the result
when the opportunity to recover from another is a sliding scale Mary
Carter agreement?

Although earlier court of appeal cases had implicitly held that a sliding
scale settlement is not subject to the offset requirement of the California
statute,[12] the California Supreme Court concluded otherwise.[13] The court
noted that sliding scale settlements are subject to the good faith requirement articulated in *Tech-Bilt, Inc. v. Woodward-Clyde & Assocs.*[14] The

---

[5] *See, e.g.,* Far W. Fin. Corp. v. D.&S. Co., 46 Cal. 3d 796, 760 P.2d 399, 251 Cal. Rptr. 202 (1988).

[6] *Id.* at n.5.

[7] *Id.* (citing Bay Dev. Ltd. v. Superior Court, S000888). *See also* Stratton v. Peat, Marwick, Mitchell & Co., 190 Cal. App. 3d 286, 292, 235 Cal. Rptr. 374, 376–77 (1987) (claim for implied contractual indemnity barred); IRM Corp. v. Carlson, 179 Cal. App. 3d 94, 109–12, 224 Cal. Rptr. 438, 446–48 (1986) (claims for equitable, express contractual, and implied contractual indemnity "by operation of law" barred); County of Los Angeles v. Superior Court, 155 Cal. App. 3d 798, 803, 202 Cal. Rptr. 444, 447 (1984) (claim allowed).

[8] 5 A. Corbin, Corbin on Contracts § 992 (1957).

[9] *See* 22 Am. Jur. 2d *Damages* § 566 (1988).

[10] *See* Grover v. Ratliff, 120 Ariz. 368, 370, 586 P.2d 213, 215 (Ct. App. 1978) and cases cited therein.

[11] Cal. Civ. Proc. Code § 877 (Deering 1988).

[12] *See* City of Los Angeles v. Superior Court, 176 Cal. App. 3d 856, 862–63, 206 Cal. Rptr. 674 (1986) (citing Riverside Steel Constr. Co. v. William H. Simpson Constr. Co., 171 Cal. App. 3d 781, 789–92, 217 Cal. Rptr. 569 (1985)).

[13] Abbott Ford, Inc. v. Superior Court, 43 Cal. 3d 858, 741 P.2d 124, 239 Cal. Rptr. 626 (1987).

[14] 38 Cal. 3d 488, 698 P.2d 159, 213 Cal. Rptr. 256 (1985). *Id.* at 875, 741 P.2d at 134, 239 Cal. Rptr. at 637.

application of the statute to a settlement agreement, the court emphasized, results in two "interrelated consequences: (1) it discharges the settling tortfeasor from all liability to other defendants for contribution or indemnity, and (2) it reduces the plaintiff's claims against the other defendants by 'the amount of consideration paid for it.'"[15] The court concluded that the "amount of consideration paid" for the release, which will be offset against the plaintiff's recovery from nonsettling defendants, should be determined by the parties to the agreement.[16] Cases in other jurisdictions have held that the amount offset against the plaintiff's recovery should be the amount of the loans or repayable "advances" paid to the plaintiff by the settling defendant(s).[17]

§ 17.5   —Adjustment of Recovery

When the terms of a Mary Carter agreement have been revealed to the court, the court may be forced to adjust the recovery against the nonsettling party so that the total recovery does not exceed or fall short of the plaintiff's total injury. Assume, for example that the Mary Carter agreement was as follows.

A defendant, the co-obligor on a general contract, agreed to pay the owner $500,000 prior to trial, and 50 cents for each dollar by which the owner's recovery against the remaining co-obligor(s) falls short of $500,000. If the total injury to the owner as a result of the breach of contract is one million dollars, the court might require the nonsettling defendant(s) to pay the owner $500,000 in order to ensure that the owner recovers no more or less than the value of his injury (the value he would have received had the contract been performed).

If the total injury to the owner was only $750,000, however, the Mary Carter agreement and the rule against damages exceeding breach of contract injury could only be reconciled if the nonsettling defendant was required to pay nothing, because the Mary Carter agreement effectively guarantees the owner a recovery of at least $750,000. If the total value of the owner's injury is less than $750,000, the two are irreconcilable.

It is not clear that courts would allow a Mary Carter agreement to function as intended in a pure contract case. However, if such agreements are permitted in a pure contract case, or in one involving both tort and contract claims, courts will be forced to perform such arithmetic gymnastics

---

[15] Abbott Ford, Inc. v. Superior Court, 43 Cal. 3d at 877, 741 P.2d at 136, 239 Cal. Rptr. at 638.

[16] *Id.* at n.21.

[17] *See* Bolton v. Zeigler, 111 F. Supp. 516 (N.D. Iowa 1953); Cullen v. Atchison, Topeka & Santa Fe Ry., 211 Kan. 368, 507 P.2d 353 (1973); Monjay v. Evergreen School Dist. No. 114, 13 Wash. App. 654, 537 P.2d 825 (1975).

or to adopt the California approach outlined in *Abbot Ford*[18] of requiring the settling parties to establish the value of their settlement, in order to prevent the terms of the settlement from producing a recovery inconsistent with principles of contract damages. On the other hand, such manipulation of the recovery by the courts might defeat the intent of the parties to the agreement, thereby defeating the policy favoring private settlement of disputes.

§ 17.6 —Disclosure of Agreements

Mary Carter agreements quite clearly encourage collusion between the plaintiff and the settling defendant. Because the real incentives are different from that which courts and juries normally attribute, the effect can be to undermine the adversary system to the point of extreme prejudice. Just imagine your codefendant, who appears to the jury to be defending, confessing in final argument his newly formed conviction of your liability (and perhaps even his own!) for the full amount of the prayer. To combat this perniciousness, many jurisdictions now require, by case law or statute, that Mary Carter agreements be subject to discovery.[19] Some go further by requiring affirmative disclosure by the agreeing parties.[20]

Once disclosed, the question of admissibility of the agreement into evidence arises. Again the jurisdictions differ, but the better rule seems to be that the agreement is admissible if it provides a basis for attacking the settling defendant's testimony. Cases following this rule typically reason that evidence of Mary Carter agreements is relevant to the jury's determination of the defendant's credibility.[21]

---

[18] 43 Cal. 3d 858, 741 P.2d 124, 239 Cal. Rptr. 626.

[19] *See, e.g.,* Maule Indus., Inc. v. Rountree, 264 So. 2d 445 (Fla. 1972).

[20] *See, e.g.,* Cal. Civ. Proc. Code § 877.5 (Deering 1988) (requiring disclosure to the court and jury of the settlement; requiring notice of intent to settle to nonsignatory defendant tortfeasors).

[21] *See, e.g.,* Maule Indus., Inc. v. Rountree, 264 So. 2d at 448 (also noting that Mary Carter agreements may be relevant to nonsigning defendant's right to set-off). For cases holding that Mary Carter agreements are discoverable and admissible into evidence, *see* Firestone Tire & Rubber Co. v. Little, 276 Ark. 511, 639 S.W.2d 726, *appealed sub nom.* Shelton v. Firestone Tire & Rubber Co., 281 Ark. 100, 662 S.W.2d 473 (1982); Grillo v. Burke's Paint Co., 275 Or. 421, 551 P.2d 449 (1976); General Motors Corp. v. Simmons, 558 S.W.2d 855 (1977), *overruled on other grounds sub nom.* Duncan v. Cessna Aircraft Co., 665 S.W.2d 414 (Tex. 1984); Ward v. Ochoa, 284 So. 2d 385 (Fla. 1973). For a case upholding the trial court's refusal to allow jury consideration of evidence of an agreement entered into between the plaintiff and one defendant, *see* Taylor v. DiRico, 124 Ariz. 513, 606 P.2d 3 (1980) (court's holding based on specific facts of case).

§ 17.7 —Alternatives to Mary Carter Agreements

There are undoubtedly many alternatives to the classic Mary Carter agreement. One would be a simple loan repayable only from the proceeds of recovery against the nonsettling defendant, perhaps on a formula basis. Another would be an immediate payment to the plaintiff in return for an assignment of some interest in the proceeds of the judgment. Depending on the case law in the jurisdiction, one of these devices might be preferable, but one would expect the Mary Carter case law to be strongly persuasive in any challenge to the validity of the arrangement.

In failure cases, particularly those featuring financially strapped plaintiffs, the race to settle may be the most important aspect of defense. Mary Carter settlements, where judicially approved, provide a device that can be attractive to both sides. Therefore, a premium is placed on early defense evaluation. If the choice is to be a nonsettling defendant, the risk of an unfair trial is great. Counsel must make all efforts to require the trial court to ameliorate the problem by permitting discovery, admitting the agreement into evidence, and allowing argument of all fair inferences. One would expect case and statutory law to continue rapid development in this area.

§ 17.8 Insolvent Defendant

If the main defendant is insolvent or bankrupt, peripheral defendants will find themselves exposed unfairly to the full loss. Moreover, the owner's counsel may count on the force of his case—furnaces are not supposed to explode—to overcome the weak link of participation by the peripheral defendant. Because the peripheral defendant is unlikely to settle for more than his fair share, these cases sometimes go to trial.

The peripheral defendant's strongest weapon is the "empty chair" defense. The real wrongdoer can be lambasted severely and without caution because he is not present to defend himself. But the defense is not perfect, because juries have a tendency to want to recompense the injured party. If it is apparent that the principal target cannot be reached, a jury will likely do the next best thing.

§ 17.9 The Technical Defense

The defendant may have a perfectly good defense written into his contract. For architects and engineers, this often takes the form of a limitation of liability clause providing that the defendant cannot be required to pay more for his errors than a fraction of the real costs. That fraction is often measured by such things as the engineer's fee or his malpractice

coverage limits. Such arrangements can be perfectly sensible. They relate
to known risks that the parties consciously choose to allocate in a certain
way, bearing in mind the economics of a different allocation and who
among them is best equipped to take on the risk.

Yet things that make sense in the negotiation room are seen differently
in the wake of disaster. The party who took the risk will feel that he never
truly understood it or, at least, that he never realized that the other party
would err so grossly. Political and economic pressure for retribution color
the picture as well. The result can be an attempt to have the jury rewrite
or ignore the contractual risk allocations in favor of a "just result."

An innovative response to this might be a countersuit requesting that
the other commercial terms of the contract also be rewritten in view of
the adjusted risk allocations. In support of the countersuit, evidence
could be offered by an engineer that his fee would necessarily have had
to be millions of dollars greater in order for him to be able to take on or
insure against the adjusted risk. Persuasive expert and industry testimony supporting this argument should be available. This should be an
effective way of demonstrating to the jury why careful contractual risk
allocations should be honored.

The trouble with the technical defense is that it is technical—that is, in
retrospect it seems unfair. It lets the wrongdoer off the hook and thus has
no jury appeal. Plaintiffs' lawyers will therefore sue anyway, and look to
the jury to do justice.

§ 17.10 —Summary Judgments

The best solution here is to get the court to enforce the contract. The procedural vehicle usually chosen is the summary judgment motion because
it can be brought on for early determination to foreclose if successful, ongoing litigation costs.

Summary judgment motions are, however, hard to win. The main impediment is that there must be no material and disputed issue of fact to
resolve in order to enter judgment.[22] Because every case requires the establishment of at least some facts, the necessary facts must be beyond dispute, usually as a result of binding admissions acquired through discovery.
But it is a rare case (and one that the opposition wants resolved by a judge
as promptly as you do) in which counsel is unable to construct some sort
of fact dispute. Furthermore, most courts permit, even require, liberal

---

[22] *See, e.g.,* Stationers Corp. v. Dun & Bradstreet, Inc., 62 Cal. 2d 412, 417, 398 P.2d 785,
788, 42 Cal. Rptr. 449, 452 (1965); McFadden v. American United Life Ins. Co., 658
S.W.2d 147, 148 (Tex. 1983); 6 J. Moore, W. Taggart & J. Wicker, Moore's Federal
Practice ¶ 56.15(1.0) (2d ed. 1985).

opportunity for discovery for counsel searching for ammunition with which to dispute the facts set up by the moving party.[23]

In failure cases, the party relying on limitation or exculpation of liability language will usually be faced with a dispute over the meaning of these words in the contract. If extrinsic evidence (for example, regarding drafter's intent) is admissible, then fact issues are presented that will ordinarily defeat summary judgment. Thus, the rigor with which the courts in the jurisdiction in question would apply the parol evidence rule is crucial. In California, for example, extrinsic evidence is almost always admissible as an aid to interpretation.[24]

If summary judgment is not possible, an order specifying certain facts or legal principles to be established without further controversy may be achieved, assuming such an order was properly requested in the alternative. There are procedural pitfalls and niceties in this area requiring careful study of local rules and practice.

§ 17.11   Repair or Replacement: The Cadillac/Ford Defense

When your perfectly good Ford car is totalled by another, the very least that you want in replacement is a new Ford even though yours was two years old. When the stadium roof collapses under a snow load, the local authorities are likely to go one step farther, demanding that the replacement be something akin to a bomb shelter. And they get what they want because they will be looking to others to design and build it. Thus the original design/build team will find itself asked to pay for replacing a Ford with a Cadillac.

The problem here is that Fords and Cadillacs look an awful lot alike in the construction context. A roof is a roof is a roof, and who can say just how much more load-carrying capacity a replacement roof should have? There is a fine line between conservative design and gilding the lily. Moreover, all jurors are sympathetic to the "once burned, twice afraid" mind set, particularly when public safety or mass disaster is concerned.

There is no effective way to defend against owner overreaching of this sort if one waits until trial to mount the effort. To be able to use the

---

[23] *See, e.g.,* Portland Retail Druggists Ass'n v. Kaiser Found. Health Plan, 662 F.2d 641, 645 (9th Cir. 1981).

[24] *See* Cal. Civ. Proc. Code § 1856 (Deering 1988); Pacific Gas & Elec. Co. v. G.W. Thomas Drayage & Rigging Co., 69 Cal. 2d 33, 37–40, 442 P.2d 641, 644–46, 69 Cal. Rptr. 561, 564–66 (1968) ("The test of admissibility of extrinsic evidence to explain the meaning of a written instrument is . . . whether the offered evidence is relevant to prove a meaning to which the language of the instrument is reasonably susceptible." (citations omitted)).

argument, the record must have been made back when the replacement decisions were being made. This means that the original designers and builders, whether asked to or not, should develop their own, demonstrably conservative, solutions and offer them. They should seek to participate in and review the suggestions of others. Finally, they should document their belief that the solutions adopted are overreactions to the problem.

It is hard to do these things credibly because of the obvious financial bias of the original team. Therefore, neutral experts should be retained and given the freedom to develop their own opinions, which should then be promptly made known to the decisionmakers.

When this sort of record has been made, the Cadillac/Ford defense can work. The downside is that a deficiency in the original work will, in effect, have been admitted in the process. Given the fact that the original work failed, this will, in most cases, not be a significant concession.

There is plenty of case law to the effect that an owner is not entitled to recover the full cost of his Cadillac replacement or repair job.[25] Instead, recovery should be limited to the reasonable cost of repair or, if the work is not repairable, to the cost of replacement according to the original design.[26] Furthermore, if an alternate, cheaper methodology is available, recovery will be limited to what that method of replacement would have cost.[27] One way to arrive at the correct result is to view the Cadillac repair or replacement as an enhancement of the value of the property and then deduct the enhancement value from the costs expended.[28]

The abundance of appellate decisions applying these rules makes a powerful point. Juries are ignoring the rules by making owners whole even when a Cadillac has replaced a Ford.

§ 17.12 Pretrial Settlement of Minor Failures

When failures occur, experts are invited to visit the scene. They are charged with discovering what went wrong, and, quite often, opining who is at fault. They may be, or hope to be, charged with creating the solution. These people are very thorough, very conservative, and very aware that

---

[25] *See, generally,* Annotation, *Damages—Breach of Construction Contract,* 41 A.L.R.4th 131 (1985 & Supp. 1988).

[26] *See, e.g.,* Temple Beth Sholom & Jewish Center, Inc. v. Thyne Constr. Corp., 399 So. 2d 525, 526 (Fla. Dist. Ct. App. 1981).

[27] Pinella City v. Lee Constr. Co. of Sanford, 375 So. 2d 293, 294 (Fla. Dist. Ct. App. 1979).

[28] State Property & Bldg. Comm'n v. H.W. Miller Constr. Co., 385 S.W.2d 211, 214 (Ky. 1964).

the work had better be right the second time around. Therefore, they refuse to limit their inquiries. They will review the whole project—the part that failed and that which did not. Not infrequently the part that failed turns out to be the least of the alleged deficiencies. The ensuing lawsuit may be largely dubious, but it will gain immeasurably by having a failure as its cornerstone.

In such a case, the defense objective should be to get rid of the cornerstone. Every effort to settle that part of the case should be made, including paying more than its value. Failing that, an appeal to the court for a bifurcated trial should be made. If all else fails, the plaintiff's strategy should at least be made plain to the jury.

No defendant wants to try a failure case, but he will if there is something unusual about it. That something always has to do with a perception that the defendant is being asked to pay a judgment out of proportion to his fault. The above discussion identifies some of the circumstances which can cause this to happen. When those circumstances are in play, a trial will occur; it will be an unpleasant experience.

TABLE OF CASES

419

Case	*Book §*
Anderson v. Liberty Lobby, Inc., 477 U.S. 242 (1986)	§ 15.22
Anderson Elec., Inc. v. Ledbetter Erection Corp., 115 Ill. 2d 146, 503 N.E.2d 246, 104 Ill. Dec. 689 (1986)	§ 3.16
Arcos Corp. v. American Mut. Liab. Ins. Co., 350 F. Supp. 380 (D.D.C. 1972)	§§ 9.9, 9.12
Arkansas Rice Growers Cooperative Ass'n v. Alchemy Indus., Inc., 797 F.2d 565 (8th Cir. 1986)	§ 12.1
A.R. Moyer, Inc. v. Graham, 285 So. 2d 397 (Fla. 1973)	§ 12.10
Artesian Water Co. v. Government of New Castle County (Artesian I), 605 F. Supp. 1348 (D. Del. 1985) and (Artesian II), 659 F. Supp. 1269 (D. Del. 1987)	§§ 6.6, 6.11
Attlin Constr., Inc. v. Muncie Community Schools, 413 N.E.2d 281 (Ind. Ct. App. 1980)	§ 3.20
Audlane Lumber & Builders Supply, Inc. v. D.E. Britt Assoc., 168 So. 2d 333 (Fla.), *cert. denied,* 173 So. 2d 146 (Fla. 1965)	§ 3.10
Bacco Constr. Co. v. American Colloid Co., 148 Mich. App. 397, 384 N.W.2d 427 (1986)	§ 11.33
Bank of Am. Nat'l Trust & Savings Assn. v. Touche Ross & Co., 782 F.2d 966 (11th Cir. 1986)	§ 11.15
Bartak v. Bell-Galyardt & Wells, Inc., 629 F.2d 523 (8th Cir. 1980)	§ 11.9
Bates & Rogers Constr. Corp. v. North Shore Sanitary Dist., 128 Ill. App. 3d 962, 471 N.E.2d 915 (1984), *aff'd on other grounds sub nom.* Bates & Rogers Constr. Corp. v. Greeley & Hansen, 109 Ill. 2d 225, 486 N.E.2d 902 (1985)	§§ 3.16, 12.10
Bates & Rogers Constr. Corp. v. North Shore Sanitary Dist., 92 Ill. App. 3d 90, 414 N.E.2d 1274 (1980)	§§ 3.15, 3.16, 3.26
Bay Dev. Ltd. v. Superior Ct., S00088	§ 17.4
Bayne v. Everham, 197 Mich. 181, 163 N.W. 1002 (1917)	§ 12.6
Bayuk v. Edson, 236 Cal. App. 2d 309, 46 Cal. Rptr. 49 (1965)	§ 12.5
Beacon Constr. Co. v. United States, 314 F.2d 501, 161 Ct. Cl. 1 (1963)	§ 3.2
Beacon Textiles Corp. v. Employers Mut. Liability Ins. Co., 355 Mass. 643, 246 N.E.2d 673 (1969)	§ 9.6
Bell v. Jones, 523 A.2d 982 (D.C. 1987)	§§ 11.26, 12.2
Bellevue School Dist. 405 v. Brazier Constr., 100 Wash. 2d 776, 691 P.2d 178 (1984)	§ 11.27
Bernard Johnson, Inc. v. Continental Constructors, Inc., 630 S.W.2d 365 (Tex. Ct. App. 1982)	§ 12.10
Bethesda Lutheran Church v. Twin City Constr., 356 N.W.2d 344 (Minn. App. 1984)	§§ 3.3, 3.5
Bielski v. Schulze, 16 Wis. 2d 1, 114 N.W.2d 105 (1962)	§ 14.9

Case	Book §

Case	*Book §*
McQuagge v. United States, 197 F. Supp. 460 (W.D. La. 1961)	§ 3.30
Metropolitan Sanitary Dist. of Greater Chicago v. A. Pontarelli & Sons, 7 Ill. App. 3d 829, 288 N.E.2d 905 (1972)	§ 11.17
MGM Grand Hotel Fire Litig., *In re,* MDL 453 (1981)	§§ 15.1, 15.12
Midland, City of v. Helger Constr. Co., 157 Mich. App. 736, 403 N.W.2d 218 (1987)	§ 11.27
Miller v. City of Broken Arrow, 660 F.2d 450 (10th Cir. 1981)	§ 12.7
Miller v. DeWitt, 37 Ill. 2d 273, 226 N.E.2d 630 (1967)	§ 12.9
Miller v. Spencer, 732 S.W.2d 758 (Tex. Civ. App. 1987)	§ 8.11
Miller v. United States Fidelity & Guar. Co., 291 Mass. 445, 197 N.E. 75 (1935)	§ 9.18
Mills v. Standard Titles Ins. Co., 39 Colo. App. 261, 568 P.2d 79 (1977)	§ 14.6
Milton J. Womack, Inc. v. House of Representatives, 509 So. 2d 62 (La. Ct. App.), *cert. denied,* 513 So. 2d 1208 & 513 So. 2d 1211 (1987)	§§ 12.2, 12.10
Mitchell v. Branch, 45 Haw. 128, 363 P.2d 969 (1961)	§ 14.12
M.L. Shalloo, Inc. v. Riccardi & Sons Constr., Inc., 348 Mass. 682, 205 N.E.2d 239 (1965)	§§ 3.2, 3.26
Monjay v. Evergreen School Dist. No. 114, 13 Wash. App. 654, 537 P.2d 825 (1975)	§ 17.4
Montijo v. Swift, 219 Cal. App. 2d 351, 33 Cal. Rptr. 133 (1963)	§ 12.8
Moore v. Pavex, Inc., 356 Pa. Super. 50, 514 A.2d 137 (1986)	§ 12.11
Moore v. Werner, 418 S.W.2d 918 (Tex. Civ. App. 1967)	§ 8.11
Moorman Mfg. Co. v. National Tank Co., 91 Ill. 2d 69, 435 N.E.2d 443 (1982)	§ 3.16
Morgan v. Bank of Waukegan, 804 F.2d 970 (7th Cir. 1986)	§ 11.15
Morse/Diesel Co. v. Trinity Indus., Inc., 664 F. Supp. 91 (S.D.N.Y. 1987)	§ 3.16
Mounds View, City of v. Walijarvi, 263 N.W.2d 420 (Minn. 1978)	§§ 3.10, 3.19, 11.9, 12.1
Moundsview Indep. School Dist. No. 621 v. Buetow & Assocs., Inc., 253 N.W.2d 836 (Minn. 1977)	§§ 10.10, 12.4
Mountain Home Contractors v. United States, 425 F.2d 1260, 192 Ct. Cl. 16 (1970)	§ 3.2
Munroe, County of v. Travelers Ins. Co., 100 Misc. 2d 417, 419 N.Y.S.2d 410 (1979)	§ 9.18
Nat Harrison Assocs. v. Gulf States Utils. Co., 491 F.2d 578 (5th Cir. 1974)	§ 6.23
Nationwide Mut. Fire Ins. Co. v. Burke, 90 App. Div. 2d 626, 456 N.Y.S.2d 223 (1982)	§ 9.18

Case	*Book §*
Peter Kiewit & Sons' Co. v. Iowa S. Utils. Co., 355 F. Supp. 376 (S.D. Iowa 1973)	§§ 12.1, 12.10, 12.16
Peter Kiewit & Sons' Co. v. United States, 109 Ct. Cl. 390 (1947)	§ 1.13
Peyronnin Constr. Co. v. Weiss, 137 Ind. App. 417, 208 N.E.2d 489 (1965)	§ 12.10
Philadelphia v. Stepan Chem. Co., 544 F. Supp. 1135 (E.D. Pa. 1982)	§§ 6.6, 6.7, 6.11
Philadelphia v. Westinghouse Elec. Corp., 210 F. Supp. 483 (E.D. Pa. 1962)	§ 5.8
Phillips v. ABC Builders, Inc., 611 P.2d 821 (Wyo. 1980)	§ 11.27
Pierringer v. Milwaukee Gas Light Co., 21 Wis. 2d 182, 124 N.W.2d 106 (1963)	§ 14.16
Pinella City v. Lee Constr. Co. of Sanford, 375 So. 2d 293 (Fla. Dist. Ct. App. 1979)	§ 17.11
Piracci Constr. Co. v. Skidmore, Owings & Merrill, 490 F. Supp. 314 (S.D.N.Y. 1980)	§ 11.27
Pittsburgh Plate Glass Co. v. Fidelity & Casualty Co. of N.Y., 281 F.2d 538 (2d Cir. 1960)	§ 9.6
Plan-Tec v. Wiggins, 443 N.E.2d 1212 (Ind. Ct. App. 1983)	§ 3.21
Portland Retail Druggists Ass'n v. Kaiser Found. Health Plan, 662 F.2d 641 (9th Cir. 1981)	§ 17.10
Prichard Bros. v. Grady Co., 407 N.W.2d 423 (Minn. Ct. App. 1987)	§ 3.16
Prier v. Refrigeration Eng'g Co., 74 Wash. 2d 25, 442 P.2d 621 (1968)	§ 3.10
Prihard Bros. v. Brady Co., 428 N.W.2d 391 (Minn. 1988)	§ 12.10
Public Constructors, Inc. v. State, 55 A.D.2d 368, 390 N.Y.S.2d 481 (1977)	§ 1.8
Pugh v. Butler Tel. Co., 512 So. 2d 1317 (Ala. 1987)	§ 4.3
Reber v. Chandler High School Dist. No. 202, 13 Ariz. App. 133, 474 P.2d 852 (1970)	§ 10.12
Redgrave v. Boston Symphony Orchestra, Inc., 557 F. Supp. 230 (D. Mass. 1983)	§ 3.19
Reliance Ins. Corp. v. Martin, 126 Ill. App. 3d 94, 467 N.E.2d 287 (1984)	§ 9.13
R.G. Wood & Assocs., 85-1 B.C.A. (CCH) ¶ 17,898 (PSBCA 1985)	§ 12.2
Richardson v. Pacific Power & Light Co., 11 Wash. 2d 288, 118 P.2d 985 (1941)	§ 14.5
Richardson Elec. Co. v. Peter Francese & Son, 21 Mass. App. 47, 484 N.E.2d 108 (1985)	§ 3.2
Riverside Steel Constr. Co. v. William H. Simpson Constr. Co., 171 Cal. App. 3d 781, 217 Cal. Rptr. 569 (1985)	§ 17.4
Robert E. Owen & Assocs. v. Gyongyosi, 433 So. 2d 1023 (Fla. Dist. Ct. App. 1983)	§ 3.11

Case	*Book §*
Shelton v. Firestone Tire & Rubber Co., 281 Ark. 100, 662 S.W.2d 473 (1982)	§ 17.6
Shoffner Indus., Inc. v. W.B. Lloyd Constr. Co., 42 N.C. App. 259, 257 S.E.2d 50, *cert. denied,* 298 N.C. 296, 259 S.E.2d 301 (1979)	§§ 12.10, 12.14
Smiley v. Manchester Ins. & Indem. Co., 71 Ill. 2d 306, 375 N.E.2d 118 (1978)	§ 9.15
Souza & McCue Constr. Co. v. Superior Ct. of San Benito County, 57 Cal. 2d 508, 370 P.2d 338, 20 Cal. Rptr. 634 (1962)	§ 3.2
State *ex rel.* Vapor Corp. v. Narick, 320 S.E.2d 345 (W. Va. 1984)	§ 14.15
State Farm & Casualty Co. v. All Elec., Inc., 660 P.2d 995 (Nev. 1983)	§ 11.27
State Highway Dept. v. Hewitt Contracting Co., 113 Ga. App. 685, 149 S.E.2d 499 (1966)	§ 3.2
State Property & Bldg. Comm'n v. H.W. Miller Constr. Co., 385 S.W.2d 211 (Ky. 1964)	§ 17.11
Stationers Corp. v. Dunn & Bradstreet, Inc., 62 Cal. 2d 412, 398 P.2d 785, 42 Cal. Rptr. 449 (1965)	§ 17.10
Steele v. Gold Kist, Inc., 186 Ga. App. 569, 368 S.E.2d 196 (1988)	§ 11.23
Steere Tank Lines, Inc. v. United States, 577 F.2d 279 (5th Cir. 1978), *cert. denied,* 440 U.S. 946 (1979)	§ 2.12
Stock & Grove, Inc. v. United States, 204 Ct. Cl. 103, 493 F.2d 629 (1974)	§ 3.3
Stone & Webster Eng'g Corp. v. American Motorist Ins. Co., 458 F. Supp. 792 (E.D. Va. 1978)	§ 9.9
Stratton v. Peat, Marwick, Mitchell & Co., 190 Cal. App. 3d 286, 235 Cal. Rptr. 374 (1987)	§ 17.4
Superior Oil Co. v. Kulmer, 785 F.2d 252 (8th Cir. 1986)	§ 11.15
Swanigan v. State Farm Ins. Co., 99 Wis. 2d 179, 299 N.W.2d 234 (1980)	§ 14.16
Swartz v. Ford, Bacon & Davis Constr. Corp., 469 So. 2d 232 (Fla. Dist. Ct. App. 1985)	§ 12.9
Tamarac Dev. Co. v. Delamater, Freund & Assocs., 234 Kan. 618, 675 P.2d 361 (1984)	§ 11.9
Taylor v. DiRico, 124 Ariz. 513, 606 P.2d 3 (1980)	§ 17.6
Tech-Bilt, Inc. v. Woodward-Clyde & Assocs., 38 Cal. 3d 488, 698 P.2d 159, 213 Cal. Rptr. 256 (1985)	§ 17.4
Telefson v. Green Bay Packers, 256 Wis. 318, 41 N.W. 201 (1950)	§ 1.13
Temple Beth Sholom & Jewish Center, Inc. v. Thyne Constr. Corp., 399 So. 2d 525 (Fla. Dist. Ct. App. 1981)	§ 17.11
The T.J. Hooper, 60 F.2d 737 (2d Cir.), *cert. denied,* 287 U.S. 662 (1932)	§ 12.2
Thomas J. Lipton, Inc. v. Liberty Mut. Ins. Co., 34 N.Y.2d 356, 357 N.Y.S.2d 705 (1974)	§ 9.12

INDEX

437

INDEX